Foundations of Behavioral Statistics

Foundations
of Behavioral Statistics

An Insight-Based Approach

BRUCE THOMPSON

THE GUILFORD PRESS
New York London

© 2006 The Guilford Press
A Division of Guilford Publications, Inc.
72 Spring Street, New York, NY 10012
www.guilford.com

Paperback edition 2008

Printed in the United States of America

This book is printed on acid-free paper.

Last digit is print number: 9 8 7 6 5 4 3 2

Library of Congress Cataloging-in-Publication Data

Thompson, Bruce, 1951–
  Foundations of behavioral statistics : an insight-based approach /
  Bruce Thompson.
    p. cm.
  Includes bibliographical references and index.
  ISBN-10: 1-59385-840-X   ISBN-13: 978-1-59385-840-7 (pbk.)
  ISBN-10: 1-59385-285-1   ISBN-13: 978-1-59385-285-6 (hardcover)
  1. Psychometrics. 2. Psychology—Statistical methods. I. Title.
BF39.T473 2006
150.1′5195—dc22

                                 2006001101

Cover monograph, *Guardians of the Morning*, by Anne Moore

Preface

Young children playing in the schoolyard may fantasize about their future careers, often across stunningly disparate ambitions. For example, very early in his schooling my younger brother struggled between the career choices of being either a pumpkin or an air conditioner.

But young children, or even young adults, *never* include statistician or psychometrician among the options they consider. Instead, a few people somewhere along the path of education discover these fields, and often they are surprised by their unanticipated interest.

I first became interested in statistics and measurement as a young, first-year high school teacher taking a required master's degree course in research methods. I was so exhausted from my new job that one night I fell asleep in class.

But that class and its content eventually captivated my interest, and even my passion, once I realized that methodology is not about math. Instead, good social science research is primarily about thinking, about reflection, and about judgment.

Moreover, studying social science phenomena is just plain interesting, because people are so interesting. Of course, this does not mean that studying people is easy. On the contrary, because people are so different from each other, studying people is really quite challenging (Berliner, 2002).

I hope that you, too, will find yourself captivated at least a bit by the methodological challenges inherent in studying people. In any case, through the years I have learned that students expect their professors to be passionate about what they teach, even when the students do not fully share these interests.

I hope that you will sense some of my excitement in this book. I also hope that this book, under a best-case scenario, will leave you with two fundamental reactions:

1. "This is the clearest book I have ever read."
2. "This book made me think, but also maybe even made me a better thinker."

The book does have several features that together I believe make it unique, in addition to what I hope is its clarity and thought-provocativeness. First, the book emphasizes the General Linear Model concepts, which involve understanding how different statistical methods are related to each other. Second, the book emphasizes effect sizes and confidence intervals; these are old statistical ideas that are now in the fore-front of contemporary social science. Third, the book includes many concrete hypothetical datasets, as well as the encouragement to use computer software (e.g., the statistical package SPSS, and the spreadsheet program Excel) to confirm and further explore statistical dynamics. For convenience, some datasets used in the book have been posted on the web at the URL *http://www.coe.tamu.edu/~bthompson/datasets.htm*. Also posted are various other datasets. These can be quite useful in exploring statistical dynamics, or to develop mastery of software via practice.

This book has *not* been written as a sterile, formal, impenetrable treatise. The book teaches formulas, not as an end in themselves, but as vehicles to facilitate understanding of key concepts. Rote memory of legions of formulas is less relevant in an environment populated by modern hardware and software. Moreover, the book is written in my voice, and I speak directly to you. My hope is that you will find this approach engaging and stimulating.

In closing, I would be remiss if I failed to thank all the students over so many years who have taught me so much about statistics, as well as clarity of thinking and articulation, among other things. Teaching is the ultimate learning experience. I learn more every time I revisit each topic in a lecture or class discussion, no matter how mundane the topic or how well traveled the road.

I appreciate the helpful suggestions from reviewers selected by the Publisher and unknown to me at the time of their reviews: Robin K. Henson, Department of Technology and Cognition, University of North Texas; Jeff Kromrey, Department of Educational Measurement and Research, University of South Florida; David Morse, Department of Psychology, Mississippi State University; Victoria Rodlin, Statistical Consultant (former faculty, Department of Psychology, California State University, Fullerton); Frank Schmidt, College of Business, University of Iowa; Paul R. Swank, Department of Pediatrics, University of Texas Health Science Center at Houston; Bruce Thyer, College of Social Work, Florida State University; Ken Wallston, School of Nursing, Vanderbilt University; David Weakliem, Department of Sociology, University of Connecticut, Storrs. Additionally, several colleagues (Laurie Goforth, Bonnie Haecker, Oi-Man Kwok, and Janet Rice) provided insightful comments on sections of the draft manuscript. I have not followed this counsel in all cases, and so necessarily must remain responsible for the work in its final form.

I also thank my Publisher, C. Deborah Laughton, with whom I have now worked for more than 10 years, for her support and encouragement. I quite vividly remember our first dinner in New Orleans in April 1994. I will also never forget some of our degustation dinners since, including a near "death-by-chef" experience in Manhattan. One has to love anybody who drives a car with personalized license plates admonishing, "BE SILLY." I am guardedly optimistic that someday she will confess what the "C" stands for.

BRUCE THOMPSON
Texas A&M University and
Baylor College of Medicine (Houston)

Contents

1 Introductory Terms and Concepts   1

    Definitions of Some Basic Terms   3

    Levels of Scale   13

    Some Experimental Design Considerations   24

    ▓▓▓ Some Key Concepts   30

    ▓▓▓ Reflection Problems   30

2 Location   31

    Reasonable Expectations for Statistics   32

    Location Concepts   33

    Three Classical Location Descriptive Statistics   36

    Four Criteria for Evaluating Statistics   46

    Two Robust Location Statistics   47

    ▓▓▓ Some Key Concepts   49

    ▓▓▓ Reflection Problems   49

3 Dispersion   53

    Quality of Location Descriptive Statistics   54

    Important in Its Own Right   54

    Measures of Score Spread   57

    Variance   62

    Situation-Specific Maximum Dispersion   67

    Robust Dispersion Descriptive Statistics   69

    Standardized Score World   70

    ▓▓▓ Some Key Concepts   72

    ▓▓▓ Reflection Problems   73

4 Shape   75

Two Shape Descriptive Statistics   76
Normal Distributions   86
Two Additional Univariate Graphics   91
■■■ Some Key Concepts   94
■■■ Reflection Problems   95

5 Bivariate Relationships   97

Pearson's r 99
Three Features of r 101
Three Interpretation Contextual Factors   110
Psychometrics of the Pearson r 116
Spearman's rho   118
Two Other r-Equivalent Correlation Coefficients   124
Bivariate Normality   128
■■■ Some Key Concepts   130
■■■ Reflection Problems   131

6 Statistical Significance   133

Sampling Distributions   135
Hypothesis Testing   142
Properties of Sampling Distributions   150
Standard Error/Sampling Error   154
Test Statistics   156
Statistical Precision and Power   169
$p_{CALCULATED}$ 177
■■■ Some Key Concepts   182
■■■ Reflection Problems   182

7 Practical Significance   185

Effect Sizes   187
Confidence Intervals   200
Confidence Intervals for Effect Sizes   207
■■■ Some Key Concepts   210
■■■ Reflection Problems   211

8 Multiple Regression Analysis: Basic GLM Concepts   215

Purposes of Regression   217
Simple Linear Prediction   220

Case #1: Perfectly Uncorrelated Predictors   232
Case #2: Correlated Predictors, No Suppressor Effects   234
Case #3: Correlated Predictors, Suppressor Effects Present   237
β Weights versus Structure Coefficients   240
A Final Comment on Collinearity   244
■ ■ ■ Some Key Concepts   245
■ ■ ■ Reflection Problems   246

9 A GLM Interpretation Rubric   247

Do I Have Anything?   248
Where Does My Something Originate?   266
Stepwise Methods   270
Invoking Some Alternative Models   278
■ ■ ■ Some Key Concepts   299
■ ■ ■ Reflection Problems   300

10 One-Way Analysis of Variance (ANOVA)   303

Experimentwise Type I Error   304
ANOVA Terminology   309
The Logic of Analysis of Variance   311
Practical and Statistical Significance   317
The "Homogeneity of Variance" Assumption   319
Post Hoc Tests   325
■ ■ ■ Some Key Concepts   329
■ ■ ■ Reflection Problems   330

11 Multiway and Other Alternative ANOVA Models   333

Multiway Models   333
Factorial versus Nonfactorial Analyses   343
Fixed-, Random-, and Mixed-Effects Models   345
Brief Comment on ANCOVA   354
■ ■ ■ Some Key Concepts   357
■ ■ ■ Reflection Problems   358

12 The General Linear Model (GLM): ANOVA via Regression   359

Planned Contrasts   360
Trend/Polynomial Planned Contrasts   375

Repeated-Measures ANOVA via Regression   380
GLM Lessons   385
▪▪▪ Some Key Concepts   390
▪▪▪ Reflection Problems   391

13 Some Logistic Models: Model Fitting in a Logistic Context   393
Logistic Regression   394
Loglinear Analysis   413
▪▪▪ Some Key Concepts   423
▪▪▪ Reflection Problems   424

Appendix: Scores (*n* = 100) with Near Normal   427
Distributions

References   431

Index   449

About the Author   457

1

Introductory Terms and Concepts

Most of us at some point have been asked to tell others the essence of who we are or to describe a friend to a third party; or friends may have described to us other people whom we had not yet met. For example, you may have been offered the opportunity for a blind date. Most of us develop the survival skills to ask a lot of questions when these opportunities arise!

The problem is that it is difficult to summarize a person by only a few characteristics. Some people may be easier to represent than others (e.g., "She is just so nice!"). But we probably perceive most people to be multidimensional, and so several different characterizations may be necessary to even begin to represent complex personalities (e.g., "He is intense, brilliant, and incredibly funny").

The kinds of characterizations of interest depend upon both who we are, and our purposes. We will ask somewhat different questions if we are deciding whom to hire for a job, from whom to receive cooking advice, or whom we should date.

Similar dynamics arise when we are trying to understand data or to characterize data to others. Maybe some data can be described by a single characterization (e.g., "the mean score was 102.5"). But more often than not *several different kinds* of characterizations are needed (e.g., "the data ranged from 83.0 to 116.5, and the most frequent score was 99.0").

And as in describing people, which characterizations are relevant when describing data *depend largely upon our purposes*. Sometimes the mean is essential; sometimes the mean is completely irrelevant.

Finally, our personal values affect which and how many characterizations may be needed to describe a potential blind date (e.g., one person may be most concerned about the blind date's wealth, but another may be most interested in the candidate's sexiness). Similarly, in statistics experts reach different decisions about how best to understand or represent data, even when their research has the same purposes. Researcher *values and interests* inherently affect how we characterize data.

In other words, statistics is *not* about always doing the same data analysis no matter what is the research purpose or situation and no matter who is the researcher. Nor is statistics about black and white or universally-right or universally-wrong analytic decisions. Instead, statistics is about being reasonable and reflective.

Statistics is about *thinking*. In the words of Huberty and Morris (1988), "As in all statistical inference, subjective judgment cannot be avoided. Neither can reasonableness!" (p. 573).

The good news for mathphobic students is that statistics and research are not really about math and computation. The bad news, however, is that statistics and research are about thinking. And thinking can be much more challenging (but also much more exciting) than rote calculation or rote practice.

Statistics is about both understanding and communicating the essence of our data. If all studies were conducted with only three or seven or nine people, perhaps no statistics would ever be necessary. We could simply look at the data and understand that the intervention group receiving the new medication did better than the control group receiving placebo sugar pills.

But when we conduct studies with dozens, or hundreds, or tens of thousands of participants, even the most brilliant researcher cannot simply stare at the data and see all (or perhaps any) of the themes within the data. With datasets of realistic size, we require statistics to help us understand the story underlying our data, or "to let the data speak." Statistics were invented by people, for people, to help us characterize the relevant features of data in a given context for a given purpose.

And even if a researcher was so astoundingly brilliant as to be able simply to examine huge datasets and understand all the underlying themes, statistics would still be needed to communicate the results to others. For example, even presuming that some researcher could look at the achievement test scores of 83,000 elementary school students and understand their performance, most newspapers and journals would balk at reprinting all 83,000 scores to convey the results to their readers. Statistics, then, are also needed to facilitate the economical communication of the most situationally-relevant characterizations of data.

Definitions of Some Basic Terms

Variables versus Constants

Research is about variables and, at least sometimes, constants. A variable consists of scores that in a given situation fall into at least two mutually exclusive categories. For example, if you have data on the gender of your classmates, as long as at least two people differ in their gender, your data constitute a variable.

If your class consists of 1 male and 16 females, the data constitute a variable. If the class consists of 8 males and 9 females, the data constitute a variable. If the class consists of 16 males and 1 female, the gender data constitute a variable.

The number of variable categories is also irrelevant in determining whether a variable is present, as long as there are at least two categories. For example, if your class consists of 5 males, 11 females, and 1 person who has split XY chromosomes, you still have a variable.

Of course, it is always possible (and sometimes desirable) to collect data consisting of a single category. A **constant** consists of scores that in a given situation all fall within a single category. For example, if all the students in a class are females, the gender data in that class on this occasion constitute a constant. Obviously, sometimes data that are constants in one situation (Professor Cook's class) are variables in another situation (Professor Kemp's class).

In some situations we purposely constrain scores on what could be variables to be constants instead. We do so to control for possible extraneous influences, or for other reasons. For example, if we are conducting studies on metabolizing huge quantities of alcohol, we may limit the study to men because we believe that men and women metabolize alcohol differently. We don't have to worry about these differences if we limit our focus to men, and examine dynamics in women in a subsequent study, or let other researchers examine alcohol phenomena involving women. Or, we might limit the study to only men, knowing that some female study participants might be pregnant, and we do not want to risk damaging any babies of mothers who may not realize they are pregnant by having them drink large quantities of alcohol during our study.

No statistics are needed either to understand or to communicate a constant. It is easy to both understand and communicate that "all the students were females."

But statistics are often needed to understand data collected on variables, even if we collect data only on a single variable. **Univariate statistics** are statistics that can be computed to characterize data on a single variable, either one variable at a time in a study with multiple variables, or when data have been collected only on a single variable.

By the way, now is as good a time as any to let you in on a secret (that actually is widely known, and thus not really secret): The language of statistics is intentionally designed to confuse the graduate students (and everyone else). This mischievousness takes various forms.

First, some terms have different meanings in different contexts. For example, univariate statistics can be defined as "statistics that can be computed to characterize data from a single variable," but in another context (which we will encounter momentarily) the same term has a different meaning.

Second, we use multiple synonymous names for the same terms. This second feature of statistical terminology is not unlike naming all seven sons in a family "George," or the Bob Newhart television show on which one of three brothers regularly made the introduction, "This is my brother Darrell, and this is my other brother Darrell."

Of course, at the annual summer statistical convention (called a coven), which statistics professors regularly attend to make our language even more confusing, an important agreement was reached long, long ago.

It is not reasonable to confuse the graduate students on unimportant terms. Thus, we have more synonymous terms for the most important concepts, and consequently the importance of a concept can be intuited by counting the number of recognized synonymous terms for the concept.

The implication is that you, unfortunately, must become facile with *all* the synonymous terms for a concept. You never know which terminology you will encounter in published research that reflects merely the arbitrary stylistic preferences of given scholars. So you must master all the relevant synonyms, even though the failure of statisticians to agree on uniform terminology is frustrating for all of us.

We may need and use statistics when we have only a single variable (e.g., to describe the spreadoutness of the scores on the midterm test or to identify the most frequently scored score on the midterm test). But when we conduct research we *always* have at least two variables.

Research is always about the business of identifying relationships that replicate under stated conditions. We never conduct scholarly inquiry investigating only a single variable. For example, we never study only depression. We may study how diet seems to affect depression, or how exercise seems related to self concept. But we never study only depression, or only self-concept.

Dependent versus Independent Variables

When we conduct research, usually there is one variable from among all the variables in which we are most interested. This variable is called the **dependent variable** (or, synonymously, the "criterion," "outcome," or "response" variable). Clearly this is an important variable, else why would this variable have so many names?

Dependent variables may be caused by or correlated with other variables. A variable of the second sort is an **independent variable** (also called a "predictor" variable).

Within the researcher's theory of causation, dependent variables always occur after or at the same time as independent variables. Outcomes cannot logically flow from subsequent events that occur after the outcome.

However, the dependent variable is the *first* variable selected by the researcher. The researcher may declare, "I care about math achievement." And then the researcher selects what is believed to be the most reasonable independent variable. The one exception to this generalization is in applied program evaluation, when we evaluate existing programs and then conceptualize various possible program effects, including effects that are either intended or unintended.

In scientific inquiry, we do *not* select independent variables, and then wander around checking for all the various things that these independent variables might or might not impact. This is not by any means meant to say that important things can only be discovered through formal scientific methods.

For example, Fleming discovered penicillin when some mold apparently drifted through an open lab window one night and landed on a petri dish, thereby killing some bacteria that he was investigating. Viagra was initially investigated as a heart medication, but male patients began reporting unexpected side effects. These initial discoveries were serendipitous, and not scientific, but nevertheless were important.

But we usually adopt as a premise the view that new discoveries will be most likely when inquiry is more systematic. We select the outcome we care about, and most want to control or predict, and only then do we identify potential causes or predictors that seem most promising, given contemporary knowledge.

Incidental Variables

Of course, in most studies many **incidental variables** are present, although not of primary interest. Some of these data may be recorded and reported for descriptive purposes, to characterize the makeup of a sample (e.g., ethnic representation or age). Other incidental variables may be of no interest whatsoever, and may not even be recorded.

For example, a researcher may investigate as an independent variable the effects of two methods of teaching statistics to doctoral students. One method may involve rote memorization and the use of formulas; the other method may be insight-focused and Socratic. Final exam scores may constitute the dependent variable.

In any study of this sort, there would be a huge number of incidental variables (e.g., length of right feet, soda preferences, political party affiliations, Zodiac signs) that occur but are of no theoretical interest whatsoever, and therefore are usually not even recorded.

Univariate versus Multivariate Analyses

Although formal inquiry always involves at least two variables (at least one dependent variable, and at least one independent variable), it is usual that a given study will involve more than two variables. Because most researchers believe that most outcomes are multiply caused (e.g., heart health is a function not only of genetics, but also of diet and exercise), most studies involve several independent variables.

By the same token, most independent variables have multiple effects. For example, an effective reading intervention will impact the reading achievement scores of sixth graders, but also may well impact the self-concepts of these students. Fortunately, just as studies may involve more than one independent variable, studies may also involve more than one dependent variable.

When a study involves two or more independent variables, but only one outcome variable, researchers use statistical analyses suitable for exploring or characterizing relationships among the variables. The class of statistical analyses suitable for addressing these dynamics is called **univariate statistics**, which invokes the second, alternative definition of this term: "methods suitable for exploring relationships between one dependent variable and one or more independent variables." Univariate analyses have names such as "analysis of variance" or "multiple regression," and are the sole focus of this book.

When a study involves two or more dependent variables, researchers may conduct a series of univariate analyses of their data. For example, if a study involves five dependent variables, the researcher might conduct five multiple regression analyses, each involving a given outcome variable in turn.

Alternatively, when a study involves two or more dependent variables, researchers may conduct a single analysis that *simultaneously* considers *all* the variables in the dataset, and all their influences and interactions with each other. This alternative to univariate statistics invokes **multivariate statistics**.

Thompson (2000a) emphasized that "univariate and multivariate analyses of the *same data* [emphasis added] can yield results that *differ night-and-day* [emphasis added] . . . and the multivariate picture in such cases is the accurate portrayal" (p. 286). However, multivariate statistics are beyond the scope of the present treatment.

Given that (a) researchers quite often conduct studies involving two or more criterion variables, and (b) multivariate analyses provide accurate insights into these data, why must we learn univariate statistics? There are two reasons. First, sometimes researchers do conduct reasonable studies with only one dependent variable. Second, understanding univariate statistics is a necessary precondition for understanding multivariate statistics. Indeed, mastery of the content of this book will make learning multivariate statistics relatively easy. Learning this content actually will be harder than learning the multivariate extensions of these concepts.

Mastery of the concepts of this book will give you the equivalent empowerment that the ruby slippers gave Dorothy in *The Wizard of Oz*. You will have the power to go to Kansas (or not) whenever you wish (or not wish). Unlike the kind Witch of the North, however, I am telling you about your empowerment at the beginning, rather than withholding this knowledge so that the information can be revealed in a surprise ending. (I have always wondered why Dorothy didn't deck the kind witch at the end of the movie, once the witch revealed to Dorothy the power she had possessed all along; Dorothy might have avoided some painful and difficult situations if the kind witch had not been so intellectually withholding.)

Symbols

When we are presenting statistical characterizations of our data, we often use Roman or Greek letters to represent the characterization being reported (e.g., M, SD, r, σ, β). This is particularly useful when we are presenting formulas, as in statistics textbooks. For example, we conventionally use M (or $\overline{X}$) as the symbol for the mean (i.e., arithmetic average) of the data for a given variable.

We also often use Roman letters (e.g., Y, X, A, B) to represent variables. Because independent variables tend to first occur chronologically, and dependent variables occur last, to honor this sequence we typically use letters from near the end of the alphabet to represent outcomes, and letters from nearer the beginning of the alphabet to represent predictor or independent variables. For example, a researcher may declare that Y represents degree of coronary occlusion, X_1 represents amount of exercise, and X_2 represents daily caloric intake. Or a researcher might investigate the effects of gender (A) and smoking (B) on longevity (Y).

The symbols for statistical characterizations and for variables can also be combined. For example, once Y has been declared the symbol representing the variable longevity, M_Y is used to represent the mean longevity.

Moderator versus Mediator Variables

In some studies we may also study the effects of a subset of independent variables called **moderator variables**. In the words of Baron and Kenny (1986), "a moderator is a . . . variable that affects the direction and/or strength of the relation between an independent or predictor variable and a dependent or criterion variable" (p. 1174).

Some variables may have causal impacts within some groups, but not others, or may have differential impacts across various subgroups. For example, taking a daily low dose of aspirin reduces the risk of stroke or infarct. But apparently about 20% of adults are "aspirin resistant," and for these patients the independent variable, aspirin dosage, has little or no effect on the outcome, infarct incidence.

As another example, Zeidner (1987) investigated the power of a scholastic aptitude test to predict future grade point averages. He found that predictive power varied across various age groups. In this example, GPA was the dependent variable, aptitude was the independent variable, and age was the moderator variable.

Moderator effects can be challenging to interpret. **Simpson's Paradox** (Simpson, 1951) emphasizes that relationships between two variables may not only disappear when a moderator is considered, but also may even reverse direction! Consider the following hypothetical study in which a new medication, Thompson's Elixir, is developed to treat patients with very serious coronary heart disease. The results of a randomized clinical trial (RCT), a 5-year drug efficacy study, are presented below:

Outcome	Control	Treatment
Live	110	150
Die	121	123
% survive	47.62%	54.95%

The initial interpretation of the results suggests that the new medication improves 5-year survival, although the elixir is clearly not a panacea for these very ill patients. However, mindful of recent real research suggesting that a daily aspirin may not be as helpful for women as for men in preventing heart attacks, perhaps some inquisitive women decide to look for gender differences in these effects. They might discover that for women only these are the results:

Outcome	Control	Treatment
Live	58	31
Die	99	58
% survive	36.94%	34.83%

Apparently, for women considered alone, the elixir appears less effective than the placebo.

Initially, men might rejoice at this result, having deduced from the two sets of results (i.e., combined and women only) that Thompson's Elixir must work for them. However, their joy is short-lived once they isolate their results:

Outcome	Control	Treatment
Live	52	119
Die	22	65
% survive	70.27%	64.67%

In short, for both women and men separately, the new treatment is less effective than a placebo treatment, even though for both genders combined the elixir appears to have some benefits.

The paradox that any relationship between variables may be changed, or even reversed, by introducing a moderator makes clear how vital is the decision of what variables will be considered in an analysis. In the present example, we might deem the results for genders combined to be the relevant analysis, and consider using the elixir, notwithstanding the paradoxical differences within the categories of the moderator variable.

In addition to investigating moderator effects, we also sometimes study the effects of **mediator variables**. Whereas moderator variables inform judgment about when or for whom effects or relationships operate, mediator variables may help us understand how or why effects or relationships occur.

Independent variables may have some combination of both direct and indirect effects. Mediator variables are used to explore and quantify the indirect versus the direct effects of an independent variable upon a dependent variable.

For example, for the largest 50 cities in the United States, there is a huge relationship between the number of churches and the number of annual murders. However, if we take into account the mediating influence of city size, there is virtually no relationship between numbers of churches and murders. That is, virtually all the "effects" of number of churches on murders is indirect, via the mediation of city size.

Any observed relationship between churches and murders is spurious. Taking into account city size, we see that churches do not apparently explain or predict murders. Nor do more or fewer murders apparently lead to building more or fewer churches!

As a second example, consider the relationship between fathers' education and oldest child's subsequent education, mediated by fathers' socioeconomic status. Fathers' education may have a mixture of both direct and indirect effects on the educational attainment of children. More educated fathers may teach children to value attainment, and may also teach their children educational content.

But fathers' education additionally impacts fathers' socioeconomic status. And fathers' socioeconomic status may, in turn, have its own impacts on the educational attainment of children, because social class may influence children's aspirations, expectations, and the knowledge exchanged by peers in classrooms and other settings.

Populations versus Samples

Whenever we conduct quantitative or mixed-methods (Tashakkori & Teddlie, 2002) research, there is the group of people (or lab rats or monkeys) about which we wish to generalize, and the group from which we have data. The group to which we wish to generalize is called the **population**. If we have data only from a subset of the population, our dataset is called a **sample**.

If I collect data in a teaching experiment from 20 doctoral students in a given time period, and these are the only students about whom I care, then this group constitutes a population. But if I give you my data, and you wish to use these data to generalize to other graduate students, or for these students to other points in time, then for you these same data constitute a sample.

The distinction between a population and a sample is solely in the eyes of the beholder. Two researchers looking at the same data may make different decisions about the generalization of interest.

The distinction is made on the basis of research purpose, and *not* on the basis of data representativeness. Indeed, there is an old cliché that much social science research involves unrepresentative samples and is conducted "on rats and college sophomores." Regardless of the mechanism of sampling (e.g., a sample of local convenience), if the researcher is generalizing to a larger population, the data constitute a sample, even though the sample may not be very good, or representative.

In practice, researchers almost always treat their data as constituting a sample. Researchers seem to be quite ambitious! For example, in conducting an intervention experiment with 10 first graders who are being taught to read, even if the sample consists only of children who are family acquaintances, scholars seemingly prefer to generalize their findings to all first graders, everywhere, for all time.

Thus, when we take courses about quantitative ways to characterize data, we tell people we are taking a "statistics" course rather than a "parameters" class or a "statistics/parameters" class. In actuality, it might be more accurate to say that we are taking a course about "statistics/ parameters."

The judgment as to whether data constitute a population or a sample is *not* semantic nit-picking. For some characterizations of data, formulas for a given characterization differ, depending on whether or not the data are deemed a sample or a population. So two researchers who are computing the same result even for the same data may obtain different numerical answers if they reach different judgments about the population of interest.

Characterizations of data computed for populations are termed **parameters**. Parameters are always represented by Greek letters. For example, if we have data for 12 doctoral students at a given time on the variable X, and we only care about these students at this single point in time, the data constitute a population. The arithmetic average, or mean, of these 12 scores would be represented by the Greek letter μ_X.

Characterizations of sample data are called **statistics**. For example, if we have the same data for 12 doctoral students at a given point in time, and we believe we can generalize their results to other doctoral students, and we desire to make this generalization, our data instead constitute a sample. The arithmetic average, or mean, of these 12 scores would be represented by a Roman letter, such as M_X or $\overline{X}$.

As another mnemonic device to help distinguish populations from samples, we will also use different symbols to represent the number of scores in populations versus samples. We will use N to quantify the number of scores in a population, and n to quantify the number of scores in samples.

Levels of Scale

Quantitative data analysis typically involves information represented in the form of numbers (e.g., the dataset for a sample of $n = 3$ people: 1, 2, 3). However, different sets of the *same* three numbers (i.e., 1, 2, and 3) may contain *different* amounts of information.

Furthermore, when we characterize different aspects of data, each characterization presumes that the numbers contain *at least* a certain amount of information. If we perform a calculation that requires more information than is present in our data, the resulting characterization will be meaningless or erroneous.

So the judgment about the amount of information each dataset contains is *fundamentally* important to the selection of appropriate formulas for data characterizations. And for every way of characterizing data, we must learn the *minimum* information that must be present to compute a given statistic or parameter.

Four Levels of Scale

Quantitative researchers characterize the amount of information contained in a given variable by using *levels of scale* conceptualized by S. Stevens (1946, 1951, 1968) and others. The four levels of scale are: (a) nominal/categorical, (b) ordinal/ranked, (c) interval/continuous, and (d) ratio. More detail on levels of scale is provided by Nunnally (1978, Ch. 1), Guilford (1954, Ch. 1), and Kirk (1972, Ch. 2).

The levels of scale constitute a hierarchy. Data at a given level of scale contain all the information unique to the given level *plus* all the information present at lower levels of scale.

For each level of scale, there are specific constraints on what numbers we may use to represent the information contained in a variable. At the same time, even given these constraints, infinitely many reasonable choices always still exist for communicating a given variable's information.

Knowing the numbers used to represent scores on a given variable tells you *nothing* about the level of scale of the data. It is the information present in the data, as determined by the mechanisms of measurement, that determines scaling. And, as might be expected by now, because these concepts are important, there are synonymous names for several of the levels of scale.

Nominal or **categorical** data represent only that (a) the categories constituting a given variable are mutually exclusive, and (b) every person scoring within a given category is identical with respect to the particular variable being measured. Human gender of a particular class of students is a variable *iff* (if and only if) at least two students in this class have a different gender. We usually take human gender in many groupings to be dichotomous (i.e., a two-category variable). Worms are an entirely different story. For people, the commonly-recognized categories are "male" and "female." Because very, very few people are hermaphrodites, presumably the categories in our given class of students are mutually exclusive.

We also consider every person in a given category to be *exactly* identical with respect to the variable, gender. All males are exactly equally male, and all females are exactly equally female. This does *not* mean that all the males, or all the females, have the same physical measurements, sex appeal, money, intelligence, or anything else. But every person in a given category of a given variable is considered exactly the same as regards that variable.

Consider the data for the following four students on the variable gender (X):

Name	X
Steve	M
Patty	F
Judy	F
Sheri	F

In quantitative research we typically represent information using numbers, rather than letters or other symbols

In converting these data to numbers, we *must* honor the two pieces of information present on the variable. Thus, we cannot assign the same number (e.g., 0) to all four students, or we would misrepresent the reality that the categories are mutually exclusive. Nor could we legitimately give Patty one number, and Judy and Sheri a different number, or we would misrepresent the reality that Patty, Sheri, and Judy are all considered equally female.

Notwithstanding these constraints, which are absolute, there remain infinitely many plausible choices. We could assign Steve "1," and the remaining students "2." Or we could assign Steve "1," and everyone else a "0." Alternatively, we could assign Steve "999,999,999," and the remaining students each "–5.87." Or we could assign Steve "6.7," and Patty, Judy, and Sheri each "–100,000."

Let us assume that a researcher selected the first scoring strategy (i.e., "M" = "1"; "F" = "2"). This is perfectly acceptable. But when analyzing our data, it is essential to remember what information is present in the data, and what information is not. Given the nominal level of scale of our data, we know *only* that we have two mutually-exclusive categories, and that everyone in a given category is identical with respect to gender. Our scoring does *not* mean that two males equal one female, or that concerning gender a male is half a female!

Given the information present in nominal data, the only mathematical operation permissible with such variables is counting. For example, we can say that female is the category with the most people, or that there are three times as many females as males.

Ordinal or **ranked** data contain the two features of nominal data but also warrant that (c) score categories have a meaningful order. Let's say we have data for our sample of $n = 4$ people on a second variable, military rank (Y):

Name	Y
Steve	General
Patty	Captain
Judy	Private
Sheri	Private

When translating this information into numerical scores, there are again both constraints, and infinitely many plausible alternatives. We can assign scores of 1, 2, 3, and 3, respectively. Or we can assign scores of 9, 8, 1, and 1. Or we can assign scores of –0.5, –2.7, –1,000,000,000, and –1,000,000,000.

We may not assign scores of 4, 4, 2, and 1, or we misrepresent characteristic #1. We may not assign scores 1, 2, 3, and 4, or we dishonor characteristic #2. We may not assign scores of 1, 3, 2, and 2, or we misrepresent characteristic #3.

If we assign the scores, 3, 2, 0.5, and 0.5, respectively, we have honored all the necessary considerations for these data. But this does not mean that Steve has exactly the same military authority as Patty, Judy, and Sheri when they act in concert, even though 2 plus 0.5 plus 0.5 does mathematically sum to 3.

With ordinal data, as with data at all the levels of scale, we can always perform counting operations. So, for these data we can say that Private is the most populous category on this variable, or that 50% of the sample had the rank of Private.

But now we can also perform mathematical operations that require ordering the scores. For example, we can now make comparative statements, such as Patty has less authority than Steve. But we cannot quantify how much less authority Patty has versus Steve.

Interval or **continuous** data contain the previous three information features, but also (d) quantify how far scores are from each other using a "ruler," or measurement, on which the units have exactly the same distances. Consider the following scores for variable X, a measure of self-concept on which scores of zero are impossible because sentient beings are presumed to have some self-image:

Name	X
Steve	183
Patty	197
Judy	155
Sheri	141

These data create a four-category intervally-scaled variable. Note that it is the interval quality of the measuring "ruler," and *not* the scores themselves, that must be equally spaced. Every additional point represents an equal amount of change in self-concept.

We can again represent these scores in infinitely many ways, as long as we do not misrepresent the information. For example, we could without distortion convert the scores by dividing each score by 10. Doing so would not dishonor the order of the scores, or the relative distances between scores. If one person had a score twice as large as another person, any reasonable reexpression of the scores would honor these (and all other relevant) facts, and be equally plausible. Indeed, any preference for one versus another of these reasonable representations would be completely a matter of personal stylistic preference, and not matter otherwise.

Finally, with interval data we can perform mathematical operations of addition and the reciprocal operation of subtraction, as well as multiplication and the reciprocal operation of division by constants, such as the sample size. It makes no sense to add scores measured with a "ruler" on which every interval is a different distance. But with interval scores these operations are sensible.

We can now quantify the distances of scores from each other. For example, we can say that the distance between the scores of Patty and Steve is the same as the distance between the scores of Judy and Sheri.

Ratio data contain the prior four information features, but also (e) include the potential score of a meaningful zero. A zero is said to be meaningful if the score of zero means the complete absence of the variable being measured. For example, if your net financial worth is $0, this means that you have exactly no money, which is both meaningful (in the sense of representing the exact absence of any money) and possible.

For many social science variables, a meaningful zero is not sensible. For example, it is impossible to imagine that a living person to whom we could administer an IQ test would have an IQ score of exactly zero (i.e., a complete absence of intelligence).

Scaling as a Judgment

Life is not always about definitively right or wrong choices, and neither is statistics. For many physical measurements, such as height in centimeters or weight in pounds, clearly data are being collected at the interval level of scale.

But most constructs in the social sciences are abstract (e.g., self-concept, intelligence, reading ability) and are *not* definitively measured at a given level of scale. For example, are IQ data intervally-scaled? Is the 10-point difference between Bill with an IQ of 60 and Jim with an IQ of 70 *exactly* the same as the difference between Carla with an IQ of 150 and Colleen with an IQ of 160?

Probably all methodologists would agree that measurements of this sort are *at least* ordinally-scaled. Furthermore, many statisticians would treat such data as interval because they judge the data to truly approximate intervally-scaled data. Other methodologists are statistically conservative, treat such data as ordinal, and only perform analyses on the data that require only ordinal scale. You can discern the two camps at professional meetings, because the latter always wear business attire and the former wear blue jeans.

You might feel more comfortable about these judgments if you recognize that even physical measurements do not really yield perfectly interval data. All measurements, even physical measurements, yield scores with some measurement error, or unreliability (see Thompson, 2003). For example, even the official clock of the United States, which measures time by measuring atomic particle decay, loses 1 second every 400 years. So, if we consider measurement reliability, no "rulers" have intervals that are perfectly, exactly equal.

Transforming Scale of Measurement

Some variables can inherently be measured only at the nominal level of scale. For example, gender, or religious preference, or ethnic background, can only be measured categorically.

At the other extreme, some variables can be measured at any level of scale, depending on how the researcher collects or records the scores. Consider the following measures of how much money these four people were carrying at a given point in time:

Name	X_1	X_2	X_3
Steve	$379	1	Rich
Patty	$9	4	Poor
Judy	$78	3	Poor
Sheri	$264	2	Rich

Given these three sets of scores, all measuring the variable wealth, X_1 is certainly *at least* intervally-scaled, because the "ruler" measuring financial worth at a given point in time in dollars measures in equal intervals. The financial value (though perhaps *not* the personal differential value) of a change in any $1 is constant throughout the scale.

The variable X_2 is ordinally-scaled. We have discarded information about the distances of datapoints from each other. We can still say that no two people have the same wealth (i.e., are in the same category), and we can still order the people. But with access only to the X_2 data, we can no longer make determinations about how far apart these individuals are in their wealth.

The variable X_3 is nominally-scaled. Although the categories are still ordered, we can no longer order the individual people. We have either collected relatively limited information, or have chosen to discard considerable information about wealth.

In general, collecting data at the highest possible scale is desirable. For example, if the researcher collects intervally-scaled data, the data can always be converted later to a lower level of scale. Conversely, once data are collected at a lower scale level, the only way to recover a higher level of scale is to recollect the data.

Because statistics require specific levels of scale to properly conduct their required mathematical operations, some statistics cannot be computed for data at some scale levels. Also, more analytic options exist for data collected at higher scale levels.

However, in statistics there are exceptions to most general rules. When we are collecting information that is particularly sensitive, people may be more likely to respond if data are collected at lower levels of scale. For example, we can ask people how many times they have sex in a month, or how frequently they go to church in a year, or how much money they made last year. These data would be intervally-scaled.

But people may be more likely to respond to such questions if we instead presented a few categories (e.g., 0–2 times/month, 3–8 times/month, more than 8 times/month) from which respondents select their answers. This measurement strategy collects less information, and thus is less personal. Research always involves many tradeoffs of the good versus bad things that occur when we make different research decisions. Nevertheless, the conscious decision to collect data at lower scale levels should be based on a reflective analysis that you can still do whatever analyses you need to do to address the research questions that are important to you.

Normative versus Ipsative Measurement

Cattell (1944) presented a related measurement paradigm that distinguishes between normative and ipsative measurements. **Normative** measurement collects data in such a way that responses to one item do not *mechanically* constrain responses to the remaining items.

Here are two items from a survey measuring food preferences:

1. Which one of the following foods do you *most* prefer?

    A. monkfish   B. filet mignon with bernaise
    C. mushroom risotto   D. crème brûlée

2. Which one of the following wines do you *most* prefer?

    A. sauvignon blanc   B. cabernet sauvignon
    C. pinot noir   D. riesling

These items yield normative scores.

The response to one item may *logically* constrain responses to other items. For example, people who love beef with bernaise sauce may have some tendency to prefer cabernet sauvignon. But responses to the first item do not *physically* constrain the choice made on the second item. People can declare that their favorite food is monkfish, and that their favorite wine is riesling. Indeed, some people may actually like that pairing.

Ipsative measurement collects data such that responses to a given item mechanically constrain choices on other items. Items of this sort have forced-choice features, such as requirements to rank-order choices or to allocate a fixed number of points across a set of items.

The following item, with one respondent's choices shown, yields ipsative data:

1. Please allocate *exactly* 100 points to show how much you like each of the following types of wine by awarding more points to wines you most prefer.

A. sauvignon blanc	10
B. chardonnay	15
C. pinot noir	20
D. merlot	10
E. cabernet sauvignon	45
F. malbec	0
G. riesling	0
TOTAL	100

This individual clearly likes cabernet.

We can at least make reasonable *intraindividual* comparisons with ipsative data. For example, we can argue that this person likes cabernet three times as much as chardonnay.

These data are ipsative, because the decision to allocate a given number of points to one choice necessarily constrains allocations for all other options. And we have no information about whether this individual despises wine, thinks wine is nice sometimes, or adores wine. This makes it difficult to use ipsative data to make meaningful *interindividual* comparisons of results *across individuals*, if that is our purpose (L. Hicks, 1970).

Related data could be collected normatively, as illustrated in these results, which measure the actual spending decisions of two hypothetical individuals:

2. Please report how many dollars you would like to spend per month on each of the following types of wine, if your income was not a consideration.

	Bruce	Julie
A. sauvignon blanc	$90	$0
B. chardonnay	$295	$125
C. pinot noir	$360	$0
D. merlot	$110	$35
E. cabernet sauvignon	$895	$45
F. malbec	$0	$0
G. riesling	$0	$0
TOTAL	$1,750	$205

These are normative and not ipsative data, because responses regarding one wine do not in any mechanical way constrain responses for the remaining wines.

Likert (1932) **scales** are often used to collect normative data about attitudes or beliefs. Likert scales present response formats with numerical scales in which some or all of the numerical values are anchored to words or phrases. The numerical value and word pairing might be: 1, Strongly Agree; 2, Agree; 3, Neutral; 4, Disagree; 5, Strongly Disagree. If the researcher judges the psychological distances between these alternatives to be equal, then the data collected are arguably intervally-scaled.

At first impression, it may seem that normative data should be preferred over ipsative data. Normative data are usually intervally-scaled, and it may seem undesirable to constrain responses when collecting data.

Ipsative data collection tends to make responding more complex, because specific response rules must be followed exactly. Respondents may resent restrictions that have no obvious basis. Also, ipsative response formats as a statistical artifact yield dependencies among item responses (Kerlinger, 1986, p. 463). That is, because responses to one item (e.g., a high allocation of points to an item) constrain responses to other items, the relationships between item responses tend to be inverse (i.e., high ratings on one item necessarily yield lower ratings on other items).

However, sometimes ipsative data collection is necessary. For example, in an investigation of phenomena involving variables that are all highly treasured, normative data collection might result in every respondent's rating every choice at the extremes of the response format. If respondents were asked to rate the importance of health, economic sufficiency, attractiveness, and honor on 1-to-5 scales, it would not be unreasonable for everyone to rate all four items "5."

In such situations, reasonable variability in scores can only be achieved by using ipsative measurement. Furthermore, in some cases it might be argued that ipsative measurement is most ecologically-valid (i e , best honors the way in which people really function in everyday life). For example, people may cherish a great many outcomes (e.g., health, economic sufficiency). But given time and other resource constraints, we cannot pursue every possible thing about which we care.

In this example, ipsative measurement not only might be necessary to produce score variability, but also may best honor the ecological reality. At least, that seems to be the thinking underlying Rokeach's (1973) development of his *Values Survey*, which requires respondents to rank-order the different human values he lists, with no ties.

Ipsative measurement is used on a variety of psychological measures. For example, ipsative measurement is used on some tests intended to measure psychopathology. Items on such measures may ask unusual questions that focus on atypical thought or preference patterns. The items may pose questions virtually of the ilk, "Would you most rather be (a) a pumpkin, (b) an air conditioner, or (c) a fork?"

Some Experimental Design Considerations

Designs

Experiments are studies in which at least one intervention group receives a treatment, and at least one control group receives the usual treatment (e.g., conventional reading instruction) or no treatment (e.g., placebo sugar pills). In *true experiments*, the mechanism for assigning participants to groups is random assignment. Random assignment has the desirable feature that groups will be equivalent at the start of the experiment on *all* variables, even those the researcher does not realize are actually important, iff the sample size is sufficiently large that the law of large numbers can function. The mechanisms of random assignment simply do not work well when sample size is very small.

Only experimental designs allow us to make definitive statements about causality, although other research designs may suggest the possibilities of causal effects (see Odom, Brantlinger, Gersten, Horner, & Thompson, 2005; Thompson, Diamond, McWilliam, Snyder, & Snyder, 2005). Recent movements to emphasize evidence-based practice in medicine (Sackett, Straus, Richardson, Rosenberg, & Haynes, 2000), psychology (Chambless, 1998), and education (cf. Mosteller & Boruch, 2002; Shavelson & Towne, 2002) have brought an increased interest in experimental design.

Classically, designs were portrayed by an array of symbols presented on an implicit timeline moving from earlier on the left to later on the right (D. T. Campbell, 1957; Campbell & Stanley, 1963). "R" indicates random assignment to groups, "O" indicates measurement (e.g., a pretest), and "X" indicates intervention. For example, a two-group true experiment with no pretesting might involve

$$
\begin{array}{ccc}
R & X & O \\
R & & O
\end{array}
$$

Or, if both groups were pretested, the design might be

R	O	X	O
R	O		O

A classic design is the Solomon four-group design. The structure of the design is:

R	O	X	O
R	O		O
R		X	O
R			O

This design involves two intervention groups and two control groups.

Designs are limited only by the researcher's creativity and thoughtfulness. Consider the design for an education intervention below:

R	O	O	O	X	O	O	O
R	O	O	O		O	O	O
R	O	O	O		O	O	O

This design involves one intervention and two control groups. Perhaps one control group receives regular reading instruction, while the second group receives no reading instruction, insofar as these participants are queued up to receive the intervention after the experiment is over (i.e., constitute a wait-list control).

The design has several positive features. First, because several posttests (e.g., annual achievement testing) are administered, the design evaluates not only whether the immediate effects of the intervention are positive, but also whether the effects are sustainable. Second, the design can be used to evaluate intervention impacts on average achievement, but because repeated measurements are taken both before and after the intervention, the design can also be used to evaluate intervention effects not only on average achievement, but also on *rates of learning*.

The six measurements can be plotted both for the groups and for individuals. The slopes of the lines drawn from contiguous points represent the rates of learning. If the intervention positively impacts the rate of learning, the lines connecting the plotted scores will be steeper after the intervention than before the intervention. Impacting rates of learning may have sustained effects even more important than immediate impacts, because changing how fast people learn may have more dramatic cumulative consequences over time than do the immediate impacts on learning. **Latent growth curve modeling** (Duncan & Duncan, 1995; Duncan, Duncan, Strycker, Li, & Anthony, 1999) evaluates these various dynamics, although this analysis is beyond the scope of the present, introductory text. Nevertheless, we can intuit the potential richness of data yielded by such designs.

Historically, designs were evaluated in terms of the ability to address two sorts of design validity issues (Campbell & Stanley, 1963). Note that *design validity* should not be confused with *measurement validity* (see Thompson, 2003, Ch. 1, for further discussion of measurement issues). The similarity of wording for these two unrelated concepts is merely another effort to invoke confusing language in statistics.

Internal Design Validity

Internal design validity addresses concerns about whether we can be certain that the intervention caused the observed effects. Without internal design validity, study results are simply uninterpretable. Campbell and Stanley (1963) listed threats to internal design validity, of which seven are considered here.

Selection threats to design validity occur if there are biases in assigning participants to groups. For example, in the following design,

if smarter students are disproportionately assigned to treatment, group selection dynamics are confounded with intervention effects. Even if we statistically adjust for initial group differences, by computing and comparing gain scores (ΔX_i = posttest$_i$ − pretest$_i$), we will not have removed the rate of learning (i.e., aptitude) differences across the groups, and the results will remain confounded. Obviously, this is why we prefer random assignment to groups.

Experimental mortality involves differential loss of participants from groups during the intervention. For example, if the intervention group showed posttest improvement, but 35% of the intervention group withdrew from the study, while only 5% of the control group dropped, the results are confounded by the presence of potentially selectively missing data.

History threats to internal design validity occur when unplanned events that are not part of the design occur during the intervention. For example, if one school is the intervention site, and another school is the control school, during the intervention school year an intervention school teacher might win hundreds of millions of dollars in a lottery, and begin showering the school with new computers, and even books. These effects may confound the intervention effects such that we are not certain what impacts are attributable to the designed intervention.

Maturation effects involve developmental dynamics that occur purely as a function of the passage of time (e.g., puberty, fatigue). For example, if the control group is a first-period high school class, and the intervention group is a last-period class, the differential impacts of fatigue and hunger may be confounded with intervention effects.

Testing involves the impacts of taking a pretest on the posttest scores. A pretest (e.g., a first-grade, spelling test) may focus participants on targeted words. These effects might become confounded with intervention effects, for example, if the design was

$$R \qquad O \qquad X \qquad O$$
$$R \qquad\qquad\qquad\qquad O$$

Instrumentation may compromise result interpretation if different measures (e.g., Forms X and Y of a standardized test) are used in different groups, or over time. For example, instrumentation effects might compromise this design:

$$R \qquad O_X \qquad X \qquad O_X$$
$$R \qquad O_Y \qquad\qquad O_Y$$

Statistical regression occurs when extreme scores exhibit the statistical phenomenon called **regression toward the mean**. The phenomenon refers to the fact that extreme scores tend to move toward the group mean over time.

Sir Francis Galton, British genius and polymath, first described this statistical phenomenon (Galton, 1886). At the Great Exhibition, Galton measured the heights of families at the event. He observed that extremely tall or short parents tended to have adult children whose heights more closely approximated typical height. Clearly, the phenomenon is purely statistical, and not some function of the exercise of will or judgment during procreation.

The phenomenon can compromise designs, for example, when participants with extreme scores are assigned to groups. Thus, in a one-group design, if people with very high blood pressure on pretest are assigned to treatment, in the long run their scores will tend toward the mean even without treatment. The effects of medication and the statistical regression effect will be confounded, and we will be unable to ascertain with confidence what are the intervention effects.

External Design Validity

External design validity involves the question of "to what populations, settings, treatment variables, and measurement variables can this effect be generalized?" (Campbell & Stanley, 1963, p. 175). Here, three threats will be considered.

Reactive measurement effects occur if pretesting affects sensitivity to the intervention. For example, a vocabulary pretest might impact the effects of a vocabulary intervention, such that the intervention effects might not exactly generalize to future nonexperimental situations in which the intervention is conducted without pretesting.

In the 1920s, the German physicist Werner Heisenberg proposed his Uncertainty Principle, which essentially says that the more precisely the position of atomic particles is determined, the less precisely the momentum of the particles can be simultaneously known. A related but more general measurement paradox says that "observing a thing changes the thing." If we don't measure, we do not know what happens. But what happens in the absence of our measurements might be different than when we measure. However, in some cases reactive measurement might be avoided by using unobtrusive measures (Webb, Campbell, Schwartz, & Seechrest, 1966).

Hawthorne effects occur when participants in the intervention group alter their behavior because they are aware that they are receiving special attention. The name of the effect originates from a 5-year study conducted at the Hawthorne Plant of the Western Electric Company in Cicero, Illinois, during the Great Depression. The researchers found that when working conditions were improved in the intervention group, productivity improved. However, even when less favorable conditions were imposed, productivity also improved. The participants were apparently responding to the generalized notion of public specialized treatment, as opposed to the intervention itself. Therefore, such intervention effects might not generalize once the intervention was applied to everyone, or at least was widely available, because the novelty of the treatment would no longer be a factor.

John Henry effects occur when participants in the control group behave differently because they know that they are in the control condition. The effect is named after the legendary John Henry, The Steel Driving Man, who fought harder than he presumably would have because he knew he was in a contest and his performance was being evaluated. In the legend, John Henry was an African American of incredible strength who drove railroad spikes when track was being laid. When a steam-driven spike drill was being introduced, John Henry competed in a race with the drill to determine whether he or the drill could drive more spikes. The race was close, and John Henry died at its end.

A **double-blind design** is one way to avoid Hawthorne and John Henry effects. In this design, the participants do not know whether they are receiving the intervention or a placebo treatment (e.g., sugar pills), and the treatment administrators (e.g., nurses) do not know what treatment they are providing. Of course, double-blind studies are feasible in medicine, but may not be possible in education or psychology in cases where the nature of the intervention simply cannot be obscured.

Design Wisdom

Here is one of the most important things I can tell you about doing research. When selecting variables and designing research, *before* you collect any data whatsoever, first "List [all] possible experimental findings [i.e., results] along with the conclusions you would draw and the actions you would take if this or another [any/every other] result should prove to be the case" (Good & Hardin, 2003, p. 4). This exercise forces early recognition of fatal design flaws before it is too late to correct problems.

Some Key Concepts

Statistics are computed so that we can understand and communicate the dynamics within data. Statistics are selected given the researcher's purpose. Usually several statistics will be needed to characterize relevant data features within a given study. Both subjective judgment and reasonableness must be exercised when selecting statistics.

Statistics may be used to characterize data involving only a single variable. But science is about the business of identifying relationships that occur under stated conditions, and so scientific studies inherently involve at least one dependent variable and at least one independent variable.

The selection of ways to characterize data is also governed by a decision about whether the data constitute a sample or a population. And the levels of scale of variables impact which statistics are and are not reasonable in a given research situation.

Only true experiments, in which treatment conditions are randomly assigned, can definitively address questions about causality. To yield definitive conclusions, studies must be organized to mitigate threats to internal and external design validity.

■■■ Reflection Problems ■■■

1. Name a nominally-scaled, an ordinally-scaled, and an intervally-scaled variable, with each of the three variables involving four categories. Then name five equally-reasonable ways to assign numbers to the categories of each of the three variables (i.e., scoring rubrics).

2. Think of a situation, not described in this book, in which ipsative measurement might be preferred over normative measurement.

3. Identify a dependent variable of particular interest to you. Then select the two independent variables that you consider the best possible predictors of this outcome. In a study using these three variables, would you hold anything constant? What moderator variable might be of greatest interest?

2

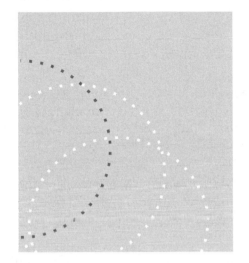

Location

escriptive statistics quantitatively characterize the features of data. Although "statistics" are always about sample data, "descriptive statistics" are about either sample or population data. (You have already been duly forewarned about the confusing language of statistics.)

Four primary aspects of data can be quantified: (a) location or central tendency, (b) dispersion or "spreadoutness," (c) shape, and (d) relationship. The first three classes are called univariate statistics, in the sense of this term meaning that these descriptive statistics can be computed even if you have data on only one variable. The fourth category of descriptive statistics requires at least two variables. In the simplest case, when there are only two variables (e.g., X and Y), or there are more than two variables but the variables are considered only in their various pairwise combinations (e.g., A and B, A and C, B and C, and never all A, B, and C simultaneously), relationship statistics encompass bivariate statistics.

The statistics computed across these four classes are independent. This means, for example, that knowing the central tendency of the data tells you *nothing* about the numerical quantification of the dispersion of the data, or that knowing the shape of the data tells you nothing about the numerical quantification of the location of the data.

The independence of the four categories is only logical. If any two of the characterizations performed the same function, there would be fewer than four categories. Even the most wild-eyed statisticians can only go so far in trying to be confusing!

■■■ Reasonable Expectations for Statistics

Formulas for descriptive statistics were not transmitted on stone tablets given to Moses, nor otherwise divinely authored. Instead, different human people developed various formulas as ways to characterize quantitative data.

Sometimes people are noble, honorable, and insightful. But sometimes people are also lazy, sloppy, or simply wrong. Because these formulas were created by fallible people, the prudent scholar does not take these equations as givens, and instead evaluates whether the formulas seem to be reasonable.

Thoughtful, critical, and responsible judgment requires initially formulating expectations about what might be deemed reasonable for a given way of characterizing data. These different expectations apply to all the entries in a given class of descriptive statistics. If the descriptive statistics are indeed reasonable, they will behave such that they *always* meet these expectations. Otherwise, the characterizations yielded by these formulas are erroneous, and should be discarded in favor of correct formulas.

There are advantages from understanding statistics (our focus), rather than merely memorizing unexplained formulas. Only when we fully understand the underlying logics of the formulas, as well as which data features do and do not affect results, do we really understand our characterizations of data (and the data we are using these characterizations to understand).

▪▪▪ Location Concepts

Location or **central tendency** descriptive statistics address the question "Which one number can I use to stand for or represent all my data?" Obviously, this can be a big job for one number to do. The quality of the characterization of the location of a dataset along a numberline is situationally conditional upon (a) the number of scores in the data and (b) the spreadoutness of the data.

When sample size is smaller, logically a single number will do a better job of characterizing central tendency. For example, when sample size is $n = 1$, a single location statistic can do a superb job of representing the dataset! Just use the one scored score to represent the entire dataset.

Central tendency descriptive statistics may be less suitable as sample size gets larger. But even at huge sample sizes, location descriptive statistics still do very well at representing data when scores are very similar to each other, and perfectly well when all the scores are identical, even if sample size is huge.

The procedures for computing the characterizations of location are the same for both sample and population data. However, we will see that for other classes of descriptive statistics (e.g., dispersion) different procedures are required for sample as against population data.

Expectations for Location Statistics

Descriptive statistics each fall into one of two "worlds": (a) the score world, or (b) the area world. Scores as they are originally measured are (obviously) in the score world, and have a particular measurement metric. For example, scores may be measured in dollars, pounds, or number of right answers.

We will first encounter area-world descriptive statistics once we consider the second class of descriptive statistics, dispersion statistics, in Chapter 3. Only then will the fundamentally important concept of the two worlds of statistics become more apparent.

The first minimal expectation for location descriptive statistics, which yield a single number to represent all the scores, is that *location descriptive statistics ought to be in the same metric as the scores themselves.* Thus, if the unit by which we measure knowledge is the number of correct test answers, the corresponding location descriptive statistics should also be in exactly the same metric. So, all location statistics are members of the score world.

However, it seems unreasonable to expect that location descriptive statistics must universally include only numbers that are actually scored. For example, if we have a large group of professional football linemen who all weigh between 275 and 285 pounds, it might be reasonable to use the number, 280 pounds, to represent the entire dataset, even if no lineman weighs exactly 280 pounds.

But it does seem reasonable to demand that the one number we use for a location descriptive statistic for a given dataset ought to be in one sense or another in the center of the scores. This leads to a second expectation when data are at least ordinally-scaled, such that the scores have a meaningful order, that *at a bare minimum, a location descriptive statistic for a given dataset should be no lower than the lowest score and no higher than the highest score.*

Univariate Location Graphics

Most of the mathematical methods for characterizing data, including descriptive statistics, were developed over the course of the previous several centuries, and many of these originated during the 1900s. These mathematically-computed characterizations of data can be very useful in efforts to understand or communicate the stories that data have to tell.

But graphics are also a very useful way to explore or disseminate the insights lurking in data (Tukey, 1977). In some cases graphics make obvious data dynamics that would otherwise be obscure. Sometimes graphics are also more economical in representing data dynamics. And when communicating our scholarly findings, we had best remember that some people prefer numbers, some people prefer pictures, and some people like to have both numbers and graphics.

The influential recommendations of the Task Force on Statistical Inference of the American Psychological Association (APA) emphasized that there are many "ways to include data or distributions in graphics. . . .

Many of these procedures are found in modern statistical packages. It is time for authors to take advantage of them and for editors and reviewers to urge authors to do so" (Wilkinson & APA Task Force on Statistical Inference, 1999, p. 602).

Histograms are commonly used to portray a single set of scores (i.e., a variable or a constant). A histogram presents a numberline oriented with lower numbers to the left and higher numbers to the right. Scores are often represented by asterisks located on the numberline at a position corresponding to score values, although some software uses symbols other than asterisks.

When datasets are relatively small, each person is represented by a unique asterisk. When datasets are larger, asterisks represent multiples of people (e.g., 5, 10) who have a common score. There is no firm rule about when datasets become small or large. In any case, when presenting such graphs, you should inform readers how many scores each asterisk represents.

Table 2.1 presents data for scores of seven people on the variables X and Y. The variable X is the number of cups of coffee consumed on one day, and Y is the number of phone calls each person placed on the same day. Figure 2.1 presents the two histograms for these two variables, with each asterisk representing the score of a single person.

TABLE 2.1. Scores of Seven People on X and Y

Participant	Variable	
	X	Y
Jennifer	5	5
Stephanie	5	4
Elizabeth	5	3
Paul	2	3
Sarah	1	3
Christopher	1	2
Michael	1	1

FIGURE 2.1. Histograms of the Table 2.1 variables

Three Classical Location Descriptive Statistics

Traditionally, three location descriptive statistics have been frequently used in the social sciences. There are other location descriptions (e.g., the geometric mean, the harmonic mean, the contraharmonic mean) that are beyond the scope of the present treatment, in part because they are less frequently reported (interested readers are referred to Glass & Stanley, 1970). As we shall see once we cover the descriptive statistics that characterize shape, for some data the three descriptive statistics yield the same three numbers for a given dataset, and for some data all three estimates may differ even for a given single dataset.

Mode

The **mode** is the most frequently scored score, and therefore, unlike the other two commonly-used location descriptive statistics, the mode is *always* a scored number. Of course, this also ensures that the mode is in the metric of the original scores, and must fall within the range of the scored scores.

For data that constitute a constant (i.e., all the scores are the same), that single scored number is always the mode. Otherwise, identifying the mode requires counting the number of scores in each variable category. No ordering of categories is required, nor are any addition or multiplication operations. Counting is permissible with data at *all* levels of scale, so the mode can be computed even for nominally-scaled data.

Because the mode is in the same score-world metric as the original data, the mode for variable Y in Table 2.1 is *not* 3.0, but is instead more descriptively reported as "3.0 phone calls." The mode for variable X in Table 2.1 is less obvious, because the scores of 1 cup of coffee and 5 cups

bimodal, more than
2 males, ~~no~~ no mode

of coffee are each scored three times, which is more than any other single
score.

Such data are said to be **bimodal**, and both modes (1 cup and 5 cups)
must be reported. When data have three or more scores that occur equally
often and are most frequently scored for a dataset, we generally deem the
data to have no mode.

As previously intimated, the mode will work perfectly to represent
data that define a constant (i.e., all the scores are the same). However, for
variables, although the mode must lie within the range of scored scores
(sometimes barely), it is troubling that the mode can literally be at the very
boundary of scored scores (e.g., the modes for variable X in Table 2.1 are
literally at both score extremes for these intervally-scaled data). Perhaps
these limitations are why the mode is infrequently reported, and in turn
why there is not a commonly-used symbol for this descriptive statistic.

The mode is a location descriptive statistic that is only "in the center"
in the loosest possible sense. However, for nominally-scaled data, the
scores have no order and no numerically-meaningful boundaries, so this
deficiency is not a consideration for nominal data. The mode is the only
location statistic that can be computed for nominally-scaled data, and so
must be used for such data, if central tendency is an interest.

Given the limitations of the mode, for data higher than nominally-
scaled the mode in practice is rarely interpreted. An exception occurs if
you are an apparel manufacturer, rather than a social scientist. People will
usually not buy brassieres or shoes that do not fit well, even if the bras-
siere or shoe *almost* fits a lot of people. So if you are in the apparel business, the first size you would select to manufacture is the mode size,
because it not only will fit people, and thus potentially be bought, but also
will indeed fit the largest audience of potential buyers.

Median

The **median**, or **50th percentile**, can be computed for data that are at least
ordinally-scaled. Conceptually, the median is the number, either scored or
unscored, that divides the ordered scores into two groups of equal sizes.
Because we cannot put nominally-scaled scores into any meaningful order
(i.e., no real ordering information is present), the median cannot be reasonably computed for nominal data. That is, you can erroneously put

nominal scores into some arbitrary order, and estimate the median, but the estimate is just as senseless as the ordering itself.

The median is "in the center" of the scores in the sense that half the scores are above the median and half are below the median. Thus, for the interval scores {1, 2, 4, 5 speeding tickets}, the median is "3.0 tickets," which is not a scored score. The median for the Y scores in Table 2.1 is also 3.0, albeit "3.0 phone calls," which in this case is a scored score, and indeed coincidentally is also the mode.

The symbol for the median on variable X is "Mdn_X." The formula for the median is

$$Mdn_X = P_{50} = L + [((q * n) - cum.f) / f] \qquad (2.1)$$

where

q is the percentile being computed, which for the median is always the number 50, so $q = 0.50$;

n is the number of scores in the distribution;

L is the lower limit of the score interval of length 1 containing the q nth frequency from the bottom of the score distribution;

$cum.f$ is the cumulative frequency up to L; and

f is the number of scores in the score interval containing the q nth frequency.

The formula for the parameter median would be the same, but we would symbolize the number of scores in the population with N.

For the sample data on X from Table 2.1, the cumulative frequency distribution presented in Table 2.2 would be computed. Here $q * n = 0.50 * 7 = 3.5$. The score interval containing the 3.5th score is the interval running from 1.5 to 2.5. The lower limit, L, of this score interval is 1.5. The cumulative frequency up to L is 3. There is $f = 1$ score in the score interval containing the 3.5th score. So, for these data we obtain:

$$
\begin{aligned}
Mdn_X &= 1.5 + [((0.50 * 7) - 3) / 1] \\
&= 1.5 + [(3.5 - 3) / 1] \\
&= 1.5 + [0.5 / 1] \\
&= 1.5 + 0.5 \\
&\ 2.0
\end{aligned}
$$

TABLE 2.2. Cumulative Frequency Distribution
for the Table 2.1 X Data

Score	Frequency	Cumulative frequency
5	3	7
4	0	4
3	0	4
2	1	4
1	3	3
	$n = 7$	

For these data, the median is "2.0 cups of coffee" (and *not* simply 2.0). In this case, the median is a scored score.

Unlike the mode, the median *cannot* be all the way at the boundaries of the ordinal or the interval scores, except when all the scores are identical. And unlike the mode, the median does have the desirable feature that all the scores are considered in computing the median.

Iff (if and only if) data are intervally-scaled, the distances of the scores from the median become meaningful. For intervally-scaled data, the median is "in the middle" of the scores in the sense that the sum of the *absolute* distances of the scores from the median will be smaller than or equal to the sum of the absolute distances of the scores from *any* other benchmark (i.e., "How far is each score from this number?") scored score or unscored number (Horst, 1931).

However, the computation of the median does not itself take into account any information about score distances. This is necessary for ordinally-scaled data, which contain no information about distances. But when we have intervally-scaled data, such information is present, and sometimes we want to capitalize on all the information features contained in the data.

Mean

The **mean** is the arithmetic average of intervally-scaled data, and does take into account score distances as part of its computation. As noted in Chapter 1, the symbol for the mean is M_X or $\overline{X}$ for sample data, and μ_X for population data.

The formula for the mean of sample data is

$$M_X = \Sigma X_i / n \qquad\qquad (2.2)$$

where the Greek capital letter sigma (Σ) means "add them all up," X_i are the scores of each of the i individuals in the dataset, and n is the number of scores in the sample. Note that M_X does not have an i subscript, because the mean is one number representing the entire dataset, and may not even be any individual's scored score in the data, and so the use of an i subscript would be inappropriate. The parameter formula for population data is

$$\mu_X = \Sigma X_i / N \qquad\qquad (2.3)$$

where N is the number of scores in the population.

For the variable X Table 2.1 data, the sample mean, M_X, equals 20.0/7, or to three decimal places, "2.857 cups of coffee." Remember that the modes were "1 cup" and "5 cups," and the median was "2.0 cups of coffee." For these data, each of these three location descriptions yields a different answer, and so the selection of a particular location description might impact our interpretation of results even for a single dataset.

Of course, we are not limited to computing only a single location descriptive statistic, if our data are higher than nominally-scaled, and computing several helps us to understand our data. But typically scholars report only one such characteristic, perhaps because journal editors are so protective of journal signature space. We will learn later in this chapter when some of these location results will be identical for a dataset, and when they will differ.

The mode is "in the center" in the loose sense of being some (any) scored score. The median, even for ordinally-scaled data, is "in the center" in the sense of dividing the ordered scores into two equal-sized groups of lower and higher scores. The mean is "in the center" in a physical sense of being the fulcrum underneath the numberline at the point that the histogram would balance.

The mean has the property that if you subtract the mean from each of the scored scores, yielding **deviation scores** (symbolized by lowercase letters, such as x_i or y_i), the deviation scores will *always* add up to exactly zero (e.g., $\Sigma x_i = 0.0$). This implies that you could create a numberline by marking equal intervals on a 2″-by-6″ board, possibly ranging from 0 pounds to 12 pounds, and then place lead objects weighing between 0 and 12 pounds at the corresponding locations on the board (e.g., a 3.5-pound object at the location 3.5 on the board/numberline); the board (or seesaw/teeter-totter) would be level if placed on a fulcrum or balance point at whatever location corresponded to the mean (e.g., "5.75 pounds" if that was the mean weight of the lead objects).

The mean also is "in the middle" of the scores in the sense that the sum of the *squared* distances of the scores from the mean will be smaller than the sum of the squared distances of the scores from *any* other benchmark (i.e., "How far is each score from this number?") scored score or unscored number. These two characteristics of the mean make the mean a great benchmark to use when we need to compare each score to some one benchmark number to help characterize dynamics within our data.

Rounding

When dividing or multiplying numbers, it is possible to obtain answers that are nonterminating. For example, 2 divided by 3 yields a nonterminating result. There are two options for reporting nonterminating results. First, the nonterminating number or set of numbers can be represented by placing a line over the nonterminating values. For example, 2 divided by 3 can be reported as 0.66. Second, rounding can be employed with nonterminating numbers, just as rounding can be employed with any decimal values in real numbers.

In the social sciences, descriptive statistics are rarely reported to more than either two or three decimal values, partly because for most of our variables extremely small differences are not meaningful or noteworthy. For example, it is usually sufficient to compute the mean number of right answers on a test as 57.6 or 57.63, but it probably makes no sense to report the mean as "57.63289366567 right answers." The "289366567" part of the number is trivial.

Reporting an excessive number of decimal values communicates more precision than is really present in most data. However, when our descriptive statistics can be employed by others to replicate our analyses (as in a textbook), or to conduct analyses different than ours (because some secondary analyses do not require the original data), then more decimal values may be used in reporting.

Rounding requires, first, a decision about the desired number of decimal places (e.g., two). Then one rounds from the number at the decimal place immediately beyond the targeted number of decimal places (e.g., the third decimal place). If the number we are rounding from is less than 5, we round down (e.g., 3.744 becomes 3.74 if we are rounding to two decimal places). If the number we are rounding from is greater than 5, we round up (e.g., 3.746 becomes 3.75 if we are rounding to two decimal places).

When the number we are rounding from is a 5, special rules apply (Tukey, 1977). There are nine possible numbers in the location from which we are rounding where rounding may be necessary (i.e., 1, 2, 3, . . . , 9). Arguably, rounding is not being performed when in a descriptive statistic a zero is to the right of the targeted number of decimal places.

When we are rounding from descriptive statistics, four numbers are below 5 and four numbers are above 5. To avoid rounding from 5, and consistently biasing rounded results upward or downward, we round half the time from 5. Specifically, we round up if the rounded number will become even (e.g., 3.735 becomes 3.74), and we do not round up if doing so would make the rounded number odd (e.g., 3.745 becomes 3.74).

Purpose of Division

In addition to rounding, division also requires some explanation. Let's consider the formula for the sample mean, $M_X = \Sigma X_i / n$, and *why* we divide by n, and especially what function division serves in statistics.

Presume that we have data about the life savings of a sample of women and a sample of men. If we were interested in the wealth of the two groups as a whole, we could compare the sums of the savings in the two groups. But if we are interested instead in savings from the perspective of the *individual people* of both genders, we need to compare location descriptive statistics, such as means, rather than score sums.

If the groups were not of equal size, and the sum of the savings of the *smaller* group was *larger* than the sum of the savings of the *bigger* group, we could be unequivocally certain that the smaller group had more savings than the larger group, even given a focus on the perspective of the individual. Of course, we still could not quantify how much more savings there were in the more frugal group. Conversely, if the groups were not of equal size, and the sum of the savings of the *bigger* group was *larger* than the sum of the savings of the *smaller* group, we could not be certain that from the individual perspective the bigger group had more savings than the smaller group.

If the two groups were exactly equal in size, we could compare the sums to make accurate judgments of wealth from both the group and the individual perspectives. But researchers do not limit themselves to studying groups that are always of equal size.

We need ways to compare data dynamics represented in descriptive statistics that will work when group sizes are equal, but also will work when group sizes differ. Happily, statisticians know that *when we divide, we are removing from our answer that which we are using to divide.*

Most statistics formulas involve division that uses some function of n (either n or $n - 1$), so that results may be compared across groups of disparate sizes. And sometimes we divide by other data characteristics, so that these too no longer impact our answers.

Of course, some analyses focus exclusively on the data in hand, at our fixed single sample size. For analyses of this sort, division by n (or $n - 1$) is unnecessary, because the sample size is a constant for within-study characterizations of data.

Outliers

The mean is fundamentally important in computing other characterizations of data in addition to location (i.e., dispersion, shape, and relationship), as we shall see in succeeding chapters. However, the mean is very sensitive to anomalous or outlying scores. And any distortions in the mean unavoidably also impact the characterizations of data that themselves invoke the mean as a benchmark reference point.

An **outlier** is a participant whose data are distinctly atypical and thus would unduly influence characterizations of the data. Some researchers have the misconception that outliers are evil people (or lab rats, etc.) who are or should be branded on their foreheads with giant, red capital letter "O's."

Instead, most people are outlying in some sense on at least some variables. We are all probably really exceptionally bad, or exceptionally good, or weird, on some things. This is part of the challenge of formulating social science generalizations involving people with so many individual differences. Of course, some people may be outliers on more variables than other people.

To complicate matters, as we shall also eventually see, an outlier is not necessarily outlying on all descriptive statistics for a given dataset. For example, a given person may be an outlier regarding the mean, but not regarding the median or other statistics.

Table 2.3 illustrates these dynamics. Jane is not an outlier regarding the mean or the median on X_1. However, Jane arguably is an outlier regarding the mean of X_4, even though she is not an outlier regarding the median of X_4.

The Table 2.3 data illustrate the relative sensitivities to outliers of the mean versus the median. The mean can be very highly influenced by relatively few anomalous scores in the data, even when the number of scores is quite large.

However, the sensitivity of the mean to unusual scores does *not* suggest that the median is always a better location statistic than the mean. In some cases, we care more about people who are extreme (e.g., people whose cholesterol is exceptionally high) and therefore would intentionally

TABLE 2.3. Heuristic Data Illustrating Impacts of Outliers on M and Mdn			
Participant	X_1	X_2	X_3	X_4
Robert	1	1	1	1
David	2	2	2	2
Karan	3	3	3	3
Jane	4	9	99	999
Median	2.50	2.50	2.50	2.50
Mean	2.50	3.75	26.25	251.25

select the mean as a descriptive statistic most sensitive to the most or least worrisome scores.

When the researcher is in a quandary about which central tendency description to use, remember that this is not necessarily an either-or choice. It may be perfectly reasonable to report several location descriptive statistics to more fully represent the scores, and to give readers a more complete understanding of the data.

Another alternative is to use more sophisticated and considerably more complex central tendency descriptive statistics. For example, the Huber (1981) estimator can be used. Statistically, this estimator for sample data in essence focuses on the mean for the core of the data distribution and on the median for more extreme portions of the distribution (Maxwell & Delaney, 2004).

The Huber estimator is *not* computed using a formula! In particularly sophisticated statistics, sometimes no formula is present. When no formula exists to derive an estimate, computationally-intensive procedures requiring computers, called "iteration," sometimes can still produce an estimate. **Iteration** is a statistical routine in which a first guess is made, then the guess is repeatedly tweaked using some statistical rule, until a satisfactory estimate is obtained. For example, in the method called exploratory factor analysis, iteration is always performed as part of what is called rotation (Thompson, 2004).

The mechanics of iteratively guessing the Huber estimator for a dataset are beyond the scope of the present treatment. The point is that there are a lot of descriptive statistics that can be used to characterize location, and no single characterization is always definitively correct.

A related question is what to do with the outliers themselves. Perhaps the better solution for dealing with outliers, rather than changing the descriptive statistic, is to eliminate or alter the scores of outliers.

The first thing to consider when encountering outlying scores is that data may have been incorrectly entered. Out-of-range values (e.g., an IQ score of 900) are obvious indications of inaccurate data entry. Out-of-range or other entry errors are simply corrected once the mistakes are identified.

Second, further investigation may shed some light on whether plausible but unlikely scores are legitimate values. For example, perhaps a grade-equivalent score of 7.2 by a doctoral student on a reading skills test is possible, but the alternative hypothesis—that the student was not working to capacity—clearly must be considered. Upon being interviewed, the student might confess lack of motivation when taking the test. Or consultation of other data for the student (e.g., a GRE verbal score of 780) might suggest that the student simply was not trying. When external information definitively indicates that scores are inaccurate, participants might be retested or their scores simply may be omitted from the dataset.

Third, when scores are in some sense extreme but possible, and no external evidence can explain the basis of the anomaly, decisions about what to do with the outlying scores become quite difficult. In general, omitting outliers simply because they are bothersome, without theoretical justification, is unreasonable. As Pedhazur and Schmelkin (1991) noted, "the onus of interpreting what the outliers and/or influential observations mean in a set of data and the decision about what to do is, needless to say, on the researcher" (p. 408). Researchers should avoid the temptation for atavistic escape inherent in using arbitrary cutoffs for degrees of score extremity as the sole basis for removing unexpected scores (Johnson, 1985).

One prudent choice may be to report results for analyses both with and without the outliers with plausible scores for whom the basis for score extremity cannot be discerned. If the interpretations are reasonably invariant (i.e., similar) across analyses, the researcher is assured that conclusions are not artifacts of analytic strategies.

▪▪▪▪ Four Criteria for Evaluating Statistics

As suggested by the previous discussion, no statistic provides a perfect characterization of sample scores under all circumstances. But methodologists have elaborated four criteria to guide evaluations of how well statistics work.

Sufficiency refers to whether a statistic makes use of all the data in the sample. For example, the mode is not a sufficient statistic, except in very small samples (i.e., $n = 2$) or when the scores delineate a constant rather than a variable. The median and the mean, on the other hand, are sufficient statistics.

Unbiasedness refers to the capacity of repeated samples invoking a statistic to yield accurate estimates of corresponding parameters. For example, M is an unbiased estimate of μ. If we draw infinitely many random samples, each of a given size (e.g., $n = 50$) from a population, and average the sample Ms, that average will equal μ.

Efficiency refers to how tightly statistics used to estimate parameters cluster around the actual parameters. For example, if we are attempting to characterize the parameter central tendency, we prefer estimates using a given sample size that fluctuate less across samples from a given population than do other plausible estimates.

Robustness refers to the capacity of a statistic to be less influenced by outlying scores. For example, as noted previously, although the mean is a sufficient, unbiased, and relatively efficient statistic, the mean is more influenced by outliers than is the median.

Two Robust Location Statistics

Statisticians have long been concerned about how to improve characterizations of data containing outliers. For example, in a short, accessible article, Wilcox (1998) argued that *a good deal of educational and psychological research probably has reached erroneous conclusions based on overreliance on classical statistics* such as the mean.

Robust statistics are variations on older classical estimates (e.g., M_X, Mdn_X) for location and other data descriptions that seek to minimize the influences of outliers. Wilcox (1997) published a book on robust statistics alternatives. Also see Keselman, Kowalchuk, and Lix (1998) and Keselman, Lix, and Kowalchuk (1998). Table 2.4 presents a heuristic dataset that can be used to illustrate two alternative "robust" location descriptive statistics that can be employed to mitigate the disproportionate influences of extreme scores.

One robust method "winsorizes" (à la statistician Charles Winsor) the score distribution by substituting less extreme values in the distribution for more extreme values. For example, in a set of 20 skewed scores, the fourth score (e.g., 433) may be substituted for scores 1 through 3, and in the other tail the seventeenth score (e.g., 560) may be substituted for

TABLE 2.4. Two Illustrative "Robust" Location Descriptive Statistics

ID	X	X'	$\overline{X}$
1	430	433	—
2	431	433	—
3	432	433	—
4	433	433	433
5	435	435	435
6	438	438	438
7	442	442	442
8	446	446	446
9	451	451	451
10	457	457	457
11	465	465	465
12	474	474	474
13	484	484	484
14	496	496	496
15	512	512	512
16	530	530	530
17	560	560	560
18	595	560	—
19	649	560	—
20	840	560	—
M	500.00	480.10[a]	473.07[b]
Mdn	461.00	461.00	461.00

[a]The arithmetic average of the third column, containing one version of altered data, is the winsorized mean.

[b]The arithmetic average of the fourth column, containing data omitting 0.15 (or 15%) of the scores in both extremes of the distribution ($n = 20 - 3 - 3 = 14$), is the trimmed mean.

scores 18 through 20. The mean of this winsorized distribution (e.g., $M_{X'} = 480.10$) thus becomes less extreme than the original value (e.g., $M_X = 500.00$).

Another robust alternative "trims" the more extreme scores and then computes a "trimmed" mean. In this example, 0.15 of the distribution is trimmed from each tail. The resulting mean (e.g., $M_{\overline{X}} = 473.07$) is thereby closer to the median of the original distribution, which has remained 461.00.

In a sense, as pointed out by Lunneborg (1999), the median can itself be thought of as a trimmed mean (i.e., a mean based on trimming essentially 50% of the scores from both tails). In theory, robust statistics may generate more replicable characterizations of data, because at least in some respects the influence of more extreme scores, which given their atypicality may be less likely to be drawn in future samples, has been minimized.

However, robust statistics have not been widely employed in contemporary research. Perhaps scholars who are not methodologists have difficulty keeping up with the burgeoning literatures in their own disciplines, much less the burgeoning methodology literature. Or some researchers may hesitate to report methods not already routinely presented in journals, for fear that if they violate normative expectations for scholarly behavior their work may be less likely to be published.

Some Key Concepts

All location or central tendency statistics, to be reasonable, must fall within the score distribution and ideally, in one sense or another, should fall near the center of the distribution. Location statistics can be very useful in understanding and explaining the story underlying our data.

However, too often researchers focus solely on location statistics, and especially the mean. And, as we shall see in our Chapter 4 treatment of shape statistics, the median is too infrequently considered. As Grissom and Kim (2005) noted, sometimes a "*sample's* [emphasis added] median can provide a more accurate estimate of the mean of the *population* [emphasis added] than does the mean of that sample" (p. 40).

▨▨▨ Reflection Problems ▨▨▨

1. Consider the scores {1″, 1″, 2″, 3″, 8″}. Determine the mean and the median. Because these data are intervally-scaled, the differences of scores from both the mean and the median are meaningful. Compute (a) the difference, (b) the absolute difference, and (c) the squared difference of each score from the *median*. Then sum up each set of three numbers.

   Then compute (a) the difference, (b) the absolute difference, and (c) the squared difference of each score from the mean. Then sum up each set of three numbers.

What are the sums of the difference scores from the mean, and from the median? Which descriptive statistic, mean or median, has the *smallest* sum of the *absolute* difference scores? Which descriptive statistic, mean or median, has the *smallest* sum of the *squared* difference scores?

2. Researchers not infrequently encounter missing data (e.g., some students skip certain test questions, or some participants were absent when a given test was administered). Even though there are better ways to deal with missing data (Little & Rubin, 1987), sometimes researchers substitute the mean of the nonmissing scores on a variable for the missing data on a given variable. What effect does using this mean imputation for missing data have on the means computed both before and after the substitution is performed?

    Imputation of missing data can be particularly problematic when the data are not missing at random. A classic example involves statistician Abraham Wald's work on aircraft survivability in World War II (Mangel & Samaniego, 1984). Researchers counted the bullet and shrapnel injuries in various locations on returning aircraft. Might a focus on reinforcing the locations on returning aircraft receiving the most hits have been less productive than focusing on the locations receiving the most hits on the planes that did *not* return? Of course, damage data for nonreturning planes was not available to the analysts, and Wald was merely emphasizing that the researchers really did not have access to the data they most needed, and should have been more cautious in using the data that were available!

3. For two independent and equally critical reasons, the influences of additive and multiplicative constants on statistics ought to be understood. First, to understand various statistics (e.g., medians, means), we must know what causes or affects them, and what does not. Second, throughout statistics, as we shall see in subsequent chapters, additive and/or multiplicative constants are used. To understand the results invoking these constants, we must understand the impacts of additive and multiplicative constants.

Consider the following data:

	Y	X1	X2	X3
Jane	1	1	0	6
Douglas	2	2	0	1
Jim	3	3	0	1
Mike	4	4	4	1

Compute the mean of each variable. Then apply the following constants to *X1*, *X2*, and *X3*, and next compute the means of the various new versions of the three variables:

a. Add 3 to each score.
b. Add −1 to each score.
c. Multiply each score by 2.
d. Multiply each score by −0.5.
e. First add −1 to each score; then multiply each result by 2.

For each original and revised version of a given variable, plot the *original* values of a given variable in a histogram in blue or black pen, and plot the *revised* values of a given variable in a histogram in red or green pen. How do the distributions move as constants are applied? How does the mean move in relation to its score distribution?

What rule can we formulate to express the effects on means of additive constants (e.g., "New mean always equals original mean . . .")? What rule can we formulate to express the effects on means of multiplicative constants (e.g., "New mean always equals original mean . . .")? Why mathematically do these rules work? When will a multiplicative constant *not* change the value of the original mean?

3

Dispersion

Dispersion or "spreadoutness" statistics quantify the answer to the question, "How dissimilar (or similar) are the scores to each other?" Dispersion statistics can be used for two purposes: (a) to characterize how well location descriptive statistics perform at representing all the data, and (b) to characterize score "spreadoutness" as an important result in its own right.

Of course, the dispersion question only makes sense in the presence of data that are at least intervally-scaled. With nominal or ordinal data, all we can do is compute the proportion 0.0 to 1.0 (or the percentages 0% to 100%) of scores within the modal score category. This is a crude dispersion characterization, but does not quantify how much the scores differ. But for nominal or ordinal data, how could we quantify how distant scores are from each other, or from some benchmark, if the scores have no meaningful, nonarbitrary information about distance on a "ruler" that is at least intervally-scaled?

▪▪▪ Quality of Location Descriptive Statistics

Recognizing that location descriptions may differ in their quality, and even have *no* value for some data, is a fundamentally important understanding. For example, presume that you and your significant other are sitting under a tree on a university park bench. Lo and behold, along comes Bill Gates, the chairperson of Microsoft Corporation.

The accumulated savings of the three of you in dollars could be measured, and the data would be intervally-scaled. Thus, the mean could be computed. But would the resulting one number fairly represent all, or even any, of the three scores? Mr. Gates might be perturbed that the mean woefully underrepresented his net worth. And you might be depressed to realize that the mean of the group was (presumably) so far above your own life savings.

As noted in Chapter 2, all the central tendency statistics work perfectly well for data that have zero dispersion. But location descriptions work less well as scores become increasingly dissimilar from each other. And at some degree of dispersion, the concept of central tendency becomes senseless. The big picture becomes only the score spread, and not the use of one number to represent all the scores.

But for other data for which central tendency is sensible and that are at least intervally-scaled, dispersion statistics are *essential* quantifications of the quality of location descriptions. The important implication is: *Never report a central tendency statistic (e.g., M_X) without reporting (usually in parentheses) right next to the location description a dispersion description.*

▪▪▪ Important in Its Own Right

Dispersion statistics can also be important in their own right. In such cases, these dispersion characterizations might be presented without even reporting central tendency descriptions.

Consider the results below for 10 first graders coincidentally all named after deceased former U.S. presidents. The students were randomly assigned to one of two methods of teaching spelling. Prior to intervention, the students completed a pretest on which the number of correctly-spelled words was recorded. After instruction, the students again completed a brief posttest measuring the number of correctly-spelled words.

Group / first grader	Pretest	Posttest
Control		
M. Fillmore	1	1
R. Hayes	2	2
C. Coolidge	3	3
H. Hoover	4	4
R. Nixon	5	5
M	3.0	3.0
Experimental		
G. Washington	1	0
T. Jefferson	2	0
A. Jackson	3	3
A. Lincoln	4	6
F. Roosevelt	5	6
M	3.0	3.0

The means for these data suggest that the process of randomly assigning participants to groups effectively created groups that were equivalent at the start of the intervention, reflected in part by the fact that both pretest means equaled "3.0 correct answers." That is the good news. The bad news is that the two posttest means suggest that the interventions were equally (in)effective.

However, upon closer scrutiny, the data do suggest intervention effects, albeit *not* on average achievement. Here the new, experimental teaching method caused student achievement to become increasingly dispersed. Clearly, understanding intervention effects requires more than looking only at group means.

The outcomes for these data (no mean change, but increased achievement variability) are obvious given that the dataset in the example is ridiculously small. This sort of impact might have been obscured in a large dataset, and might have gone completely unnoticed by researchers who sadly have "obsession with only means" personality disorder.

The pattern here of no growth during educational intervention is not typical. But the pattern of interventions impacting score spread is reasonably common. Indeed, educational interventions frequently yield "fan" spreads reflecting differential impacts for students starting at different levels. Figure 3.1 illustrates such a "fan" effect for the five participants in the intervention group whose scores became more dispersed following the intervention.

Less able students over the course of intervention may stay about the same or only slightly improve. More able students may not only improve, but may even improve more dramatically than their less able counterparts. This dynamic reflects the fact that pretest achievement scores involve estimated abilities at a given point in time, but may involve as well differential rates of learning.

The challenge in many educational interventions is not only to help students learn, but also to impact rates of learning. The take-home message is to remember that means only characterize one aspect of data, and that other characterizations of data dynamics may also be important, or may even be more or most important.

FIGURE 3.1. Plot of pretest to posttest changes for intervention participants

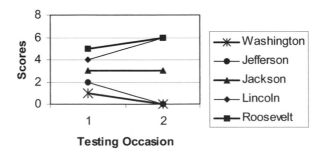

▩▩▩ Measures of Score Spread

Expectations for Dispersion Statistics

The least "spreadout" that scores could be would occur if all the scores were identical, regardless of what the identical scores were. In this case, the scores would have exactly zero spread. We expect statistics describing score variability or dispersion to *all* yield numerical answers of exactly zero (i.e., 0.00) when the scores have no spreadoutness.

A negative numerical answer for any statistic describing dispersion would assert that "the scores are less 'spreadout' than the scores would be if the scores were all identical." This does not seem plausible!

When any two scores differ from each other, we expect dispersion descriptive statistics to be greater than zero. As scores are increasingly more dissimilar to each other, we also expect statistics describing score variability to increase in value.

Logically, because scores can take on infinitely many different values, the scores can also be infinitely dispersed from each other. Therefore, there is no *universal* mathematical limit on the upper-bound or maximum values of descriptive statistics for dispersion.

Range

The simplest descriptive statistic that characterizes score dispersion is the **range**. The range is the largest score minus the smallest score. We cannot compute the range for nominal data, because the scores of the variable's categories have no meaningful order, so there is no highest or lowest. We cannot compute the range for ordinal data, because addition or subtraction is not reasonable unless the scores are intervally-scaled.

The range has the expected feature that we obtain zero if all the scores are identical, in which case we subtract any one person's score from any one other person's score to compute the range. The range is nonzero if any two people have different scores, as reasonably expected of all dispersion statistics.

The range, like all the location descriptive statistics, is in the score world. So, if the scores are {$1.00, $3.00, and $5.00}, the mean is not 3.0, but $3.00. Similarly, the range would be $4.00.

The range has the disadvantage that only two scores are considered in its computation. This means that different datasets, each involving different score variabilities, may nevertheless have the same range. For example, the following three datasets (years 2006, 2008, and 2010) all have a range of $2M, even though the datasets differ in spreadoutness, going from least dispersion in the 2006 data to the most dispersion in 2010.

Person	2006	2008	2010
George	$2M	$2.0M	$2M
Wenona	$0	$1.5M	$2M
Steve	$0	$1.0M	$2M
Patty	$0	$1.0M	$0
Judy	$0	$0.5M	$0
Sheri	$0	$0	$0

Of course, the insensitivity of the range to all but two scores is completely irrelevant at every sample size, if the scores are a constant, and so the range equals zero. So, for example, at $n = 1,000,000$, for range = 0.0, this descriptive statistic does a perfect job of characterizing the dispersion of all 1,000,000 scores.

However, for scores that constitute a variable, the range is less and less satisfactory as n increases, because more and more scores are ignored, or because data with different dispersions can have the same ranges. We need a dispersion descriptive statistic that considers *every* score and yields a different result for datasets with different "spreadoutness."

Sum of Squares

If we wish to compare each score with every other score, there would be $[n(n-1)] / 2$ pairwise comparisons. For example, for the previous data, involving the scores of six people, there are $[6(6-1)] / 2 = [6(5)] / 2 = 30 / 2 = 15$ unique comparisons. As a starting point, we could compute how far every score deviated from George's score, and then add up or average the "George deviations."

Which person we use as the benchmark score makes no difference. If all the scores are the same, the sum of the "George deviations" or the "Wenona deviations" or any of these deviations will be zero, and the average of these will then also be zero. Alternatively, we could use any number (e.g., 0.0) as the comparative benchmark, even a number outside the score range.

However, as noted in Chapter 2, the mean has some very special properties. For example, M is "in the center" of the scores, even in the sense that physical weights balance on a fulcrum positioned at M. These properties of the mean make the mean particularly desirable as our benchmark from which we may measure dispersion for each score.

One candidate for a descriptive dispersion statistic is the sum of the individual deviation scores from the mean, where each $x_i = X_i - M_X$. The $\Sigma x_i = 0.0$ when the data constitute a constant, which is desirable. The sum of the deviation scores also has the desirable feature of considering each and every score. However, the sum of the deviation scores would be a completely unsatisfactory measure of score dispersion, because Σx_i is *always* zero, even for variables, as emphasized in Chapter 2.

One alternative would be to compute the sum of the absolute deviations from the mean or some function of this sum, such as the **mean absolute deviation** (i.e., $MAD_X = \Sigma|x_i| / n$). For example, for the scores {$1, $3, and $5}, the sum of the absolute deviations is | $2| + |$0| + |$2| = $2 + $0 + $2 = $4. And $MAD_X = $4 / 3 = $1.3\overline{3}$. This description of dispersion is not unreasonable, but the description is rarely used because this characterization lacks a statistical "theoretical undergirding," and "the mathematical statistician finds the process of 'taking absolute values' presents special difficulties for certain mathematical derivations" (Glass & Stanley, 1970, p. 86).

Another alternative is to square the deviation scores, and then sum the squared deviations. Doing so yields the **sum of squares** (SOS_X). For example, the SOS of the following three IQ scores is 200.0:

Person	X_i	$-$	$\overline{X}$	$=$	x_i	x_i^2
Geri	125	$-$	135	$=$	-10	100
Murray	145	$-$	135	$=$	10	100
Wendy	135	$-$	135	$=$	0	0
Σx_i					0	
SOS_X						200

Thus, the formula for the SOS_X can be expressed as

$$SOS_X = \Sigma(X_i - \overline{X})^2 \qquad (3.1)$$

or equivalently as

$$SOS_X = \Sigma \, x_i^2 \qquad (3.2)$$

An algebraically equivalent formula uses the original scores (or "raw scores") rather than the mean and the deviation scores:

$$SOS_X = \Sigma X_i^2 - [(\Sigma X_i)^2 / n] \qquad (3.3)$$

For our data we have $[125^2 + 145^2 + 135^2] - [(405^2) / 3] = [15625 + 21025 + 18225] - [164025 / 3] = 54875 - 54675 = 200$. The "raw score" formula is computationally easier. However, computational ease of use was more relevant when statistics were computed on hand-cranked calculators. And the raw score formula has the very serious heuristic downside that the formula completely obscures (a) the underlying nature of *SOS* and (b) the role of the mean in computing several dispersion statistics.

The sum of squares cannot be negative, because of the squaring operation. The *SOS* will be zero iff (if and only if) the scores constitute a constant. The *SOS* will be nonzero for all variables and, for a fixed n, will become larger as scores become more dissimilar from each other. Conceptually, the *SOS* is *information about both the amount and the origins of individual differences.*

The social sciences presume that people differ as individuals. These individual differences create challenges in formulating theoretical generalizations, and may make universal statements impossible. Even medicines do not work equally well in different people! But these individual differences are exactly the focus of scholars in the social sciences. Thus, our definition of the *SOS* makes the *SOS* sound critically important in quantitative research in the social sciences, because the *SOS* indeed is critically important in quantitative research.

As we shall see, the *SOS* has some limitations as a descriptive statistic. However, the *SOS* is used ubiquitously in various other statistical analyses, as will be illustrated over and over again in later chapters.

The *SOS* in this case quantifies the *amount* of information we have in our data as "200.0 squared IQ points." In general, we prefer more rather than less information (i.e., variability) about the variables of interest to us. If we are investigating childhood depression, and the *SOS* of the depression scores of our study participants is zero, we will have considerable difficulty (actually, an impossibility) in understanding the nature and causes of depression.

But a nonzero *SOS* can also be used to explore the *origins* of our information about individual differences. First, we can partition the *SOS* information based on the degree to which the scores are reliable, and the degree to which the information is unreliable. This is a *measurement* study application that focuses on score psychometric integrity, and is beyond the scope of the present treatment, but the interested reader is directed to Dawson (1999) or Thompson (2003).

Second, we can perform a *"who"* partition of our information. Because each person's contribution to our information is unique, nonoverlapping, or uncorrelated, x_i^2 for a given person quantifies how much information a given study participant contributed to the dataset. We can even secure graph paper and draw a Venn diagram, portraying the information by using different color pens for each participant.

In the present example, we will draw in red a rectangle or square containing 100 graph paper boxes to represent Geri's contribution. We can draw a contiguous rectangle or square in blue to represent Murray's contribution of 100 area world units of information. We can draw Wendy's contribution in chartreuse, but here there will be no problem if we do not have this color of pen, because Wendy contributed no information about individual differences on this particular variable. Persons scoring at the mean never contribute any information about individual differences, at least on this given variable.

Third, we can perform a *substantive* partition to explore how our 200 squared units of information originated, or how well other variables might predict or explain our information. Substantive partitioning applications are the focus of the "Bivariate Relationships" chapter in this book and of all subsequent chapters.

The mean of our three IQ scores is "135 IQ points." However, the sum of squares is *not* "200.0 IQ points." Instead, the SOS_X is "200.0 *squared* IQ points." In other words, although the three scores and the central tendency descriptive statistics for the scores are all in the "score" world, the sum of squares is the first statistic we have encountered that is in the squared or "area" world.

Variance

The *SOS* meets many of our expectations for a dispersion descriptive statistic and has many, many uses in applications that are not descriptive (e.g., that are explanatory or substantive). The *SOS* is quite useful in quantifying how much information we have on a given variable in a study with a fixed number of participants to the extent that we focus only on a given dataset.

However, problems may arise if we wish to compare score spread across subgroups within our study, or if we wish to compare dispersion of scores in our study with score dispersion in some other study. We *can* compare score spreads apples-to-apples using *SOS* if the scores in the groups are all constants, and the sums of squares are all zero.

But if the scores create a variable (*SOS* > 0.0), there may be difficulties. If two groups (or subgroups) of scores involve exactly the same number of participants, we can (a) make definitive statements about which set of scores is more dispersed and (b) quantify in squared information units how different dispersion is by subtracting the smaller *SOS* from the larger *SOS*.

If two groups have different numbers of participants, and the *SOS* in the smaller group is larger than the *SOS* in the larger group, we can be certain that the scores are more dispersed in the smaller group than in the larger group. However, we cannot quantify the amount of differential score dispersion on the average by subtracting the sums of squares one from the other, because this computation would not recognize the difference in the group sizes.

Things are particularly problematic if the *SOS* for the variable in the larger group is larger than the *SOS* in the smaller group. Now we cannot determine whether the larger group's *SOS* is due to (a) cumulating squared deviation scores over more participants, (b) greater average dispersion in the larger group, or (c) both these factors. Nor can we quantify the amounts of differential average score spreads in the two groups.

As explained in Chapter 2, these problems can be overcome by removing the influence of group size from our descriptive statistic via division. At first impression, the solution seems very straightforward: Divide by n for samples, and N for populations. Unfortunately, the correct solution is a bit more complex.

Dividing the *SOS* by a function of the number of participants yields an area-world descriptive statistic, the **variance**. The parameter symbol for the population variance is σ^2_X. The statistic symbol for the sample variance is Var_X (or SD^2_X, for reasons that will become clear in the next section).

However, it turns out that we must use different divisors, depending on whether our data constitute a population or a sample. For the parameter, we use the formula

$$\sigma^2_X = SOS_X / N \qquad (3.4)$$

For the statistic, we use

$$Var_X = SD^2_X = SOS_X / (n - 1) \qquad (3.5)$$

Obviously, the variance cannot be computed for sample data with $n = 1$, because division by $n - 1 = 0$ is impermissible, but dispersion is a moot point of little or no interest when n equals 1 anyway.

Note that dividing by $n - 1$ rather than by n for sample data will *always* result in a larger answer, iff $SOS \neq 0$. The difference in our result from dividing by $n - 1$ versus n (iff $SOS \neq 0$) is fairly dramatic when n is small (e.g., when n is 2 or 3). How much larger our answer will be, however, iff $SOS \neq 0$, differs for every value of n. This dynamic is illustrated by the following list of potential values for n:

n	$n - 1$	Difference
2	1	50.00%
3	2	33.3$\overline{3}$%
4	3	25.00%

5	4	20.00%
6	5	16.6$\overline{6}$%
7	6	14.28%
8	7	12.50%
9	8	11.1$\overline{1}$%
10	9	10.00%
100	99	1.00%
1,000	999	0.10%
1,000,000	999,999	0.0001%

Division by $n - 1$ rather than by n is a correction for statistical bias that would otherwise occur in our answer. Problems of systematic bias in research present no difficulty as long as we (a) recognize that bias is present and (b) know the appropriate correction factor.

For example, people may have a tendency to either lie or unconsciously exaggerate how much money they earn, how often they go to church, or how often they have sex. When we are conducting door-to-door surveys, if we know the correction factor is to divide by 2, there is simply no point in confronting the study participant for being dishonest when we knock on the door, and pose our research question, and they respond "eight times per week." We simply record 4.0 on our data collection form and move on to the next house, hoping that we will not get punched in the nose for asking intensely personal questions.

Similarly, statistical bias in estimating score dispersion in sample data is not problematic as long as we know the "fix." When we are characterizing score dispersion in the sample, we are using the statistic as an estimate of the population dispersion. Samples always imply ultimate interest in the population. Otherwise, we would instead call the data the population, and use Equation 3.1. But *why* do sample data tend to underrepresent the score dispersion present in the population, when we are drawing strictly random samples from the population?

The tendency of sample data to underrepresent score dispersion in the population is actually *conditional* on the shape of the population data, a topic covered in more depth in Chapter 4. However, for now, let us assume that the population consists of the nine scores portrayed in the Figure 3.2 histogram of the Table 3.1 data.

On each successive selection from the population when creating the

TABLE 3.1. Population Scores ($N = 9$)	
Person	X
Molly	1
Geri	2
Murray	2
Peggy	3
Carol	3
Anne	3
Donna	4
Deborah	4
Wendy	5

sample, each person's probability of being drawn is exactly equal, by definition of what simple random sampling means. For example, the probability of drawing Molly first is 1 / 9, the probability of drawing Geri is 1 / 9, and the probability of drawing Wendy is 1 / 9. After the first draw, on the second draw, every person's probability of being selected is now exactly 1 / 8.

But (and this is a very big "but"), the probability of drawing each of the five scores is *not* equal. The probability of drawing scores 1 or 5 is 1 / 9 each. But the probability of drawing scores 2 or 4 is instead 2 / 9 each. And the probability of drawing score 3 is 3 / 9, or 1 / 3.

This means that random samples from populations such as that portrayed in Figure 3.2 tend to overrepresent scores in the middle, and underrepresent scores in the two extremes. Consequently, scores in random samples for populations like this one tend to be less dispersed than the populations from which the samples are drawn! This is the dynamic

FIGURE 3.2. Histogram for a population consisting of nine scores

```
                    *
            *       *       *
    *       *       *       *       *

    1       2       3       4       5
```

for which we are correcting for bias by dividing by $n - 1$ rather than by n when we have sample data.

Standard Deviation

The variance meets our expectations for describing score spread. The variance (like every other dispersion statistic) can be no less than zero and is zero iff the scores are a constant. The variance gets larger as scores become more dissimilar to each other (or differ more from a score benchmark, the mean). And the variance can be used to compare score dispersion across groups of unequal sizes, even when the scores are not a constant.

Of course, the variance is in a squared metric (e.g., "580 squared pesos," "76 squared pounds," "350 squared IQ points"). Mathematically, this poses no difficulty. However, most of us are more comfortable working in the unsquared metric of the score world. For example, if we ask a store clerk whether 100 squared dollars is sufficient to pay for our purchase, the clerk may look at us quizzically, and we may even be arrested.

Taking the square root of the variance puts our descriptive statistic back in the score world, and in the metric of the original score. The square root of the variance is the **standard deviation** (i.e., σ_X for the parameter, and SD_X for the statistic). The parameter formula is

$$\sigma_X = SQRT[\sigma^2_X] = [SOS_X / N]^{0.5} \qquad (3.6)$$

Note that raising a value to the exponential power of 0.5 is equivalent to taking the square root of the value. The statistic formula is

$$SD_X = SQRT[Var_X] = [SOS_X / (n - 1)]^{0.5} \qquad (3.7)$$

Thus, if the scores are measured in the units of number of correct test answers, and the variance is "4.0 squared correct answers," the standard deviation would be "2.0 correct answers."

We have noted previously that the mean has some special features as a measure of central tendency, including the fact that $\Sigma x_i = 0.0$. The mean is used as the benchmark from which we quantify degree of score dispersion.

We initially invoke a squaring function to quantify score spread from the mean. Consequently, the standard deviation is sometimes called the "first moment about the mean." Other descriptive statistics also use the mean as the benchmark from which to quantify deviations, but use higher-order exponential powers of the deviations (i.e., 3 and 4), thereby defining the second and third moments about the mean. These two additional statistics are presented in Chapter 4.

■■■ Situation-Specific Maximum Dispersion

Deep understanding of statistical characterizations of data requires insight into what expectations ought apply to different results, and what universal limits (e.g., minimum possible results) apply for various descriptive statistics. Understanding also requires knowledge of *situation-specific* mathematical restrictions on possible results.

For example, dispersion descriptive statistics have a *universal* mathematical lower-bound limit. Dispersion statistics cannot be less than zero, and will be zero only for data that constitute a constant.

Dispersion statistics have no universal mathematical upper-bound limit. For example, *SOS* can equal 1,000,000,000, and *SD* can equal 1×10^{27}. But dispersion statistics *do* have an upper-bound mathematical limit if we constrain the description as regards (a) how many participants there are, and (b) what the lowest and highest scores are.

Scores are most dispersed *when half the scores are at one extreme, and half the scores are at the other extreme.* For example, if we constrain the scores of six participants to be numbers 1.0 through 5.0, at maximum score dispersion (i.e., three scores of 1.0 and three scores of 5.0) the mean will equal

$$[(n_1 * X_{MIN}) + (n_2 * X_{MAX})] / n \qquad (3.8)$$
$$[(3 * 1.0) + (3 * 5.0)] / 6$$
$$[3 + 15] / 6$$
$$18 / 6$$
$$3.000$$

where, for an even number of scores, $n_1 = n_2 = n / 2$, and for an odd number of scores, $n_1 = n / 2 + 0.5$, and $n_2 = n / 2 - 0.5$; X_{MIN} is the lowest possible score; and X_{MAX} is the highest possible score.

The maximum situation-specific SOS will equal

$$[n_1 * ((X_{MIN} - M_X)^2)] + [n_2 * ((X_{MAX} - M_X)^2)] \qquad (3.9)$$
$$[3 * ((1.0 - 3.000)^2)] + [3 * ((5.0 - 3.000)^2)]$$
$$[3 * (-2.00^2)] + [3 * (2.00^2)]$$
$$[3 * 4.000] + [3 * 4.000]$$
$$12.000 + 12.000$$
$$24.000$$

The maximum variance equals $SOS_X / (n - 1) = 24.000 / (6 - 1) = 24.000 / 5 = 4.800$. The maximum $SD_X = Var_X^{0.5} = 4.800^{0.5} = 2.191$.

If we change the previous example for the case in which $n = 7$, the mean under the condition of maximum score dispersion will equal

$$[(n_1 * X_{MIN}) + (n_2 * X_{MAX})] / n$$
$$[(4 * 1.0) + (3 * 5.0)] / 7$$
$$[4 + 15] / 7$$
$$19 / 7$$
$$2.714$$

Thus SOS_{MAX} would equal

$$[n_1 * ((X_{MIN} - M_X)^2)] + [n_2 * ((X_{MAX} - M_X)^2)]$$
$$[4 * ((1.0 - 2.714)^2)] + [3 * ((5.0 - 2.714)^2)]$$
$$[4 * (-1.714^2)] + [3 * (2.286^2)]$$
$$[4 * 2.939] + [3 * 5.224]$$
$$11.76 + 15.67$$
$$27.429$$

The maximum variance equals 4.571 (i.e., 27.429 / 6) and the maximum SD equals 2.138 (i.e., $4.571^{0.5}$). Note that the same results will be obtained if we instead perform the calculations with $n_1 = 3$ and $n_2 = 4$.

Robust Dispersion Descriptive Statistics

In Chapter 2 it was emphasized that outliers have more effect on the mean than on the median. Also, some robust central tendency descriptive statistics were presented.

Outliers also impact dispersion descriptions. Indeed, because the SD is the first moment about the mean, and the calculation of SD invokes the squaring of deviation scores, outliers have a disproportionately *greater* impact on dispersion than on central tendency statistics. And the effects of outliers on higher-order moments are even more pronounced.

Consider the following data, a count of how many recipes chefs will present during a selected cooking lecture:

Chef	Recipes	–	M_X	–	x_i	x_i^2
Emeril	1	–	2.00	=	–1	1
Flay	2	–	2.00	=	0	0
Mario	2	–	2.00	=	0	0
Stewart	3	–	2.00	=	1	1
M	2.00					
SOS						2.00
Var						0.67
SD	0.82					

Assume that Chef J. Child is then added to the dataset:

Chef	Recipes	–	M_X	=	x_i	x_i^2
Emeril	1	–	3.40	=	–2.4	5.76
Flay	2	–	3.40	=	–1.4	1.96
Mario	2	–	3.40	=	–1.4	1.96
Stewart	3	–	3.40	=	–0.4	0.16
J. Child	9	–	3.40	=	5.6	31.36
M	3.40					
SOS						41.20
Var						8.24
SD	2.87					

Chef Child's score is somewhat anomalous for this dataset. Her score does pull the mean up from the original value of "2.00 recipes" to the new value of "3.40 recipes." However, her score has an even more dramatic effect on the SD, which goes from the original value of "0.82 recipes" to the new value of "3.44 recipes."

One way to create a more robust description of dispersion is to trim extreme scores out of the dataset, as was done in the case of some robust central tendency statistics. A popular trimmed dispersion statistic trims 25% of the scores at both distribution ends and then computes the trimmed range.

This **interquartile range** (*IQR*) can be computed by first invoking Equation 2.1; for values of $q = 0.25$ and $q = 0.75$, respectively, compute the 25th score percentile (i.e., P_{25}, or first quartile [Q_1], the score below which 25% of the scores lie) and the 75th score percentile (i.e., P_{75}, or third quartile [Q_3], the score below which 75% of the scores lie). Then the interquartile range is computed as $P_{75} - P_{25}$. The *IQR* can be painlessly obtained using statistical software (e.g., the EXAMINE procedure in SPSS).

■■■ Standardized Score World

I have indicated that all statistics are either in the score world or the area world and that the statistics in these two worlds have different uses. We will see that there are result comparisons that we can make in one world but not in the other. Also, some analyses are conducted in the score world, but other analyses must be performed in the area world.

However, one world is not inherently superior to the other. We can always beam across the barrier between the worlds by either squaring or by taking the square root. The worlds are just different, and are used for different purposes.

It is now time to complicate matters by subdividing the score world into two parts: (a) the unstandardized score world, which is what we have actually been considering until now, and (b) the standardized score world.

Scores (and descriptive statistics) in the unstandardized score world are in the same metric as the original scores (e.g., pounds, inches, number of right answers). But scores in the standardized score world are *metric-*

free. These scores have no measurement metric, except standard deviation units, because the original metric has been removed from the scores via division.

The most commonly-used standard score is the z score. These scores can be easily obtained in SPSS by using the SAVE option within the DESCRIPTIVES procedure. The z scores actually are both *standardized*, because the original metric has been removed by division, and *centered*, because the original mean has also been converted to zero. The formula for converting a given person's X_i score into an equivalent z_i score is

$$z_i = (X_i - M_X) / SD_X \qquad (3.10)$$

For example, if Carol scored 87 right answers, and the dataset mean was 68.9 right answers, and the SD was 8.5 right answers, Carol's z score would be $[(87 - 68.9) / 8.5] = 18.1 / 8.5 = 2.13$ (*not* 2.13 right answers).

Standardized scores are *not* naturally occurring. But scores can always be converted into z scores as long as the SD is greater than zero. If the scores were a constant, division by zero to create the z scores would be an impermissible operation.

Any set of scores that have (a) a mean (and a sum) of zero, and (b) an SD of 1.0 (and a variance of 1.0) are z scores. We use the lowercase, italic letter z to symbolize z scores because z scores are by definition always in a deviation score metric. That is, Carol's z score of 2.13 tells us that her score is 2.13 standard deviations from the mean. Because her z score is positive, we know that specifically her score was 2.13 standard deviations *above* the mean.

These z scores are used for various purposes. First, some statistical computations are simplified if the data are both standardized and centered prior to conducting remaining calculations. This was particularly relevant when calculations were performed by hand and the computations for a given dataset were performed repeatedly as a check against human error. But even modern software still invokes this standardization for some analyses to expedite calculation speed.

Second, standardization is sometimes done as a first step in integrating results across studies so that results can be compared apples-to-apples. For example, if I give three 100-item tests in a doctoral class, Colleen might score $X_1 = 77$ right answers, $X_2 = 84$ right answers, and $X_3 = 90$ right answers.

I might either compute an average test score for each student, including Colleen ($M_{COLLEEN} = 83.67$ right answers), or alternatively add up the number of right answers for each student ($\Sigma_{COLLEEN} = 251$) and then assign letter grades. But if $M_1 = 87.0$, $SD_1 = 5.0$; if $M_2 = 90.0$, $SD_2 = 3.0$; and if $M_3 = 94.0$, $SD_3 = 2.0$; these two strategies do not take into account that Colleen did better on tests that were progressively more easy and on which scores were progressively less dispersed.

Consider Mary, whose scores were 90 right answers, 84 right answers, and 77 right answers, respectively. Mary's total (i.e., 251) and mean number of right answers (i.e., 83.67) are the same as Colleen's mean and total. Do the z scores of these two individuals also suggest that both people performed equally well across the semester? Colleen's z scores of -2.00, -2.00, and -2.00 average to -2.00. Mary's z scores of 0.60, -2.00, and -8.50, respectively, average to -3.30. Which comparison affords an apples-to-apples-to-apples view of the data, controlling for test difficulty and score dispersion, and which does not?

Third, z scores are computed in the essential, initial step of converting observed scores into other standardized metrics, such as IQ scores ($M = 100.0$; $SD = 15.0$) or SAT/GRE scores ($M = 500.0$; $SD = 100.0$). These are not naturally occurring scores either. But standardized scores of this sort become so familiar that there is no need to communicate to friends or family the relevant Ms or SDs. One need only say, "I have an IQ of 130.0."

Some Key Concepts

Dispersion statistics quantify how similar or dissimilar the scores are to each other, or to a benchmark (e.g., the mean). Because central tendency statistics more accurately represent all the scores as dispersion is smaller, dispersion statistics (e.g., the SD) characterize how well central tendency statistics do at representing the data. Therefore, *always* report the SD whenever reporting the mean.

And as Grissom and Kim (2005) perceptively noted,

> Because treatment may affect the variabilities as well as the centers of distributions, and because changes in the variances can be of as much practical significance as are

> changes in means, researchers should think of variances not just with regard to whether their data satisfy . . . [statistical variance assumptions] but as informative aspects of treatment effects. (p. 13)

So in some studies, dispersion may be interesting in its own right.

▣▣▣ Reflection Problems ▣▣▣

1. When is $SD_X > SD_X^2$, when is $SD_X = SD_X^2$, and when is $SD_X < SD_X^2$?

2. What is the SOS of z scores for different values of n?

3. What is the minimum number of scores that may create a variable (i.e., $SOS_X > 0$, $Var_X > 0$, $SD_X > 0$)?

4. If some data are missing for variables, how does substituting the mean for missing values impact the SD of the data using imputed values as against the SDs of the data computed by simply omitting any cases with missing data?

5. Use the z scores presented in the Appendix within SPSS to compute other standardized scores. For example, if you use the SPSS command

```
COMPUTE iq = (z * 15) + 100 .
```

what is the mean and the standard deviation of the new scores? If you use a multiplicative constant of 3, and an additive constant of 15, what is the mean and the standard deviation of the new scores?

6. Using the data and additive and multiplicative constants in Reflection Problem 3 in Chapter 2, what rule can we formulate to express the effects on SDs of additive constants (e.g., "new SD always equals original SD . . .")? What rule can we formulate to express the effects on SDs of multiplicative constants (e.g., "new SD always equals original SD . . .")? Why mathematically do these rules work? When will a multiplicative constant *not* change the value of the original SD?

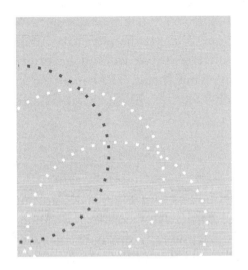

Shape

I n Chapter 1, I noted that sometimes we try to characterize an acquaintance unknown to our friends. Typically, more than one characterization is required to capture essential features of personality. And which characterizations will be relevant depends upon our purposes and our personal values. The same dynamics apply to using descriptive statistics to characterize data.

In some cases, characterizing the shape of the distribution, such as the data presented in a histogram, is of interest. Two descriptive statistics constitute this third class of characterizations—the second and third moments of deviations about the mean as a benchmark—and they apply third and fourth powers to deviation scores as part of their computations. These two statistics were conceptualized by Karl Pearson, whose interest in shape also influenced his work on relationship statistics, as will be seen in Chapter 5.

▦▦▦ Two Shape Descriptive Statistics

Most of us have experienced the horrors of blind dating. When confronted with these opportunities, survival skills are quickly heightened. We soon learn to ask questions—LOTS of questions. If the physical attractiveness of the blind date candidate is a consideration, we will be prudent and request some characterizations involving shape. The same two kinds of issues arise when attempting to characterize the shape of data distributions.

Symmetry

When we are considering the possibilities of a blind date, an important starting point for many of us will be the symmetry of the candidate. In general, for aspects of human anatomy usually involving two of a given feature, many of us prefer to see exactly two of these features (e.g., ears, eyes), and we often prefer them to be located in roughly the same location in reference to the centerline of the body.

So, we may aspire for two eyes, or two ears, roughly equidistant from the nose. For features that we would usually expect to be represented by one feature (e.g., a nose), we may prefer that this is located on or near the centerline. These are not the only shape features of interest. But symmetry may well be an essential starting point in the blind-dating dialogue. (Assume nothing, or you may be hugely sorry!)

Conceptually, data are **symmetrical** when we draw a line through the median and the distribution shapes on either side of the median are identical. Mathematically, data are symmetrical whenever $M_X = Mdn_X$. Indeed, the discrepancy between M_X and Mdn_X is a crude index of the degree to which data diverge from symmetry.

Perfectly symmetrical distributions should yield descriptive characterizations (including $M_X - Mdn_X$) of symmetry of zero iff the data are perfectly symmetrical in shape. And these descriptive statistics should get increasingly large in absolute value as the data increasingly diverge from perfect symmetry.

When data are asymmetrical, the distributions are said to be **skewed**. Specifically, if $M_X < Mdn_X$, the distribution is said to be "negatively skewed" or "skewed left." If $M_X > Mdn_X$, the distribution is said to be "positively skewed" or "skewed right."

The **coefficient of skewness** is a descriptive statistic characterizing whether or not a distribution is symmetrical and, if the distribution is asymmetrical, how much so. The coefficient of skewness$_X$ can be computed using the unstandardized (or "raw scores") formula:

$$[n / ((n - 1)(n - 2))][\Sigma(((X_i - \overline{X}) / SD_X)^3)] \qquad (4.1)$$

An algebraically equivalent formula is

$$[n / ((n - 1)(n - 2))](\Sigma(z_i^3)) \qquad (4.2)$$

Equation 4.2 makes clear that the coefficient of skewness is in the standardized score world. However, the characterizations of symmetry that are derived in this world also describe the scores in the unstandardized score world. Indeed, for a given set of scores, we will obtain identical answers if we apply (a) Equation 4.1 to the raw scores in the unstandardized score world, (b) Equation 4.2 to the scores in the standardized score world, or (c) Equation 4.1 to the scores in the standardized score world.

Note that the coefficient of skewness can never be computed unless n is at least 3, because of the use of $(n - 2)$ within a divisor. Of course, conceptually distributions consisting of only one or two scores could not be skewed anyway. Nor can the coefficient be computed at any sample size for any constant, because of the use of SD as a divisor in Equation 4.1 or as a divisor in the computation of the z scores required for Equation 4.2.

Table 4.1 presents symmetrical scores of five participants on two variables, X and Y. For the variable X, using the "raw score" formula, for the leftmost portion of the formula we have $[n / ((n - 1)(n - 2))] = [5 / ((5 - 1)(5 - 2))] = [5 / (4)(3)] = [5 / 12] = 0.41\overline{6}$.

For the rightmost portion of the "raw score" formula, we have

X_i	$-$	M	$=$	x_i	SD_X	x_i / SD_X	$(x_i / SD_X)^3$
0	$-$	4.0	$=$	-4	3.16	-1.26	-2.02
2	$-$	4.0	$=$	-2	3.16	-0.63	-0.25
4	$-$	4.0	$=$	0	3.16	0.00	0.00
6	$-$	4.0	$=$	2	3.16	0.63	0.25
8	$-$	4.0	$=$	4	3.16	1.26	2.02
Sum							0.00

TABLE 4.1. Two Examples of Symmetrical Distributions

Participant/Statistic	X_i	Y_i	Z_X	Z_Y
Bob	0	1	−1.265	−1.414
Hilda	2	3	−0.632	0.000
Marilyn	4	3	0.000	0.000
Gloria	6	3	0.632	0.000
Bruce	8	5	1.265	1.414
M	4.00	3.00	0.00	0.00
Mdn	4.00	3.00	0.00	0.00
SOS	40.00	8.00	4.00	4.00
SD^a	3.16	1.41	1.00	1.00

[a]Note that this is the statistic SD, not the parameter σ.

So, the coefficient of skewness for variable X is $0.41\overline{6}$ times 0.00, or 0.00. This corresponds to the Table 4.1 report that the mean and the median are both 4.00. This also corresponds to the representation of the data in Figure 4.1, which illustrates that the distribution is clearly symmetrical.

For variable Y—using the standardized score formula—because the sample size is still 5, we again have $[n / ((n − 1)(n − 2))] = [5 / ((5 − 1)(5 − 2))] = [5 / (4)(3)] = [5 / 12] = 0.41\overline{6}$. The rightmost portion of the formula can be computed as

z	z^3
−1.41	−2.83
0.00	0.00
0.00	0.00
0.00	0.00
1.41	2.83
Sum	0.00

So, the coefficient of skewness$_Y$ is $0.41\overline{6}$ times 0.00, or 0.00.

Table 4.2 presents two examples of skewed distributions, one negatively skewed and one positively skewed. The inequalities of the respective

```
F  4
r  3
e  2
q  1    *         *         *         *         *    X
u     0   1   2   3   4   5   6   7   8
e  1    *         *         *                   Y
n  2              *
c  3              *
y  4
```

FIGURE 4.1. Histograms of the Table 4.1 symmetrical data

means and medians portend the nonzero results we will obtain for these data.

Figure 4.2 also graphically (rather than mathematically) suggests that the data are skewed. For variable $X1$, the corpus of the scores cluster around −1 or −2. The more anomalous score(s) (here −5) constitute the "tail" of the distribution. Because the tail of the distribution is to the left of the body of scores, this distribution is "skewed left" or "negatively skewed."

For $X1$, using the "raw score" formula, we obtain

TABLE 4.2. Two Examples of Skewed Distributions

Participant/ Statistic	$X1_i$	$X2_i$	Z_{X1}	Z_{X2}
Bob	−1	1	0.577	−0.447
Hilda	−1	1	0.577	−0.447
Marilyn	−1	1	0.577	−0.447
Gloria	−2	1	0.000	−0.447
Bruce	−5	9	−1.732	1.789
M	−2.00	2.60	0.00	0.00
Mdn	−1.00	1.00	.58	−0.45
SOS	12.00	51.20	4.00	4.00
SD^a	1.73	3.58	1.00	1.00

[a]Note that this is the statistic SD, not the parameter σ.

```
F  4
r  3                          *
e  2                          *
q  1  *              *        *
u    -5  -4  -3  -2  -1   0   1   2   3   4   5   6   7   8   9        X1
e  1                             *                          *    X2
n  2                             *
c  3                             *
y  4
```

FIGURE 4.2. Histograms of the Table 4.2 skewed data

$X1_i$	$-$	M	$=$	$x1_i$	SD_{X1}	$x1_i / SD_{X1}$	$(x1_i / SD_{X1})^3$
-1	$-$	-2.0	$=$	1	1.73	0.577	0.192
-1	$-$	-2.0	$=$	1	1.73	0.577	0.192
-1	$-$	-2.0	$=$	1	1.73	0.577	0.192
-2	$-$	-2.0	$=$	0	1.73	0.000	0.000
-5	$-$	-2.0	$=$	-3	1.73	-1.732	-5.196
Sum							-4.619

Given that the leftmost portion of the equation remains $0.41\overline{6}$, for the coefficient of skewness, we obtain $0.41\overline{6}$ times -4.619, or -1.924.

For $X2$, using the standardized scores, we obtain

z	z^3
-0.447	-0.089
-0.447	-0.089
-0.447	-0.089
-0.447	-0.089
1.789	5.724
Sum	5.366

For the coefficient of skewness, we obtain $0.41\overline{6}$ times 5.366, or 2.236.

Relative Height (Relative Width)

Having confirmed that the potential blind date candidate is reasonably symmetrical, surely there is more to the story of shape. Blind dating is harrowing stuff. We had best exercise extreme, absolute caution. Are all reasonably symmetrical people equally attractive?

What if the candidate is hugely tall, or extraordinarily short? What if the candidate is hugely wide, or amazingly narrow? Clearly, another consideration may be height or width. But it is really some function of height to width, or of width to height, that is of primary import. Maybe tall people can be quite wide and look "just right" regarding their weight. Maybe narrow people can look "just right" if they are not too tall.

The statistic that measures this and related features of data is called the coefficient of kurtosis. The "raw score" formula for the coefficient is

$$\{[(n(n+1)) / ((n-1)(n-2)(n-3))][\Sigma(((X_i - \overline{X}) / SD_X)^4)]\} \quad (4.3)$$
$$- [(3((n-1)^2)) / ((n-2)(n-3))]$$

The standardized score formula is

$$\{[(n(n+1)) / ((n-1)(n-2)(n-3))](\Sigma(z_i^4))\} \quad (4.4)$$
$$- [(3((n-1)^2)) / ((n-2)(n-3))]$$

As in other cases we have seen, the raw score formula is computationally easier, but the standardized score formula for the coefficient of kurtosis makes more obvious the logic of the computation and makes more obvious the fact that the formula's home is in the standardized score world.

Note that the coefficient of kurtosis can never be computed unless n is at least 4, because of the use of $(n-3)$ in a divisor. Nor can the coefficient be computed at any sample size for any constant, because of the use of SD as a divisor in Equation 4.3 or as a divisor in the computation of the z scores required for Equation 4.4.

As suggested by Equation 4.4, kurtosis focuses on how many scores are near to or far from the mean in the metric of deviation scores measured in SD units. This statistic focuses on the concentration of scores near the mean versus away from the mean. And because the third moment takes scores to the fourth power (i.e., a quartic function), outliers are going to REALLY impact this statistic.

Distributions that have exactly the same number of scores throughout the distribution are called **rectangular** or **uniform**. Distributions that have relatively the same number of scores in the extremes versus near the mean are called **platykurtic**. Distributions that have relatively few scores in the extremes versus having many scores near the mean are called **leptokurtic**. Distributions that are unimodal and neither platykurtic nor leptokurtic are called **mesokurtic**. Let's consider three distributions to get some feel for how the coefficient of kurtosis functions.

Table 4.3 presents the scores of nine people on the variable $X3_i$, on which the scores are bimodal and define a U-shaped distribution. We can see this shape graphically in Figure 4.3.

To break down the computations into manageable blocks, let's redefine the raw score coefficient of kurtosis as equaling $a * b - c$, where

$$a = [(n(n + 1)) / ((n - 1)(n - 2)(n - 3))] \qquad (4.5)$$

$$b = [\Sigma(((X_i - \overline{X}) / SD_X)^4)] \qquad (4.6)$$

TABLE 4.3. Leptokurtic, Platykurtic, and Mesokurtic Distributions

Participant/ Statistic	$X3_i$	$X4_i$	$X5_i$	Z_{X3}	Z_{X4}	Z_{X5}
Deborah	1	4	1	−1.000	−0.943	−1.633
Donna	1	5	3	−1.000	−0.236	−0.816
Molly	1	5	3	−1.000	−0.236	−0.816
Geri	1	5	5	−1.000	−0.236	0.000
Catherine	5	5	5	−1.000	−0.236	0.000
Peggy	9	5	5	−1.000	−0.236	0.000
Carol	9	5	7	−1.000	−0.236	0.816
Anne	9	5	7	−1.000	−0.236	0.816
Murray	9	9	9	−1.000	2.593	1.633
M	5.00	5.33	5.00	0.00	0.00	0.00
SOS	128.00	16.00	48.00	8.00	8.00	8.00
SD^a	4.00	1.41	2.45	1.00	1.00	1.00

[a]Note that this is the statistic SD, not the parameter σ.

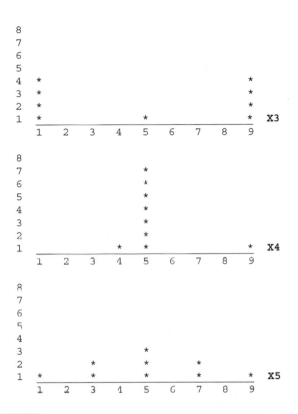

FIGURE 4.3. Histograms of the Table 4.3 data

$$c = [(3((n - 1)^2)) / ((n - 2)(n - 3))] \qquad (4.7)$$

For any dataset involving nine participants, such as the Table 4.3 data, we have

$$
\begin{aligned}
a &= [(n(n + 1)) / ((n - 1)(n - 2)(n - 3))] \\
&= (9(9 + 1)) / ((9 - 1)(9 - 2)(9 - 3)) \\
&= (9(10)) / ((8)(7)(6)) \\
&= 90 / ((8)(7)(6)) \\
&= 90 / (56(6)) \\
&= 90 / 336 \\
&= 0.268
\end{aligned}
$$

Similarly, for any dataset involving nine participants, for c we have

$$c = [(3((n - 1)^2)) / ((n - 2)(n - 3))]$$
$$= (3((9 - 1)^2)) / ((9 - 2)(9 - 3))$$
$$= (3(8^2)) / (7(6))$$
$$= (3(64)) / (7(6))$$
$$= (3(64)) / (42)$$
$$= 192 / 42$$
$$= 4.571$$

For the Table 4.3 data on variable $X3_i$, for which $M_X = 5.00$ and $SD_X = 4.00$, we now solve for b as the sum of $(x_i / SD_X)^4$:

X_i	$-$	$\overline{X}$	$=$	x_i / SD_X	$=$	x_i / SD_X	$(x_i / SD_X)^4$
1	$-$	5.0	$=$	$-4.0 / 4.0$	$=$	-1	1
1	$-$	5.0	$=$	$-4.0 / 4.0$	$=$	-1	1
1	$-$	5.0	$=$	$-4.0 / 4.0$	$=$	-1	1
1	$-$	5.0	$=$	$-4.0 / 4.0$	$=$	-1	1
5	$-$	5.0	$=$	$0.0 / 4.0$	$=$	0	0
9	$-$	5.0	$=$	$4.0 / 4.0$	$=$	1	1
9	$-$	5.0	$=$	$4.0 / 4.0$	$=$	1	1
9	$-$	5.0	$=$	$4.0 / 4.0$	$=$	1	1
9	$-$	5.0	$=$	$4.0 / 4.0$	$=$	1	1
Sum							8.00

So the coefficient of kurtosis for these platykurtic data is $(0.268 * 8.00) - 4.571 = 2.143 - 4.571 = -2.428$.

Table 4.3 presents the scores of nine people on the variable $X4_i$, which has a leptokurtic shape. We can see this shape graphically in Figure 4.3. We can compute the coefficient of kurtosis using the z-score Equation 4.4. Values of a and c remain unchanged, given a fixed sample size of nine participants, but in this algebraically equivalent standardized score formula, $b = (\Sigma(z_i^4))$. For the Table 4.3 data, we have

X_i	$-$	$\overline{X}$	$=$	x_i / SD_X	$=$	z_i	z_i^4
4	$-$	5.33	$=$	$-1.33 / 1.41$	$=$	-0.943	0.790
5	$-$	5.33	$=$	$-0.33 / 1.41$	$=$	-0.236	0.003
5	$-$	5.33	$=$	$-0.33 / 1.41$	$=$	-0.236	0.003
5	$-$	5.33	$=$	$-0.33 / 1.41$	$=$	-0.236	0.003
5	$-$	5.33	$=$	$-0.33 / 1.41$	$=$	-0.236	0.003
5	$-$	5.33	$=$	$-0.33 / 1.41$	$=$	-0.236	0.003
5	$-$	5.33	$=$	$-0.33 / 1.41$	$=$	-0.236	0.003
5	$-$	5.33	$=$	$-0.33 / 1.41$	$=$	-0.236	0.003
9	$-$	5.33	$=$	$3.67 / 1.41$	$=$	2.593	45.188
Sum							46.000

So the coefficient of kurtosis for these leptokurtic data is $(0.268 * 46.00) - 4.571 = 12.321 - 4.571 = 7.750$.

Variable $X5_i$ in Table 4.3 is approximately mesokurtic. Using raw score Equation 4.3, for this variable we solve for b as the sum of $(x_i / SD_X)^4$:

X_i	$-$	$\overline{X}$	$=$	x_i / SD_X	$=$	x_i / SD_X	$(x_i / SD_X)^4$
1	$-$	5.0	$=$	$-4.0 / 2.449$	$=$	-1.633	7.111
3		5.0	$=$	$2.0 / 2.449$	$=$	-0.816	0.444
3	$-$	5.0	$=$	$-2.0 / 2.449$	$=$	-0.816	0.444
5		5.0	$=$	$0.0 / 2.449$	$=$	0.000	0.000
5	$-$	5.0	$=$	$0.0 / 2.449$	$=$	0.000	0.000
5	$-$	5.0	$=$	$0.0 / 2.449$	$=$	0.000	0.000
7	$-$	5.0	$=$	$2.0 / 2.449$	$=$	0.816	0.444
7	$-$	5.0	$=$	$2.0 / 2.449$	$=$	0.816	0.444
9	$-$	5.0	$=$	$4.0 / 2.449$	$=$	1.633	7.111
Sum							16.000

So the coefficient of kurtosis for these mesokurtic data is $(0.268 * 16.00) - 4.571 = 4.286 - 4.571 = -0.285$.

▓▓▓ Normal Distributions

Judgments of symmetry are rather straightforward and require no arbitrary benchmark. We can judge quite well when people (or data) are symmetrical without invoking a standard. But how can height relative to width of a blind date candidate be evaluated without a standard for how much of the person (or data) should be in the extremes, and how much should be in the middle?

In conventional blind-date negotiations, one invariably turns to a standard (e.g., "She is shaped like Marilyn Monroe" or "He is shaped like Clark Gable" [younger readers may wish to substitute Brad Pitt, Paris Hilton, or some other choice, as a standard]). So, too, there is a standard in evaluating when data are Goldilocks just right, or mesokurtic, in the distribution of height relative to width.

Normal distributions are used as the gold standard for evaluating kurtosis (Henson, 1999). There are *infinitely many* different normal distributions. Every normal distribution is perfectly mesokurtic (i.e., has a coefficient of kurtosis of exactly zero).

Normal distributions were conceptualized by de Moivre, later used by Laplace, and popularized by Gauss in 1809 in the analysis of astronomical data. Normal distributions have many very important uses in statistics. Consequently, these distributions are given several synonymous names, for reasons that by now are evident to the reader. The synonymous names include "normal distributions," "Gaussian distributions," and somewhat colloquially, "bell-shaped distributions."

There is *only one* normal distribution for a given combination of M and SD. However, there are *infinitely many* normal distributions, because there are infinitely many values of M and SD. Of course, two different normal distributions may have (a) different means but the same SDs, (b) the same means but different SDs, or (c) both different means and different SDs.

For a given score on X_i, the height of the histogram can be determined using the equation

$$u = [1 / (SD)((2(pi))^{0.5})][e^{-\{((Xi-M)(Xi-M)) / (2(SD)(SD))\}}] \qquad (4.8)$$

Substituting the approximate value of 2.718 for *e* (the base of the system of natural logarithms) and 3.142 for *pi* (the ratio of the circumference of any circle to its diameter), and given that $((2(3.142))^{0.5}) = 6.284^{0.5} = 2.5067$, we have

$$u = [1 / (SD)(2.5067)][2.718^{-\{((Xi-M)(Xi-M)) / (2(SD)(SD))\}}] \qquad (4.9)$$

Although the formula looks intimidating, the computation can be easily performed using a spreadsheet such as Excel. Assuming the *M* value is stored in cell A\$1, the *SD* is stored in cell A\$2, and the specified value of X_i is stored in cell A\$3, the command is

$$+(1/(A\$2*2.5067))*(2.718^\wedge (((A\$3\ A\$1)^\wedge 2)/(2*(A\$2^\wedge 2))))$$

In a spreadsheet, the character "*" means "times," and "^" means "raised to the exponential power of."

Iff a normal distribution has a mean of zero and a standard deviation (and variance) of 1.0, the distribution is said to be **standard normal** (or *unit normal*). This is *not* meant to imply that all normal distributions are in *z*-score form. This is also *not* meant to imply that all *z*-score distributions are normal. But for a standard normal distribution, given its values $M = 0.0$ and $SD = 1.0$, for the score of $z_i = 1.0$, for example, the value of *u* would equal

$$(1 / (1.0 * 2.5067)) * (2.718^{-(((1.0 - 0.0)^\wedge 2) / (2 * (1.0\ ^\wedge 2))))})$$
$$(1 / 2.5067) * (2.718^{-(((1.0 - 0.0)^\wedge 2) / (2 * (1.0\ ^\wedge 2))))})$$
$$0.3989 * (2.718^{-(((1.0 - 0.0)^\wedge 2) / (2 * (1.0\ ^\wedge 2))))})$$
$$0.3989 * (2.718^{-(((1.0)^\wedge 2) / (2 * (1.0\ ^\wedge 2))))})$$
$$0.3989 * (2.718^{-((1.0) / (2 * (1.0\ ^\wedge 2))))})$$
$$0.3989 * (2.718^{-((1.0) / (2 * (1.0))))})$$
$$0.3989 * (2.718^{-((1.0) / (2.0)))})$$
$$0.3989 * (2.718^{-0.5})$$
$$0.3989 * 0.607$$
$$0.242$$

Table 4.4 presents values of *u* for selected values of X_i for normally distributed McCall's *T* scores, which always have a mean of 50.0 and a

TABLE 4.4. Values of u for 61 Values of X_i for a Normal Distribution When M = 50 and SD = 10

X_i	u	X_i	u	X_i	u
20	0.0004	40	0.0242	60	0.0242
21	0.0006	41	0.0266	61	0.0218
22	0.0008	42	0.0290	62	0.0194
23	0.0010	43	0.0312	63	0.0171
24	0.0014	44	0.0333	64	0.0150
25	0.0018	45	0.0352	65	0.0130
26	0.0022	46	0.0368	66	0.0111
27	0.0028	47	0.0381	67	0.0094
28	0.0035	48	0.0391	68	0.0079
29	0.0044	49	0.0397	69	0.0066
30	0.0054	50	0.0399	70	0.0054
31	0.0066	51	0.0397	71	0.0044
32	0.0079	52	0.0391	72	0.0035
33	0.0094	53	0.0381	73	0.0028
34	0.0111	54	0.0368	74	0.0022
35	0.0130	55	0.0352	75	0.0018
36	0.0150	56	0.0333	76	0.0014
37	0.0171	57	0.0312	77	0.0010
38	0.0194	58	0.0290	78	0.0008
39	0.0218	59	0.0266	79	0.0006
				80	0.0004

standard deviation of 10.0. Figure 4.4 is an SPSS graphic of a plot of values of u against corresponding values of X_i, which displays as a bell shape.

All normal distributions have certain properties. First, normal distributions are symmetric and unimodal, with mode = Mdn = M. Second, nor-

FIGURE 4.4. Normal distribution for M = 50.0 and SD = 10.0

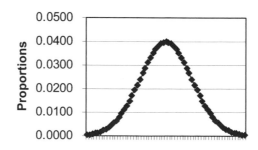

mal distributions are asymptotic to the horizontal (i.e., X) axis, which means that the further scores are from the mean, the more their frequencies decrease, but the frequencies never reach zero.

The asymptotic properties of the normal distribution can be concretely understood if we determine the proportion (or, if multiplied by 100, the percentage) of datapoints below a given score, X_i, in a given normal distribution. The spreadsheet Excel will return this value if we invoke the statistical function:

```
=normdist(X,M,SD,true)
```

where X is the given score, M is the mean of the normal distribution of interest, and SD is the standard deviation of the normal distribution of interest.

For example, if we presume that IQ scores are exactly normally distributed and if we input

```
=NORMDIST(175,100,15,TRUE)
```

Excel will return the value

$$0.999999713$$

This means that 99.9999713% of all people have an IQ score less than 175. But, by the same token, 0.0000287% of all people (or roughly 287 people out of a billion) have an IQ of 175 or more. Asymptotic in this context means, at least theoretically, that there is (or eventually will be) always somebody smarter out there!

The normal distribution has the interesting property that fixed proportions of scores are in the six regions defined by the mean plus or minus zero, one, two, or three times the standard deviation. For our IQ score example, we obtain

M	Multiplier	SD	IQ	% below
100.0	−3	15.0	55	00.135
100.0	−2	15.0	70	02.275

100.0	−1	15.0	85	15.866
100.0	0	15.0	100	50.000
100.0	1	15.0	115	84.134
100.0	2	15.0	130	97.725
100.0	3	15.0	145	99.865

Fixed percentages (or proportions) of scores fall between these boundaries. For example, 68.27% (84.134 − 15.866) of the scores fall between $M - 1(SD)$ and $M + 1(SD)$, and 95.45% of the scores fall between $M - 2(SD)$ and $M + 2(SD)$. The percentage of additional scores captured by going out successive multipliers of the SD can also be computed (e.g., 68.27% − 0.0% = 68.27%; 95.45% − 68.27% = 27.18%; 99.73% − 95.45% = 4.28%). So we have for *each and every* one of the infinitely many normal distributions

Region	Cumulative % in region	Unique to one more SD in both directions
$M - 1(SD)$ to $M + 1(SD)$	68.27	68.27%
$M - 2(SD)$ to $M + 2(SD)$	95.45	27.18%
$M - 3(SD)$ to $M + 3(SD)$	99.73	4.28%

By the same token, because all normal distributions are symmetric, 34.13% (68.27% / 2) of the scores fall specifically in the region from $M - 1(SD)$ to M, and 34.13% of the scores fall in the region from $M + 1(SD)$ to M. Similarly, 13.59% (27.18% / 2) of the scores fall specifically in the region from $M - 2(SD)$ to $M - 1(SD)$, and 13.59% of the scores fall in the region from $M + 1(SD)$ to M to $M + 2(SD)$ to M. So we have, for the six regions consuming 99.73% of scores, for *each and every* one of the infinitely many normal distributions,

Region	% in region
$<M - 3(SD)$	0.135
$M - 3(SD)$ to $M - 2(SD)$	2.14
$M - 2(SD)$ to $M - 1(SD)$	13.59
$M - 1(SD)$ to $M - 0(SD)$	34.13

$$M - 0(SD) \text{ to } M + 1(SD) \qquad 34.13$$
$$M - 1(SD) \text{ to } M + 2(SD) \qquad 13.59$$
$$M - 2(SD) \text{ to } M + 3(SD) \qquad 2.14$$
$$>M + 3(SD) \qquad\qquad\qquad\quad 0.135$$

Knowledge of these relationships is useful because intervally-scaled data, at least when collected on large numbers of participants, tend to be normally-distributed. Thus, these percentages tend to be approximately accurate in many research situations.

If I give an examination to a huge number of doctoral students, and the data are normally distributed, with $M = 15.0$ and $SD = 3.0$, I can answer such questions as these:

1. What percentage of students had a score less than 21.0?
   [Answer: 50.0% + 34.13% + 13.59% = 97.72%]
2. What is the score below which 15.865% of the students score?
   [Answer: 12.0]
3. What percentage of students score between 12.0 and 21.0?
   [Answer: 34.13% + 34.13% + 13.59% = 81.85%]

Indeed, if we employ the Excel NORMDIST statistical function, we can determine the percentages for any score, or the score for any multiple (including noninteger multiples) of the standard deviation.

■■■ Two Additional Univariate Graphics

As noted in Chapter 2, histograms are a useful univariate graphic. Histograms provide insight about score location, dispersion, and shape. Histograms can be readily obtained in SPSS by using the HISTOGRAM procedure under the GRAPHS menu. And as an option, SPSS will draw a normal curve over the histogram for comparative purposes.

Another useful univariate graphic is the **stem-and-leaf plot**. These plots can be produced in SPSS using the EXAMINE procedure under the SUMMARIZE submenu in the ANALYZE menu. Assume we have 34 scores: {1, 10, 10, 11, 12, 12, 13, 14, 14, 15, 16, 16, 17, 18, 18, 19, 20, 20, 21, 22,

22, 23, 24, 24, 25, 26, 26, 27, 28, 28, 29, 30, 30, 45}. Figure 4.5 presents a stem-and-leaf plot for these data.

The "stem" of the stem-and-leaf plot is the leading digit of the numbers (i.e., here 0, 1, 2, 3, or 4). The "leaf" is the next digit defining a given datapoint. For example, the Figure 4.5 plot indicates that one person had a score with a stem of 0 and a leaf of 1 (i.e., one person had a score of 01). Eight people had the stem of 1, and two of these eight people had leafs of 0 (i.e., scores of 10). One of these eight people had a leaf of 1 (i.e., a score of 11). Two of these eight people had leafs of 2 (i.e., scores of 12). One person had a score labeled "extreme" (i.e., 45).

A third, wonderful univariate graphic is the **box plot** (or the **box-and-whiskers plot**). The SPSS EXAMINE procedure will also produce this plot. Figure 4.6 presents the box plot for these data.

The initial step in creating the box plot is to compute the *median location*, truncating any fractional values. For $n = 34$, the median location is $(n + 1) / 2 = (34 + 1) / 2 = 35 / 2 = 17.5$, which we truncate to 17. The median itself for these data is 20.0. The dark horizontal line within the vertical box plot is drawn at Mdn_X.

We next compute *hinge locations*, which equal (median location + 1) / 2. For our data, we have $(17 + 1) / 2 = 18 / 2 = 9$. We use this to find the *hinges*, which here are the scores located ninth from the bottom (i.e., 14) and ninth from the top (i.e., 26). For our data, the hinges are 14.0 and 26.0.

For large samples, the hinges correspond to the first and third quartile scores, and will be near these scores for small samples. Thus, some computer programs create the box plot using Q_1 and Q_3 (i.e., the 25th and the 75th percentiles, using Equation 2.1) rather than the hinges.

Next, we compute the *hinge spread*, which is simply the range between the two hinges (i.e., here $26.0 - 14.0 = 12.0$) and either equals or approximates the IQR_X. We then use the hinge spread to compute the *inner fences* that we will use as boundaries for identifying outlying scores. The lower inner fence equals the lower hinge (here 14.0) minus the constant of 1.5 times the hinge spread (i.e., $14.0 - 1.5(12.0) = 14.0 - 18.0 = -4.0$). The upper inner fence equals the upper hinge (here 26.0) plus the constant of 1.5 times the hinge spread (i.e., $26.0 + 1.5(12.0) = 26.0 + 18.0 = 44.0$).

Finally, we compute the *adjacent values* by comparing our actual

```
Frequency     Stem &   Leaf
    1.00          0 *   1
     .00          0 .
    8.00          1 *   00122344
    7.00          1 .   5667889
    8.00          2 *   00122344
    7.00          2 .   5667889
    2.00          3 *   00
    1.00 Extremes       (45)
```

FIGURE 4.5. Stem-and-leaf plot from SPSS

scores to the inner fences. The lower adjacent value is the smallest score greater than or equal to the lower inner fence. For our data, our smallest score greater than or equal to –4.0 is 1. The upper adjacent value is the largest score less than or equal to the upper inner fence. For our data, our smallest score less than or equal to 44.0 is 30.

We now have the requisite information with which to draw the box-and-whiskers plot. In a vertical box plot, a box is drawn using the lower and upper hinges to define the lower and upper horizontal lines of the box. So, the box captures approximately the inner 50% of the scores, or exactly 50% of the scores if we are using $Q_1 = P_{25}$ and $Q_3 = P_{75}$ instead of

FIGURE 4.6. Normal distribution for M = 50.0 and SD = 10.0

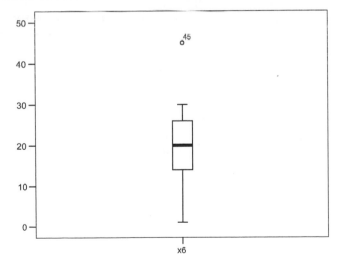

hinges. A dark horizontal line is drawn within the box to represent the median.

A "whisker" is drawn off the bottom of the vertical box down to the lower adjacent fence value (i.e., 1). A whisker is also drawn off the top of the vertical box up to the upper adjacent fence value (i.e., 30).

Any scores below the lower adjacent fence are portrayed as asterisks (or circles) within our plot. Here we have no scores below our lower adjacent fence of 1. Any scores above the upper adjacent fence are also portrayed as asterisks (or circles). We have one score (i.e., 45) above the upper adjacent fence of 30.

The box plot tells us a good deal about our data. If the data are approximately symmetrical, the median will be about halfway between the smallest and the largest scores and roughly in the middle of the box, and the whiskers will be of roughly equal length.

Box plots are also useful in identifying potential outlying scores, as regards location, dispersion, and shape. The plots also give an impression of just how extreme outlying scores may be. Of course, an outlier on one variable may not be outlying on any other variables. And, as we shall see in Chapter 5, an outlier as regards location, dispersion, and shape may not be an outlier on descriptions of relationships among the variables.

Some Key Concepts

The shapes of data distributions that are at least intervally-scaled may be characterized by computing statistics that quantify (a) symmetry (i.e., the coefficient of skewness) and (b) height relative to width (i.e., the coefficient of kurtosis). Kurtosis evaluates shape against the standard of the normal curve, which has a coefficient of skewness of zero and a coefficient of kurtosis of zero.

There are infinitely many normal distributions. But for data with *both* (a) a given mean and (b) a given *SD*, only one normal distribution exists. Iff the data are in *z*-score form, the normal distribution is called "standard normal." Distributions may be standard, normal, or both. Symmetry may be established visually by examining histograms of the data, but the normality of symmetrical data cannot be established merely by examining histograms.

When data that are at least intervally-scaled are collected with large samples, often the data are normal or near normal. In such cases we can invoke knowledge of what percentages of scores fall within score ranges in the normal distribution in order to more fully understand the dynamics within our data.

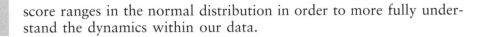

Reflection Problems

1. If we are given the score range for a normal distribution, how can we use only this information to solve for the approximate *SD* of the scores?

2. For a given dataset, how will using mean substitution for missing values impact the coefficient of skewness for data that were initially skewed? How will using mean substitution for missing values impact the coefficient of kurtosis? How does mean substitution differentially impact postsubstitution means, *SD*, skewness, and kurtosis?

3. Draw a distribution for which $M_X < Mdn_X$, but $mode_X > M_X$ and $mode_X > Mdn_X$. Draw a distribution for which $M_X > Mdn_X$, but $mode_X < M_X$ and $mode_X < Mdn_X$.

4. The scores presented in the Appendix are nearly normally distributed. Enter these *z* scores into SPSS. Then click on ANALYZE, then on DESCRIPTIVE STATISTICS, and then on FREQUENCIES. Use the STATISTICS subcommand to obtain the score mean, median, *SD*, and coefficients of skewness and kurtosis. Also, graph the scores by using the CHARTS subcommand; select HISTOGRAM and check WITH NORMAL CURVE. After the chart is generated, double left click on the chart to enter the CHART EDITOR. Click on EDIT, then SELECT X AXIS, and set the *X* axis minimum value to –5 and the maximum value to 55. This allows comparisons of graphs with different data because the *X* axis will be scaled consistently.

    Now use the command

    $$COMPUTE \ x2 = (z * 4) + 20 \ .$$

    to create another set of scores. Compute the same statistics for these data, and plot the scores. How do the skewness and kurtosis coefficients of the two sets of scores compare? How well does each histogram fit the respective normal curve plot? What does this imply about whether there is only one normal distribution?

5. Using the data and additive and multiplicative constants in Reflection Problem #3 in Chapter 2, what rule can we formulate to express the effects on coefficients of skewness and kurtosis of additive constants? What rule can we formulate to express the effects on coefficients of skewness and kurtosis of multiplicative constants? When will a multiplicative constant *not* change the value of the original coefficient of skewness? When will a multiplicative constant change the value of the original coefficient of skewness?

5

Bivariate Relationships

The descriptive statistics explained in Chapters 2 through 4 are univariate statistics. That is, these descriptions can be formulated to characterize data even when only one variable is present.

However, real science is always about the investigation of relationships that occur under stated conditions. Though we can describe features of data even if we only have data on a single variable, and such univariate descriptions may hold some personal interest for us or satisfy our curiosity, only when we have at least two variables do things really get serious.

In the simplest case of true science, we have exactly two variables. The statistics that describe relationships between two variables are **bivariate statistics**. We can only compute these statistics when we have two variables.

But the bivariate relationship descriptive statistics discussed here, although important in and of themselves, are also critical in laying the conceptual foundation for understanding the sophisticated analyses that accommodate even more than two variables. Indeed, even very complicated multivariate statistics can be explained using bivariate statistics concepts (Fan, 1996; Kimbell, 2001; Thompson, 1991a).

Parametric statistics presume that the dependent variable is intervally-scaled, and make shape assumptions as well. An important theme of this book, which we are building toward, is that *all statistical analyses are correlational* and are part of a global **general linear model** (Bagozzi, Fornell, & Larcker, 1981; Cohen, 1968; Knapp, 1978). The general linear model (GLM) has important implications for how we conduct and interpret quantitative analyses.

Of course, just as levels of scale drive what descriptive statistics can be computed for univariate characterizations, levels of scale also impact options in the bivariate case. However, now the levels of scale of two variables must be simultaneously considered.

We will emphasize four combinations of scale: (a) the Pearson r, which requires that both variables are at least intervally-scaled; (b) Spearman's rho (ρ), which requires that both variables are at least ordinally-scaled (but one or both variables may be scaled higher); (c) phi (ϕ), which can be used with two variables that are dichotomous; and (d) point–biserial correlation (r_{pb}), which is used when one variable is dichotomously scored and the other variable is at least intervally-scaled.

Additional descriptive relationship statistics (e.g., biserial and tetrachoric correlation, Kendall's tau (τ)) are beyond the scope of the present treatment, but the four coefficients listed in the previous paragraph will stand you in good stead in commonly-encountered research situations.

These four coefficients are all score-world descriptive statistics. Furthermore, ϕ and r_{pb} are merely *algebraically-equivalent* formulas that can be used in place of an explicitly Pearson r formula, but yield exactly the same result as a Pearson r computation, and so *are* the Pearson r for certain levels-of-scale combinations. And Spearman's ρ is merely the Pearson r (or an algebraic equivalent) applied to data either expressed originally as ranks, or data converted to ranks.

Pearson's *r*

When both variables are at least intervally-scaled, we can compute the Pearson product–moment correlation coefficient (r) as

$$r_{XY} = COV_{XY} / (SD_X * SD_Y) \tag{5.1}$$

where COV_{XY} is also a description of bivariate relationship, called the covariance, and which is computed for a sample as

$$COV_{XY} = (\Sigma(X_i - M_X)(Y_i - M_Y)) / (n - 1) \tag{5.2}$$

The standard deviations are computed using the statistic formula that assumes we have sample data. Equation 5.2 for the COV_{XY} invokes deviation scores, as do the first, second, and third moment about the mean, and can be reexpressed as

$$COV_{XY} - (\Sigma(x_i[y_i])) / (n - 1) \tag{5.3}$$

The fact that the numerator of the COV_{XY} uses deviation scores suggests the possibility of using z scores in an algebraically equivalent formula, because *all z scores are themselves deviation scores* (thus the lowercase z). And Equation 5.1, given z scores, because both standard deviations equal 1.0, simplifies to $r_{zXzY} = COV_{zXzY}$. For a given dataset, r_{XY} always exactly equals r_{zXzY} (for reasons that we will encounter later). So we can also compute the Pearson r for either the X with the Y scores or the z_X with the z_Y scores (or the z_X with the Y scores, or the X with the z_Y scores) as

$$r_{XY} = (\Sigma(z_{Xi}[z_{Yi}])) / (n - 1) \tag{5.4}$$

Equation 5.1 makes obvious that the Pearson r is a *standardized covariance* (i.e., a covariance with the standard deviations removed by division), and that r is not only in the score world, but also is specifically in the standardized score world. Equation 5.4 makes even more apparent the fact that r is a standardized, score-world descriptive statistic. The COV_{XY}, on the other hand, is an area-world descriptive statistic.

Given that the covariance is a description of bivariate relationship, also requiring interval scaling of both variables, why is COV_{XY} not itself used as a description of bivariate association? To answer this question, first we look at an algebraic rearrangement of Equation 5.1:

$$COV_{XY} = r_{XY} * SD_X * SD_Y \qquad (5.5)$$

where "*" means "multiplied by."

This formula asserts that three factors influence the covariance as a descriptive result, and thus makes the description confounded and ambiguous, at least in some cases. We can see this in the following data for pairs of variables, all of which have COV_{XY} approximately equal to 10,000:

COV_{XY}	=	r_{XY}	*	SD_X	*	SD_Y
10000.0	=	1.00	*	100.00	*	100.00
10000.1	=	0.75	*	0.25	*	53334.00
10000.0	=	0.50	*	100.00	*	200.00
10000.0	=	0.25	*	1.00	*	40000.00
10000.0	=	0.01	*	100.00	*	10000.00
10000.0	=	0.01	*	0.50	*	2000000.00

Thus, the covariance is of limited descriptive value, because a given result may reflect a lot of relationship and little score spread on either variable, or a little relationship and a lot of score dispersion on one or both variables, or many other possibilities!

This is not meant to suggest that the covariance is unimportant for other purposes not involving description. The covariance is important in its own right as part of the computation of r. And the covariance is also used as the primary basis for many multivariate analyses (i.e., analyses simultaneously considering multiple dependent variables, an important topic, but one not covered in this book).

Several things are made obvious by thinking about Equation 5.1. First, r is a bivariate statistic. It is truly excellent that r *cannot* be computed unless both X and Y are variables. If either or both X and Y are constants, r is undefined, because division by zero is impermissible. Having r

be undefined unless there are two variables is fantastic, because this means we don't have to hire statistics police to monitor all statistics calculations throughout the world to make sure that no one is computing r unless both X and Y are variables.

Remember that

$$\text{undefined} \neq 0 \tag{5.6}$$

Two variables *may* have a correlation of zero. But having an undefined r does *not* (i.e., not) mean that the correlation is zero. If you know that an $r = 0$, you know *certainly* that both X and Y must have been variables, or there simply would be no r.

If we think further about Equation 5.1, rather than rotely memorizing the equation, we can extrapolate additional revelations (i.e., the intellectual orgasms that learning is really all about). First, because the two SDs can *never* be negative, r_{XY} and the COV_{XY} *always* have the same sign. Second, r_{XY} and COV_{XY} will *always* be equal if (but *not* iff) the two standard deviations have a crossproduct of 1.0, which will occur iff the two SDs are reciprocals of each other (e.g., $SD_X = 1.0$, $SD_Y = 1.0$; $SD_X = 0.5$, $SD_Y = 2.0$). Third, r_{XY} and the COV_{XY} will *always* be equal (and zero) if (but *not* iff) either the r_{XY} or the COV_{XY} is zero, regardless of the standard deviations, as long as both X and Y are variables (i.e., $SD_X \neq 0$ and $SD_Y \neq 0$).

▦▦▦ Three Features of *r*

r Describes Only Linear Relationship

A **scattergram** (or **scatterplot**) is a bivariate graphic displaying the pairs of scores for each individual in the dataset. Just as a histogram is ubiquitous in the univariate case, the scattergram is ubiquitous in bivariate statistics.

Table 5.1 presents the scores of 12 people on the variables X and Y. Figure 5.1 presents the scattergram of these data. As is the case in a histogram, unless otherwise declared in a figure note, each asterisk (or diamond or square or other object) represents one person. But in a scattergram, each asterisk (diamond, or other object) represents *two* scores for a given person, rather than only one score. For example, in the Figure 5.1 scatter-

TABLE 5.1. Scores of n = 12 Participants on Two Variables

Participant/statistic	X_i	Y_i	x_i	y_i	xy_i
Paul	1	1	−3.0	−4.5	13.5
Christopher	2	2	−2.0	−3.5	7.0
Michael	3	3	−1.0	−2.5	2.5
Ralph	5	5	1.0	−0.5	−0.5
Randy	6	6	2.0	0.5	1.0
Steve	7	7	3.0	1.5	4.5
Jennifer	1	4	−3.0	−1.5	4.5
Stephanie	2	5	−2.0	−0.5	1.0
Elizabeth	3	6	−1.0	0.5	−0.5
Sarah	5	8	1.0	2.5	2.5
Judy	6	9	2.0	3.5	7.0
Patty	7	10	3.0	4.5	13.5
Sum	48.00	66.00	0.00	0.00	56.00
M	4.00	5.50	0.00	0.00	
SD	2.26	2.75			

Note. Selected entries for the five people who scored below the means on both variables are presented in **bold**. Selected entries for the five people who scored above the means on both variables are presented in *italics*.

gram, note that Paul is the lowest, leftmost asterisk, and Patty is the highest, rightmost asterisk. Paul's asterisk communicates that his X and Y scores were 1 and 1, respectively.

One way to conceptualize r is to think of r as addressing the question "How well does the line of best possible fit capture the asterisks in the

FIGURE 5.1. Scattergram of the Table 5.1 data

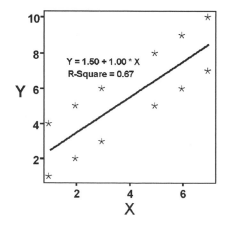

scattergram?" The line of best fit has been drawn in Figure 5.1 for the Table 5.1 data.

The Pearson r will be at its minimum or maximum limits (-1 or $+1$, respectively) iff all the asterisks in the scattergram are on the line. An r of $+1$ or -1 is called a *perfect* relationship. When there is no *linear* relationship between the two variables, any line of best fit that we draw will capture the asterisks equally badly, and r will equal zero.

When r is positive, the relationship between the two variables is said to be *direct* or *positive*. When the linear relationship is positive, as scores on one variable become larger, scores on the other variable tend to also be larger (or the converse; i.e., scores on both variables tend to get smaller together). For example, the number of calories people consume on average each day tends to be *directly* related to their weights.

When the linear relationship (and Pearson's r) is negative, as scores on one variable become larger, scores on the other variable tend to be smaller (or vice versa). For example, the number of miles people jog each day tends to be *inversely* related to their weights.

In the unstandardized score world, the line of best fit is a function of $\overline{Y}$, $\overline{X}$, SD_Y, SD_X, and r_{XY}. The line of best fit will be horizontal (flat) iff r is zero, and otherwise will *not* be flat.

Table 5.1 presents the means and standard deviations of the two variables, computed in the manner explained in previous chapters. Let's now solve for the Pearson product–moment correlation coefficient. For these data, as reported in Table 5.1, the sum of the 12 crossproducts (i.e., $\Sigma x_i[y_i]$) is 56.00, which according to Equation 5.3 yields a COV_{XY} of 5.09 (i.e., 56.00 / 11). Thus, r_{XY} for these data is COV_{XY} / [$(SD_X)(SD_Y)$] = 5.09 / [(2.26)(2.75)] = 5.09 / 6.22 = 0.82.

Now, how do we know where to draw the line of best fit within the scattergram? We can identify (fix) the location of a line as long as we can solve for any two points on the line.

An important implication of Equation 5.2 is that the intercept of the two means is *always* on the line of best fit. Indeed, the line of best fit *always* pivots on this point. In fact, this point is so important that rather than call this point the Cartesian coordinate of the two means, we instead call this location the **centroid**. (If we called the point defined by the means of all the measured variables "the means of all the measured variables," everybody would know what we were talking about, and that would be unsatisfactory.)

So one point defining our line of best fit for our data is the location, 4.00 on X, and 5.50 on Y. We can solve for a second point on the line of best fit, if we know the Pearson correlation coefficient (here $r_{XY} = 0.82$). The point where the line of best fit crosses the Y (or vertical axis; i.e., Y when $X = 0$) is called a.

We can solve for a as

$$a = \overline{Y} - [r_{XY}(SD_Y / SD_X)](\overline{X}) \qquad (5.7)$$

For our data we have a as

$$5.50 - [0.82(2.75 / 2.26)](4.00)$$
$$5.50 - [0.82(1.22)](4.00)$$
$$5.50 - [1.00](4.00)$$
$$5.50 - 4.00$$
$$1.50$$

Notice that the line of best fit does *not* capture *any* of the asterisks in the Figure 5.1 scattergram. Note also that r does *not* ask "how many" asterisks we can catch with a line, but instead focuses on "how close" we can come to capturing the asterisks, under a restriction that we cannot focus exclusively on some asterisks (e.g., the top six asterisks in the scattergram) unfairly at the expense of *any* other asterisks.

I want to emphasize that r measures linear, and *only* linear, relationship, because we are trying to catch all the asterisks with a *line*. However, never forget that curvilinear (i.e., nonlinear) relationships are also entirely possible. Consider the data in Table 5.2 for George, which involve measuring how much pleasure he experiences upon being given daily various amounts of vanilla ice cream.

George is what statisticians call "a vanilla ice-cream hound." George LOVES ice cream. George would eat a shoe if the shoe had ice cream on it. But in this case, as in many others, at some point you can get too much even of a good thing (e.g., teacher praise of first-grade students) or even a *very* good thing (e.g., use your imagination).

A hypothetical "pleasure-ometer" is used to measure how much joy

TABLE 5.2. Pleasure-ometer Readings for George over 10 Days of Ice Cream Deliveries		
Day	Gallons delivered	Pleasure
1	1	1
2	2	4
3	3	7
4	4	9
5	5	10
6	6	10
7	7	9
8	8	7
9	9	4
10	10	1

or, conversely, unhappiness George experiences. On this pleasure-ometer, the maximum pleasure a human can experience yields a score of +10. The maximum unhappiness a human can experience yields a score of −10.

The Pearson r for the Table 5.2 data is 0.00. There is *no* linear relationship between these data. However, if we examine the Figure 5.2 plot of the Table 5.2 data, it becomes obvious that there is a systematic and, indeed, virtually perfect relationship between these variables. The relationship, however, is *curvilinear*.

When given successively more vanilla ice cream each day, from 1 to 5 gallons, George's pleasure increases each time. However, the incremental

FIGURE 5.2. Scattergram of the Table 5.2 data

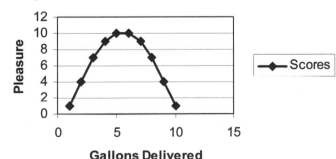

increase in his pleasure decreases with each successive increment in ice cream. There is no difference in pleasure experienced when moving from 5 to 6 gallons. And every increase in ice cream from 6 to 10 gallons causes a reduction in pleasure.

Indeed, Figure 5.2 suggests that going from 10 to 11 and then to 12 gallons of ice cream actually causes unhappiness, even for an ice-cream hound! The projected pleasure-ometer readings for these amounts of ice cream would be −3.7 and −9.2.

The Pearson r for these data is zero even though there is a near-perfect curvilinear relationship between the variables, because *the Pearson r only measures linear relationship*. This means that when $r = 0.0$, there may be anywhere from a zero relationship of all kinds (including curvilinear) to a perfect relationship of all kinds (including curvilinear).

The *only* time that r tells us both (a) about linear relationship and (b) that there is zero curvilinear relationship is when r is perfect (either −1 or +1). The reason is that when there is a perfect linear relationship, there is no possibility of any curvilinear relationship. If all the asterisks define and are on a line in the scattergram, no curvilinear pattern is possible.

Relationships between variables are often either partially or primarily linear, although variables often also have elements of curvilinear relationship at some point. Thus curvilinear relationships, as well as linear relationships, are of interest in research.

There are two ways to investigate curvilinear relationship. First, graphics like the scattergram can be used to inform judgment about curvilinear relationship. Second, some descriptive statistics that we will encounter in subsequent chapters can be used to quantify the amount of curvilinear relationship.

r Is in an Ordinal Metric

The Pearson r is a descriptive statistic quantifying the amount of linear relationship between two variables that are at least intervally-scaled. However, this does *not* mean that the r statistic itself is intervally-scaled.

In fact, r itself is ordinally-scaled as regards the variance common to the two variables. This means that $r_{AB} = +1.0$ is larger than $r_{XY} = +0.5$ or that $r_{AB} = +1.0$ in one sample is larger than $r_{AB} = +0.5$ in a separate sample. However, the r of $+1.0$ is *not* twice as large as the r of $+0.5$. Two transforms of Pearson r are fairly common, although they are typically done for different purposes.

Fisher's r-to-z Transform

One way of reexpressing r is to invoke a transformation, called the r-to-z transformation, developed by Sir Ronald Fisher. Fisher developed a number of statistical methods, for which he was knighted in Great Britain (we will hear more about him in Chapter 10, when we discuss the analysis of variance). This transform was developed for statistical purposes such as hypothesis testing, a topic covered in Chapter 6.

The r-to-z transform yields a score-world statistic. The formula for Fisher's r-to-z transformation is

$$0.5 * (LN((1 + ABS(r)) / (1 - ABS(r)))) \tag{5.8}$$

where LN means "take the natural logarithm of" and ABS means "take the absolute value of." After the computation, if r was negative, the negative sign is restored to the r-to-z value. This formula can be easily executed in Excel, presuming that the r value has been inserted into spreadsheet cell A1, using the following command:

```
=.5*(@ln((1+@abs(A1))/(1-@abs(A1))))
```

For example, for $r = 0.82$, we obtain

$$= 0.5(LN((1 + 0.82) / (1 - 0.82)))$$
$$= 0.5(LN((1.82) / (0.18)))$$
$$= 0.5(LN(10.11))$$
$$= 0.5(2.31)$$
$$= 1.16$$

As another example, consider the extreme value of $r = 0.99$. Now we have

$$= 0.5(LN((1 + 0.99) / (1 - 0.99)))$$
$$= 0.5(LN((1.99) / (0.01)))$$
$$= 0.5(LN(199.00))$$
$$= 0.5(5.29)$$
$$= 2.65$$

Note that the r-to-z transform, not unlike the z scores in a normal distribution, tends to range between roughly -3 and $+3$.

r^2 as a Descriptive Statistic

The squared value of r (r^2), unlike r, is itself intervally-scaled as regards the variance common to the two variables. Thus, $r_{AB}^2 = +1.0$ (or 100%) is *four times* larger than $r_{XY}^2 = +0.25$ (or 25%). And the result also means that $r_{AB} = +1.0$ is *four times* larger than $r_{XY} = +0.5$.

The descriptive statistic r^2 is called the **coefficient of determination** or the **common variance**. Of course, unlike r, which is in the standardized score world, r^2 is in the area world. The interval properties of r^2 have led to the popular (albeit extremely brief) hit rap song, the only lyrics of which are "Square, before you compare!"

Table 5.3 presents some interesting uses of the coefficient of determination in comparing the correlation coefficients of IQs of family members under various situations (Erlenmeyer-Kimling & Jarvik, 1963). Some researchers prefer to always express r^2 as a percentage (e.g., 25%) because doing so helps them remember that common variance is a squared, area-world statistic.

The number 1 minus the glass-full coefficient of determination yields the glass-empty perspective of the **coefficient of alienation**. For example, according to the Table 5.3 data, with knowledge of one set of identical twins' IQs, we can linearly predict or explain all but 22.6% (100% – 77.4%) of the set of paired identical twins' IQ scores, provided the twins were reared together.

Although the coefficient of determination has considerable utility, one

TABLE 5.3. Correlations of IQs of Family Members
across Various Living Conditions

Person pair	r	r^2	Increase	Ratio to foster parent
Identical twins reared together	0.88	77.4%	37.7%	21.5
Identical twins reared apart	0.75	56.3%	100.2%	15.6
Fraternal twins	0.53	28.1%	3.9%	7.8
Parent with own child	0.52	27.0%	12.6%	7.5
Siblings reared together	0.49	24.0%	13.5%	6.7
Siblings reared apart	0.46	21.2%	486.1%	5.9
Foster parent with child	0.19	3.6%	—	—

of the statistic's downsides is that we lose the sign of the relationship (direct or inverse) once we square. The implication is that we usually use both r and r^2 when investigating bivariate relationship, because both descriptive statistics provide useful, although different, information.

The descriptive statistic r_{XY}^2 is called the coefficient of determination (or common variance), because the statistic tells us that with knowledge of the scores on X we can explain or predict a given percentage of the variability (either the variance or the sum of squares) on Y. For example, with knowledge of the Table 5.1 scores on X, we can explain or predict $r_{XY}^2 = 0.82^2 = 67.2\%$ of the information about individual differences on Y (i.e., SOS_Y or SD_Y^2).

This does *not* mean that we can explain exactly 67.2% of the variability of each of the 12 individual scores on Y. All statistics are *on the average*. Given $r^2 = 67.2\%$, we *might* be able to explain exactly 67.2% of each individual Y score's squared deviation from M_Y, because 67.2% of each individual squared deviation does yield a group average of 67.2%. But the more likely outcome for most datasets is that we can explain 67.2% of the score variability (i.e., SOS_Y or SD_Y^2) on the average, and we may do better at predicting some squared deviations and worse at explaining or predicting others. In Chapter 8, we will learn how to determine what exact portion of specific, individual scores, as well as of their squared deviations, can be determined with knowledge of predictor variable scores.

For example, the variance of the Y scores is $SD_Y^2 = 2.75^2 = 7.56$ squared units of Y. With knowledge of the X scores, we can explain 5.08

squared units of Y out of the 7.56 variance in squared units of Y [7.56(67.2%) = 5.08].

Because, for a given dataset, n is fixed (here 12), we can work with the SOS rather than with some average of the SOS, such as the SD^2. For a fixed sample size, we do not have to divide all our results by $n - 1$, or 11, and may simply work with the sum of squares, which still yields apples-to-apples comparisons for a given single fixed sample size.

Given that $SD_Y = 2.75$, for a sample n of 12, we can solve for the SOS_Y as

$$SD_Y^2(n - 1) \tag{5.9}$$

For our data this yields $SOS_Y = SD_Y^2 (n - 1) = 2.75^2(12 - 1) = 2.75^2(11) = 7.56(11) = 83.19$. For these data, with knowledge of the scores on X, we can explain or predict 55.94 (i.e., 67.2%(83.19)) squared units of information on Y out of the 83.19 squared units of information that are available for these 12 people.

Three Interpretation Contextual Factors

Causality and Third Variable Problems

A major theme of this book is that *all* statistics are correlational. However, not all research *designs* are correlational (or nonexperimental). Some research designs invoke randomized clinical trials (RCTs, in which cases are randomly assigned to treatment conditions) and are therefore truly *experimental*. Only experimental designs (including single-subject designs) can definitively answer questions about causality (Thompson, Diamond, McWilliam, Snyder, & Snyder, 2005).

Because causal issues are so important in education, psychology, and medicine, RCTs are very highly regarded and appropriate once inquiry has ripened to the point where their expense is justified (Mosteller & Boruch, 2002; Shavelson & Towne, 2002). Serious problems can occur if researchers attempt to extrapolate conclusive causal inferences from nonexperimental research involving correlation coefficients.

To make this discussion concrete, consider the quasi-hypothetical data (i.e., the data are approximate but real for a recent point in time) presented in Table 5.4. The table presents data on three variables for 10 cities in the United States. The first two variables are the numbers of houses of worship (e.g., churches, mosques, synagogues) and the numbers of murders in a given year.

The Pearson r for the first two variables for these data is 0.91. The r^2 is 82.8%. Does this result mean that large numbers of churches cause people to murder each other? Does this result mean that large numbers of murders cause people to build more houses of worship?

These data reflect the difficulties of making causal inferences from nonexperimental descriptive statistics. The example reflects what statisticians call the **third variable problem** (i.e., the problem that a third, fourth, et cetera variable may *spuriously inflate* a correlation coefficient or, conversely, that a third, fourth, et cetera variable may *spuriously attenuate* a correlation coefficient).

The third variable problem may also be described as the **mediator variable** discussed in Chapter 1. As Baron and Kenny (1986) explained, "In general, a given variable may be said to function as a mediator to the extent that it accounts for the relation between the predictor and the criterion" (p. 1176).

For these data, once the researcher obtains the result $r_{AB} = 0.91$, the reasonable researcher would immediately invest considerable thought in trying to understand the result. Most researchers would eventually realize

TABLE 5.4. Scores on Three Variables for 10 Cities

City	Houses of worship	Murders	Population
New York City	3,500	1,980	7,322,600
Los Angeles	2,020	1,060	3,485,600
Chicago	2,860	920	2,783,700
Houston	2,010	450	1,629,900
Philadelphia	1,710	420	1,585,600
San Diego	580	140	1,110,600
Detroit	1,480	590	1,028,000
Dallas	1,310	370	1,007,600
Phoenix	660	130	983,400
San Antonio	940	210	935,400

that a third variable, population size, confounds the correlation coefficient computed between numbers of houses of worship and numbers of murders.

The **partial correlation coefficient** can be computed to estimate the correlation of two variables, controlling for the influence of a third variable. The partial correlation can be used to explore either spurious inflation or spurious attenuation of the bivariate coefficient. And the formula can be expanded to simultaneously consider several extraneous variables at a time.

The formula for the partial correlation coefficient (i.e., $r_{AB.C}$) controlling for only one extraneous variable is

$$[r_{AB} - (r_{AC})(r_{BC})] / [((1 - r_{AC}^2)^{.5})((1 - r_{BC}^2)^{0.5})] \qquad (5.10)$$

For the Table 5.3 data we have

$$= [0.91 - (0.85)(0.97)] / [((1 - 0.85^2)^{0.5})((1 - 0.97^2)^{0.5})]$$
$$= [0.91 - 0.82] / [((1 - 0.85^2)^{0.5})((1 - 0.97^2)^{0.5})]$$
$$= [0.09] / [((1 - 0.85^2)^{0.5})((1 - 0.97^2)^{0.5})]$$
$$= [0.09] / [((1 - 0.72)^{0.5})((1 - 0.94)^{0.5})]$$
$$= [0.09] / [(0.28^{0.5})(0.06^{0.5})]$$
$$= [0.09] / [(0.53)(0.25)]$$
$$= [0.09] / [0.13]$$
$$= 0.65$$

Thus, churches and murders in these 10 cities had 0.91^2, or 82.8%, common variance. But after controlling for population size, the two variables had only 0.65^2, or 42.2%, common variance. The common variance might be even smaller if we controlled for additional variables (e.g., income or education levels).

The problem is that, unlike our current example, we may quite conceivably be correlating two variables for which neither (a) the spurious r inflation or attenuation nor (b) the extraneous variables are obvious. The example should make it abundantly clear that drawing causal inferences from correlation coefficients can easily lead to erroneous conclusions. Thus, considerable caution must be exercised when interpreting correlational results in nonexperimental designs.

Moderator Effects

In Baron and Kenny's (1986) conceptualization, whereas "mediators speak to *how or why* ... [emphasis added] effects occur," as in the murders–churches example, "moderator variables specify *when* certain effects will hold" (p. 1176). The Pearson *r* is "on the average." It is also possible that different averages, or *r* values, occur within different subgroups of the data. Sometimes identifying subgroup variations in *r* may be quite useful.

Table 5.5 presents hypothetical data for testing done on 16 high school students at the beginning and the end of a school year. The correlation of pretest with posttest scores is 0.87, suggesting that the scores are highly and positively linearly associated.

But when we compute the correlation coefficients separately for the nongifted (*r* = 0.74) and the gifted (*r* = 0.96), it becomes clear that the predictive or explanatory power of the pretest scores differs somewhat across the groups. These differences may be noteworthy, given that $r_{TOTAL}^2 = 0.87^2 = 75.7\%$, $r_{NONGIFTED}^2 = 0.74^2 = 55.6\%$, and $r_{GIFTED}^2 = 0.96^2 = 91.8\%$, and thus the association for the gifted students is 1.65 times larger (i.e., 91.8% / 55.6% = 1.65) than the association for the nongifted students.

The take-home message is that when computing *r*, considerable

TABLE 5.5. Pretest and Posttest Scores
for Eight Gifted and Eight Nongifted Students

Group	Pretest	Posttest
Gifted	140	200
Gifted	140	180
Gifted	130	170
Gifted	130	150
Gifted	120	140
Gifted	120	120
Gifted	110	110
Gifted	110	90
Nongifted	100	40
Nongifted	100	60
Nongifted	70	30
Nongifted	70	50
Nongifted	40	20
Nongifted	40	40
Nongifted	10	10
Nongifted	10	30

insights may be realized by disaggregating the data. Some subgroups may have quite divergent association patterns. And even when the r for the total group is relatively small in absolute value, some subgroups may have stronger patterns of linear relationships.

Restriction of Range

It is widely believed by applied researchers that **restriction of range** (i.e., disproportionately small SD of one or both sample variables relative to the population) always attenuates r (Walsh, 1996). However, this should seem counterintuitive. As noted previously, when we divide we are attempting to remove from our answer whatever we are using as a divisor. Because $r_{XY} = COV_{XY} / [SD_X(SD_Y)]$, we might reasonably assume that the standard deviations do not affect r, because their influence is being removed from r by division.

The dynamics involved in range restriction are actually fairly complicated (see Huck, 1992; Huck, Wright, & Park, 1992). In exploring these issues, it is critical to distinguish the degree of *correspondence* of the sample r to the population parameter from questions about the *replicability* of r across samples.

The replicability of r statistics across samples can be affected by two sample features, one of which, indeed, does involve score dispersion. First, the number of pairs of scores affects the replicability of r statistics (as is generally true for all statistics). The r computation takes into account the ordering of cases across the rows of the raw data matrix. There is simply *more compelling evidence of generalized row-ordering effects* when they are replicated over more and more rows of data.

Second, the score dispersion does also affect replicability of r results. The further scores are from other datapoints, the harder it is for small movements of scores for given cases across replication to shift their ordinal positions. Thus, *greater SD* does tend to lead to *more replicable* estimates for r.

However, having a sample with restricted range (i.e., disproportionately small SD relative to the population) does *not* always attenuate r so that r is closer to zero. Instead, a sample with restricted range can either attenuate *or* increase the magnitude of *r*, depending upon the circumstances.

Consider the Table 5.6 hypothetical paired scores for 14 students completing the SAT and then receiving GPAs for their first year of college. The data are graphically presented in the Figure 5.3 scattergram.

For these data, the Pearson *r* is 0.44 (r^2 = 19.4%). However, if only students with SAT scores higher than 675 had been admitted to college, the SAT variable's range would have been restricted, with a concomitant narrowing of GPA score dispersion. For these four cases, the *r* with restricted range is actually *higher* in absolute magnitude (*r* = –1.00; r^2 = 100.0%), and larger by a factor of roughly five.

Clearly, restricted range does *not* always lead to attenuated results for *r*. Selective subsamples with restricted score ranges may yield *r* values that are smaller, or larger, or equal to the values for the larger dataset.

But what if the population parameter correlation coefficient for billions of score pairs is +1.0? Now all samples of two or more score pairs, even score pairs drawn at the narrow extremes of the two distributions, will yield subgroup *r* values that exactly match those of the population!

TABLE 5.6. Hypothetical Sample
of 14 Paired SAT and GPA Scores

ID	SAT	GPA
1	431	3.20
2	434	3.50
3	528	3.25
4	509	3.45
5	517	3.70
6	583	3.40
7	587	3.90
8	626	3.70
9	662	3.20
10	665	3.50
11	685	3.90
12	705	3.80
13	724	3.70
14	744	3.60

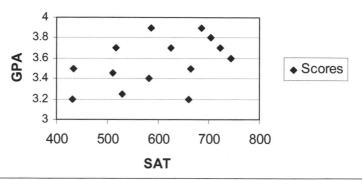

FIGURE 5.3. Scattergram of the Table 5.6 SAT and GPA data

▪▪▪ Psychometrics of the Pearson *r*

The Pearson *r*, as a standardized covariance, can only range between its mathematical limits of −1 and +1, inclusive. To see this, let's think of the exceptional case of computing the *covariance* of a variable with itself (e.g., COV_{XX}). Here we can reexpress Equation 5.2 to characterize the association of *X* with *X*:

$$COV_{XX} = (\Sigma(X_i - \overline{X})(X_i - \overline{X})) / (n - 1) \qquad (5.11)$$

This is the formula ($SOS_X / (n - 1)$) for the variance. Thus, the *covariance of a variable with itself is the variance* (i.e., $COV_{XX} = SD_X^2$) of the variable.

Now let's think of the *correlation* of a variable (never a constant for which $SD_X^2 = 0$) with itself (e.g., r_{XX}). Now we have $r_{XX} = COV_{XX} / SD_X^2 = SD_X^2 / SD_X^2 = 1.0$. Conceptually, the most highly correlated a variable could be is the correlation with itself, and that correlation must be 1.0. Therefore, the upper limit on *r* is +1. The most inversely related a correlation would be is the correlation with the inverse of itself. Therefore, the lower limit on *r* is −1.

Examination of the numerator (i.e., $\Sigma(X_i - \overline{X})(Y_i - \overline{Y})$) of the covariance numerator in the calculation of *r* further reveals the nature and sensitivities of *r*. As noted previously, this numerator declares *focal interest in the bivariate centroid as a pivot point* for drawing in the scattergram the line of best fit to the asterisks as a set.

We can also think of the two reference lines drawn at the means of Y and X within the scattergram as dividing the scattergram into four quadrants. For all asterisks in the *upper right* quadrant, all these cases had scores on both Y and X above their respective means. Therefore, all their deviation scores on both Y and X are positive, and thus *all* their crossproducts (i.e., xy_i) are positive.

For all asterisks in the *lower left* quadrant, all these cases had scores on both Y and X below their respective means. Therefore, all their deviation scores on both Y and X are negative. But a negative times a negative yields a positive, and thus *all* their crossproducts (i.e., xy_i) are positive.

For all asterisks in the *upper left* quadrant, all these cases had scores on Y above the Y mean, and scores on X below the X mean. Therefore, all their deviation scores on Y are positive, but all their deviation scores on X are negative. Thus, *all* their crossproducts (i.e., xy_i) are negative.

For all asterisks in the *lower right* quadrant, all these cases had scores on Y below the Y mean and scores on X above the X mean. Therefore, all their deviation scores on Y are negative, but all their deviation scores on X are positive. Because a negative times a positive yields a negative, *all* their crossproducts (xy_i) are negative.

The denominator of the covariance (i.e., $n - 1$) can never be negative, and neither can the r denominator (i.e., $SD_X(SD_Y)$) ever be negative. Therefore, the numerator of the covariance (i.e., Σxy_i) completely determines the sign of r. So, the preceding discussion implies that one of the several situations in which r will always be positive is if all the asterisks in the scattergram are only in the lower left and the upper right quadrants defined by the means. And one of the several situations in which r will always be negative is if all the asterisks in the scattergram are only in the upper left and the lower right quadrants defined by the means.

In all other cases in which some of the asterisks are in all four quadrants defined by the two means, counting the number of asterisks in the quadrants (i.e., lower left and upper right versus upper left and lower right) is *insufficient* for determining the sign of the Pearson r. In this last case, the *magnitudes of the deviation scores* are determinative.

For example, for the Table 5.1 data, five people are in the lower left quadrant: Paul, Christopher, Michael, Jennifer, and Stephanie. Five people are in the upper right quadrant: Randy, Steve, Sarah, Judy, and Patty. One person is in the upper left quadrant: Elizabeth. And one person is in the lower right quadrant: Ralph.

Because the magnitudes of the xy_i of Ralph and Elizabeth are small (i.e., -0.5 and -0.5), the sum of the crossproducts quickly becomes positive once we add in the other 10 crossproducts (e.g., 13.5, 7.0, 2.5). And so the covariance and r are both positive for these data.

It also becomes clear that for r to be zero, some asterisks must be in all four quadrants, and the sum of the crossproducts must be zero. For example, COV_{XY} and r_{XY} will be zero for the four pairs of scores: {1,1; 3,1; 1,3; 3,3, on Y and X, respectively}.

Now the natures of the covariance and of r become clear. In the scattergram, when we compute the deviation score y_i, we are measuring the *vertical* distance of y_i from M_Y; and when we compute the deviation score x_i, we are measuring the *horizontal* distance of X_i from M_X.

These two distances (from the Cartesian score coordinate X_i, Y_i to the M_Y or the $\overline{Y}$ line, and from the Cartesian score coordinate X_i, Y_i to the M_X or the $\overline{X}$ line) define a 90° angle. We can therefore invoke the Pythagorean theorem to solve for the length of the hypothenuse, d_i. For a given person, $d_i^2 = y_i^2 + x_i^2$; so $d_i = (y_i^2 + x_i^2)^{0.5}$.

The length of this hypothenuse is the distance of a given case's score pair (i.e., X_i, Y_i) from the centroid (i.e., $\overline{X}, \overline{Y}$). Cases near the centroid (i.e., small d_i) *inherently* exert less leverage on determining the sign and the magnitude of r.

Cases farther from the centroid *may* exert greater leverage on determining r. However, cases with large d_i values will still *not* exert this potential leverage, notwithstanding a large d_i, iff either of their y_i and x_i scores are zero or near-zero, because their crossproduct (i.e., xy_i) will be small if *either* y_i or x_i are small.

■■■ Spearman's rho

Pearson's product–moment correlation coefficient invokes the product (i.e., xy_i) of first-moment unsquared deviation scores from the two means (i.e., x_i and y_i). The r statistic quantifies how well a straight line captures all the asterisks in a scattergram. This means that the Pearson r asks the following two questions:

1. How well do the two variables order the cases in exactly the same (or the opposite) order?, and
2. To what extent do the two variables have the same shape?

This second consideration necessarily comes into play, because *a straight line can catch all the asterisks in a scattergram if and only if (iff) the two variables have the same shape.*

The Pearson r will be +1 (or −1) iff (a) the two variables identically order the cases (or perfectly order the cases in inverse directions) and (b) the two variables both have identical coefficients of skewness and kurtosis. An important implication of this realization is that the limits of r cannot be rigidly used when interpreting results unless the two variables have the same shapes or the researcher considers shape differences equally as important as ordering differences. Two rs of 0.50 and 0.77 might both involve variable pairs that order cases identically, but different degrees of result attenuation due to univariate shape differences.

Consider the following intervally-scaled data:

Participant	X	Y
Murray	1	3
Deborah	2	4
Geri	3	5
Donna	97	99

The standard deviations of these two variables do not affect r, as long as neither is zero, because we remove the SDs from r by dividing the covariance by the two SDs. In our example, these two variables have identical SDs, but this is irrelevant to our computation of r as long as both SDs > 0.0. The two variables have different means, but location also does not affect r.

Only (a) variable ordering and (b) variable shape affect r. Here both variables identically order the four participants. And both variables have identical shape. So the Pearson r for these data is +1.0.

By the way, note that Donna is extremely unusual in some respects, but is quite typical in others. Donna is an outlier as regards the means, the dispersions, and the shapes of both X and Y.

But if we plot these data in a scattergram, Donna's asterisk would lie directly on the line of best fit, as would all the asterisks. And if we took Donna's two scores out of the dataset, the r would still be +1.0. Donna is clearly *not* an outlier as regards relationship.

Remember now and for always that (a) people can be outliers on some variables but not others, and (b) people can be outliers on some statistics but not others, even for the same dataset. And don't feel too bad if you are an outlier on some variables and/or some statistics. Healthy people probably are outliers on something, somewhere, some of the time.

But what if we had the following data?

Participant	X	Y
Robert	1	1
David	2	2
James	3	3
Douglas	4	999,999,999

Assuming the data are at least intervally-scaled, we could compute the Pearson r. However, even though both variables identically order the four cases, r will not be perfect because the two variables do not have identical shape. The Pearson correlation coefficient can only reach its mathematical limits when both variables are identically shaped.

Here the r equals 0.77. The result reflects the shape differences of the two variables. The result is not inherently problematic. But we must remember that an r less than +1 or greater than −1 does *not* mean that the two variables *necessarily* order the cases differently. A given coefficient may instead merely reflect shape differences in the two variables.

So unless we consult our data further when confronted with $r = 0.77$, we must interpret the result as reflecting different ordering of the cases across the two variables, or different variable shapes, or both. We can only get an unambiguous interpretation by also computing shape statistics for the two variables, or plotting the two variables (e.g., a histogram, or a box plot).

However, when we have data that are at least intervally-scaled, if we wish to ask *only* the first of the two questions posed by the Pearson r (i.e., whether the two variables order the cases identically), we can compute an alternative descriptive relationship statistic, Spearman's rho (ρ).

Spearman's ρ can also be computed when both or either of the two variables are only ordinally-scaled. Spearman's ρ assumes that the two variables contain no information about distance, and consequently completely ignores shape or other issues presuming at least interval scaling, even when one or both variables are in fact intervally-scaled.

For both our small datasets, ρ would be +1.0. That is, ρ has the same mathematical limits as Pearson's r (i.e., −1 to +1), and will be perfect whenever the two variables order the cases identically (or perfectly but inversely).

Computing both r and ρ for a dataset characterizes the relationships between the two variables in different ways. For the first dataset (i.e., Murray, Deborah, Geri, and Donna), $r = +1$, and $\rho = +1$. The result that $r = +1$ tells us that the variables both ordered the cases identically and had identical shapes. Here, ignoring shape when computing ρ has no effect, because ignoring shape when shapes for the two variables are identical has no effect.

For the second dataset, for which $r = 0.77$, and $\rho = 1.00$, we can compare these two results to quantify the magnitude of the effect of paying attention to both variable ordering and shape versus paying attention to only variable ordering. Of course, we must make the comparisons in the area world. The difference of $r^2 = 0.77^2 = 59.3\%$ versus $\rho^2 = 100.0\%$ tells us that shape differences produced a difference of 0.407 (1.000 − 0.593) in the two coefficients for these data.

No Tied Ranks

Spearman's ρ is the *Pearson product–moment r between two variables if the variables are expressed as ranks.* However, iff the data involve ranks with no ties, the formula for r can be algebraically reexpressed. When both variables in a pair have the same number of cases, and no tied ranks, the denominator SDs in the r formula are necessarily both equal.

This means that the denominator of the r formula, $(SD_X)(SD_Y)$, becomes the variance of either X or Y, because the two standard deviations are equal. And when we are computing the variance of ranks with no ties, a formula equivalent to computing the parameter variance by dividing SOS by n is

$$\sigma^2_{RANKS} = (n^2 - 1) / 12.0 \qquad (5.12)$$

The Table 5.7 ranks for variables A, B, and C can be used to illustrate these computations. Because there are no tied ranks on variables A and B, and $n = 7$, the variance of the scores is $(7^2 - 1) / 12.0 = (49 - 1) / 12.0 = (48) / 12.0 = 4.0$. As noted in Table 5.7, the SOS of the ranks on A and B is 28.0, and computing the parameter variance instead using the SOS we again obtain $28.0 / 7 = 4.0$.

Iff the data are ranks with no ties, in addition to reexpressing the computation of the r denominator, we can also algebraically reexpress (see Siegel, 1956) the various ways of computing $COV_{XY} / (SD_X(SD_Y))$ as

$$\rho = 1 - \{[6(\Sigma(X_i - Y_i)^2)] / [n(n^2 - 1)]\} \qquad (5.13)$$

TABLE 5.7. Ranks of Seven People on Three Variables

Participant/ statistic	A	a	a^2	B	b	b^2	C	c	c^2	$(A-B)^2$	$(A-C)^2$	$(B-C)^2$
Eileen	7	3	9	2	-2	4	1	-3	9	25	36	1
Ida	6	2	4	3	-1	1	2	-2	4	9	16	1
Kathy	5	1	1	1	3	9	3	-1	1	16	4	4
Mary	4	0	0	4	0	0	4	0	0	0	0	0
Molly	3	-1	1	5	1	1	5	1	1	4	4	0
Nancy C.	2	-2	4	6	2	4	6.5	2.5	6.25	16	20.25	0.25
Nancy H.	1	-3	9	7	3	9	6.5	2.5	6.25	36	30.25	0.25
M	4.0			4.0			4.0					
Sum		0.0	28.0		0.0	28.0		0.0	27.50	106.0	110.5	6.5
Sum / n		0.0	4.0		0.0	4.0		0.0	3.93			

For example, in Table 5.7, variables A and B have no tied ranks. For these data, as noted in Table 5.7, $\Sigma(X_i - Y_i)^2 = 106.0$, and ρ:

$$
\begin{aligned}
&= 1 - \{[6(106)] / [7(7^2 - 1)]\} \\
&= 1 - \{[6(106)] / [7(49 - 1)]\} \\
&= 1 - \{[6(106)] / [7(48)]\} \\
&= 1 - \{[6(106)] / [336]\} \\
&= 1 - \{[636)] / [336]\} \\
&= 1 - 1.89 \\
&= -0.89
\end{aligned}
$$

The fact that Equation 5.13 yields Spearman's ρ for the case of no tied ranks does *not* mean that we must use this formula to obtain ρ. If instead we apply any formula for the Pearson r to data with no tied ranks, we will obtain exactly the same result. Spearman's ρ is nothing more (or less) than the Pearson r between ranks, and we can also *always* compute ρ by applying any formula for the Pearson r to any ranked data, to address the sole question that ρ poses: How well do the two variables order the cases in exactly the same (or the opposite) order?

Tied Ranks

When intervally-scaled data are converted into ranks, it is conventional to assign tied ranks to cases with tied interval scores. For example, if two rising high school seniors both had GPAs of 3.92 and eight students had higher GPAs, with the highest GPA being assigned the rank of 1, the two students with 3.92 GPAs would both be assigned the class rank of 9.5 ((9 + 10) / 2).

Assigning ranks for tied scores in this manner has the property that the mean is preserved as equaling what the mean would be if there were no tied ranks. For example, for the Table 5.7 data, the means of all three variables are 4.0, even though on variable C Nancy C. and Nancy H. both have tied ranks of 6.5.

However, when some ranks are tied, scores inherently become less dispersed. For example, as reported in Table 5.7, the variance of C is not 4.0, but instead is 3.93 (i.e., SOS_C / n). The implication is that we cannot use Equation 5.12 or 5.13 when the ranks include any ties.

When data include tied ranks, we *must* compute ρ by using one of the algebraically equivalent formulas for the Pearson r. Notice that we are computing both a Pearson r and SDs when both variables are ordinally-scaled (i.e., ranks). But in this exceptional case, the results are nevertheless sensible. We honor the exception by calling the result ρ even when the Pearson r formula is invoked for the computation. Note also that this exception does *not* mean that r can be computed for ordinal data that are in any form other than ranks!

Why does ρ only address the single question about fidelity of case ordering by the two variables? Because when the variables are ranks with no ties, the shapes of the two distributions are constrained to be identical; thus questions of shape differences are moot. And when the data include ties, the presumption that there are relatively few ties, especially in the presence of a large n, means that the influences of shape differences in the ranks may be presumed to be negligible.

Two Other *r*-Equivalent Correlation Coefficients

Phi (ϕ)

Yet another algebraically-equivalent formula for r exists for the special case in which both variables are dichotomous. Actually, dichotomous data are a bit of an anomaly in that they can be conceptualized as nominal (e.g., gender), but also might be conceptualized as interval (e.g., male, versus the absence of maleness; or female, versus the absence of femaleness).

Table 5.8 presents data ($n = 1,000$) that are hypothetical, but correspond closely to an actual study in which 22,071 physicians in a double-blind study (i.e., neither the participants nor the people actually distributing the drugs knew what drugs were being administered) were randomly assigned to take either aspirin or placebos daily (Steering Committee of the Physicians' Health Study Research Group, 1988). Figure 5.4 presents the corresponding layout of cells described by two such dichotomous variables (i.e., aspirin/placebo and heart attack/no heart attack).

TABLE 5.8. Modeled Heart Attack Data			
	Heart attack		
Treatment	Yes	No	Total
Aspirin	5	495	500
Placebo	9	491	500
Total	14	986	1000

Using the Figure 5.4 definitions, the **phi** coefficient can be computed as

$$\phi = |bc - ad| / \{[(a + c)(b + d)(a + b)(c + d)]^{0.5}\} \quad (5.14)$$

For the Table 5.8 data, ϕ is

$$[(495)(9) - (5)(491)] / \{[(5 + 9)(495 + 491)(5 + 495)(9 + 491)]^{0.5}\}$$
$$[4{,}455 - 2{,}455] / \{[(5 + 9)(495 + 491)(5 + 495)(9 + 491)]^{0.5}\}$$
$$[2{,}000] / \{[(5 + 9)(495 + 491)(5 + 495)(9 + 491)]^{0.5}\}$$
$$[2{,}000] / \{[(14)(986)(500)(500)]^{0.5}\}$$
$$[2{,}000] / \{[(14)(986)(250{,}000)]^{0.5}\}$$
$$[2{,}000] / \{[(14)(246{,}500{,}000)]^{0.5}\}$$
$$[2{,}000] / \{[3{,}451{,}000{,}000]^{0.5}\}$$
$$[2{,}000] / \{58{,}745.21\}$$
$$0.034$$

However, ϕ is nothing more (or less) than the Pearson r between the two dichotomous variables. We can apply any algebraically-equivalent

FIGURE 5.4. Layout of the Table 5.8 Aspirin Study Data

	Heart Attack		
Treatment	Yes	No	Total
Aspirin	a	b	a+b
Placebo	c	d	c+d
Total	a+c	b+d	a+b+c+d

formula for r to these data and we will obtain exactly the same result produced by Equation 5.14. If you do not believe it, enter 5 pairs of {1,1}, 495 pairs of {1,0}, 9 pairs of {0,1}, and 491 pairs of {0,0} scores, for a total of 1,000 cases, into SPSS, and compute the Pearson r. You will obtain 0.034.

This 0.034 value for ϕ is incredibly small ($\phi^2 = 0.1\%$)! Yet, the aspirin study was discontinued once these preliminary findings emerged, because to do otherwise would have unethically denied the control-group participants the life-saving benefits of daily aspirin.

Note that even though $\phi^2 = 0.1\%$, among the physicians who had heart attacks ($n = 9$), the ratio of physicians taking aspirin to the physicians taking the placebo was about half (i.e., $5 / 9 = 0.56$). (In the actual study, the ratio was $104 / 189 = 0.55$.) Clearly, these are dramatic differences, even though ϕ^2 is so small. Of course, considerable credence was placed in the actual results, because the real sample size ($n = 22,071$) was so large.

This discussion hopefully makes the general point that interpreting common variance statistics can be challenging, even for seasoned statisticians (Rosenthal, 1994; Rosenthal & Rubin, 1979). Remember that a *very small coefficient of determination for a very important outcome may nevertheless be quite noteworthy.*

Point–Biserial Correlation (r_{pb})

A final algebraically-equivalent form of the Pearson r is the point–biserial correlation coefficient (r_{pb}). The point–biserial coefficient characterizes the bivariate relationship between one variable that is dichotomous (e.g., male–female, right–wrong) and another variable that is at least intervally-scaled.

For convenience, we will restrict the dichotomous variable to the scores 0 and 1. Dichotomous data can always be converted to these two values, even if the scores were not originally recorded in this manner. Table 5.9 presents scores on one dichotomous variable (i.e., item 1: 0 = wrong; 1 = right), total scores (i.e., number of right answers) on the remaining items 2 through 9 (potentially 0–8), and total scores on all nine test items (potentially 0–9).

TABLE 5.9. Item and Total Test Scores of Five Participants

Participant/Statistic	Item #1	Items 2–9	Items 1–9
Tom	0	2	2
Dick	0	3	3
Harry	0	4	4
Sally	1	5	6
Spot	1	8	9
M_1		6.50	7.50
M_0		3.00	3.00
SOS		21.20	30.80
$SOS/(n-1)$		5.30	7.70
SD		2.30	2.77

We will correlate the item scores with the total test scores. The resulting item-to-total correlation coefficient is what in item analysis is called an *uncorrected discrimination coefficient*, which is computed to determine whether the appropriate people are getting a test item right and wrong, and the test item is performing in the desired fashion. Generally, people with higher test scores should be disproportionately likely to get a given item correct (i.e., item score = 1).

The algebraically-equivalent form of the Pearson r for this combination of levels of scale is

$$r_{pb} = [(M_1 - M_0) / SD_X][(n_1(n_0) / (n(n-1)))^{0.5}] \qquad (5.15)$$

where M_1 is the mean X score of cases scoring 1 on the dichotomously-scored item, M_0 is the mean X score of cases scoring 0 on the dichotomously-scored item, SD_X is the standard deviation of the intervally-scaled X scores, n_1 is the number of people scoring 1, n_0 is the number of people scoring 0, and n is the total number of cases. For the correlation of the scores on item #1 with the total scores on the remaining test items, excluding item #1, we have r_{pb}

$$= [(6.5 - 3.0)/2.30][(2(3)/(5(5 - 1)))^{0.5}]$$
$$= [(6.5 - 3.0) / 2.30][(6 / (5(5 - 1)))^{0.5}]$$
$$= [(6.5 - 3.0) / 2.30][(6 / (5(4)))^{0.5}]$$
$$= [(6.5 - 3.0) / 2.30][(6 / (20))^{0.5}]$$
$$= [(6.5 - 3.0) / 2.30][(0.30)^{0.5}]$$
$$= [(6.5 - 3.0) / 2.30][(0.548]$$
$$= [3.5 / 2.30][(0.548]$$
$$= [1.520][(0.548]$$
$$= 0.83$$

So, if we compute the Pearson r between scores on item #1 with total scores on the remaining test items 2–9, using Equation 5.15, or any formula for the Pearson r, we will obtain 0.83 as our result. Similarly, if we correlate scores on item #1 with scores on *all* the items, including item #1, we obtain 0.89.

The second r_{pb} (0.89) is larger than the first r_{pb} (0.83), because in computing the second coefficient, we use the scores on item #1 both as one variable, and as part of the total scores, thus producing a spuriously inflated "uncorrected item discrimination coefficient." The first r, 0.83, is a more realistic appraisal of whether the appropriate students are getting item #1 right and wrong, and is called a "corrected item discrimination coefficient."

Bivariate Normality

The Pearson r as a descriptive statistic tests, in part, whether both variables with at least interval scale have the same univariate shape. One, but only one, case of two variables having identical shape arises when both variables are univariate normal, as described in Chapter 4.

When both variables are univariate normal, they may or may not be **bivariate normal**. Univariate normality of two variables is a necessary but not sufficient condition for bivariate normality.

Bivariate normality is an important precursor for discussions of multivariate normality, which is beyond the scope of this book. However, many if not most social science datasets require multivariate analyses, so we will briefly discuss bivariate normality to lay the foundation for your potential future studies.

The concept of bivariate normality requires that we draw perpendicular X and Y axes on a two-dimensional surface. We also will require a vertical axis drawn perpendicular to the floor and rising from the $\{X,Y\}$ intercept, which we will use as a frequency axis to count how often a given pair of X and Y scores occurs.

To make this clear, we will use an example that is a bit silly, but that has the irresistible appeal of being absolutely, completely concrete. Let's presume that you put on a coat and enter a refrigerated room with a smooth concrete floor. You might paint on the floor an X axis (get permission first) that you mark off in inches, and a perpendicular Y axis that you mark off in the same manner.

You will paint the X axis subject to the restriction that the X axis passes through the mean of the the Y scores (i.e., $\overline{Y}$, or M_Y), and the Y axis subject to the restriction that the Y axis passes through the mean of the X scores ($\overline{X}$, or M_X). Then, you will attach the string that runs straight up to the ceiling from the floor at the centroid (i.e., $\{\overline{X}, \overline{Y}\}$, or $\{M_X, M_Y\}$). You also mark off a string in units of 0.25" (i.e., the exact height of a pat of butter).

Now let's say that you have scores of 4,000 (or 6,000) people on two variables, X and Y, both of which are univariate normal. Then you bring 4,000 pats of butter into the refrigerated room. You put down a pat of butter to mark the Cartesian coordinates of all 4,000 score pairs. For example, if Colleen's X and Y scores are both 1.0, you will place a pat of butter to represent her score at the $\{1,1\}$ coordinate. If you then deal with Martha's data, and her two scores also are both 1.0, you will place a pat of butter representing her two scores directly on top of Colleen's.

When you are done, iff the data are bivariate normal, you will have created a giant object made of butter and shaped exactly like a very large bell. Iff your data are bivariate normal, your butter bell will have two properties.

First, iff the data are bivariate normal, and you cut through the butter, using a very hot, very large knife, along the string that runs from the floor to the ceiling, your cut will create a univariate normal distribution. Indeed, if $r \neq -1$ and $r \neq +1$, and if you cut along the string at any of infinitely many locations, *every* cut will produce a univariate normal distribution.

Second, iff the data are bivariate normal, and you draw on the floor around the pats of butter, the outline will be a circle, an ellipse, or a line. If you use your very hot, very large knife to cut through the butter, doing so perfectly parallel to the floor, you will create a ring concentric to your tracing on the floor. Each concentric ring will narrow as you slice closer to the ceiling, until you cut at the very apex of your butter bell.

Some Key Concepts

Bivariate relationship statistics quantify the degrees of relationships between variables. The Pearson r presumes that both variables are at least intervally-scaled. However, with respect to the common variance of the two variables, r is not intervally-scaled, but r^2 is. The Pearson r is a score-world statistic, whereas the coefficient of determination is an area-world statistic. The Pearson r asks two questions:

1. How well do the two variables order the cases in exactly the same (or the opposite) order?
2. To what extent do the two variables have the same shape?

Spearman's ρ only asks the first question. The Spearman ρ (unlike r) can be computed when both variables are ordinally-scaled. Rho also can be computed when either variable, or both, are intervally- or ratio-scaled, but the researcher wishes to address only this second question.

Phi (ϕ) and point–biserial correlation (r_{pb}) are algebraically-equivalent alternative formulas for computing r when the variables are (a) both dichotomous or (b) one variable is dichotomous and the other variable is at least intervally-scaled, respectively. However, the Pearson r formula may also be applied in these cases, will yield identical results, and the results still may be correctly labeled as ϕ and r_{pb}. Regardless of how we obtain these results, we would typically call the results ϕ and r_{pb}, to call attention to the scaling of the variables.

▦▦▦ **Reflection Problems** ▦▦▦

1. Consider that the numerator of the covariance formula, which in turn is the numerator of the r formula, is $(\Sigma(X_i - M_X)(Y_i - M_Y))$. If you substitute mean values for missing data, what tends to be the effect of the estimated covariance and r values after imputation, as against the corresponding values when cases with missing data are instead omitted from the analysis?

2. Reconsider the butter bell example, limiting the discussion to bivariate normal data. First, if (a) $r = 0$ and (b) $SD_X = SD_Y$, will the tracing on the floor of the perimeter of the bell create a circle, an ellipse, or a line? Will every cut through the butter bell along the string be only normal, or will every cut univariate distribution be both univariate normal and exactly match every other cut?

   Second, if (a) $r = 0$ and (b) both variables are z scores, will every one of the infinitely many possible cuts along the string yield nonstandard normal distributions, or standard normal distributions?

   Third, if $r = -1$ or $+1$, will the tracing of the perimeter of the bell on the floor yield a circle, an ellipse, or a line? How many cuts through the bell along the string will yield a univariate normal distribution?

3. Using the data and the additive and multiplicative constants in Reflection Problem 3 in Chapter 2, successively compute the product–moment correlations for Y with $X1$, $X2$, and $X3$ both before and after the application of the constants. What rule can we formulate to express the effects on the Pearson r of additive constants? What rule can we formulate to express the effects on r of multiplicative constants? When will a multiplicative constant *not* change the value of the Pearson r? When will a multiplicative constant change the value of r?

   Draw separate scattergrams for each original set of score pairs, and draw your best "guesstimate" of the line of best fit, using a blue or black pen. Within the same plots, draw the asterisks after a given constant has been applied, and the "guesstimated" line of best fit, using a red or green pen. How do the constants affect the locations of the asterisks and of the lines of best fit? You can check your drawings by using the SPSS GRAPH menu, clicking on INTERACTIVE and then on SCATTERPLOT. In the FIT menu, for METHOD, select REGRESSION to obtain the line of best fit within a given scattergram.

4. What are the Pearson r's and the Spearman rho's between all possible variable pairs for the Appendix data? How can this be, given their divergent means and SDs?

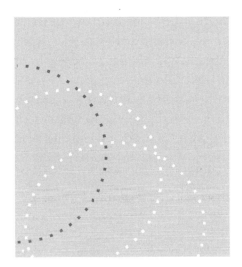

6

Statistical Significance

A s explained in Chapter 1, when we characterize aspects of data that constitute a sample, we are computing statistics. When we characterize features of data that constitute what we deem a population, we are computing parameters. In subsequent chapters, we learned various ways to compute descriptive statistics to characterize location (or central tendency), dispersion (or "spreadoutness"), shape, and bivariate relationship.

It has also been previously noted that researchers almost always presume that their data represent samples, rather than populations, and try to generalize their descriptive results to much larger populations (e.g., *all* third graders, *all* adults with depression now or ever in the future). This impulse is observed even when the data are from samples of convenience (e.g., available sophomores on the local campus), rather than from random samples drawn from an identified, specific population.

Characterizing data as creating a sample inescapably implies the existence of a larger population from which the sample data were obtained. In the presence of samples, researchers often want to know whether sample descriptive statistics accurately approximate the related population parameters. For example, does the statistic median approximate the parameter median?

There is no way to know for certain how accurate our descriptive statistics are. Indeed, as long as we are working with samples, rather than with populations, our particular sample will always imperfectly represent the data in the full population, at least to some degree.

Given descriptive statistics for imperfect sample data, researchers still seek ways to evaluate the noteworthiness of their data characterizations. Researchers may address as many as three questions when evaluating their sample results. Today, researchers typically use at least two of these evaluations when interpreting their results.

First, researchers can evaluate the **statistical significance** of their statistics (Cohen, 1994; Thompson, 1996). This evaluation requires an inferential linkage of sample and population data and thus is also referred to as **inferential statistics**. Inferential statistics always implies the presence of sample data. In inferential statistics, we go beyond our descriptive statistics by calculating the estimated probability (i.e., $p_{\text{CALCULATED}}$) of the *sample* statistics' occurrence, assuming the sample was drawn from a given population. These p values range from 0 to 1 (think of these as percentages, ranging from 0% to 100%). Statistics with smaller $p_{\text{CALCULATED}}$ values are relatively unlikely (e.g., $p_{\text{CALCULATED}} = 0.02 = 2\%$), whereas statistics with larger $p_{\text{CALCULATED}}$ values (e.g., 0.97, or 97%) are estimated to have more likely been drawn from the population we are assuming.

Second, researchers can evaluate the **practical significance** of their statistics (Kirk, 1996; Thompson, in press; Vacha-Haase & Thompson, 2004). Statistical significance yields a mathematical estimate of the probability of statistics. But the computation of $p_{\text{CALCULATED}}$ values does *not* incorporate any information about the personal values of the researcher; therefore, p values inherently *cannot* contain information about result import and *cannot* inform value judgments about results. But other statistics can be computed to help evaluate the practical significance of results. Practical significance focuses on how much difference an intervention makes or how related various variables are (e.g., how much longer, on average, will you tend to live if you do not smoke; how related are different amounts of obesity to various blood pressures).

Third, iff the research involves a dependent variable for which there are recognized diagnostic cut scores (e.g., you are considered to have high blood pressure if your diastolic pressure is greater than 90), researchers can also evaluate the **clinical significance** of the statistics (T. C. Campbell, 2005; Kendall, 1999; Kendall, Marrs-Garcia, Nath, & Sheldrick, 1999). Clinical significance focuses on estimating the extent to which an intervention given to participants who initially met diagnostic criteria no longer do so (and thus do not require further intervention) following treatment. For example, when clinically depressed people are randomly assigned to talk therapy or to a control condition, what percentages of the participants in talk therapy versus the control condition are no longer depressed at the end of the intervention? Two studies with identical statistical significance, and identical practical significance, may nevertheless differ with respect to clinical significance.

All three types of significance require calculations and yield numerical results. For the last half of the twentieth century, statistical significance dominated investigators' evaluations of research results (Hubbard & Ryan, 2000). Although ways of quantifying practical significance have been available for decades (Huberty, 2002), during roughly the past dozen years scholars have moved practical significance toward the forefront of their evaluations of research results (e.g., Wilkinson & APA Task Force on Statistical Inference, 1999).

In this and the following chapter, we will focus on statistical and practical significance, respectively, because these estimates can be computed for studies even when diagnostic criteria are not relevant. Readers interested in pursuing the issues involved in evaluating clinical significance are directed elsewhere (e.g., T. C. Campbell, 2005; Kendall, 1999).

Sampling Distributions

Previously we have learned that the *population* distribution consists of the *scores* of the N entities (e.g., people, laboratory mice) of interest to the researcher, regarding whom the researcher wishes to generalize. The *sample* distribution *also* consists of *scores*, but only a subsample of n scores from the population.

Statistical significance testing estimates the calculated probability (i.e.,

$p_{\text{CALCULATED}}$) of sample statistics (e.g., for 10 women the median IQ is 102, whereas for 10 men the median IQ is 98). The estimation of the probability of our sample results (i.e., the $p_{\text{CALCULATED}}$ for our statistic medians of 102 and 98, given $n_{\text{WOMEN}} = 10$ and $n_{\text{MEN}} = 10$) requires the use of a third distribution, called the **sampling distribution**. The sampling distribution consists *not* of scores, but instead consists of *statistics* (e.g., the median) computed from repeated sampling from the population, each at the exact sample size(s) in our actual sample.

Heuristic Example

A heuristic example will clarify the distinctions among (a) the population distribution of *N* scores, (b) the sample distribution of *n* scores, and (c) the sampling distribution of statistics. Even though "sample" and the first word of "sampling distribution" are similar, the two distributions are distinct. Do *not* be tricked because the terms include a similar word, and therefore incorrectly confuse the sample with the sampling distribution, or vice versa.

We'll draw on football for the heuristic example. In the early 1980s, the New Orleans Saints not only were playing terribly, losing virtually every game, but the Saints also lost virtually every coin flip at the start of every game.

Let's imagine that at the start of one game, just as the referee was about to flip the coin to determine who would kick off, the Saints' captain said to the referee, "Wait a minute. I don't think this coin is a fair coin. I want to test whether this coin is fair."

Now the referees in the National Football League are actually pretty bright, well-educated people. Included among referees are lawyers and doctors and others with graduate degrees. Such a referee might then respond,

> Well, we could determine for certain if this coin was a fair coin, if we knew the population of all possible flips for this particular coin. If we flipped this coin infinitely many times, there would be an exactly equal number of heads and tails for a fair coin.

> But it will take infinitely long to flip this coin infinitely many times.

We're going to make these 80,000 fans here in the stadium mighty mad to have to wait infinitely long for the game to start, not to mention some mighty mad television viewers and television executives. So we can't reasonably create this population. Doing so would be impractical.

The Saints' captain might then respond, "Well, what we could do is create a sample, the number of heads obtained over $n = 10$ flips. If we get approximately 5 heads, that result would be consistent with a conclusion that the coin is fair. If we get either approximately zero, or approximately 10 heads, the result would be improbable for a set of 10 flips sampled for a fair coin. Based on only 10 flips, we won't know for certain whether our coin is fair, but at least we will have some empirical evidence bearing upon the fairness of the coin."

However, the referee might then object, "How will we know where to draw the boundary for deciding whether the coin is fair or unfair?" And the Saints' captain might then say, "Let's estimate the probability of our sampled number of heads out of 10 flips, assuming that the results were sampled from a population of flips for a fair coin. To reject our coin as not being fair, let's require that our coin produce the number of heads that is 5% or less likely to occur for a coin sampled from a population involving results for a fair coin. We will call this cutoff value for deciding coin fairness, which we pick subjectively rather than mathematically, '$p_{CRITICAL}$.' "

Now the referee might say, "But how can we obtain the $p_{CALCULATED}$ value for the results for our coin, which we will then compare against our $p_{CRITICAL}$ value of 0.05 (i.e., 5%) or less?" And the captain might respond, "Let's approximate a sampling distribution for a fair coin flipped 10 times. Let's assume that all 80,000 fans in the audience have a fair coin on their persons. We will ask every fan to flip a coin 10 times, and then we will create a distribution indicating how many heads resulted for each of the 80,000 sets of coin flips."

Table 6.1 presents the resulting empirically-approximated sampling distribution. Note that although 0 or 10 heads in a set of 10 flips are both very rare, in 80,000 sets of flips of a fair coin, 78 sets of 0 heads, and 78 sets of 10 heads will nevertheless result even for a fair coin.

Simultaneous to the creation of the sampling distribution via the 80,000 fans, the referee creates the sample by flipping the coin that is

TABLE 6.1. Empirically-Derived Sampling Distribution

Number of heads	Number of samples	Percentage	Cumulative % from Sample Space Ends
0	78	0.10%	0.1%
1	781	0.98%	1.1%
2	3,516	4.40%	5.4%
3	9,375	11.72%	
4	16,406	20.51%	
5	19,688	24.61%	
6	16,406	20.51%	
7	9,375	11.72%	
8	3,516	4.40%	5.4%
9	781	0.98%	1.1%
10	78	0.10%	0.1%
Total	80,000	100.00%	

Note. The cumulative percentages are reported here only for the three results from the two extremes of the sample space.

being evaluated 10 times. Let's say that the result is 2 heads. This is not the expected result, given 10 flips and the presumption that the coin is fair. The presumptive most-likely outcome is that there will be 5 heads. However, even for a fair coin, flips yielding 2 (and indeed even 0 or 10) heads out of 10 may occur, as reflected in Table 6.1.

How can we use the Table 6.1 sampling distribution to obtain a $p_{CALCULATED}$ value for our sample result of two heads, which we can then compare with our subjectively (i.e., nonmathematically) derived $p_{CRITICAL}$ value of 5% (or 0.05)? The *sampling distribution* (or some related distribution based on the sampling distribution) is *used to obtain the required $p_{CALCULATED}$ values* associated with our sample statistics.

The Table 6.1 sampling distribution allows us to make statements such as:

1. The probability of obtaining 0 heads in 10 flips with a fair coin is 0.1%.
2. The probability of obtaining 1 *or fewer* heads in 10 flips of a fair coin is 1.1%.
3. The probability of obtaining 2 *or fewer* heads in 10 flips of a fair coin is 5.4%.

4. The probability of obtaining 9 *or more* heads in 10 flips of a fair coin is 1.1%.
5. The probability of obtaining 10 heads in 10 flips of a fair coin is 0.1%.

To use the $p_{CALCULATED}$ values *derived from our sampling distribution*, we must first think further about our 5% $p_{CRITICAL}$ value. We want to reject the presumption that the referee's coin is fair if the referee's coin gets either wildly too many heads or wildly too few heads. This means that we need to conduct what is called a **two-tailed test** by splitting our 5% $p_{CRITICAL}$ value to cover both extreme eventualities.

For two-tailed tests, we typically divide our $p_{CRITICAL}$ value by 2 to create equal-sized **regions of rejection** in both tails of the sampling distribution (0.05 / 2 = 0.025 = 2.5%). So here we will reject the presumption that the referee's coin is fair if the number of obtained heads has a calculated probability less than 2.5%, regardless of whether we obtain too few or too many heads. According to the sampling distribution in Table 6.1, only a sample statistic involving either 0 heads or 1 head is sufficiently rare for us to conclude that the coin is probably unfair (i.e., 1.1% < 2.5%). Conversely, at the other extreme, only a sample statistic involving either 9 or 10 heads is sufficiently rare, given our subjectively selected $p_{CRITICAL}$, for us to conclude that the coin is probably unfair (i.e., 1.1% < 2.5%).

In this example, which involves discrete outcomes (i.e., only integer numbers of heads), the rejection region constitutes 2.2% (i.e., 1.1% + 1.1%) of the sampling distribution rather than exactly 5%. But for most hypotheses involving other outcomes (e.g., medians, SDs, coefficients of kurtosis) which are real numbers (numbers with values to the right of the decimal) rather than integers, we can create rejection regions that exactly match either $p_{CRITICAL}$ or $p_{CRITICAL}$ / 2.

So, for the present example, our statistic of two heads is somewhat unlikely to come from a population created by a fair coin. However, the statistic is *not sufficiently* unlikely, given our subjective a priori selection of a cutoff of $p_{CRITICAL}$ = 0.05, to decide that the referee's coin is unfair.

Complete mastery of the full mechanics of our example is not necessary. Here are the "take-home" messages:

1. Samples and populations and sampling distributions are three different distributions.

2. Samples and populations are distributions of *scores* for different cases (e.g., people, lab rats); sampling distributions are distributions of *statistics* for different samples, each involving the same n as the actual sample.

3. When we perform inferential statistics, we subjectively select a p_{CRITICAL} cutoff value, *before* we collect our sample data, that is later used to evaluate the $p_{\text{CALCULATED}}$ value.

4. The obtained sample statistics for our actual sample are plugged into the relevant sampling distributions to obtain the $p_{\text{CALCULATED}}$ value *of our sample statistics*.

Finite Sampling Distributions

The number of samples drawn for the sampling distribution from a given population is a function of the population size, and the sample size. The number of such different samples (C) for a population of size N and a sample of size n, called **combinations**, is

$$_{N}C_{n} = N! \,/\, [n!(N - n)!] \tag{6.1}$$

If the population is finite in size, the sampling distribution itself involves a finite number of samples. For example, for a finite population of scores for $N = 20$ people, presume that we wish to evaluate a sample mean for $n = 3$ people. Here the problem is manageable, given the relatively small population and sample sizes. The number of statistics creating this sampling distribution is

$$_{N}C_{n} = \frac{N!}{n!(N - n)!}$$

$$\frac{20!}{3!(20 - 3)!}$$

$$\frac{20!}{3!(17)!}$$

$$\frac{20 \times 19 \times 18 \times 17 \times 16 \times 15 \times 14 \times 13 \times 12 \times 11 \times 10 \times 9 \times 8 \times 7 \times 6 \times 5 \times 4 \times 3 \times 2}{3 \times 2 \times (17 \times 16 \times 15 \times 14 \times 13 \times 12 \times 11 \times 10 \times 9 \times 8 \times 7 \times 6 \times 5 \times 4 \times 3 \times 2)}$$

$$\frac{2.433E + 18}{6 \times 3.557E + 14}$$

$$\frac{2.433E + 18}{2.134E + 15}$$

$$= 1,140$$

Table 6.2 presents a hypothetical population, the scores of 20 people. As reported in Table 6.2, for these data, $\mu = 500.00$ and $\sigma = 97.73$.

Table 6.3 presents the first 15 and the last 10 of the 1,140 samples and statistic means for samples of $n = 3$. The full sampling distribution takes quite a few pages to present, and so is not presented here in its entirety. Although the full sampling distribution for this situation is tedious to compute, and boring to read, this sampling distribution is finite, and could be

TABLE 6.2. Heuristic Dataset 3, Defining a Population of $N = 20$ Scores	
ID	X
1	430
2	431
3	432
4	433
5	435
6	438
7	442
8	446
9	451
10	457
11	465
12	474
13	484
14	496
15	512
16	530
17	560
18	595
19	649
20	840
μ	500.00
σ	97.73

TABLE 6.3. The Sampling Distribution for the Mean of $n = 3$ Scores Drawn from the Table 6.2 Population of $N = 20$ Scores

Sample	Cases 1	2	2	X_1	X_2	X_3	Mean
1	1	2	3	430	431	432	431.00
2	1	2	4	430	431	433	431.33
3	1	2	5	430	431	435	432.00
4	1	2	6	430	431	438	433.00
5	1	2	7	430	431	442	434.33
6	1	2	8	430	431	446	435.67
7	1	2	9	430	431	451	437.33
8	1	2	10	430	431	457	439.33
9	1	2	11	430	431	465	442.00
10	1	2	12	430	431	474	445.00
11	1	2	13	430	431	484	448.33
12	1	2	14	430	431	496	452.33
13	1	2	15	430	431	512	457.67
14	1	2	16	430	431	530	463.67
15	1	2	17	430	431	560	473.67
. . . .							
1131	16	17	18	530	560	595	561.67
1132	16	17	19	530	560	649	579.67
1133	16	17	20	530	560	840	643.33
1134	16	18	19	530	595	649	591.33
1135	16	18	20	530	595	840	655.00
1136	16	19	20	530	649	840	673.00
1137	17	18	19	560	595	649	601.33
1138	17	18	20	560	595	840	665.00
1139	17	19	20	560	649	840	683.00
1140	18	19	20	595	649	840	694.67

computed by anyone wanting to do so. Figure 6.1 presents the full sampling distribution of 1,140 estimates of the mean based on samples of size $n = 3$ from the Table 6.2 population of $N = 20$ scores. The figure also portrays the normal curve given the mean and SD of these data.

Hypothesis Testing

Social scientists have traditionally applied inferential statistics for the purpose of making decisions about whether their prior expectations were right or wrong. These prior expectations are expressed as **research hypotheses** (e.g., "Adults who take a daily vitamin pill are less likely to develop cancer than adults who do not").

However, the hypotheses that are *actually tested* in inferential statistics are called **null hypotheses**. In practice, null hypotheses are almost always expressed as what Cohen (1994) called "nil" null hypotheses (i.e., hypotheses predicting zero differences, or zero relationship).

Here are some illustrative (nil) null hypotheses:

FIGURE 6.1. Graphical presentation of the sampling distribution for the mean of n − 3 scores drawn from the population of N = 20 scores in Table 6.2.

```
Count  Midpoint
  60    433  I************:**
 146    446  I******************:********************
 160    459  I*******************:********************
 135    472  I************************:**********
 123    485  I**************************:****
  96    498  I***********************     .
  97    511  I***********************     .
  67    524  I*****************         .
  30    537  I**********
  21    550  I*****             .
  28    563  I*******        .
  50    576  I*********:***
  35    589  I******.**
  24    602  I***:**
  17    615  I**:*
  17    628  I*:**
  14    641  I:***
   6    654  I**
   4    667  I*
   1    680  I
   1    693  I
              +----+----+----+----+----+----+----+----+----+
              0        40        80       120       160      200
                           Histogram frequency
```

Mean	500.000
Median	486.000
SD	53.395
Skewness	1.052
Kurtosis	.418
Minimum	431.000
Maximum	694.670

1. The median IQ of men equals the median IQ of women (or H_0: $Mdn_{MEN} = Mdn_{WOMEN}$, or H_0: $Mdn_{MEN} - Mdn_{WOMEN} = 0$).
2. The standard deviations of IQ scores of right-handed, left-handed, and ambidextrous adults are all equal (or H_0: $SD_{RIGHT-HANDED} = SD_{LEFT-HANDED} = SD_{AMBIDEXTROUS}$).
3. The Pearson r between amount of time spent in study and class grades is zero ($r_{XY} = 0$, or equivalently, $r_{XY}^2 = 0$).

The null hypothesis expresses expectations for *parameters* (i.e., for the population). We ultimately wish to determine the probability (i.e., $p_{CALCULATED}$) that our *sample statistics* are consistent with the sample having been drawn from populations in which the null hypotheses are exactly true.

Frequently, null hypotheses predict an outcome that is the opposite of the research hypotheses (i.e., what we want or expect to happen). For example, we might want (and expect) to reject the null hypothesis: "The mean longevity of AIDS patients randomly assigned to take a new drug equals the mean longevity of AIDS patients randomly assigned to take a placebo medication." But in other cases, we may not want to reject the null hypothesis: "The proportion of side effects occurring with new AIDS drug equals the proportion of side effects occurring in AIDS patients taking a placebo medication."

It is the content, expressing an expectation of no difference or no relation, that makes a hypothesis null. The researcher's expectations and hopes are *not* the basis for this determination.

The inferential statistics process of making decisions about whether to reject or not reject null hypotheses is called **null hypothesis statistical significance testing** (NHSST) or sometimes merely **statistical significance testing**. Mulaik, Raju, and Harshman (1997) and Huberty (1999) provide brief histories of the evolution of this statistical logic.

However, when we decide whether or not to reject the null hypothesis, based on our statistics, once we have our sample data, we can conceivably make an incorrect decision. We can never be certain we avoided an erroneous decision, unless we collect data from the entire population, and thus are no longer invoking inferential statistics.

It is always conceivable that we can draw an unusual, fluky sample from a population where the null is true, and the aberrant sample is so unlikely that we (erroneously) decide to reject our null hypothesis. In our football example, if the team captain flips the referee's coin 10 times and obtains 0 heads, at our $p_{CRITICAL}$ we would reject the null hypothesis that the coin is not different from a fair coin.

But the referee's coin might actually be perfectly fair, even though the coin produced a fluky sample. Whenever we are dealing with inference, and probability, because we are using sample rather than population data, there is always the possibility of making an inferential error. Short of collecting population data, all we can do is attempt to minimize (but never eliminate) the probabilities of making erroneous decisions.

Two errors are possible whenever we perform statistical significance testing. In recognition of their importance, these two errors are given proper names (i.e., they are capitalized and enumerated with Roman numerals). A **Type I error** occurs when we decide to reject a null hypothesis that in truth accurately describes the population from which our sample was derived. A **Type II error** occurs when we decide to *not* reject a null hypothesis that in truth does *not* accurately describe the population from which our sample was derived.

In statistical significance testing, we can never be certain whether or not we are making a Type I or a Type II error. However, we can determine the probabilities of these two errors. Like all probabilities, these two probabilities range between 0 and 1. And, unless we are perverse, evil scientists, we want the probabilities of making decision errors to be small (i.e., close to zero). These errors can never be zero, unless we have population data, in which case we are not performing inferential statistics. But we can take steps to ensure that the probabilities are small.

The probability of a Type I error is represented as α, or synonymously as $p_{CRITICAL}$. We obtain this probability, not through calculation, but instead merely by *subjective judgment* about what is an acceptable probability of a Type I error, given the context of our study, as was done in our football coin example.

Note that this probability, α, has nothing to do with the score reliability coefficient called Cronbach's alpha (Thompson, 2003). Some Greek letters are used to represent multiple things, partly just to be gratuitously confusing, and to rub salt in the wounds of other Greek letters that unfairly are not used as symbols at all, or only rarely.

Conventionally, we set α (or p_{CRITICAL}) at 0.05, 0.01, or 0.001. But there is no reason—especially given modern computers and software, which perform the necessary related calculations—that precludes our use of any other values, such as 0.029, 0.04, or whatever value between 0 and 1 we prefer. Because the determination is subjective, wrong decisions are impossible as long as the selected value falls in the mathematically plausible range of a probability (i.e., 0 to 1), and is what we deem reasonably small (i.e., reasonably close to 0).

We set α *before* we collect our sample data and compute our statistics. If the consequences of an error are quite serious (e.g., an erroneous decision about a drug might result in deaths), we will set α smaller than we would in studies with less serious implications. But because human values drive this subjective decision, two researchers testing the same null hypothesis might reasonably select different values for α, simply because they have different personal priorities or human values.

The probability of a Type II error is β. Again, the Greek letter β is used for multiple purposes, and the probability β has nothing to do with beta weights, which we will discuss in our coverage of multiple regression, beginning in Chapter 8.

Figure 6.2 clarifies how we perform tests of statistical significance. We pick α (i.e., p_{CRITICAL}) before we collect the sample data. Next, we collect sample data and compute our statistics. We then somehow obtain a sampling distribution, or some distribution that is a function of the sampling distribution, from which we can determine the $p_{\text{CALCULATED}}$ *of our statistics*.

When an author of a journal article says that "($p < 0.05$)," the author is telling you that the study α (or p_{CRITICAL}) was whatever number is to the

---

FIGURE 6.2. Contingency table for NHSST

Decision on H_0	Truth (Unknown) in Population		Decision Rule	Called
	H_0 True	H_0 False		
Reject	Type I error ☹ α, or p_{CRITICAL}	☺ Power $(1 - \beta)$	$p_{\text{CALCULATED}} < p_{\text{CRITICAL}}$ OR $TS_{\text{CALCULATED}} > TS_{\text{CRITICAL}}$	"Statistically Significant"
Not Reject	☺	Type II error ☹ β	$p_{\text{CALCULATED}} > p_{\text{CRITICAL}}$ OR $TS_{\text{CALCULATED}} < TS_{\text{CRITICAL}}$	"Not Statistically Significant"

right of this expression involving either "<" or ">" (i.e., here $\alpha = 0.05$). As another example, if the author reported that for the study's sample statistics "$(p > 0.10)$," this author used an α of 0.10.

When alpha is reported in this manner, the $p_{CALCULATED}$ is not being specifically reported. But if the author says that "$(p < 0.05)$," we do at least know that the $p_{CALCULATED}$ value was smaller than 0.05, or 5%. If a p value is instead reported with an equal sign, such as "$(p = 0.047)$," the author is instead telling you the specific value of $p_{CALCULATED}$.

As the decision rule in Figure 6.2 says, if $p_{CALCULATED}$ is less than $p_{CRITICAL}$, we therefore make the decision "reject the null hypothesis." On the other hand, if $p_{CALCULATED}$ is greater than $p_{CRITICAL}$, we therefore make the decision to "not reject the null hypothesis." Theoretically, because these probabilities are real (i.e., noninteger) numbers, the possibility of the two numbers being equal is infinitely small, and need not concern us.

The decision to reject the null can be communicated by saying, "The results were statistically significant." All this expression means is that you rejected the null hypothesis, because the sample statistics were very unlikely.

Obtaining a "statistically significant" result does *not* mean that the results are important, or valuable (or unimportant, or unvaluable). The decision is merely a mathematical decision that indicates (and *only* indicates) that the statistics were unlikely under a premise that the sample came from a population exactly described by the null hypothesis.

Similarly, obtaining a "statistically nonsignificant" result does *not* mean that the results are unimportant, or unvaluable (or important, or valuable). For example, if you are investigating the side effects of a powerful new cancer treatment, and do not reject a null that side effects equal zero, that could be very important. Conversely, if you were investigating whether hospital patients prefer nurses to wear chartreuse versus lavender uniforms, the results might not be valuable, if you don't care about hospital patients, or if you don't care about what uniforms nurses wear.

The characterization of decisions to reject or not reject as "statistically significant" or "not statistically significant" is one of the most damaging language choices in the history of statistics (Thompson, 1996). Confusion arises because the common meaning of "significant" in nontechnical conversation as being synonymous with "important" has *no relevance whatsoever* to the use of this same language in inferential statistics.

Some researchers telegraphically describe results for which H_0 was rejected as being "significant," rather than "statistically significant." Using the full phrase, "statistically significant," has appeal because at least some readers will recognize that the use of the two-word phrase has a meaning completely distinct from the use alone of the single word, "significant." Thus, *always* say results were "statistically significant" or achieved "statistical significance," rather than describing results as "significant" or as achieving "significance."

Relationships among Errors

Figure 6.2 is also useful in clarifying other features of NHSST. Note that once a decision is made about the null, you are either in the top two boxes, if you rejected, or you are in the bottom two boxes, if you failed to reject. Consequently, the following relationships are implied by Figure 6.2:

1. You cannot make both a Type I and Type II error on a given hypothesis test.
2. Once you reject, you could not have made a Type II error, and Type II error is irrelevant.
3. Once you fail to reject, you could not have made a Type I error, and Type I error is irrelevant.

"Accepting" the Null

When we are in the bottom row of Figure 6.2, we say that we "failed to reject" or "did not reject" instead of saying that we "accepted the null hypothesis." Another heuristic example may be helpful in explaining why.

I taught at the University of New Orleans for 11 years, thus fulfilling a lifelong dream to live and work in that city, now ravaged by Hurricane Katrina. The present heuristic (and entirely fictitious) example draws on this experience.

Roughly 6 weeks before Easter Sunday there is a celebration in New Orleans called Mardi Gras, or Fat Tuesday. On Mardi Gras and the days leading up to Mardi Gras, there are numerous parades throughout the city. The people riding on the garish floats are dressed in costume. Other people line the streets and greet the passing riders with the traditional salutation, "Throw me something, Mister!" When the riders are impressed with the request, they respond by throwing some inexpensive plastic beads, or a plastic cup, or in some cases, intriguing underwear.

On the whole, these parades are family-centered events through much of the city, and it is the children who are showered with "throws." But in the French Quarter, the celebration often takes on a different hue. In essence, all laws are suspended in the French Quarter on Mardi Gras. The only exception involves laws against violence. If you are violent in any way, you will be promptly arrested and escorted to an area near Canal Street that is fenced off with metal barricades. Over this holding area and attached to the nearby building is a billboard-sized reproduction of the Monopoly card that says, "Go directly to jail. Do not pass Go. Do not collect $200." This is where you will be held until transport to the real jail can be organized.

But nonviolent celebrants roaming the French Quarter may notice a few people (actually, hoards) who are imbibing somewhat excessively. Many of these people will be masked, many will be costumed, and some will be walking the streets virtually naked. But being virtually naked is not considered being violent.

Let's say I wake up the day after Mardi Gras (i.e., Ash Wednesday), naked in an alley. Perhaps I have enjoyed myself too much and I am uncertain whether I am in New Orleans, or whether some of my friends have maliciously transported me to another city while I was unconscious. I am concerned, because the consequences of walking around naked on Ash Wednesday are probably different in New Orleans than elsewhere. In New Orleans, people may merely laugh, and offer a loan of clothing and other assistance. Elsewhere, I may be charged with a crime and get taken to jail.

Let's say I look down my alley and see a sign alternating between displaying the time, which is noon, and the temperature. The temperature I observe is my sample statistic. This information may be useful in testing the null hypothesis that I am in a city no different than New Orleans.

If the sign reports that it is 32°F, I will be quite cold, and unhappy to be naked in an alley. But I will nonetheless be empowered to make a probability statement about the null hypothesis that I am in New Orleans.

I have some idea what the sampling distribution is for temperatures at noon the day after Mardi Gras in New Orleans. Mardi Gras occurs in February or March. Temperatures this cold are rare. I would conclude that I may be in New Orleans, but that this is highly unlikely. I would reject my null hypothesis.

The same thing would occur if the temperature was 95°. I may be in New Orleans, but the probability that I am, based on my notion of this sampling distribution, would be quite small. I would reject under these circumstances also.

However, let's say the temperature was 65°. This is probably a fairly common temperature in New Orleans the day after Mardi Gras. This sample statistic is fairly likely under the assumption that I am in New Orleans. Now I would *not* reject the null that I am in New Orleans, because my statistic has a reasonably large $p_{CALCULATED}$.

But have I proven that I am in New Orleans? Do I have evidence for the truth of the null? Or do I instead merely have evidence that is consistent with my null, but that *may also be consistent with other null hypotheses*? For example, maybe my malicious friends have transported me to Mobile, Alabama, or to Jackson, Mississippi. If they are particularly perverse, perhaps they have transported me to College Station, Texas!

In other words, when we reject the null, we have indications that our particular null hypothesis is false. The indications involve probability of falseness, never certainty. But when we fail to reject, we have not proven that our particular null hypothesis is *the* correct null hypothesis. Our sample result, although consistent with our particular null, is nevertheless ambiguous because other null hypotheses—in particular, non-nil nulls—may also be consistent with our sample result. Thus, it is appropriate to say that we have "failed to reject the null hypothesis," but it is inappropriate to say that we have "accepted" or "proven" our null hypothesis.

■■■ Properties of Sampling Distributions

For a finite population, we can compute a sampling distribution for any statistic (e.g., the median, the coefficient of skewness, Spearman's ρ). There will be a different sampling distribution for different sample sizes, even for a given statistic. There will also be a different sampling distribution for every statistic, even for fixed n.

The sampling distributions of different statistics for a fixed n from a population may themselves have different locations, dispersions, or shapes. For example, the mean of the sampling distributions for $n = 5$ for all possible sample medians may be 57.5, whereas the mean of the sampling distributions for $n = 5$ for all possible sample coefficients of skewness may be 0.0.

Some properties apply to *all* sampling distributions. Other properties apply to sampling distributions for certain statistics (e.g., the mean), but not to sampling distributions for other statistics (e.g., Pearson's r).

Table 6.4 presents a finite population consisting of $N = 6$ scores. For the purposes of formulating features that apply to the sampling distributions of all statistics, here we will arbitrarily focus on the sampling distributions for the mean, and compute the sampling distributions for ns of 1, 2, and 3.

Table 6.5 presents (a) all the possible samples of scores, and the related statistic means, and (b) descriptive statistics for the three sampling distributions. Of course, if we can compute descriptive characterizations of samples (called statistics), and of populations (called parameters), there is no impediment to also using these formulas to characterize the data in sampling distributions (i.e., to computing statistics of statistics).

The first sampling distribution of the mean, for $n = 1$, is heuristically very interesting. From a population of $N = 6$ scores, there are six possible samples at $n = 1$. Sampling distributions are *always* distributions of statistics.

TABLE 6.4. Hypothetical Population ($N = 6$)	
Case/parameter	X_i
1	1
2	2
3	3
4	4
5	5
6	5
μ	3.33
σ	1.63
Skewness	−0.38
Kurtosis	−1.48

TABLE 6.5. Sampling Distributions for the Mean
for Three Sample Sizes ($n = 1$, $n = 2$, and $n = 3$)

Sample result	$n = 1$		$n = 2$			$n = 3$			
	X_1	M	X_1	X_2	M	X_1	X_2	X_2	M
1	1	1.00	1	2	1.50	1	2	3	2.00
2	2	2.00	1	3	2.00	1	2	4	2.33
3	3	3.00	1	4	2.50	1	2	5	2.67
4	4	4.00	1	5	3.00	1	2	5	2.67
5	5	5.00	1	5	3.00	1	3	4	2.67
6	5	5.00	2	3	2.50	1	3	5	3.00
7			2	4	3.00	1	3	5	3.00
8			2	5	3.50	1	4	5	3.33
9			2	5	3.50	1	4	5	3.33
10			3	4	3.50	1	5	5	3.67
11			3	5	4.00	2	3	4	3.00
12			3	5	4.00	2	3	5	3.33
13			4	5	4.50	2	3	5	3.33
14			4	5	4.50	2	4	5	3.67
15			5	5	5.00	2	4	5	3.67
16						2	5	5	4.00
17						3	4	5	4.00
18						3	4	5	4.00
19						3	5	5	4.33
20						4	5	5	4.67
M		3.33			3.33				3.33
SD		1.63			0.98				0.68
Skewness		−0.38			−0.12				0.00
Kurtosis		−1.48			−0.46				−0.38

However, in this exceptional case, this particular sampling distribution is a distribution of *both* statistics and scores, because at $n = 1$ the mean of the sample also equals the only score in the given sample. Notice that the scores and all of the characterizations (i.e., location, dispersion, shape) of both the population and the sampling distribution all exactly match for this sampling distribution.

For the sample size of $n = 2$, we can apply the following formula to determine the number of unique *pairwise combinations* of six things drawn two at a time:

$$C_{PW} = [N(N - 1)] / 2 \qquad (6.2)$$

By applying the equation, we see that there are 15 different samples of size $n = 2$ that can be drawn from our population of $N = 6$ people: $[n * (n - 1)] / 2 = [6 * (6 - 1)] / 2 = [6 * 5] / 2 = 30 / 2 = 15$.

By the way, Equation 6.2 applies when determining the number of pairwise combinations for *any* situation. For example, the equation also (correctly) suggests that 15 unique Pearson r coefficients can be computed in a study involving six intervally-scaled variables.

Notice that the dispersion of the sampling distribution has gotten smaller (i.e., changed from sampling distribution $SD = 1.63$ to 0.98). This reflects the fact that when we use samples to estimate parameters, we can obtain atypical or fluky samples from the population, even if the samples are drawn randomly. Indeed, every possible sample, as well as the related statistic, is equally likely to be drawn in a given instance.

But as the sample size increases toward the population size, fluky samples are less and less likely for each increase in sample size. The sample statistics bounce around less and, as a set (or sampling distribution), become more homogeneous. This leads us to our first generalization about *all* sampling distributions:

> 1. For *all* sampling distributions, *the standard deviation of the sampling distribution gets smaller as sample size increases.*

We can see this dynamic reflected in the sampling distribution for the mean for $n = 3$. Using Equation 6.1, we can determine how many different samples of size $n = 3$ can be drawn from a population of $N = 6$. We have $(6)(5)(4)(3)(2)(1) / (3)(2)(1)(3)(2)(1) = 720 / 36 = 20$ different combinations. Again, as expected, the standard deviation of the sampling distribution gets smaller (i.e., 0.68 versus 0.98 versus 1.63) as n gets larger.

One (correct) way to think about this dynamic is to say that samples become more representative as n approaches N. But another (also correct) way to think about this is to say that this pattern reflects favorably on the qualities of our statistical formulas. Formulas that are statistically *efficient*, a desirable property of statistics explained in Chapter 2, will yield results honoring the expectation that estimates should become less fluky as sample size increases.

Notice also that the means of the statistics in all three of the sampling distributions in Table 6.5 exactly equal the population parameter. Here

$\mu = 3.33$, and the means of the statistics in the three sampling distributions are also all 3.33. This result reflects an expectation that formulas for statistics should also be statistically *unbiased*, as noted in Chapter 2. So another feature of all sampling distributions is that:

2. *The mean of the statistics in a sampling distribution for unbiased estimators will equal the population parameter being estimated.*

A third pattern in Table 6.5 occurs *not* for sampling distributions for all statistics, but does occur for the sampling distribution for the mean. Notice that even though the population scores have a somewhat skewed distribution (parameter coefficient of skewness = –0.38; parameter coefficient of kurtosis = –1.48), the shapes of the sampling distributions approach normality (i.e., skewness and kurtosis of zero) as sample size, n, increases. This reflects a dynamic stated in what is called the **central limit theorem**, which says that as n becomes larger, the sampling distribution of the mean will approach normality even if the population shape is nonnormal. This theorem is useful in developing an equation to estimate the standard deviation of the sampling distribution of the mean when we do not have the sampling distribution, such that this *SD* of the sampling distribution cannot be directly computed using the statistics housed in the sampling distribution.

Standard Error/Sampling Error

The standard deviation of a sampling distribution is really, really, really important in statistics. Given important applications, by now logically we would expect that this standard deviation will not be called "the standard deviation of the sampling distribution." Too many people would know what this was. Instead, to keep everybody on their toes, we call the standard deviation of the sampling distribution the **standard error of the statistic** or the **standard error** (i.e., the *SE*).

Still, perhaps a logical case can be made for naming standard deviations of the sample and the population *SD*s, and the standard deviation of the sampling distribution *SE*. The names distinguish *SD*s of scores from *SD*s of statistics. This particular *SD*, of a sampling distribution, not of the population or the sample, is used for two purposes.

First, the *SE* can be used *descriptively* to quantify how much precision we believe we have for our given sample statistic. Just as the sample statistic *SD* is a very important characterization of how well the sample mean represents the *n* scores, the *SD* of the sampling distribution informs us about the quality of a statistic as a parameter estimate, *whatever* statistic we are computing.

For example, if in one study we compute the statistic median for longevity for *n* = 10 cancer patients receiving treatment, and the statistic is 24.0 months postdiagnosis, and we somehow knew that the standard deviation of the sampling distribution for the estimate is 30.5, we would not vest excessive confidence in an interpretation that the new treatment prolongs life, given the ratio of the statistic to its SE_{MEDIAN} (i.e., 24.0 / 30.5 = 0.79). We might vest more confidence in our statistic if this ratio was large, or at least larger. However, the 0.79 ratio is not entirely unexpected, because we probably expect that median estimates based on *n* = 10 tend to bounce around a lot. And we have no way to know whether our particular estimate, 24.0 months, came from the middle, or the low, or the high end of the sampling distribution.

On the other hand, in a second study with *n* = 200, if the statistic median was 24 months postdiagnosis, and SE_{MEDIAN} was 2 months, we would vest considerable faith in an inference that this new treatment increases longevity by roughly 2 years after initial diagnosis. In other words, even two identical statistics with different *SE*s have quite different implications.

Second, standard errors of statistics can be used *inferentially* to test the statistical significance of a parameter estimate. One way to perform a statistical significance test in this manner is to divide the statistic by its standard error. This ratio is so fundamental in statistics that the ratio is given three synonymous names: **t statistic**, **Wald statistic** (in honor of a statistician with that name), and **critical ratio**. This takes us to the topic of yet another kind of distribution, in addition to sample distribution, population distribution, and sampling distribution: test statistic distributions.

▓▓▓ Test Statistics

At this point in our discussion of NHSST, several questions may (and should) have been bothering you. How do we get the sampling distribution, if all we have is a sample? If we had the population, we would not fool with a sample, and we would not care about the sampling distribution for a given statistic at a given sample size.

Historically, researchers conducted statistical significance tests *not* with sampling distributions, but with related distributions, called **test statistic distributions**. Researchers soon realized that although $p_{CRITICAL}$ (or α) is easy to obtain, because $p_{CRITICAL}$ is obtained by subjective judgment, $p_{CALCULATED}$ on the other hand was very difficult to compute.

Of course, you must bear in mind that until around the 1970s, statistics were performed on mechanical calculators, and computations also had to be performed repeatedly until the same results were achieved on some two of the repeated calculations. So the difficulty of estimating $p_{CALCULATED}$ was no small thing. Indeed, only in the last few years has software, such as SPSS, routinely provided $p_{CALCULATED}$ when statistical analyses are being performed.

Happily, researchers eventually realized that distributions, called test statistics (*TS*) distributions, can be used in place of *p* values. And test statistics are much easier to calculate than are $p_{CALCULATED}$ values.

There are numerous *TS* distributions. You have probably heard of some test statistics, such as *t*, *z* (not to be confused with the score distribution, called *z*), *F*, and χ^2. Other test statistics, such as the binomial, poisson, and gamma distributions, may be less familiar.

Test statistics are all directly related to sampling distributions of statistics. However, test statistics are not distributions of statistics, but instead are a function of statistics divided by the standard error of the statistic (i.e., by the standard deviation of the sampling distribution). Conceptually, test statistics are **standardized sampling distributions**.

As indicated in the "Decision Rule" column of Figure 6.2, for a given set of sample results, the comparison of a given $p_{CALCULATED}$ with a given $p_{CRITICAL}$ will *always* (always, always . . .) yield the same decision about the comparison of a given $TS_{CALCULATED}$ with a given $TS_{CRITICAL}$. The only thing that is different in invoking the decision rules is that *the signs of the rules are reversed*.

For example, if $p_{CALCULATED}$ is 0.049, and $p_{CRITICAL}$ (i.e., α) is 0.05, we will reject. If $t_{CALCULATED}$ is 2.05, and $t_{CRITICAL}$ is 2.00, we will reject. Conversely, if $F_{CALCULATED}$ is 4.00, and $F_{CRITICAL}$ is 4.10, we will *not* reject the null.

We will not delve very far into the murky world of test statistics, and especially the more esoteric test statistics. Modern statistical software has been programmed to select the appropriate test statistics with which to evaluate given hypotheses.

Furthermore, in recent years commonly used statistical software has now been programmed to print $p_{CALCULATED}$ values always. This means that test statistics are largely historical artifacts, now that with modern software and computers we can painlessly compare $p_{CALCULATED}$ against $p_{CRITICAL}$. So here we will only briefly explore the computation of test statistics for three research situations.

Test statistics are actually related to each other. For example, a t can be converted into an F, and so forth. The full set of relations among test statistics is beyond the scope of our treatment, but the interested reader may wish to consult Glass and Stanley (1970, pp. 236–238).

H_0: $\sigma_1^2 = \sigma_2^2$

Let's say that on the midterm exam in your class, the 11 male students had $SD_M = 10.0$ right answers and the 21 female students had $SD_F = 8.0$ right answers. You want to test the null hypothesis that the test score dispersions of males and females are equal. For your sample data, given statistic SDs of 10.0 and 8.0, you want to know whether or not to reject H_0: $\sigma_M = \sigma_F$. Let us presume that you are using $\alpha = 0.05$.

For convenience of computation in the test of the null that two standard deviations are equal, we will test the equivalent hypothesis that H_0: $\sigma_M^2 = \sigma_F^2$. This is permissible because, for a given pair of sample dispersion statistics, the test of H_0: $\sigma_M^2 = \sigma_F^2$ yields an identical $p_{CALCULATED}$ as the test of H_0: $\sigma_M = \sigma_F$.

The test statistic suitable for this null is the *F* **ratio**, named to honor Sir Ronald Fisher, a famous statistician who computed many test statistics tables and developed various formulas for conducting NHSST. The *F* test statistic is *always* a ratio of two variances. Because $F_{CALCULATED}$ is *always* computed by dividing one variance by another variance, F itself is also in a squared, area-world metric.

For the test of the null that two variances are equal (but not necessarily for other applications involving different hypotheses), the formula for the test statistic is

$$F_{\text{CALCULATED}} = SD^2 / SD^2 \qquad (6.3)$$

For our data, we have $F_{\text{CALCULATED}} = 10.0^2 / 8.0^2 = 100.0 / 64.0 = 1.56$.

We now have p_{CRITICAL} and $F_{\text{CALCULATED}}$. We can only compare $p_{\text{CALCULATED}}$ with p_{CRITICAL}, or $TS_{\text{CALCULATED}}$ with TS_{CRITICAL}. We need either $p_{\text{CALCULATED}}$ or TS_{CRITICAL}. F_{CRITICAL} is easier to obtain.

Statistics textbooks traditionally contained appendices for various test statistics, for various sample sizes, and for various values of α (i.e., usually 0.05 and 0.01). Indeed, some books consisted *only* of TS_{CRITICAL} values for various research situations. These books were invaluable for decades. But today most microcomputers have a spreadsheet with functions built in that yield TS_{CRITICAL} for all commonly used test statistics, any sample sizes, and any α. Thus, the books reporting page after page after page of values for F and t and other test statistics are primarily useful for treating insomnia, because they make dull reading even for a statistician.

However, to find either F_{CRITICAL} or $p_{\text{CALCULATED}}$ for our sample using Excel, we will first need to compute an additional pair of numbers for our research situation. **Degrees of freedom** quantify *how many scores in a dataset are free to vary in the presence of a statistical estimate.*

For example, if we have the scores {1, 2, and 3} in the presence of an estimate that $M = 2.0$, the degrees of freedom for this mean are 2. If I know the mean is 2.0, and I know any two of the three scores, the remaining score is fully statistically determined. For example, if I know the mean is 2.0, and that two scores are {1 and 2}, the third score can only be 3. If I know the mean is 2.0, and that two scores are {2 and 3}, the third score can only be 1.

For the F ratio, which is computed as the ratio of two statistic variances, we must determine the degrees of freedom for the numerator statistic and for the denominator statistic. The degrees of freedom for the variance, like the degrees of freedom for the mean, also equal $n - 1$. So for our situation, the degrees of freedom associated with the variance in the numerator of $F_{CALCULATED}$ are 10 (i.e., $n_{MALES} = 11 - 1$). The degrees of freedom for the denominator are 20 (i.e., $n_{FEMALES} = 21 - 1$).

When people report $F_{CALCULATED}$ values, they may report the degrees of freedom in various ways. For example, a researcher may report that "the $F_{10/20}$ was computed to be 1.56" or "the calculated F ($df = 10, 20$) was 1.56." Of course, even if the author does not report sample sizes, for the test of this particular null hypothesis we know from these degrees of freedom that sample sizes were 11 (10 + 1) and 21 (20 + 1).

We are now ready to determine the $F_{CRITICAL}$ that is associated with our particular degrees of freedom and our preselected α. The abridged tables in older textbook appendices (and even the books consisting entirely of test statistics tables) reported $F_{CRITICAL}$ values only for selected sample sizes, and only for selected values of α (e.g., 0.05, 0.01, 0.001). Indeed, one reason so many articles use $\alpha = 0.05$ (or 0.01 or 0.001) is that these were the common values reported in abridged test statistic tables. But, as noted previously, most modern computers have software with built-in test statistic distributions for any sample sizes and any alpha values.

For our problem, we will again use a two-tailed test. We have no reason to predict that males' scores will be more dispersed than will scores of females, or the converse. We only wish to evaluate whether the scores are equally dispersed, or not. So we will divide the test statistic distribution into two equal rejection regions, using $\alpha = 0.05 / 2 = 0.025$.

We can find the $F_{CRITICAL}$ value for our results by typing into Excel our $\alpha / 2$ value, and our degrees of freedom numerator and denominator, respectively,

$$=FINV(.025,10,20)$$

or

$$=FINV(.05/2,10,20)$$

and hitting the ENTER key. The computer will report that $F_{CRITICAL} = 2.77$. Because our $F_{CALCULATED}$ (i.e., 1.56) is less than our $F_{CRITICAL}$ (i.e., 2.77), according to the Figure 6.2 decision rule, this means we will decide not to reject H_0: $\sigma_M^2 = \sigma_F^2$ (or H_0: $\sigma_M = \sigma_F$).

However, with modern computers and software, we can just as easily (and in a more straightforward manner) make the same determination by comparing p values. We can type our $F_{CALCULATED}$ into Excel:

$$=FDIST(1.56,10,20)$$

and hit the ENTER key. The computer will report that $p_{CALCULATED} = 0.19$. Because our $p_{CALCULATED}$ is greater than our $p_{CRITICAL}$, according to the Figure 6.2 decision rule, this means we will decide not to reject $H_0: \sigma_M^2 = \sigma_F^2$ (or $H_0: \sigma_M = \sigma_F$).

We would never perform comparisons of both the pairs of F and the pairs of p values, because the decisions reached by these two rules are *always* the same. Of course, we could conduct all our computations to more decimal places, if we were concerned about mathematical precision. But in practice, we will usually conduct NHSST using software, such as SPSS, which will use more precision in all the relevant computations.

Frequently, different test statistics, or different formulas for the same test statistics, may be used to test selected null hypotheses. In the present example, a formula developed by Levene (1960) might have been used. Indeed, newer versions of SPSS use the Levene test rather than the test described here.

$H_0: \mu_M = \mu_F$ ($\sigma_M^2 = \sigma_F^2$ Assumed)

Using the same research situation, let's say that you wanted to evaluate whether the mean numbers of midterm right answers of the males and females were equal ($H_0: \mu_M = \mu_F$). Year after year, you have noted that the score variances of the two groups are equal, and so a comparison of these variance statistics is not of interest. The equality of these two variances in the population is judged to be a given.

The sample statistics are $M_M = 97.0$ ($SD_M = 10.0$) and $M_F = 103.0$ ($SD_F = 8.0$). The test of $H_0: \mu_M = \mu_F$ can be accomplished by using the test statistic distribution, t, developed in 1908 by Gossett ("Student," 1908), a worker in the Guinness brewery in Dublin. Because the employer prohibited publication by employees under their own names, Gossett wrote under the pseudonym "Student," and so this test statistic is sometimes referred to as Student's t.

We will use these data to test H_0: $\mu_M = \mu_F$, assuming the researcher's interest in looking for any difference in the means, regardless of which group has a higher mean. The researcher's expectation is expressed in terms of an **alternative hypothesis** (H_A). For the two-tailed test appropriate for these circumstances, the related alternative hypothesis is H_A: $\mu_M \neq \mu_F$.

For heuristic purposes only, we will also conduct a one-tailed test, under the alternative hypothesis that H_A: $\mu_F > \mu_M$. Simultaneous use of both two-tailed and one-tailed tests for a given null hypothesis is *never* done in practice. However, the heuristic comparison allows us to see differences in the two procedures, as well as how the procedures can lead to different NHSST outcomes even for one dataset.

For both tests, we will use $\alpha = 0.05$. This is a very commonly used value for $p_{CRITICAL}$, although the choice is partially an artifact of space limitations governing the length of abridged test statistic distributions presented in outdated textbooks.

H_A: $\mu_M \neq \mu_F$

In Chapter 3, it was emphasized that the SD characterizes how well a mean does at representing the scores in a dataset. An M of 97.0 with $SD = 0.5$ represents the scores in a dataset much better than an M of 97.0 with $SD = 20.0$. Logically, this suggests that score dispersion *must* be taken into account when comparing two means.

We require an estimated parameter score variance across both groups of scores when testing the equality of two means. This is called a **pooled variance** (σ^2_{POOLED}). If the two groups were of equal size, we could compute the estimated pooled variance as the simple average of the two group variances (i.e., $\sigma^2_{POOLED} = [SD_1^2 + SD_2^2] / 2$). However, the following formula for the pooled variance takes into account the difference in group ns, and can be used even when group sizes are unequal:

$$\sigma^2_{POOLED} = [(n_1 - 1)SD_1^2 + (n_2 - 1)SD_2^2] / [n_1 + n_2 - 2] \quad (6.4)$$

For our data, we have

$$[(11 - 1)10.0^2 + (21 - 1)8.0^2] / [11 + 21 - 2]$$
$$[(11 - 1)100.0 + (21 - 1)64.0] / [11 + 21 - 2]$$
$$[(10)100.0 + (20)64.0] / [11 + 21 - 2]$$
$$[1000.0 + 1280.0] / [11 + 21 - 2]$$
$$2280.0 / [11 + 21 - 2]$$
$$2280.0 / 30$$
$$\sigma^2_{POOLED} = 76.0$$

Remembering that test statistics are *always* a function of the ratio of a parameter estimate (such as mean difference, $M_1 - M_2$) to the standard error of this estimate, we require $SE_{M1 - M2}$ for the current problem. When (a) two groups are independent (i.e., the composition of the first group did not affect who was assigned to group two, except that the two groups are mutually exclusive), and (b) we assume $\sigma_M^2 = \sigma_F^2$, then

$$SE_{M1 - M2} = [\sigma^2_{POOLED}((1 / n_1) + (1 / n_2))]^{0.5} \qquad (6.5)$$

For our data we have

$$[76.0((1 / 11) + (1 / 21))]^{0.5}$$
$$[76.0(0.09 + 0.05)]^{0.5}$$
$$[76.0(0.14)]^{0.5}$$
$$10.53^{0.5}$$
$$SE_{M1 - M2} = 3.24$$

Last, we need to compute $t_{CALCULATED}$. For the nondirectional, or two-tailed, test involving H_A: $\mu_M \neq \mu_F$, we can compute the mean difference by subtracting M_F from M_M, or M_M from M_F. For research involving two sample means that are not identical, one choice would yield a mean difference (and a $t_{CALCULATED}$) that is negative, and the other choice would yield a mean difference (and a $t_{CALCULATED}$) that is positive. However, the $p_{CALCULATED}$ for either choice would be identical regardless of this decision because the t test statistic distribution, unlike the F distribution, is symmetrical (i.e., not skewed); therefore, the rejection regions for the two-tailed test are unaltered by this decision.

We will compute the mean difference (i.e., "mean difference" = "difference of the two means") as $M_F - M_M$, which for our data yields $103.0 - 97.0 = 6.0$. We compute $t_{CALCULATED}$ as $(M_F - M_M) / SE_{M1 - M2}$. For our data, we obtain $t_{CALCULATED} = 6.0 / 3.24 = 1.85$. Is this mean difference sufficiently large, given the score standard deviations and our two sample sizes, to reject H_0: $\mu_M = \mu_F$?

Again, to honor historical practice required before the ready access in recent years (via modern software) to $p_{CALCULATED}$, we can invoke the Figure 6.2 decision rule comparing $t_{CALCULATED}$ to $t_{CRITICAL}$. We have $t_{CALCULATED} = 1.85$. We can obtain $t_{CRITICAL}$ for our α and our sample size by using the Excel spreadsheet function TINV. We require the degrees of freedom for a mean difference. Unlike the F ratio, which has degrees of freedom for both the numerator and the denominator, the df of t is a single number, and for this application equals $n_1 + n_2 - 2$, which for our data is 30 (i.e., $11 + 21 - 2$). We input the alpha and the df into the spreadsheet as

$$=\text{TINV}(.05,30)$$

and hit the ENTER key. The $t_{CRITICAL}$ is 2.04. Because $1.85 < 2.04$, using the decision rule in Figure 6.2, we fail to reject H_0: $\mu_M = \mu_F$.

We could have instead compared our $p_{CRITICAL}$ of 0.05 with $p_{CALCULATED}$. Our statistical computer software (e.g., SPSS) would have printed this, and our work would be done. But we can also use Excel to determine the $p_{CALCULATED}$. We type in

$$=\text{TDIST}(1.85,30,2)$$

where 1.85 is $t_{CALCULATED}$, 30 = df, and 2 indicates that we are performing a two-tailed test of a "no difference" (or "nondirectional") alternative hypotheses. The computer returns a $p_{CALCULATED}$ value of 0.074, and because $0.074 > 0.05$, we fail to reject H_0: $\mu_M = \mu_F$.

H_A: $\mu_F > \mu_M$

For heuristic comparison purposes, let's presume that prior to collecting sample data you expected the women students to outperform the male students, resulting in $M_F > M_M$. This expectation might have been based on years of observing this pattern in various semesters. Or perhaps there is a psychological theory predicting that women are more verbal than men, and that therefore women should do better than men, at least when statistics are taught with an emphasis on concepts as opposed to an emphasis on the rote memorization of statistical formulas.

All the calculations (i.e., the pooled variance and the standard error) in the previous example remain the same. However, for a one-tailed, directional test, the mean difference *must* be computed as the mean for the group expected to have the higher average minus the mean of the other group.

We have already computed the mean difference and t, reflecting an expectation that $\mu_F > \mu_M$. Therefore, the mean difference remains 6.0, and still $t_{CALCULATED} = 6.0 / 3.24 = 1.85$. However, the test statistic critical value, $t_{CRITICAL}$, will differ for a directional, one-tailed test, because rather than splitting α to create rejection regions in both tails of the test distribution, we will put *all* of α into a single tail. For the current problem, we can find $t_{CRITICAL}$ by typing into Excel

```
=TINV(.10,30)
```

where 0.10 equals α times 2.0, or

```
=TINV(.05*2,30)
```

and hitting the ENTER key. The $t_{CRITICAL}$ value is 1.70.

We learn that now we must reject the null hypothesis, because now $t_{CALCULATED} = 1.85$ is greater than $t_{CRITICAL} = 1.70$. Clearly, testing directional alternative hypotheses can result in statistical significance that would not otherwise be achieved.

What is to keep the nefarious, perverse researcher from pretending to have had a directional alternative hypothesis all along? Of course, the integrity of scholars hopefully precludes such treachery. Another barrier to such pretense is that directional hypotheses should not be tested or reported without either an empirical or a theoretical basis for the tests. Reports of directional tests in the absence of clear rationales should be treated with skepticism.

Directional alternative hypotheses do have the appeal that they honor more specific expectations, when such expectations are possible. However, it should also be noted that directional tests can result in the failure to reject when rejection would occur for the same data under a two-tailed, nondirectional test.

For example, let's say the researcher was testing H_A: $\mu_F > \mu_M$, and that the sample statistics were $M_M = 597.0$ ($n_M = 11$; $SD_M = 10.0$) and $M_F = 3.0$ ($n_F = 21$; $SD_F = 8.0$). When statistics are different in the direction opposite to expectation, the null hypothesis will never be rejected, no matter how wildly different are the sample means!

This is because the rejection region is vested in a single tail of the test distribution (or the sampling distribution). No matter where the sample statistics occur in the far extremes of the sampling distribution opposite our one-tailed expectations, the decision is "fail to reject."

Conducting one-tailed tests is a bit like betting on specific numbers rather than on a color when playing roulette. If you're right, the payoffs can be big. But if you're wrong, you can lose it all. However, it must be said that directional tests honor a science in which researchers are trying to develop theory that says more than only that things differ, or only that things have a nonzero relationship.

H_0: $\mu_1 = \mu_2$ ($\sigma_1^2 \neq \sigma_2^2$)

More typically when testing H_0: $\mu_1 = \mu_2$, we may have no firm basis for assuming that the population variances are equal. Indeed, if we test and reject the null that the variances are equal, the most reasonable assumption is that the population variances are unequal.

Table 6.6 presents hypothetical data that will be used to compare results when t tests are used to evaluate the equality of two means when the two samples are independent (e.g., boys and girls) rather than dependent or paired (e.g., participants are sampled as marriage partners). For this independent t test example, the dependent variable is "X1," and the independent variable is named "GROUP."

In this example, there are six people in group 1, and six people in group 2, and so group sizes are equal. This is permissible but *not* required for the independent samples t test of H_0: $\mu_1 = \mu_2$. However, equal group sizes are required for the dependent samples t test, because participants are sampled as pairs.

TABLE 6.6. Hypothetical Data for Use in Comparing
Independent and Dependent (Paired) t Tests

X1	X2	GROUP
1	1	1
2	3	1
3	5	1
4	7	1
5	9	1
6	11	1
1	.	2
3	.	2
5	.	2
7	.	2
9	.	2
11	.	2

Note. The data layout and variable names honor the format required for inputting the data in a statistical software package, such as SPSS. "." reflects missing data, which would be input as empty cells in the input window, or as blank spaces in a datafile.

When parameter variances are not assumed to be equal, the $t_{\text{CALCULATED}}$ is still the ratio of the mean differences to the *SE* of the mean differences, but now the standard error is computed as

$$SE_{M1 - M2} = [(\sigma_1^2 / n_1) + (\sigma_2^2 / n_2))]^{0.5} \qquad (6.6)$$

For our data we have

$$[(1.87^2 / 6) + (3.74^2 / 6)]^{0.5}$$
$$[(3.50 / 6) + (13.99 / 6)]^{0.5}$$
$$[0.58 + 2.33]^{0.5}$$
$$2.91^{0.5}$$
$$SE_{M1 - M2} = 1.71$$

So our $t_{\text{CALCULATED}}$ value is $M_1 - M_2 = 3.50 - 6.00 = -2.50 / SE_{M1 - M2} = -2.50 / 1.71 = -1.46$.

However, for this situation, *df* no longer equals $n - 2$ (Satterthwaite, 1946). Rather, the *df* are

$$[(SD_1^2 / n_1) + (SD_2^2 / n_2)]^2 / [\{(SD_1^2 / n_1)^2 / (n_1 - 1)\} + \{(SD_2^2 / n_2)^2 / (n_2 - 1)\}] \quad (6.7)$$

For our data we have

$$[(1.87^2 / 6) + (3.74^2 / 6)]^2 / [\{(1.87^2 / 6)^2 / (6 - 1)\} + \{(3.74^2 / 6)^2 / (6 - 1)\}]$$
$$[(3.50 / 6) + (13.99 / 6)]^2 / [\{(3.50 / 6)^2 / (6 - 1)\} + \{(13.99 / 6)^2 / (6 - 1)\}]$$
$$[(3.50 / 6) + (13.99 / 6)]^2 / [\{(3.50 / 6)^2 / 5\} + \{(13.99 / 6)^2 / 5\}]$$
$$[0.58 + 2.33]^2 / [\{0.58^2 / 5\} + \{2.33^2 / 5\}]$$
$$2.91^2 / [\{0.58^2 / 5\} + \{2.33^2 / 5\}]$$
$$8.47 / [\{0.34 / 5\} + \{5.43 / 5\}]$$
$$8.47 / [0.07 + 1.09]$$
$$8.47 / 1.16$$
$$df = 7.30$$

We can now use the Excel spreadsheet to solve for $p_{CALCULATED}$. However, because $t_{CALCULATED}$ is a symmetrical (nonskewed) distribution, $p_{CALCULATED}$ at a fixed df is the same for –1.46 and 1.46. Excel only programs solutions for the positive values of $t_{CALCULATED}$. So we enter

$$=\text{TDIST}(1.46, 7.30, 2)$$

and obtain $p_{CALCULATED} = 0.188$. Assuming $\alpha = 0.05$ (or *any* value < 0.188), our decision is "not reject."

H_0: $\mu_1 = \mu_2$ (Paired Scores)

When means are from dependent samples (e.g., paired twins generate scores on a variable X, or given participants generate both midterm and final exam scores), an additional complication arises. Dependent or paired sampling structurally tends to induce a relationship between the paired scores. This makes a given mean difference more or less impressive, depending on how correlated the two sets of paired scores are. We must take the degree of this correlation into account when computing the *SE* of the mean difference, and this in turn impacts $t_{CALCULATED}$, even for a fixed mean difference.

Here we treat the Table 6.6 data now as paired data, using the *X1* scores of the last six people also as the *X2* scores of the first six people, and now presuming that we had n = 6 paired scores (*X1* and *X2*) of one group of people, rather than two groups of participants with n = 12 scores on one dependent variable (*X1*). This is for heuristic comparative purposes only. Real data are treated *only* as independent, or as dependent.

The standard error of mean differences for paired scores can be computed as

$$SE_{M1-M2} = [(SD_1^2 / n) + (SD_2^2 / n) - (2(r)\{(SD_1 * SD_2) / n\})]^{0.5} \qquad (6.8)$$

where n is the number of paired scores. Note the logically expected use of the Pearson r of the paired scores in the formula for the *SE*. If r is zero, the rightmost portion of Equation 6.8 will zero out, and the formula will equal Equation 6.6 (i.e., the *SE* formula for evaluating mean differences in independent samples)!

As Equation 6.8 intimates, when r is positive, as r gets larger, the standard error of the mean difference will become smaller. This, in turn, will make $t_{CALCULATED}$ larger, and statistical significance more likely. Conversely, when r is negative, the standard error of the mean difference will become larger. This, in turn, will make $t_{CALCULATED}$ smaller, and statistical significance less likely.

For these data, the second set of six scores was computed by (a) doubling the original scores and then (b) subtracting 1. The mean of the first set of scores was 3.50 (*SD* = 1.87). As we learned in the very important Reflection Problems for previous chapters, the use of multiplicative and additive constants has predictable impacts on location, dispersion, and relationship:

1. The new mean (i.e., 6.00) equals the old mean (3.50) times the multiplicative constant (3.50 * 2 = 7.00) minus 1 [(3.50 * 2) − 1 = 7.00 − 1 = 6.00)].
2. Given that only multiplicative constants can affect *SD*, the new standard deviation (i.e., 3.74) equals the old *SD* times the absolute value of the multiplicative constant (1.87 * 2 = 3.74).
3. Given that (a) scores correlate +1.0 with themselves, and (b) additive and positive multiplicative constants do not affect r, the r of the two sets of scores is +1.0.

So, for these data, with $n = 6$ paired scores, we have

$$[(1.87^2 / 6) + (3.74^2 / 6) - (2(1.0)\{(1.87 * 3.74) / 6\})]^{0.5}$$
$$[(3.50 / 6) + (13.99 / 6) - (2(1.0)\{(1.87 * 3.74) / 6\})]^{0.5}$$
$$[0.58 + 2.33 - (2(1.0)\{6.99 / 6\})]^{0.5}$$
$$[0.58 + 2.33 - (2\{1.16\})]^{0.5}$$
$$[0.58 + 2.33 - 2.33]^{0.5}$$
$$0.58^{0.5}$$
$$SE_{M1 - M2} = 0.76$$

And thus $t_{CALCULATED}$ is again the mean difference divided by the standard error of the mean difference, which here yields $(3.50 - 6.00) / 0.76 = -2.50 / 0.76 = -3.29$.

The degrees of freedom for this test are $n - 1 = 6 - 1 = 5$. So we enter

$$=TDIST(3.29,5,2)$$

into Excel and obtain $p_{CALCULATED} = 0.022$. Assuming $\alpha = 0.05$ (or *any* value > 0.022), our decision now is "reject."

These results make the heuristic point that, for the same numbers, evaluating a mean difference across two groups with independent versus dependent tests can yield quite different results. One implication is that the correct selection of the appropriate test statistic can be vitally important. Another implication is that using paired or repeated measures can have considerably more statistical power against Type II error, as we shall eventually see in Chapter 12.

▪▪▪ Statistical Precision and Power

Precision as a Function of *n*

When we are using statistics to estimate parameters, we would certainly prefer our estimates to be more rather than less precise. In other words, we would like our estimates to have small standard errors, even if we are not conducting statistical significance tests. Thus, in the first instance, if we estimate that $M_X = 100.0$ and that $SE_M = 1.5$, we would be considerably more confident in our estimate of the mean than if $M_X = 100.0$ but $SE_M = 15.0$.

Precision of estimates also benefits us if we are conducting statistical significance tests. *All* test statistics are *a function of a parameter estimate divided by the standard error of the statistic*, although this relationship is most obvious for the t test. For a given statistic, we will obtain larger $TS_{CALCULATED}$, and be more likely to obtain statistical significance, as the standard error becomes smaller.

From our previous discussion of the sampling distribution, it should be clear that for given statistics, as n gets larger, the sampling distribution gets narrower, reflecting less flukiness being likely in a given sample, and less flukiness being present in all the possible estimates of the statistic. And when the sampling distribution gets narrower, so, too, does the standard error measuring the dispersion of the statistics in the sampling distribution get smaller.

However, the impact on precision of adding each new person is not equal, and instead *lessens as each new person is added*. Thus, the impact on precision of going from $n = 5$ to $n = 10$ may be considerable, but the impact would be less going from $n = 10$ to $n = 15$, and would be less still when going from $n = 15$ to $n = 20$, *although each increase in sample size does improve precision*.

We can get a more concrete understanding of these dynamics by further considering the standard error of the mean. If we have the sampling distribution of the mean (which we wouldn't, or we wouldn't be doing NHSST), we can apply the formula for the standard deviation to the statistics in the sampling distribution, and obtain SE_M directly via computation.

Otherwise, we can estimate the SE_M by invoking the following equation:

$$SE_M = SD_X / n^{0.5} \qquad (6.9)$$

which is a theoretical estimate, but one that works reasonably well if the population scores are normally distributed or the sample size is sufficiently large that the central limit theorem can be invoked. Table 6.7 presents a

TABLE 6.7. Statistical Precision for M as a Function of SD_X and n

SD_X	n	SE_M	Change
4.0	4	2.000	
4.0	16	1.000	50.0%
4.0	64	0.500	50.0%
4.0	256	0.250	50.0%
4.0	1024	0.125	50.0%
4.0	4096	0.063	50.0%
4.0	16384	0.031	50.0%
2.0	4	1.000	
2.0	16	0.500	50.0%
2.0	64	0.250	50.0%
2.0	256	0.125	50.0%
2.0	1024	0.063	50.0%
2.0	4096	0.031	50.0%

range of standard errors for the mean, associated with two arbitrarily selected values for SD_X, and for a range of sample sizes.

As suggested by Table 6.7, one way to increase the precision of the mean statistic is to decrease the score standard deviation estimated for the population. For example, for a given n, if we halve the SD_X, we also double the precision of our estimate (i.e., SE_M is halved). Thus, at $n = 4$, when we move from $SD_X = 4.0$ to $SD_X = 2.0$, SE_M changes from 2.00 to 1.00.

This only makes sense. I have repeatedly said that SD_X characterizes how well M_X does at representing a set of scores. Means that better capture the features of sample scores should be more generalizable. Restricted sample score ranges also suggest that the population scores are more homogeneous, which implies that all means at a given n from such populations should bounce around less than if σ_X was larger.

Of course, as a practical matter, making SD_X smaller is not always feasible. In some instances, we can attempt to achieve this objective. For example, in an intervention study, perhaps if the treatment is continued longer, treatment responses will become more uniform or homogeneous.

But the most practical way of impacting precision is to increase sample size. Table 6.7 shows that to halve SE_M, for a fixed SD_X, we must quadruple the sample size! Indeed, to change SE_M by a factor of Q, we must change the sample size by a function of the square of the reciprocal of Q

(e.g., for $Q = 1 / 2$, sample size must be increased by $(2 / 1)^2$, or 4.0; for $Q = 1 / 3$, sample size must be increased by $(3 / 1)^2$, or 9.0).

Nature of Power

In our initial discussion of Figure 6.2, we noted that α is obtained by subjective judgment (i.e., α is *not* computed). We simply declare what we believe is an acceptable maximum likelihood of a Type I error, given what we are investigating, and our personal values system. This selection of α is then taken into account in our remaining use of the NHSST logic.

However, no explanation was offered as to how the probability of a Type II error, β, is obtained. In fact, β, unlike α, is computed. However, the calculations are quite complex. The interested reader is referred to Cohen's (1988) seminal book.

Specialized software can be used to estimate β. Of course, the calculation is irrelevant in the presence of a reject decision, because you *cannot* make a Type II error if you are in one of the top two boxes in Figure 6.2. The β probability is relevant only (a) before you conduct the study, and do not yet know the resulting decisions regarding H_0, or (b) after the study, only if the decision was "not reject."

Although we will not cover the computations of β, the related concepts are quite important, and are the focus here. As usual, we eschew excessive mathematical detail because modern software so painlessly implements the required computations.

The concept of the complement of β, called **power** (i.e., power = $1 - \beta$), is important. From the formula for power (i.e., $1 - \beta$), clearly if we have either β, or alternatively power, the complement can be computed by an easy subtraction. Power is the probability of rejecting the null hypothesis when the null hypothesis is false, as reflected in Figure 6.2.

To understand power (and thus β), we must understand the relationships of four features of a given study: (a) n, (b) α, (c) β, and (d) effect size. An **effect size** is a statistic quantifying the extent to which sample statistics diverge from the null hypothesis.

Effect size is perhaps the most important single concept in statistics, and is covered in considerably more detail in Chapter 7 (see also Thompson, 1996, 2002a). For now, suffice it to say that there are dozens of effect size statistics (Kirk, 1996, 2003; Rosenthal, 1994; Thompson, in press).

But commonly-used effect sizes are zero when sample statistics exactly match the null hypothesis. For example, if the differences in the coefficients of kurtosis of IQ scores of left-handed, right-handed, and ambidextrous persons are being tested under a nil null and the statistics are −1.3, −1.3, and −1.3, the effect size is zero. If these statistics at the same sample sizes were −1.3, −1.3, and −1.2, the effect size would not be zero. The effect size would be larger still if the three statistics at the same sample sizes were −2.2, 0.5, and 3.1.

We will approach power analysis (i.e., the estimation of β and the mathematical complement of β, $1 - \beta$) conceptually rather than mathematically. Think of every research study as involving a quagmire of uncertainty, which we will label "the blob."

The blob incorporates four non-overlapping elements: (a) n, (b) α, (c) β, and (d) effect size. For a given study, the blob has a fixed and knowable area. This means that if we know (or can estimate) any three of the areas, by subtraction we can solve for the area taken up by the remaining fourth element. The blob can be used to conduct power analyses in two contexts.

First, *prospectively*, before we conduct a study, we can subjectively select desired values for α and β. We can estimate the expected effect size either by (a) computing some kind of location statistic (e.g., median, mean, weighted average) across the effect sizes in the related prior studies, *or* (b) identifying the smallest effect size that would have to be obtained in our future study that we personally would deem noteworthy. Then we can solve for the required n for our study, perhaps adding a few extra participants as a safety measure.

Of course, this presumes that our sole focus is (a) statistical significance and (b) economy. In general, because precision is enhanced as we add participants, we would usually like to have the largest sample size we can feasibly obtain.

Second, *retrospectively*, after the study has been conducted, we can conduct a power analysis to solve for β. In this case we invoke the α we selected before conducting the study, and the n we actually used in the study. We now compute the actual effect size we obtained, rather than having to estimate or guess the effect size, and we then solve for β and power (i.e., $1 - \beta$). Of course, we would never perform this analysis if we rejected the null hypothesis (i.e., the results were "statistically significant"), because Type II error is irrelevant in the presence of a decision to reject the null.

One reason we rarely see retrospective power reported in journal articles is that historically authors have been reluctant to submit, and editors have been reluctant to publish, articles in which results were statistically nonsignificant. In a literature plagued by what Rosenthal (1979) labeled the "file drawer" problem, referring to the historical tendency of authors to file such manuscripts away rather than submit them for possible publication, Type II error is of no interest. However, the field is moving, and the "file drawer" problem may become less dominant, in which case Type II error rates will be seen more often in journal articles.

Power Analyses via "What-If" Analyses

One easy way to conduct power analyses is to create "what-if" spreadsheets in software such as Excel (Thompson & Kieffer, 2000), although specialized statistical software for power analysis is also widely available. Figure 6.3 shows the setup for a research problem involving the Pearson r. Spreadsheets define cells referenced by columns labeled by letters (e.g., "A", "B", "C") and rows referenced by numbers (e.g., "1", "2", "3"). To create the Figure 6.3 spreadsheet, type "A1" into the uppermost, leftmost cell (i.e., cell "A1"). Type "B" into the "B1" cell. Type all the cell entries, as they are displayed in Figure 6.3.

Once the spreadsheet entries have been typed, *never* change any entries, except the entries for the Pearson r in cell "C6," and for the sample size, n, in cell "C7." Figure 6.4 illustrates the output for a problem in which the researcher presumed an r of 0.50 and an n of 33. For this research situation, the $p_{CALCULATED}$ (to six decimal places) is 0.003047. What-if spreadsheets can be used in two ways.

First, for a fixed effect size (both r and r^2 are among the dozens of effect size statistics), the sample sizes at which the fixed result transitions from statistically significant to statistically nonsignificant (or vice versa) can be determined. Simply type in the r and the n, and then alter n until the transition point is detected at a given α.

For example, for a fixed effect size of $r = 0.50$ ($r^2 = 25\%$), at $\alpha = .05$

```
A1 B          C          D         E        F        G                      H
 2 FOR Pearson r:
 3 whatif.wk1
 4
 5 ***************** CHANGE ENTRIES BELOW ************************
 6 r =
 7 n =
 8 ***************** CHANGE NOTHING BELOW THIS LINE *************
 9 r sq =    +C6^2
10                                                                          Effect
11 Source    SOS        df        MS       Fcalc    pcalc                   Size
12 Model     +C14*H12          1  +C12/D12 +E12/E13 =FDIST(F12,D12,D13)     =C9
13 Residual  +C14-C12  +D14-D12  +C13/D13
14 Total     100       +C7-1     +C14/D14
```

FIGURE 6.3. Spreadsheet **setup** for Pearson r "What If" Analyses

the result goes from being statistically significant at $n = 16$ to statistically nonsignificant at $n = 15$. So, if we are going to conduct a study and expect an r^2 of 25%, and we want a statistically significant result, we need to use a sample size of at least 16 participants.

Second, for a fixed sample size, the minimum effect size required to achieve statistical significance can be determined. For example, using the Figure 6.3 spreadsheet, for $n = 20$, what is the minimum r^2 required to achieve statistical significance?

What-if spreadsheets are extraordinarily valuable, for two reasons. First, these spreadsheets are *practically* useful. The spreadsheets can be used prospectively before a study to estimate the n required for an antici

FIGURE 6.4. Spreadsheet **output** for Pearson r – 0.50 and n – 33

```
A1 B          C          D         E        F        G          H
 2 FOR Pearson r:
 3 whatif.wk1
 4
 5 ***************** CHANGE ENTRIES BELOW ************************
 6 r =       0.5
 7 n =       33
 8 ***************** CHANGE NOTHING BELOW THIS LINE *************
 9 r sq =    0.25
10                                                             Effect
11 Source    SOS        df    MS        Fcalc    pcalc        Size
12 Model     25         1         25    10.3333  0.003047     25.00%
13 Residual  75         31    2.41935
14 Total     100        32    3.125
```

pated effect size. Or they can be used retrospectively to flesh out the import of a statistically significant effect. What does it mean to obtain a statistically significant result when, at half the actual n, the result would have remained statistically significant? What does it mean to fail to reject if, with an additional one or two participants and the same effect size, the statistically nonsignificant result would have been statistically significant?

Second, and more importantly, what-if spreadsheets are *heuristically* valuable. Persons who use these spreadsheets to explore outcomes for a wide range of effect sizes, and a wide range of sample sizes, will develop an intuitive feel for the sample sizes required to obtain statistical significance for a range of effect sizes. These exercises help us to remember that "surely, God loves the .06 [level of statistical significance] nearly as much as the .05" (Rosnow & Rosenthal, 1989b, p. 1277).

The really critical point is that what-if exercises can help promote the realization that sample results will *always* be statistically significant at some sample size, and sample size is a key driver in the decision to reject or fail to reject (see Cohen, 1994). The only sample effect size that will never be statistically significant for a null hypothesis of no difference or no relationship is an effect size of exactly zero.

The likelihood of obtaining a zero effect size is infinitely small, and thus not worth considering. This is because effect sizes are continuous. The range of all possible effect sizes defines a number line consisting of infinitely many points. The probability of sampling a zero out of infinitely many possible effect sizes is infinitely small, because one outcome (i.e., effect size = 0) out of infinitely many yields an infinitely small probability of that effect being sampled (i.e., $1 / \infty$ is infinitely small).

The spreadsheet can be used to own the fact that all nonzero effect sizes will be statistically significant at some sample size. Use the what-if spreadsheet to determine the minimum sample size required to obtain statistical significance for $r^2 = 0.0000001$. The required n may be large, but is finite.

These realizations change the context for framing statistically significant results. The implication is this:

Statistical significance testing can involve a tautological logic in which tired researchers, having collected data from hundreds of subjects [today called "participants" instead], then conduct a statistical test to evaluate whether there were a lot of subjects, which the researchers already know, because they collected the data and know they're tired. (Thompson, 1992c, p. 436)

In part, statistical significance tests evaluate whether researchers are ambitious regarding sample size, or lazy. Would we rather know about the personality of the researcher (e.g., drive, ambition), or (a) the effect size magnitude and (b) the replicability of the research results?

Matters really get dicey when we compare NHSST results (apples to oranges versus apples to apples) across a related literature involving different sample sizes. As Thompson (1999a) explained,

> Because p values are confounded indices, in theory 100 studies with varying sample sizes and 100 different effect sizes could each have the same single $p_{CALCULATED}$, and 100 studies with the same single effect size could each have 100 different values for $p_{CALCULATED}$. (pp. 169–170)

▩▩▩ $p_{CALCULATED}$

The implication is not that excessive NHSST causes blindness, but instead is that $p_{CALCULATED}$ must be interpreted with caution, and correctly. Researchers ought to understand both what statistical significance tests do *not* mean, and what they do mean. Empirical studies suggest that not all researchers have these understandings (e.g., Mittag & Thompson, 2000; Nelson, Rosenthal, & Rosnow, 1986; Oakes, 1986; Rosenthal & Gaito, 1963; Zuckerman, Hodgins, Zuckerman, & Rosenthal, 1993). As Thompson (1999b) noted, "parroting mumbled words about 'due to chance,' even when accompanied by enthusiastic hand flapping, doesn't count as real understanding" (p. 164).

What Does $p_{CALCULATED}$ Not Mean?

There are two misconceptions about $p_{CALCULATED}$ that remain somewhat common. The first equates small $p_{CALCULATED}$ values with result import, and the second equates small $p_{CALCULATED}$ values with result replicability.

Result Import

As noted previously in this chapter, $p_{\text{CALCULATED}}$ is not useful in evaluating result importance. Thompson (1993) explained, "If the computer package did not ask you your values prior to its analysis, it could not have considered your value system in calculating p's, and so p's cannot be blithely used to infer the value of research results" (p. 365).

In his classic dialogue between two hypothetical graduate students, Shaver (1985, p. 58) poignantly illustrated the folly of equating result improbability with result importance:

> CHRIS: I set the level of significance at .05, as my advisor suggested. So a difference that large would occur by chance less than five times in a hundred if the groups weren't really different. An unlikely occurrence like that surely must be important.

> JEAN: Wait a minute, Chris. Remember the other day when you went into the office to call home? Just as you completed dialing the number, your little boy picked up the phone to call someone. So you were connected and talking to one another without the phone ever ringing. . . . Well, that must have been a truly important occurrence then? (p. 58)

Result Replicability

The $p_{\text{CALCULATED}}$ computation presumes that the null hypothesis exactly describes the population, and then evaluates the probability that the sample came from this presumed population. The direction of the inference is population to sample, *not* sample to population.

If NHSST really did make an inference from sample to population, then (and only then) the outcome of the statistical significance test would bear upon result replicability. Future samples drawn from the population about which an inference would be drawn should yield somewhat comparable results. But it ain't so. In Cohen's (1994) immortal words, the statistical significance test "does not tell us what we want to know, and we so much want to know what we want to know that, out of desperation, we nevertheless believe that it does!" (p. 997).

What Does $p_{CALCULATED}$ Mean?

The $p_{CALCULATED}$ estimates the *probability of the sample statistic(s) (and sample results even more extreme in their divergence from the null hypothesis than our sample results), assuming (a) the sample came from a population exactly described by the null hypothesis, and (b) given the sample size.* Why must these two assumptions be invoked?

First, the sample size must be taken into consideration, because sample size impacts the precision of statistical estimates, and impacts the dispersion of the sampling distribution. If a sample result diverged wildly from H_0, the divergence may not be grossly unlikely, when sample size is small. Small samples *may* not always be fluky and yield fluky and inaccurate parameter estimates, but conversely, fluky statistics *may* certainly occur when n is small. However, as sample size gets larger, estimation precision should increase, and so statistics that diverge from the null are less and less likely.

Second, why *must* the null be assumed to describe the population? Well, we are estimating the probability that the sample and its statistics came from the population. Clearly, the population from which the sample is presumably drawn must impact the results expected in the sample.

If we draw two samples from two populations with coefficients of kurtosis parameters of −1.5 and +1.5, respectively, the most likely (not guaranteed, but most likely) sample statistics are −1.5 and +1.5, respectively. Similarly, if we draw three samples from a single population in which the coefficient of skewness is 0.0, the most likely three sample statistics are equal (and all 0.0).

If we have four samples with statistic SDs of 0.75, 1.00, 1.25, and 1.33, we would obtain one $p_{CALCULATED}$ value if $p_{CALCULATED}$ was computed under a premise that the parameter SDs were 0.75, 1.00, 1.25, and 1.33, respectively. For the same sample statistic SDs, we would obtain a different $p_{CALCULATED}$ value if $p_{CALCULATED}$ was computed under a premise that the parameter SDs were equal.

Literally, infinitely many population parameters can be assumed. For each of these infinitely many population assumptions, for a given set of sample statistics (e.g., SDs of 0.75, 1.00, 1.25, and 1.33, respectively) there is one *single $p_{CALCULATED}$* value.

We *must* assume one single population with given parameters, so that there will be one single $p_{CALCULATED}$ value for a given set of sample statistics. If we assume infinitely many populations, there are infinitely many equally plausible and arguably correct values for $p_{CALCULATED}$, and $p_{CALCULATED}$ becomes mathematically "indeterminate."

This discussion does *not* mean that we have to assume that H_0 describes the population. We could obtain $p_{CALCULATED}$ as long as we assumed *any* one set of population parameters. But the historical tradition is to assume that the population is perfectly described by H_0. And this assumption does make $p_{CALCULATE}$ mathematically determinate, using the procedures described in this chapter.

NHSST is one of the single most important concepts in statistics. Mastery of this (somewhat convoluted) logic is imperative, so that the limitations of NHSST will be truly understood.

Here are four questions that test your understanding of NHSST. Note that answering these questions correctly does not require any math. These are conceptual questions, testing your understanding of $p_{CALCULATED}$ as a concept (i.e., real understanding or mastery, not rote memorization of words or formulas):

1. Three studies, each involving three groups of 350 students, are conducted. The medians in study A were 68, 92, and 120; in study B were 52, 48, and 61; and in study C were 40, 50, and 60. Which of the following correctly lists these studies in the order of **largest to smallest** $p_{CALCULATED}$?

    A. A, B, and C   B. B, C, and A
    C. A, C, and B   D. B, A, and C
    E. C, A, and B

2. In each of three studies, $SD_1 = 6.8$ and $SD_2 = 7.5$. In study Gamma, $n = 100$; in study Delta, $n = 1,000$; and in study Epsilon, $n = 580$. Which of the following lists the studies from **largest to smallest** $p_{CALCULATED}$?

    A. Delta, Epsilon, Gamma   B. Epsilon, Delta, Gamma
    C. Gamma, Epsilon, Delta   D. Gamma, Delta, Epsilon
    E. none of the above, because here $p_{CALCULATED} = 0$.

3. Four studies each include four groups of 25 participants. Given the sample means listed below, which study would produce the **largest** $p_{CALCULATED}$?

      A. 26, 38, 45, 50   B. 30, 31, 29, 30
      C. 20, 22, 47, 49   D. 21, 58, 58, 58

4. Four studies were conducted to determine the correlation between gender and response time on spatial tasks. In Study 1, 50 males and 50 females were tested. In Study 2, 150 males and 150 females were tested. In Study 3, 25 males and 25 females were tested. In Study 4, 200 males and 200 females were tested. Remarkably, in all four studies, $r = +0.61$. Which of these four studies had the **smallest** $p_{CALCULATED}$ value?

      A. Study 1   B. Study 2
      C. Study 3   D. Study 4

Here are three hints for addressing such questions.

First, as long as the numbers are reasonable (e.g., an SD is not less than zero, r is not greater than $+1$ or less than -1), ignore the statistic being evaluated. The logic of NHSST generalizes across *all statistics*, including statistics that are fictitious, or of which you have never heard.

Second, compare $p_{CALCULATED}$ values as percentages, rather than proportions. We are taught percentages in early elementary school, and instinctively comprehend that 10% ($p = 0.1$) is larger than 5% ($p = 0.05$). Nonmathematicians have greater intuitive understanding of percentages than of proportions.

Third, convert $p_{CALCULATED}$ as a concept into its actual conceptual meaning (i.e., more or less likely sample statistics, assuming that the sample originated in a population described by the null hypothesis). Whenever you see (or hear) "smaller (or smallest) $p_{CALCULATED}$," think instead of "less (or least) likely sample statistics." Whenever you see (or hear) "bigger (or biggest) $p_{CALCULATED}$," think instead of "more (or most) likely sample statistics."

Some Key Concepts

Statistical significance testing does *not* evaluate result importance. Valid deductive logic cannot contain in conclusions any information missing from deductive premises, and because NHSST does not require a declaration of the researcher's personal values, p does not contain *any* information about the value of results.

Nor does p evaluate result replicability (Cohen, 1994; Thompson, 1996). Therefore, because result replicability is important to establish, so that we know our effect sizes are not serendipitous, other methods discussed in subsequent chapters that help evaluate replicability are important in quantitative research.

A given hypothesis test may yield a Type I error, or a Type II error, but never both. Type II error is irrelevant once the null hypothesis is rejected, because a Type II error is not possible in the presence of a decision to reject, by definition. "What-if" analyses may be practically useful in selecting a desired sample size given an expected effect size, such as r^2. What-if analyses are also instructionally powerful in helping us to realize that (a) a nonzero effect size will always be statistically significant at some sample size, and (b) sample size is a very important determinant of $p_{\mathrm{CALCULATED}}$.

▩▩▩ Reflection Problems ▩▩▩

1. What is asserted by saying that "$p_{\mathrm{CALCULATED}}$ = 0.000"? Can $p_{\mathrm{CALCULATED}}$ ever really equal zero? Should anyone ever report in an article or dissertation that "$p_{\mathrm{CALCULATED}}$ = 0.000"?

2. Use the Figure 6.3 spreadsheet layout to obtain $p_{\mathrm{CALCULATED}}$ for the following research study.

    A researcher, using a single predictor variable, conducts an n = 10,001 study to predict how long people live. The r^2 was 100.0%.

   What is $p_{\mathrm{CALCULATED}}$ whenever the r^2-type effect size is perfect? What implications does this $p_{\mathrm{CALCULATED}}$ have as regards your ability to publish results that allow perfect prediction of important outcomes, such as how long people will live?

3. Either using the Figure 6.3 spreadsheet, or the spreadsheet suggested by Thompson and Kieffer (2000), find the contiguous transitional sample sizes (e.g., $n = 22$, $n = 23$) at which the following effect sizes are and are not statistically significant: $r^2 = 0.1\%$, 1%, 2%, 3%, 4%, 5%, 10%, 25%, 50%, 75%, 85%, 95%.

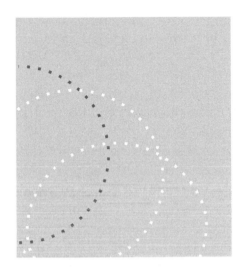

7

Practical Significance

M ost of the well-known statistical analyses (e.g., Student's *t*, Pearson's *r*, Spearman's ρ), and their associated statistical significance tests, were developed roughly a century ago. But criticisms of these accompanying NHSST applications are almost as old as the methods themselves (cf. Berkson, 1938; Boring, 1919). Harlow, Mulaik, and Steiger (1997) have provided a balanced and comprehensive treatment of whether journal editors should ban statistical significance tests in their book *What If There Were No Significance Tests?*

The criticisms have been presented with increasing frequency over recent decades (Anderson, Burnham, & Thompson, 2000). The concerns have been published in disciplines as diverse as economics (e.g., Ziliak & McCloskey, 2004), education (e.g., Carver, 1978; Thompson, 1996), psychology (e.g., Cohen, 1994; Schmidt, 1996), and the wildlife sciences (e.g., Anderson et al., 2000).

To convey the tenor of the commentary of critics, Schmidt and Hunter (1997) can be cited as arguing that "Statistical significance testing retards the growth of scientific knowledge; it *never* [emphasis added] makes a positive contribution" (p. 37). Rozeboom (1997) was equally emphatic:

> Null-hypothesis significance testing is surely the most bone-headedly misguided procedure ever institutionalized in the rote training of science students.... [I]t is a sociology-of-science wonderment that this statistical practice has remained so unresponsive to criticism.... (p. 335)

However, NHSST has been defended with corresponding vigor by advocates (cf. Abelson, 1997; Robinson & Wainer, 2002).

The criticisms of NHSST have substantially affected scholars' views of what counts as evidence in quantitative research. Today, the social sciences have now moved toward the view that indices of practical significance should be reported and interpreted. This movement was largely influenced by the Task Force on Statistical Inference, appointed by the American Psychological Association (APA) in 1996. The Task Force published recommendations three years later (Wilkinson & APA Task Force on Statistical Inference, 1999).

The Task Force recommendations, in turn, affected the reporting expectations presented in the revised APA (2001) *Publication Manual*, used by more than 1,000 journals, although it has also been argued that the *Manual* should have gone further in promulgating expectations for changed reporting and interpretation practices (Fidler, 2002). The field of medicine has moved further and faster in emphasizing practical significance, in part due to the cohesion of editors of medical journals who came together to articulate *uniform* author guidelines for the discipline as a whole (International Committee of Medical Journal Editors, 1997).

The editors of several dozen social science journals have articulated expectations that surpass those of the APA *Publication Manual* (e.g., Snyder, 2000). Indeed, as Fidler (2002) recently observed, "Of the major American associations, only all the journals of the American Educational Research Association have remained silent on all these issues" (p. 754).

Two forms of evidence for practical significance have been emphasized in the APA Task Force report, the *Publication Manual*, and the supplementary editorial policies of several dozen journal editors: effect sizes and confidence intervals. After discussing these in turn, we will also consider the use of them together.

■■■ Effect Sizes

The APA Task Force on Statistical Inference urged authors to "*Always* [emphasis added] provide some effect-size estimate when reporting a *p* value" (Wilkinson & APA Task Force, 1999, p. 599). The Task Force further emphasized, "reporting and interpreting effect sizes in the context of previously reported effects is *essential* [emphasis added] to good research" (p. 599). And the 2001 APA *Publication Manual* labeled the "failure to report effect sizes" as a "defect in the design and reporting of research" (p. 5). Today, because such encouragements to report effects have had demonstrably limited impact (Vacha-Haase, Nilsson, Reetz, Lance, & Thompson, 2000), 24 journals (cf. K. Harris, 2003; Thompson, 1994a) have gone further and now explicitly *require* the reporting of effect sizes. Unfortunately, textbooks still emphasize NHSST over effect sizes (Capraro & Capraro, 2002). However, as Grissom and Kim (2005) emphasized, journal and dissertation readers "have a right to see estimates of effect sizes. Some might even argue that not reporting such estimates in an understandable manner . . . may be like withholding evidence" (p. 5).

As previously noted in Chapter 6, an **effect size** is a statistic quantifying the extent to which sample statistics diverge from the null hypothesis. For a study of the relationship between handedness (right or left) and gender, using the ϕ coefficient, the ubiquitous nil null might be H_0: $\phi_{FRESHMEN} = \phi_{SOPHOMORES} = \phi_{JUNIORS} = \phi_{SENIORS}$. If the statistic ϕ coefficients were all 0.73 in all four groups, the effect size for the study would be zero. If the four ϕ coefficients were 0.69, 0.69, 0.69 and 0.70, the effect size would be nonzero, but small. The effect size would be bigger if the four statistic ϕ coefficients were 0.50, 0.55, 0.60, and 0.65. And the effect size would be considerably larger if the four statistics were −0.95, −0.05, 0.45, and 0.88.

Why can't $p_{CALCULATED}$ values themselves be used as indices of practical significance? One reason is that $p_{CALCULATED}$ values are confounded indices of effect, because *both* effect size and sample size impact $p_{CALCULATED}$. As previously noted in Chapter 6,

> Because *p* values are confounded indices, in theory 100 studies with varying sample sizes and 100 different effect sizes could each have the same single $p_{CALCULATED}$, and 100 studies with the same single effect size could each have 100 different values for $p_{CALCULATED}$. (Thompson, 1999a, pp. 169–170)

Furthermore, as Good and Hardin (2003) explained,

> [T]he p value is a random variable that varies from sample to sample. . . .
> Consequently, it is not appropriate to compare the p values from two distinct
> experiments, or from tests on two variables measured in the same experi-
> ment, and declare that one is more significant than the other. (p. 100)

These are exactly the reasons why effect sizes, and not $p_{\text{CALCULATED}}$ values,
are used in meta-analyses.

There are literally dozens of effect sizes. Kirk (1996) cataloged 41,
and his list did not include some indices proposed by Carl Huberty and his
colleagues (Hess, Olejnik, & Huberty, 2001; Huberty & Holmes, 1983;
Huberty & Lowman, 2000)! Furthermore, more effect size variations will
doubtless be proposed now that the social sciences have moved toward an
increased emphasis on practical significance.

Some of the statistics that have already been discussed are actually
themselves effect sizes. For example, for the null H_0: $r = 0$ (or equivalently,
H_0: $r^2 = 0$), the actual statistic r (or r^2) computed in the sample is an effect
size for this null.

Here we will not cover all the numerous possibilities. For exposure to
the full landscape, the reader is referred to Grissom and Kim (2005), Kirk
(1996, 2003), or Rosenthal (1994). However, the most commonly-used
effect sizes will be considered.

The effect size indices presented here can be organized into three categories. A few effect sizes (e.g., group overlap indices, Huberty & Holmes,
1983; number-needed-to-treat, Schulzer & Mancini, 1996; probability of
superiority, Grissom, 1994) fit instead into a fourth, "miscellaneous" category. But three categories work for the effects considered here.

One dimension for the organizational framework involves whether
the indices are score-world (i.e., in an unsquared metric) or area-world
(i.e., in a squared metric). As noted in previous chapters, some statistics
are in the score world (e.g., M_X, Mdn_X, SD_X, coefficients of skewness and
kurtosis, r), whereas others are in the area world (e.g., SOS_X, SD_X^2, r^2).
Similarly, some test statistics are in an unsquared metric (e.g., the z and t
distributions), whereas others are in a squared metric (e.g., F, χ^2). By the
same token, some effect size indices are in the score world, whereas others
are in the area world.

A second dimension for the categorization focuses on whether the effect sizes are "uncorrected" estimates, focusing on sample effects, or "corrected" (or "adjusted") estimates, attempting to take into account sample features (e.g., n) that impact the flukiness of the sample and its estimates. So, here we will consider three classes of effects: (a) uncorrected, standardized difference effect sizes; (b) uncorrected, variance-accounted-for effect sizes; and (c) corrected, variance-accounted-for effect sizes.

Uncorrected, Standardized Difference Effect Sizes

In medicine, researchers conventionally report effect sizes for experiments as mean (or median, or proportion) differences between treatment and control groups. For example, physicians will report that, on average, adults who take vitamin pills daily live 2 years longer than adults who do not do so. Or physicians will report that there are half as many heart attacks among adults who take 81 milligrams of aspirin every day than among adults who do not do so.

Medical researchers have the advantage that their mean, or median, or proportion differences are measured in natural and universally accepted metrics. For example, everywhere in the world cholesterol is measured in milligrams per deciliter. And everywhere in the world disease mortality is measured in deaths per thousand patients. Moreover, these measures have known parameter standard deviations.

But in the social sciences, there are no universally accepted measures of our constructs. For example, there may be 5 widely accepted measures of academic achievement or 10 widely accepted measures of self-concept. And these measures may have different parameter standard deviations, because some achievement (or self-concept) tests are harder or are scaled differently than others.

A fundamentally important aspect of science is the ability to compare results across studies. The comparability of results allows the cumulation and integration of findings across studies. And it is primarily through the integration of our new results with prior related results that we can evaluate the replicability of our own new results. As emphasized in Chapter 6, statistical significance is *not* a viable vehicle for testing result replicability.

But how can results across studies be compared if the dependent (or criterion) variables are measured in different metrics? As noted in Chapter 2, in statistics, when we divide by a number, we are removing from our answer the influence of whatever we are using to divide. For example, we divide by n when computing the mean so that we can compare means apples to apples across two or more samples with different sample sizes. And we divide the mean deviation scores (x_i) by the group SD to obtain standardized (i.e., SD is removed) deviation scores, z_i, from which we have removed SD.

Two popular standardized effect sizes (i.e., Glass' Δ, and Cohen's d) compute a standardized (i.e., SD is removed) mean difference by dividing the mean difference of the experimental and the control groups by some estimate of the σ of the outcome variable. Of course, a standardized median difference might also be computed. Because they have both been standardized, Δ and d are in the standardized score world.

By the way, note the use for the Glass effect size of a Greek letter to represent, in this case, a sample statistic. This is just another effort by statisticians to be confusing. Usually Greek letters are used only for parameters.

Glass' Δ

Historically, researchers attempted to integrate results across related studies in various ways, including averaging p values and especially "vote counting" the number of statistically significant versus statistically nonsignificant results (Kulik & Kulik, 1992). However, because $p_{\text{CALCULATED}}$ values are confounded jointly by effect sizes and sample sizes, researchers soon realized that these strategies were doomed to create irreconcilable, contradictory integrations of previous findings.

Building on other strategies for integrating results, Glass (1976; Glass, McGaw, & Smith, 1981) proposed methods for the meta-analytic integration of studies using the effect size Δ. Glass reasoned that the experimental intervention could not have impacted dependent variable dispersion in the control group, because the control group presumably received no intervention. Therefore, he reasoned that the effect size should be computed as

$$\Delta = (M_E - M_C) / SD_C \qquad (7.1)$$

where SD_C is the standard deviation of the outcome variable scores of only the control group.

Cohen's d

Cohen (1969, 1988), on the other hand, noted that the precision of the estimate of the σ, which is critical to the correct estimation of the effect size, would be enhanced by using both the experimental and the control group to compute the SD, because $n_E + n_C > n_C$. A weighted, pooled average SD can be computed as a weighted (taking into account group sizes) average of the outcome variable dispersions in the two groups, using a formula such as Equation 6.4 to compute SD_{POOLED}^2 and, from that result, SD_{POOLED}. Then we can obtain

$$d = (M_E - M_C) / SD_{POOLED} \qquad (7.2)$$

Δ versus d

The comparison of Δ versus d affords the opportunity to emphasize the fundamentally important point that statistics is about thinking, rather than about black-versus-white decisions or the rote memorization of formulas. As Huberty and Morris (1988, p. 573) argued, "As in all statistical inference, subjective judgment cannot be avoided. Neither can reasonableness!"

When should researchers reflectively select Δ as an effect size? First, if sample size is huge, there may be relatively little gain in precision in estimating σ by combining both groups. Remember, too, that the impacts on precision from increasing sample size are not equal for each change in sample size, and may be small at large sample sizes. Second, if theory or previous empirical results suggest that the intervention impacts not only central tendency, but dispersion as well, then Δ may be a preferred choice. It is not unusual for interventions, such as educational or psychological treatments, to affect both location and dispersion.

Conversely, if sample size is small, and the intervention seems not to have affected dispersion, Cohen's d may be the preferred effect size. Of course, if both Δ and d are computed and found to be comparable, the researcher can be more assured that the effect estimate is not an artifact of effect size choice.

Uncorrected, Variance-Accounted-for Effect Sizes

Effect sizes for various research designs can also be computed as analogs of r^2. For example, for the two-group problem associated with the independent t test, a variance-accounted-for effect size can be computed as the squared point–biserial correlation (r_{pb}^2) between the dichotomous group membership variable and the outcome variable. And as we shall see in subsequent chapters (e.g., Chapter 10), related effect sizes can be computed in situations involving three or more groups and an intervally-scaled dependent variable.

Finally, when all the variables are intervally scaled, r^2 can be computed as an effect size for the bivariate case, as noted previously. And when multiple intervally-scaled variables are used to predict a single intervally-scaled outcome variable, a related variance-accounted-for effect size (R^2) can be computed, as we shall see in Chapter 8.

Of course, just as r can be converted into r^2, and vice versa, score-world d and r can be converted into each other's metrics. For example, Cohen (1988, p. 24) provided the following formula for deriving r from d when the groups of interest are of approximately the same size:

$$r = d \,/\, [(d^2 + 4)^{0.5}] \tag{7.3}$$

Thus, for the effect size that Cohen characterized as "medium" (i.e., $d = |0.50|$) with respect to typicality, based on his subjective impression of the social science literature as a whole, we have

$$0.5 \,/\, [(0.5^2 + 4)^{0.5}]$$
$$0.5 \,/\, [(0.25 + 4)^{0.5}]$$
$$0.5 \,/\, [4.25^{0.5}]$$

$$0.5 / 2.06$$
$$r = 0.242,$$
$$\text{and } r^2 = 0.058$$

For what Cohen deemed a "large" d (i.e., $|0.8|$), the d converts to an r of 0.388, and an r^2 of 15.0%. For what Cohen deemed a "small" d (i.e., $|0.2|$), the d converts to an r of 0.097, and an r^2 of 0.9%. Aaron, Kromrey, and Ferron (1998) provided more detail on this d-to-r conversion for cases in which group sizes are disparate.

Conversely, Friedman (1968, p. 346) proposed the following formula to approximate d from r:

$$d = [2(r)] / [(1 - r^2)^{0.5}] \qquad (7.4)$$

For $r = 0.242$ we have

$$[2(0.242)] / [(1 - 0.242^2)^{0.5}$$
$$0.484 / [(1 - 0.242^2)^{0.5}$$
$$0.484 / [(1 - 0.059)^{0.5}$$
$$0.484 / 0.941^{0.5}$$
$$0.484 / 0.970$$
$$d = 0.499$$

Corrected, Variance-Accounted-for Effect Sizes

As explained in Chapter 6, all samples have some degree of flukiness. The only way to eliminate flukiness is to collect population rather than sample data.

The bottom line is that some of the score variance, SD^2, in the sample data reflects true variance that exists in the population (i.e., σ^2). But some of the score variance (SD^2) in the sample does *not* exist in the population, and instead reflects the flukiness introduced by the sampling process. This latter score variance is called **sampling error variance**.

Note that "sampling error variance" should not be confused with other statistical phrases that you may hear, such as "measurement error variance" or "model specification error." Even though all three phrases include the word "error," mainly to try to confuse everybody, the three terms are conceptually discrete from each other (Thompson, 2003).

Every sample has its own, *unique* sampling error variance (i.e., variance that does not exist in the population, and also differs from the sampling error found in other samples). That is, samples are like people. And, like people, some samples are wildly weird, and some samples are only a little bit weird.

Sampling error variance consistently tends to inflate effect sizes. This is because when we compute the r^2 (or r_{pb}^2, or Spearman ρ^2, or R^2) for sample data, the computations do not take into consideration the fact that some of the sample score variance does not exist in the population, and is instead peculiar to the given sample.

But, if we could somehow estimate how much the sampling error variance in a given sample was inflating the effect size, we could then remove this estimated distortion, and compute a "corrected" or "adjusted" effect size that better estimated the effect size in the population. Happily, we know the three factors that influence sampling error variance, and so we can estimate sampling error variance, and we can then estimate corrected effect sizes.

First, as suggested in the previous chapter, there is more sampling error variance in samples with smaller ns than in samples with larger ns. So every formula for corrected effect sizes from among the dozens of possible choices must logically include n as an element.

Second, there is more sampling error in samples with more variables than in samples with fewer measured variables. As explained in Chapter 2, an outlier is a case whose data disproportionately impacts statistical estimates. Outliers are *not* bad, evil people who distort all statistics for all variables. Instead, probably everybody is an outlier on some statistics for some variables, although some people may be outliers on a lot of statistics for a lot of variables.

The implication is that for a fixed n of cases, as we sample the scores on more variables, we provide greater opportunity for the weirdnesses of people to be manifested. So, logically, any formula for corrected effect sizes must take into account the number of variables being measured.

Third, for a given n and number of measured variables, there is more sampling error in samples drawn from populations with smaller effect sizes than in samples drawn from populations with larger effect sizes. This dynamic is harder to follow intuitively.

Thompson (2002a) explained this dynamic via discussion of the bivariate case in which the Pearson r is being estimated in sample data. Imagine a population scattergram, where ρ is +1.0. In this scattergram billions of asterisks will define an upward-sloping perfect line. Thompson (2002a) then noted,

> In this instance, even if the researcher draws ridiculously small samples, such as $n = 2$ or $n = 3$, and no matter which participants are drawn, we simply cannot incorrectly estimate the variance-accounted-for effect size. That is, *any* two or three or four people will always define a straight line in the sample scattergram, and thus [sample] r^2 will always be 1.0. (p. 68)

The implication is that any formula used to estimate a corrected effect size must include the estimated or assumed population effect size as an element. Of course, this suggests the paradox that if we knew the population effect size, we would not need the corrected effect size estimate, and if we lack knowledge of the population effect size, we cannot accurately correct the sample effect size.

In practice we deal with this paradox by presuming that the sample effect size is a reasonable estimate of the population effect, and we correct the sample estimate with itself. Alternatively, we could take an average of previously reported effect sizes in the related literature, and use this value to correct our sample estimate.

Ezekiel (1930) proposed one frequently used correction formula that can be used with r^2 (or with the multiple regression R^2). This correction is automatically produced when the SPSS REGRESSION procedure is executed to compute the Pearson r^2, and so will be the only focus in the present chapter, although dozens of related correction formulas have been proposed and this formula is not without limitations (Carter, 1979; Rencher & Pun, 1980). The "corrected" or "adjusted" variance-accounted-for estimate for a squared correlation coefficient can be computed as

$$1 - ((n - 1) / (n - v - 1))(1 - r^2) \qquad (7.5)$$

where n is the sample size and v is the number of predictor variables. The equation can be equivalently expressed as

$$r^2 - ((1 - r^2)(v / (n - v - 1))) \qquad (7.6)$$

Notice that, as expected, the correction formula contains the expected three elements, and only these, as elements that change across samples. For the Pearson r^2 situation, the number of predictor variables is always $v = 1$, and Equation 7.5 simplifies to

$$r^{2*} = 1 - ((n - 1) / (n - 2))(1 - r^2) \qquad (7.7)$$

where r^{2*} is the corrected variance-accounted-for effect size.

The corrected estimate is sometimes called the "shrunken" r^2, because r^{2*} is always less than or equal to r^2. And the difference in the uncorrected and the corrected estimate divided by the uncorrected estimate quantifies the percentage of the sampling error variance's impact on the effect estimate. For example, if $r^2 = 50.0\%$ and $r^{2*} = 40.0\%$, sampling error is estimated to have produced 20.0% [(50.0% − 40.0%) / 50.0%] of the original uncorrected effect size estimate.

Table 7.1 presents a range of values for r^2 and the corrections associated with various sample sizes. Notice that the impacts of increasing sample size are again not equal. For example, for $r^2 = 50.0\%$ and $n = 5$, $r^{2*} = 33.3\%$, which represents a shrinkage of 0.167, or 33.3% of the original r^2 value. For $r^2 = 50.0\%$ and $n = 6$, the shrinkage is 0.125, or 25.0% of the original r^2 value. For $r^2 = 50.0\%$ and $n = 7$, the shrinkage is 0.100, or 20.0% of the original r^2 value. Each increase in sample size brings reduced shrinkage, but less and less of an improvement with each increase.

Table 7.1 also indicates that the amount of correction is not uniform throughout the range of estimated r^2 values. When the estimated r^2 value is large (e.g., approaching |1.0|), the shrinkage will be quite small, even when sample size is relatively small. But when r^2 is small (e.g., 1.00%) and even at $n = 320$, shrinkage is 31.1% of the original estimate.

Conversely, this discussion can be reframed as reflecting the fact that even when the population effect size is zero, the expected sample r^2 is *not* zero. Equations 7.6 or 7.7 can be plugged into a spreadsheet, and "what-if" analyses can be conducted to solve for $r^{2*} = 0.0$ for various ns. For the Pearson r^2, for example, if $n = 8$ and the population parameter is zero, the expected sample statistic at this n is $r^2 = 14.3\%$. If $n = 7$ and the population parameter is zero, the expected sample statistic is $r^2 = 16.7\%$. If $n = 6$ and the population parameter is zero, the expected sample statistic is

TABLE 7.1. Corrected Estimates of r^2 for Various Sample Sizes and Original Uncorrected Estimates

r^2	n	r^{2*}	Shrinkage	Percentage shrinkage
0.50	5	0.333	0.167	33.3%
0.50	6	0.375	0.125	25.0%
0.50	7	0.400	0.100	20.0%
0.50	8	0.417	0.083	16.7%
0.50	9	0.429	0.071	14.3%
0.50	10	0.438	0.063	12.5%
0.50	20	0.472	0.028	5.6%
0.50	80	0.494	0.006	1.3%
0.50	320	0.498	0.002	0.3%
0.25	5	0.000	0.250	100.0%
0.25	6	0.063	0.188	75.0%
0.25	7	0.100	0.150	60.0%
0.25	8	0.125	0.125	50.0%
0.25	9	0.143	0.107	42.9%
0.25	10	0.156	0.094	37.5%
0.25	20	0.208	0.042	16.7%
0.25	80	0.240	0.010	3.8%
0.25	320	0.248	0.002	0.9%
0.125	5	−0.167	0.292	233.3%
0.125	6	−0.094	0.219	175.0%
0.125	7	−0.050	0.175	140.0%
0.125	8	−0.021	0.146	116.7%
0.125	9	0.000	0.125	100.0%
0.125	10	0.016	0.109	87.5%
0.125	20	0.076	0.049	38.9%
0.125	80	0.114	0.011	9.0%
0.125	320	0.122	0.003	2.2%
0.0625	5	−0.250	0.313	500.0%
0.0625	6	−0.172	0.234	375.0%
0.0625	7	−0.125	0.188	300.0%
0.0625	8	−0.094	0.156	250.0%
0.0625	9	−0.071	0.134	214.3%
0.0625	10	−0.055	0.117	187.5%
0.0625	20	0.010	0.052	83.3%
0.0625	80	0.050	0.012	19.2%
0.0625	320	0.060	0.003	4.7%
0.03125	5	−0.292	0.323	1033.3%
0.03125	6	−0.211	0.242	775.0%
0.03125	7	−0.163	0.194	620.0%
0.03125	8	−0.130	0.161	516.7%
0.03125	9	−0.107	0.138	442.9%
0.03125	10	−0.090	0.121	387.5%
0.03125	20	−0.023	0.054	172.2%
0.03125	80	0.019	0.012	39.7%
0.03125	320	0.028	0.003	9.7%
0.01	320	0.007	0.003	31.1%
0.01	640	0.008	0.002	15.5%
0.01	1280	0.009	0.001	7.7%

$r^2 = 20.0\%$. And if $n = 5$ and the population parameter is zero, the expected statistic $r^2 = 25.0\%$!

Note also that corrected variance-accounted-for effect sizes can become negative, even though the r^{2*} estimates are theoretically in a squared metric. Such corrected estimates suggest the use of a ridiculously small sample size for a given research study.

Corrections such as Equations 7.5 and 7.6 make adjustments to estimates of the population parameter. If all studies invoked the same correction of this sort, researchers would be comparing results apples to apples in the world of the *population*.

An alternative corrects the sample statistic to estimate effect size in a subsequent *sample* (e.g., Herzberg, 1969). Corrections of this ilk honor the reality that researchers never have the population, and compare their results across studies. These corrections tend to be more severe, because the adjustment must take into account the sampling error in two samples, rather than in only one sample (Snyder & Lawson, 1993).

Interpretation of Effect Sizes

Some researchers interpret single-study effect sizes by invoking Cohen's (1988) benchmarks for "small," "medium," and "large" effects. However, Cohen intended these only as general guidelines, mainly useful when working in unexplored territory, and he emphasized that

> these proposed conventions were set forth throughout with much diffidence, qualifications, *and invitations not to employ them if possible* [emphasis added]. . . . They were offered as conventions because they were needed in a research climate characterized by a neglect of attention to issues of [effect size] magnitude. (p. 532)

As noted elsewhere, "if people interpreted effect sizes [using fixed benchmarks] with the same rigidity that $\alpha = .05$ has been used in statistical testing, we would merely be being stupid in another metric" (Thompson, 2001, pp. 82–83).

As emphasized in Chapter 5 with respect to the aspirin/heart attack study, a very, very small, but replicable effect size for a very important outcome can be strikingly important. In the same vein, Gage (1978) pointed out that even though the relationship between cigarette smoking and lung cancer is relatively "small" (i.e., $r^2 = 1\%$ to 2%),

> Sometimes even very weak relationships can be important. . . . [O]n the basis of such correlations, important public health policy has been made and millions of people have changed strong habits. (p. 21)

Isolating a very, very small impact on death rates from a previously incurable and potentially pandemic disease (e.g., Ebola) will generally be deemed more important than finding a very, very large effect for a new treatment for a nonfatal disease for which numerous treatments are already widely available (e.g., jock itch).

At least in relatively established areas of research, "there is no wisdom whatsoever in attempting to associate regions of the effect-size metric with descriptive adjectives such as 'small,' 'moderate,' 'large,' and the like" (Glass, McGaw, & Smith, 1981, p. 104). Or, as Cohen (1977) himself said, "These qualitative adjectives . . . may not be reasonably descriptive in any specific area. Thus, what a sociologist may consider a small effect may be appraised as medium by a clinical psychologist" (p. 277).

Another complication is that effect sizes must be interpreted within the context of a given unit of analysis. Smaller effects for clusters of people (e.g., schools, hospitals) may be more noteworthy than identical effect sizes for individuals, because more people may be impacted by smaller effects at a larger unit of analysis (McCartney & Rosenthal, 2000).

However, it is also important to realize that what is called the ecological fallacy may compromise comparisons of effect sizes across units of analysis. For example, W. S. Robinson (1950) illustrated how effects even for the same data can differ not only in magnitude across units of analysis (e.g., individuals versus states), but in direction as well!

In any case, single-study effect sizes should be interpreted via *direct, explicit* comparison of the effects in related research. As Schmidt (1996) noted,

> Meta-analysis . . . has revealed how little information there typically is in any single study. It has shown that, contrary to widespread belief, a single primary study can rarely resolve an issue or answer a question. (p. 127)

Even single studies ought to be interpreted within a meta-analytic perspective, using **meta-analytic thinking** (cf. Cumming & Finch, 2001). Thompson (2002b) defined meta-analytic thinking as

> both (a) the prospective formulation of study expectations and design by explicitly invoking prior effect sizes and (b) the retrospective interpretation of new results, once they are in hand, via *explicit, direct* comparison with the prior effect sizes in the related literature. (p. 28, emphasis added)

Such comparisons will be facilitated once everyone routinely reports effect sizes. Of course, the comparisons require given effects to be converted into a common metric.

Confidence Intervals

The 2001 APA *Publication Manual* argued that confidence intervals (CIs) are "in general, *the best* reporting strategy. The use of confidence intervals is therefore *strongly recommended*" (p. 22; emphasis added). These admonitions are not new. For example, five decades ago Jones (1955) argued that

> an investigator would be misled less frequently and would be more likely to obtain the information he seeks were he to formulate his experimental problems in terms of the estimation of population parameters, with the establishment of confidence intervals about the estimated values, rather than in terms of a null hypothesis against all possible alternatives. (p. 407)

However, empirical studies of journals show that confidence intervals are published very infrequently (Finch, Cumming, & Thomason, 2001; Kieffer, Reese, & Thompson, 2001). And as Thompson (2002b) suggested, "It is conceivable that some researchers may not fully understand statistical methods that they (a) rarely read in the literature and (b) infrequently use in their own work" (p. 26).

In Chapter 6 I noted that a statistic could be divided by its *SE* to yield calculated t (or Wald statistic, or critical ratio). This ratio and its variations can be reexpressed in terms of a variety of related test statistics (e.g.,

F, χ^2). The ratio of a statistic to its standard error can be used to evaluate the statistical significance of a statistic using the nil null that the related parameter is zero.

But the standard error can also be used for *descriptive* purposes. As emphasized in Chapter 6, when the *SE* is large in relation to the value of a statistic, we know that the precision of our estimate may be compromised.

Indeed, the previous logic suggests the potential utility of creating **standard error bars** by adding and subtracting the *SE* from the point estimate of the statistic:

$$SE \text{ bar} = \text{statistic} \pm (k)SE_{\text{STATISTIC}} \qquad (7.8)$$

where k is some multiplicative constant and is often either 1 or 2. We would vest more confidence in the precision of point estimates when the standard error bars were narrower. In fact, such standard error bars are reported quite frequently in medical research (Cumming & Finch, 2001, 2005).

However, as noted previously, the APA Task Force advocated in particular the use of confidence intervals, which are related to standard error bars, but are a bit different. A confidence interval (CI) for a statistic is

$$CI_{\text{CONFIDENCE \%}} = \text{statistic} \pm TS_{\text{CRITICAL}}(SE_{\text{STATISTIC}}) \qquad (7.9)$$

where TS_{CRITICAL} is the critical value of a relevant test statistic at the study's *df* and α.

Confidence intervals for statistics can be easily derived using modern statistical software. But here we will explore some specific examples to make these procedures more concrete. For example, the CI for *M* with population variance assumed known and either large sample size or population normality assumed is computed as

$$CI_M = M \pm z_{\text{CRITICAL}}(SE_M) \qquad (7.10)$$

Let's say that a group of 30 statistics students have $M = 60.0$ ($SD = 10.0$) on a measure of clinical depression for which higher scores indicate greater depression. The parameter mean score on the measure is known to be 50.0 across all types of adults (e.g., students, nonstudents, clerics, elected politicians), where scores below 50.0 indicate less than average depression.

Based on our point estimate of the mean (i.e., 60.0), it appears that the students are, on the average, somewhat depressed. Of course, this does *not* indicate that all the students are depressed. Indeed, if the scores were normally distributed in our sample—because in a normal distribution 99% of the scores fall between $M \pm 3(SD)$—the sample scores would range between roughly 30.0 and 90.0, and some students would have lower than average or expected depression.

However, we know that our statistic point estimate is not perfectly precise, because we are working with a sample. Thus, we cannot conclude that all statistics students have a mean depression score of exactly 60.0.

We can compute the SE_M to obtain some idea about the precision of our point estimate. For these data we have $SE_M = SD_X / n^{0.5}$, or $10.0 / 30^{0.5}$ = 10.0 / 5.48 = 1.82. The result reflects an expectation that the standard error of the mean (i.e., SD of the sampling distribution) will be roughly 1.82 if we draw repeated samples of $n = 30$ from a population in which σ = 10.0.

For n of at least 30, one plausible test statistic distribution is the z test statistic distribution (*not* to be confused with a sample distribution of z scores). To construct a CI at a given confidence level, we compute the complement of the desired confidence level, and then divide by 2. For example, if we seek a 95% confidence interval, we need the z test statistic for $[(1 - 0.95) / 2]$, or 0.025. The necessary value can be obtained in Excel with the command

```
=NORMINV(0.025,0,1)
```

which returns a z test statistic value of 1.96. Thus, the 95% CI for our mean of 60.0 equals $60.0 \pm 1.96(1.82) = 60.0 \pm 3.57$, or [56.4, 63.6].

Let's say instead that we had sought a 68.4% confidence interval for our estimated mean. Inputting the related information into Excel yields a z test statistic of 1.00. Thus, the 68.4% CI would be [58.2, 61.8]. The standard error bar for our mean is also 58.2 to 61.8. The implication is that error bars about the mean created by $\pm 1(SE_M)$ are equivalent to 68.4% confidence intervals, and vice versa.

Misconceptions about CIs

Three common misconceptions about confidence intervals should be avoided. First, some researchers, either consciously or unconsciously interpret CIs constructed using large confidence levels (e.g., 90%, 95%, 99%) as if the intervals yield a result involving 100% certainty. The fallacy of this misinterpretation is obvious: although 95% is close to 100%, 95% simply does not equal 100%.

If I put only one bullet in a six-shot revolver, randomly spin the cylinder, point the gun at you, and pull the trigger, there is a 16.7% probability that you will be shot, and an 83.3% probability that you will not be shot. Would it make a difference to you if I was shooting at you with a revolver with which you were 83.3% likely to be safe, or with a different revolver with which you were 100.0% likely to be safe? Do not confuse these two different revolvers, and do not confuse 95% probability with 100% certainty.

Second, some researchers erroneously believe that confidence intervals are just null hypothesis statistical significance tests in a different guise (e.g., Knapp & Sawilowsky, 2001). One basis for clearly discriminating between NHSST and CI use involves the fact that you can construct confidence intervals completely absent a null hypothesis, but you simply cannot do NHSST without a null hypothesis (Thompson, 2001).

The confusion may arise because asking whether a CI, constructed at a confidence level $1.0 - \alpha$, does or does not subsume a given parameter does always yield an outcome equivalent to either rejecting or not rejecting the related null hypothesis. For example, if we have $M_{IQ} = 104.27$ ($SD_{IQ} = 15.0$) of $n = 50$ left-handed people, the SE_M is 2.12. In a two-tailed, nondirectional test of whether 104.27 equals an IQ of 100, $t_{CALCULATED}$ is 2.012.

In other words, our sample M is 2.012 standard errors distant from 100. The $t_{CRITICAL}$ value at $\alpha = 0.05$ is 2.0090. The $p_{CALCULATED}$ is 0.0496. We reject H_0: $\mu = 100$. The corresponding 95% confidence interval is [100.0, 108.5]. Note that the lower boundary of the 95% CI is near our hypothesized value, just as $TS_{CALCULATED}$ and $TS_{CRITICAL}$ are close. Both sets of results show that the sample M is at the boundary of a result leading to a decision to reject H_0 at $\alpha = 0.05$.

But the thoughtful interpretation of CIs usually does *not* involve evaluating whether a given interval subsumes an hypothesized parameter. Instead, the most thoughtful use of CIs bases interpretation upon comparison of CIs for parameter estimates *across studies*. The beauty of such integrative comparisons is that by comparing CIs across studies (*not* by evaluating CIs by whether they subsume an hypothesized expectation) we will eventually discover the true parameter, even if our initial expectations are wildly wrong (Schmidt, 1996)!

Third, some researchers interpret a CI in a given study as if they were X% certain that *their particular single* interval captured the population parameter. But the certainty level involved in constructing a given sample CI applies to the construction of *infinitely many* CIs drawn from a population, and not to the *single* CI constructed in a single sample.

Figure 7.1 illustrates what CIs do, and what CIs do *not* do. Figure 7.1 was created using one of the many modules in the Exploratory Software for Confidence Intervals (ESCI) developed by Geoff Cumming (see Cumming & Finch, 2001, 2005).

For the present example, a population of normally-distributed scores, with $\mu = 50.0$ and $\sigma = 10.0$, has been created. This population is portrayed in the topmost portion of Figure 7.1

Samples of $n = 15$ are randomly drawn from the population. "Randomly drawn" means that in a given draw all the remaining, undrawn cases in the population are equally likely to be selected. However, as noted in Chapter 3, random sampling does *not* mean that every possible score in a normally-distributed population is equally likely to be drawn.

The first set of 15 scores is represented by small circles at the top of the "Successive samples" section of Figure 7.1. Note that in this sample, 1 score of roughly 50 was drawn, as well as 1 extreme score of almost 78.

The 95% CI for the mean is presented immediately below the 15 circles representing the scores in the first sample. The M_X for the first sample was roughly 56. The 95% CI for the statistic mean of ~56 for the first sample ranged from just below 50 to ~62.

The bottom portion of Figure 7.1 presents 25 95% CIs for the mean. Notice that the sample means bounce around a fair amount. This merely reflects the expected influences of sampling error variance. The SE_M would be smaller if (a) n was larger, or (b) σ (i.e., the population score standard deviation) was smaller. Indeed, if σ was zero, the SE_M would be zero at every sample size!

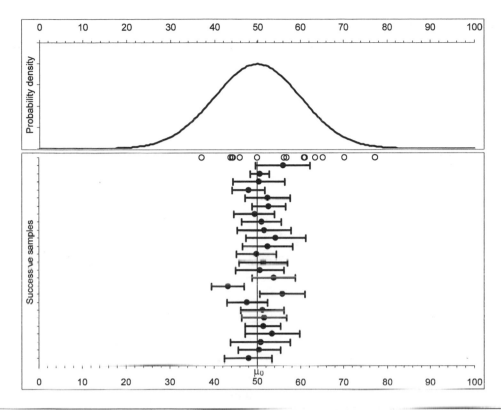

FIGURE 7.1. Twenty-five randomly drawn 95% CIs for M when μ = 50.0 and σ = 10.0

Of course, each of the 25 sample means is associated with an independent, randomly drawn sample. The implication is that each of the portrayed samples is *equally likely*. And the major take-home message is that we cannot vest too much confidence in a sample point estimate when *SE* is large. A large *SE* implies instability in statistic estimates across repeated sampling. So, the message is "Don't fall in love with your point estimate," at least when *SE* is large.

Confidence intervals provide information about the point estimate *and* the *SE*, and thus about the precision of the estimate. Wider CIs imply less precise estimates.

Note that the Figure 7.1 CIs vary in width, even though all 25 sample sizes were *n* = 15, and all the intervals were constructed at the 95% confidence level. This is because the *SD*s differed across the 25 samples. If we had known that $\sigma = 10.0$, but somehow still did not know μ, we could have drawn CIs to estimate μ, and at fixed n, fixed and known σ, and a fixed confidence level, the CIs would have been identical in length. In practice, when we are estimating μ, we rarely presume at the same time that somehow we know σ.

In Figure 7.1, two of the 95% CIs for the M do not capture μ, which in the present heuristic example is known to be 50.0. These are the 16th and the 17th intervals in Figure 7.1. Of course, in real research, we will *never* know that our sample CI does not capture a parameter. Indeed, the estimated precision for the 16th CI is fairly narrow. For this sample result, we might fall in love with our statistic $M = \sim43$, especially given the relatively narrow width of the 95% CI. But our love would be misplaced.

If we drew a huge or infinite number of random samples from the population portrayed in Figure 7.1, and constructed 95% CIs for the parameter estimate (e.g., M, SD, coefficient of kurtosis), exactly 95% of the intervals would capture the true parameter, and exactly 5% of the intervals would fail to capture the parameter. In other words, when we construct a confidence interval, the confidence level statement applies, *not* to a single interval, but to infinitely many intervals. As Thompson (in press) emphasized, never forget that $1 \neq \infty$. In the words of Good and Hardin (2003), "It is not true that the probability that a parameter is included in a [single] 95% confidence interval is 95%" (p. 101).

Thus CIs cannot magically tell us what the parameter we are estimating is. Nevertheless, CIs communicate both the point estimate, and information about the precision of the estimate. And CIs have the wonderful feature that sets of CIs for a literature can readily be presented in a single picture. As has been intimated elsewhere (Wilkinson & APA Task Force, 1999), a picture may be worth a thousand p values. Such graphics can be easily constructed with the Excel CHART WIZARD and by inputting CI lower and upper bounds, as well as the point estimates from a series of studies, as STOCK wizard option low, high, and close values.

Modern software painlessly computes CIs for various statistics, or provides the relevant SEs. Some very good books that flesh out related concepts have been provided by Altman, Machin, Bryant, and Gardner (2000) and Smithson (2000, 2002). The recent article by Cumming and Finch (2005) provided useful, practical suggestions. As Good and Hardin (2003) explained,

Point estimates are seldom satisfactory in and of themselves. First, if the observations are continuous, the probability is zero [actually infinitesimally small] that a point estimate will be correct and equal the estimated parameter. Second, we still require some estimate of the precision of the point estimate. (p. 45)

▨▨▨ Confidence Intervals for Effect Sizes

If effect sizes are essential, and confidence intervals are "the best" reporting strategy, then the marriage of CIs and effect sizes seems appealing. However, some technical difficulties confront this proposal.

Formulas are available for computing (a) the commonly-used statistics discussed in this book, (b) standard errors for these statistics, and (c) confidence intervals for these statistics. But a formula cannot be used to compute the CI for an effect size.

The problem with computing a confidence interval for an effect size is that, unlike CIs for statistics, even for a fixed n the widths of the CIs for an effect size are different for different values of the effect. In essence, a different formula for computing an effect CI has to be used for each of the infinitely many values of the effect size (see Cumming & Finch, 2001).

Nevertheless, CIs for effect sizes may still be computed, but the process does not involve execution of a formula. Instead, a computer intensive statistical process called iteration must be used. As conventionally performed, **iteration** involves a process of initially guessing a solution, and then repetitively tweaking the guess until some statistical criterion is reached.

Here the logic of iterative estimate of the CI for an effect size is briefly described. For more detail, the reader is referred to Cumming and Finch (2001) and the excellent book by Kline (2004).

In the case of a two-tailed CI, there is a sampling or a test distribution that is associated with each end of the interval. When we construct an interval at a given confidence level, $1 - \alpha$, for the test statistic distribution for the *left* side of the CI, we want $\alpha / 2\%$ (e.g., $5\% / 2 = 2.5\%$) of area in the test statistic distribution to be to the *right* of the point estimate (e.g., the computed M, the computed d). Conversely, for the test statistic distribution for the *right* side of the CI, we want $\alpha / 2\%$ (e.g., $5\% / 2 = 2.5\%$)

of area in the test statistic distribution to be to the *left* of the point estimate (e.g., the computed *M*, the computed *d*).

For CIs for *statistics*, this outcome can be easily accomplished by
invoking the appropriate computational formula, because only one test
statistic distribution, one assuming the nil null is true, is always used to
identify both endpoints of the confidence interval. But because there are
infinitely many possible test statistic distributions for effect sizes, which
vary in shape for each different effect size, CIs for *effect sizes* must be
iteratively estimated.

The test statistic distributions used in estimating CIs (and also for
computing power or β) for nonzero effect sizes are **noncentral** distributions. These are *not* the *central* test statistic distributions discussed in
Chapter 6, which assume a zero effect size, which is the required assumption when testing nil null hypotheses. When people say "test statistic,"
they are talking about the central test statistics discussed in Chapter 6,
unless they explicitly say "noncentral."

To compute a CI for an effect size, an initial guess is made about the
appropriate noncentral test statistic (see Cumming & Finch, 2001, or
Smithson, 2001) for the left arm of the CI. Then the computer tweaks the
selection of the test statistic distribution, associated with different nonzero
effect sizes, until $\alpha / 2$ of the area in the rightmost part of the distribution is
just to the right of the calculated effect. Then the same process is followed independently for the rightmost arm of the effect size CI, or vice versa.

Various computer programs are readily available for iteratively, pain-
lessly estimating the CIs for effect sizes. Some run stand-alone (Steiger &
Fouladi, 1992), or under SPSS or SAS (Algina & Keselman, 2003; Algina,
Keselman, & Penfield, 2005; Smithson, 2001), or Excel (Cumming &
Finch, 2001).

Table 7.2 presents a hypothetical literature consisting of 10 studies,
and the related Cohen's *d* and $p_{CALCULATED}$ values. Nine of the 10 original
studies and the new 11th study were created to honor Rosnow and
Rosenthal's (1989b) view that "surely, God loves the .06 [level of statistical significance] nearly as much as the .05" (p. 1277).

In a literature prejudiced against statistically nonsignificant results,
the first study with an anomalous negative effect size ($d = -0.50$;
$p_{CALCULATED} = 0.043$) will be afforded priority for publication. The remaining studies with positive values for *d*, but *p* is approximately 0.06, may
never see the light of the publication day.

TABLE 7.2. Integration of *d* across 11 Hypothetical Studies

Study	*d*	*n*	$t_{CALCULATED}$	$p_{CALCULATED}$
		Previous research		
1	−0.50	19	−2.18	0.043
2	0.25	60	1.94	0.058
3	0.50	17	2.06	0.056
4	1.00	6	2.45	0.058
5	0.75	9	2.25	0.055
6	0.30	43	1.97	0.056
7	0.85	7	2.25	0.066
8	0.20	90	1.90	0.061
9	0.57	13	2.06	0.062
10	0.45	19	1.96	0.065
		Pooled weighted (by *n*) average		
	0.281	283	4.73	<.001
		Current study		
11	0.28	45	1.88	0.067
		Revised weighted average		
	0.281	328	5.09	<.001

These dynamics are troubling. If 1,000 researchers all drew random samples from a population exactly described by the nil null, and in each of the 1,000 independent studies α = 0.05, exactly 50 studies should obtain statistically significant results. These Type I errors will be afforded publication priority. But subsequently, any researchers replicating the 50 published studies, each involving Type I errors, will have difficulty publishing their failures to replicate statistical significance. In this manner the self-correcting features of science may be compromised by the bias against statistically nonsignificant results. Greenwald (1975, pp. 13–15) cited real-world examples of these dynamics.

Figure 7.2 graphically presents the CIs for the Cohen's *d* values from the 11 studies. The figure also portrays the weighted (by *n*) averages for effects across the studies, and the related CIs. (In real meta-analytic integrations of effect sizes, more sophisticated forms of weighted averages are actually used.)

The figure illustrates how a literature can be summarized in a picture.

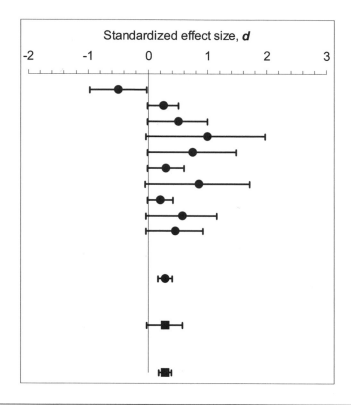

FIGURE 7.2. Plot of 95% confidence intervals for d values

Even a relatively large literature could be summarized economically. Pictures such as Figure 7.2 make clear the patterns of effects across related studies. More importantly, such pictures also convey the precisions of studies.

Pictures such as Figure 7.2 are too rarely seen today. Such pictures might lead to disturbing conclusions about the precisions of various literatures on which we depend for evidence-based practices (Odom, Brantlinger, Gersten, Horner, & Thompson, 2005).

Some Key Concepts

Effect sizes should *not* be interpreted using fixed benchmarks or ignoring the context of the study. Instead, effects should be interpreted by invoking personal value judgments informed by "meta-analytic thinking" and the direct, explicit comparison of effects across related studies (Thompson, 2002b, in press). Effect sizes must be interpreted considering the study's context. Small effects for critically important outcomes, given evidence of replicability, may nevertheless be quite noteworthy (Breaugh, 2003).

Confidence intervals have great power to support the explication of the story that data have to tell. Intervals inform judgment about the precision of point estimates. And experience in using CIs will also teach you the very powerful lesson that "apparently inconsistent results in the literature may be revealed later by the use of a confidence interval for each study to be more consistent than traditional analyses originally seemed to indicate" (Grissom & Kim, 2005, p. 24).

▓ ▓ ▓ Reflection Problems ▓ ▓ ▓

1. The r^{2*} / R^{2*} correction can be used either retrospectively or prospectively. Retrospectively, once we complete a study, we know all three elements of the correction with certainty, including the actual r^2 / R^2. We can then adjust our final effect size using these elements.

    Prospectively, before we conduct our study, but once we know our intended sample size and number of predictor variables, a useful exercise is to compute the expected sample r^2 / R^2 under an assumption that the population parameter r^2 / R^2 is zero. The expected sample r^2 / R^2 is not zero. Program the following spreadsheet.

	A	B	C	D	E	F	G
1			'= R sq				
2			'= n predictors				
3			'= n				
4							
5	R sq	1	R sq	Vars	n	Vars	1
6	+a1	1	+a6	+a2	+a3	+d6	1
7	+a6		+b6-c6	+d6	+e6	+f6	+g6
8	+a7		+c7	+d7	+e7-f7-g7		
9	+a8		+c8	+d8/e8			
10	+a9		+c9*d9	'= Shrinkage %			
11	+a10-c10		'= Adj R sq (i.e., R sq - shrinkage)				

The output for $r^2 = 90.0\%$, $n = 10$, and one predictor variable will yield these results.

```
       A     B  C                D      E      F       G
1      0.9  = R sq
2         1  = n predictors
3        10  = n
4
5  R sq      1  R sq      Vars       n        Vars    1
6   90.00%  1   0.9000          1       10       1   1
7   90.00%      0.1000          1       10       1   1
8   90.00%      0.1000          1        8
9   90.00%      0.1000    0.125
10  90.00%         1.250%  = Shrinkage %
11  88.75%      = Adj R sq (i.e., R sq - shrinkage)
```

Under an assumption that the population parameter r^2 is zero, solve for $r^{2*} = 0$ by varying the input values of r^2 and declaring use of only a single predictor variable for the bivariate problem. The final r^2 isolated in this manner for a given design is the expected sample r^2 for the design under our assumption, and will *not* be zero, notwithstanding our assumption. Find the expected sample r^2 for (a) $n = 15$, (b) $n = 50$, and (c) $n = 500$, under an assumption that the population value is zero.

2. Of course, the standardized difference effect sizes are biased by sampling error, just as other effect sizes are impacted by these same dynamics. Thus, Hedges (1981; Hedges & Olkin, 1985) proposed a correction factor for Glass' Δ. The "adjusted Δ" can be computed by multiplying the original value by the correction factor:

$$1 - (3/((4 * (n_c - 1))-1))$$

where n_c is the sample size in the control group. For example, for $n_c = 10$, the correction factor is the multiplicative constant of 0.91428. Use a spreadsheet to compute the correction factor for $n_c = 5$, 10, 20, 30, and 40. What does the result suggest about the bias of Δ?

3. Classical effect sizes are "on the average." Grissom (1994; Grissom & Kim, 2005) proposed the intriguing alternative idea of a probability of superiority (*PS*) effect size that is not on the average, and is computed by

making all possible pairwise comparisons of scores across the treatment and control groups to evaluate which treatment is likely to help the greater number of people. With no or few ties, this computation can be vastly expedited by invoking the Mann–Whitney U in SPSS, and then dividing U by $n_{TREATMENT}(n_{CONTROL})$.

Consider the following data.

Case	DV	GRP
1	1	0
2	3	0
3	5	0
4	7	0
5	2	1
6	4	1
7	6	1
8	8	1

For these data, 2 > 1; 4 > 1, 4 > 3; 6 > 1, 6 > 3, 6 > 5; and 8 > 1, 8 > 3, 8 > 5, 8 > 7, for a total of 10 occasions in which group 1 scores are larger than group 0 scores. There are $4 \times 4 = 16$ score comparisons, so $PS_{10} = 10 / (4)(4) = 0.625$. SPSS returns a value of 6.0 for the Mann–Whitney U. Dividing U by $n_{TREATMENT} \times (n_{CONTROL})$ yields 6.0 / (4)(4) – 0.375. This is the proportion of scores in the group with overall lower scores (i.e., group 0), so $PS_{10} = 1 - 0.375 = 0.625$. Confirm these or similar analyses using SPSS.

Multiple Regression Analysis

Basic GLM Concepts

The initial chapters in this book considered situations in which you wish to characterize features of a single variable. Univariate statistics characterize features of a single variable as regards (a) location, (b) dispersion, or (c) shape.

Of course, quantitative science focuses on relationships that recur under stated conditions. So real science at a minimum requires the measurement of at least two variables, sometimes conceptualized as a dependent (or criterion or outcome) variable, and at least one independent (or predictor) variable. And in science, the analytic focus is directed specifically at the relationship between these two variables. The bivariate statistics that can be used to quantify these relationships include the Pearson product–moment r (or alternatively r^2), Spearman's ρ (or alternatively Spearman's ρ^2), and the ϕ coefficient (or alternatively ϕ^2).

However, a fundamental premise of statistics is that each researcher presumes some (conceivably implicit) model of reality. Furthermore, every statistical analysis tests the fit of a model to data. Consequently, a critical imperative of social science research is that we ought to *insure the fit of our analytic model with our model of reality*. Otherwise we are using our analyses to investigate something other than the reality that we believe exists, which is not sensible!

Our model of reality may posit that the outcome variables of interest to us are multiply caused, or require multiple predictors to attain reasonable predictive accuracy. Given this model of reality, we may well use univariate statistics, or even bivariate statistics, to understand and describe our variables. But the primary analysis used to address our main research questions usually must be able to accommodate multiple predictor variables (and, indeed, sometimes multiple criterion variables).

Multiple regression analysis is a statistical technique that can be used to investigate relationships between a single outcome variable and two or more predictor variables. Multiple regression is a univariate statistical analysis in the second meaning of the word "univariate" (i.e., analyses involving only one outcome variable). Regression is one of many analyses that can be conducted when only one outcome variable is of interest.

Multiple regression analysis is often of practical value because the analysis can yield important insights into data dynamics. But regression is just as important from a heuristic point of view, because regression is the univariate case of the parametric general linear model (GLM). That is, regression (but not vice versa) can be used to conduct the commonly-used univariate statistical analyses.

As Cohen (1968) argued in a seminal article years ago, scholars who understand regression understand how the various univariate methods are part of a single general linear model, what all univariate statistical analyses have in common, and what features differentiate the analyses. All statistical analyses (a) are correlational, (b) either explicitly or implicitly compute weights that are applied to measured (or observed) variables to estimate scores on latent variables (also called synthetic or composite variables), and (c) yield variance-accounted-for effect sizes analogous to r^2.

Indeed, there is a broader version of the univariate GLM. Multivariate analyses (e.g., MANOVA, descriptive discriminant analysis, canonical correlation analysis) simultaneously consider two or more outcome variables and one or more predictor variables. Knapp (1978) and others (e.g., Thompson, 1991a, 2000a) have explained that canonical correlation analysis is the multivariate general linear model. And there is an even larger GLM umbrella called structural equation modeling (SEM; Bagozzi, Fornell, & Larcker, 1981).

The existence of the multivariate GLM is noteworthy here, because once someone has truly mastered interpretation of results for the regression case, one has all the requisite skills for interpreting multivariate results. Mastering univariate GLM concepts is like being in Oz with ruby slippers. You can easily branch out to Kansas or multivariate statistics whenever a good witch (or nice scholar) explains that you now have powers beyond those that may at first glance be obvious.

Purposes of Regression

Regression can be used for two purposes: prediction and explanation (i.e., theory testing). Of course, these purposes are not mutually exclusive. When in real life we do prediction, even when the prediction is very accurate, we probably would feel more comfortable if we understood why the prediction worked so well. Conversely, when we test theory, although our initial purpose may be basic science (i.e., knowledge for its own sake), we do usually presume that our insight will ultimately have some practical use of some sort. However, in both cases (and throughout the general linear model), the dependent variable is the focus of all analyses.

Focal Role of Dependent Variables

In science, dependent variables are the foci of our thinking, and of all analyses. Scientists identify dependent variables that are important to them, or to society. After making the necessary value judgment that given outcomes are important, *only then* will independent variables be selected. We use theory, or previous research, or both to inform the selection of those independent variables that we believe causally control, or predict, or explain the dependent variables upon which we have decided to direct our attention.

Scholars are systematic in the selection of these independent variables. True, very important insights can be discovered through happenstance. For example, Fleming discovered penicillin when some mold apparently came in through an open basement window, landed on some Petri dishes, and killed some of the bacteria growing there. The happenstance was particularly fortuitous because this happened just before World War II, when penicillin was especially needed in treating very large numbers of wound-related infections. But real science is more than the capitalization on fortuitous discoveries.

By the same token, in science we do not typically select possible causal variables and then ask what outcomes these variables might produce. We do not usually mix chemicals in various random ways in the hope that something important may eventually occur. Instead, we presume that the most productive progress in generating knowledge occurs when we first select outcomes that we value, and then systematically identify promising potential predictor variables.

Prediction

Prediction of important outcomes can be valuable, even when we have no understanding as to why the prediction works. For example, long ago in England smallpox epidemics were killing large proportions of the populace. Jenner discovered that milkmaids died infrequently from smallpox, and subsequently realized that cows get a disease like smallpox in appearance, but that is rarely fatal. Jenner reasoned that the milkmaids also got smallpox from their cows, which somehow inoculated the milkmaids against subsequent smallpox infection. His informal experiment, in which he applied cowpox puss only to selected friends, yielded the confirmation of a causal mechanism, although his social circle was somewhat more constricted following his research!

In predictive applications of regression, the existence of two groups of participants is always implied. We have an outcome that we want to predict in our second group of participants (e.g., the grade point averages of doctoral students upon their graduation) that has not yet occurred. Perhaps we wish to use these predicted outcome scores of the applicants to make admission decisions.

We also have our first group of participants. For these participants (e.g., doctoral students who graduated at the university during the previous 3 years), we know the scores on the outcome variable of interest. We also have available for this group scores on a range of predictor variables that might predict graduate grade averages. We conduct the regression analysis within group 1.

Iff the prediction works reasonably well in group 1, we then may consider using the same predictor variables in group 2. We also will apply the weights generated in group 1 to the predictor variable scores in group 2. The role of these weights is to optimize the accuracy of the prediction.

This use of group 1's weights with group 2's predictor variables turns on the fundamentally important assumption that the two groups of students are reasonably similar. This assumption might not be tenable, for example, if the two student groups were measured at disparate times, or at two very different universities, or if the academic majors of the two groups were very different.

Explanation

Sometimes basic science is conducted simply for the joy of knowing, without any expectation of an immediate application of the new knowledge. For example, when we practice science to discover the age of the universe, or its origins, we have little expectation of some immediate use for our new insights.

Kerlinger (1977) argued that sometimes theories deemed potentially useless at their origination prove in the long term to have greater application than even the findings from some applied or predictive research, and "science, then, really has no other purpose than theory" (p. 5). For example, in the 1930s, three scientists working at Bell Laboratories— funded by the then monopoly of the national telephone system—passed an electrical current through a silicone crystal structure and observed a change in features of the current. They did not envision the hugely important applications of their discovery in the form of transistors and, later, computer chips. Similarly, in 1905, when Einstein published a series of papers presenting his relativity theory, that objects moving faster experience time more slowly, and his theory that energy and matter are interchangeable, he did not envision that only a few decades later he would type a letter to Franklin Roosevelt to inform the President of the potential use of theory to guide the creation of an atomic bomb.

▪▪▪ Simple Linear Prediction

Ultimately, we will consider three multiple regression situations: (a) uncorrelated predictor variables, (b) correlated predictor variables, and (c) correlated predictor variables involving suppression effects. However, first we will spend considerable time elaborating **simple regression** (i.e., regression involving only a single predictor variable). Although not true multiple regression, this simple situation will facilitate laying the groundwork for consideration of the more complicated (and realistic cases) involving two or more predictor variables.

It might be noted that the situation involving a single predictor is a special case (i.e., a subset) of situation #1, because when only a single predictor is involved, there is no correlation between variables within the predictor variable set. Thus, many of the conclusions about simple linear regression, involving a single predictor, will generalize to the multiple regression situation involving multiple predictor variables that are perfectly uncorrelated with each other.

Table 8.1 presents the hypothetical data for 20 participants that will be employed to make this discussion more concrete. The interested reader can readily reproduce or further explore the results presented in this chapter for these data by analyzing the data using SPSS or another statistical package.

Form of the Regression Equation

As an example of simple linear regression, one might wish to predict the height of adults (Y_i) using information about their heights at 2 years of age (X_i). Or, alternatively, we might wish to predict the height of adults (Y_i) using information about the participants' IQ scores measured at age 6 (X_i).

Regression analysis employs two types of weights: an additive constant, a, applied to every individual ith participant, and a multiplicative constant, b, applied to the predictor variable for each individual ith participant. We do *not* use i subscripts for these constants, because their values do not change across individual participants. Thus, the weighting system takes the form of a regression equation:

$$Y_i \longleftarrow \hat{Y}_i = a + b\,(X_i)$$

TABLE 8.1. Heuristic Data for Three Regression Situations

ID/statistic	Y	X1	X2	X3	X4	X5	X6	X7
				Predictor variables				
1	49.553	48.473	51.610	49.338	49.162	49.718	49.488	50.240
2	50.094	48.812	50.537	51.545	50.576	49.640	49.925	51.286
3	50.799	49.152	49.732	49.890	50.386	49.662	49.889	50.641
4	50.778	49.491	49.195	48.786	49.646	50.297	51.399	51.116
5	50.296	49.830	48.927	49.338	50.579	49.924	49.732	49.904
6	51.420	50.170	48.927	50.662	50.598	50.704	50.303	50.223
7	49.582	50.509	49.195	51.214	48.595	49.350	48.549	49.095
8	50.345	50.848	49.732	50.110	49.087	51.979	49.566	48.004
9	49.988	51.188	50.537	48.455	50.386	48.923	49.148	51.652
10	50.860	51.527	51.610	50.662	50.806	50.068	49.481	49.781
11	49.753	50.170	48.927	50.662	49.768	51.384	49.325	48.400
12	50.491	50.509	49.195	51.214	51.681	49.026	50.357	49.841
13	48.415	50.848	49.732	50.110	48.873	49.657	50.294	49.378
14	49.474	51.188	50.537	48.455	51.746	48.945	51.679	50.997
15	49.506	51.527	51.610	50.662	49.755	50.467	50.510	50.224
16	47.166	48.473	51.610	49.338	48.393	49.058	47.365	49.210
17	50.480	48.812	50.537	51.545	50.857	48.217	50.556	51.488
18	51.158	49.152	49.732	49.890	50.760	50.537	50.344	49.275
19	49.067	49.491	49.195	48.786	49.834	50.541	51.022	50.030
20	50.778	49.830	48.927	49.338	48.512	51.904	51.070	49.216
M	50.000	50.000	50.000	50.000	50.000	50.000	50.000	50.000
SD	1.000	1.000	1.000	1.000	1.000	1.000	1.000	1.000

The **regression equation** is the set of weights generated in a given analysis.

Just to keep people on their toes by creating potential confusion, the b weights are also sometimes synonymously referred to as **unstandardized regression weights**. This label is especially confusing, because a constant cannot be standardized. The intent presumably is to refer to "weights applied to measured variables in their unstandardized form."

For example, it is known that the following system of weights works reasonably well in predicting height at age 21 from height at age 2:

$$Y_i \longleftarrow \hat{Y}_i = 0.0 + 2.0 \, (X_i)$$

Thus, an individual such as Kelly, who is $X_{KELLY} = 27''$ tall at age 2, is predicted to have a height of $\hat{Y}_{KELLY} = 54''$ ($0.0 + 2.0 \times 27 = 0.0 + 54.0 = 54.0$) at age 21.

We can also compute a fourth score in regression. If Kelly's actual height at age 21 is $Y_{KELLY} = 60''$, we can compute an "error" score as the deviation between Kelly's actual height (i.e., $Y_{KELLY} = 60''$) and Kelly's predicted height (i.e., $\hat{Y}_{KELLY} = 54''$). Because $e_i = Y_i - \hat{Y}_i$, for Kelly we have $e_{KELLY} = 6$ (i.e., $60 - 54$). Any individual whose actual Y_i score is perfectly predicted has $e_i = 0.0$, and iff all participants' Y_i scores are perfectly predicted, all the e_i scores will be zero.

The regression problem can also be conceptualized using a scattergram plot. The line of best fit to the data points is the graphical representation of the regression equation (i.e., the regression line actually is the regression equation, and vice versa). The a weight is the point on the vertical Y axis at which the regression line crosses the Y axis when X is 0; this is called the intercept. The b weight is the slope (i.e., change in rise/change in run) of the regression line (e.g., the line changes in b units of Y for every change of 1 unit of X, 2 times b units of Y for every 2 units of change in X, etc.).

Two Types of Variables

A foundational concept in statistics is the fact that all analyses involve at least two each of two kinds of variables: **measured** and **latent**. In the present example, both height at age 2 and height at age 21 are measured (or observed) variables. These are directly measured, without invoking any weights. But the $\hat{Y}_i$ and the e_i scores are latent (or synthetic or composite) variables.

In actuality, the latent variables are the focus of statistical analysis. These are the variables that represent estimated scores on unobservable theoretical constructs. And the latent variable $\hat{Y}_i$ (a) encapsulates all the useful predictive variability in the predictors and (b) discards all the useless (nonpredictive) variability in all the predictors. For this reason, the r of Y_i with $\hat{Y}_i$ always equals the r of Y_i with X_i (and the r^2 of Y_i with $\hat{Y}_i$ always equals the r^2 of Y_i with X_i).

Function of the Weights

The function of the weights is to make the Y_i and the $\hat{Y}_i$ scores of a given ith individual match as closely as possible, given the predictive power of a given X_i. We can think of a range of possibilities, running from perfect prediction (i.e., every $Y_i = \hat{Y}_i$ for each ith individual, and every $e_i = 0.0$) to prediction involving a useless predictor.

Let's consider the worst-case scenario first, and then compare these dynamics to those occurring in a best-case scenario. Of course, in actual research we invariably find ourselves somewhere along this continuum of outcomes, rather than at one of the two conceptual extremes.

Worst Case

In a worst-case scenario, we have access only to useless predictors. For example, let's assume we are predicting the height of adults (Y_i) using information about their IQ scores measured at age 6 (X_i), and the predictive information is completely useless.

In a best-case scenario, every $Y_i = \hat{Y}_i$ for each ith individual, and every $e_i = 0.0$. In the best-case scenario, because every $Y_i = \hat{Y}_i$, every statistic (e.g., M, Mdn, SOS, SD, coefficient of skewness) computed for Y exactly equals the corresponding statistic (e.g., M, Mdn, SOS, SD, coefficient of skewness) computed for $\hat{Y}_i$, because in fact in this extreme scenario the two variables have exactly the same data.

But even in a worst-case scenario, we use our weights to optimize the fit of $\hat{Y}_i$ to Y_i. What, if anything, can our weights accomplish in the unfavorable situation of a worst case prediction?

In a worst-case scenario, we will want to obliterate our useless predictor variable. Use of a b weight of zero will accomplish this objective quite nicely. When $b = 0.0$, X_i can have no impact on the estimation of Y_i, as quite rightly should be the case. Multiplication by 0.0 kills, and so multiplication of X_i by $b = 0.0$ kills the useless predictor.

So now the job of optimizing the fit of $\hat{Y}_i$ to Y_i falls solely to the a weight. Our expectation is not that the weights always do a perfect job of optimizing fit. Instead, our expectation is that the weights must optimize the fit $\hat{Y}_i$ to Y_i *within the limits of our data.*

We may not be able to do a very good job of optimizing this fit within a worst-case scenario, but what is the best we can do? Remember from Chapter 2 that the mean has the property that the sum of the deviation scores from M is always zero. The implication is that in a worst-case predictive scenario the best (not good, just best) prediction we can accomplish is to set every $\hat{Y}_i$ to equal M_Y.

In a worst-case scenario, because $b = 0.0$, we can set every $\hat{Y}_i$ equal to M_Y by setting $a = M_Y$. Doing so will optimize the fit of $\hat{Y}_i$ to Y_i, because the e_i scores will be minimized, just as M minimizes the sum of the deviation scores.

In a worst-case scenario, Y_i, X_i, and e_i will be variables (two measured, one latent), but the $\hat{Y}_i$ will be a constant (each equaling M_Y). There will be only three variables, not four.

Notice that even in a worst-case scenario the mean of the $\hat{Y}_i$ scores will equal M_Y. Of course, at the other extreme of best case, perfect prediction, the mean of the $\hat{Y}_i$ scores would also equal M_Y because these two variables would involve identical data. The implication is that the a and b weights can make the means of the Y_i and the $\hat{Y}_i$ scores equal *throughout every situation, ranging from worst-case to best-case scenario.*

Ideally, we would also like the dispersion of the Y_i and the $\hat{Y}_i$ scores to be equal. However, in the worst-case scenario, the $\hat{Y}_i$ scores have their minimum possible dispersion—such that range, *SOS*, variance, and *SD* all equal zero—because the $\hat{Y}_i$ scores in a worst-case scenario are all equal to M_Y, and define a constant.

Best Case

In the best-case scenario, every $Y_i = \hat{Y}_i$ for each ith individual, and every $e_i = 0.0$. So, in the best-case scenario, Y_i, X_i, and $\hat{Y}_i$ are variables (two measured and one latent), but the e_i scores are a constant. In all other situations, regression involves at least two measured variables and exactly two latent variables.

Of course, in the best-case scenario, as in *every* possible scenario, the mean of the $\hat{Y}_i$ scores equals M_Y. But in the best-case scenario, because the data for the Y_i and the $\hat{Y}_i$ scores are identical, the *SOS*s of the Y_i and the $\hat{Y}_i$ scores are also now equal. And because the ns for the two variables are equal, the variances and the *SD*s of the Y_i and the $\hat{Y}_i$ scores are also equal.

Indeed, the dispersion of the $\hat{Y}_i$ scores can *never* exceed the dispersion of the Y_i scores. If the SOS_Y scores equals 22.2, even before conducting any analyses, we know that the dispersion of the $\hat{Y}_i$ scores cannot be less than zero (ever) and that for our data the SOS of the $\hat{Y}_i$ scores cannot exceed 22.2 (and will only equal 22.2 in a best-case scenario).

Of course, as we learned in the Reflection Problems for Chapters 2 and 3, additive weights applied to variables do not affect dispersion. But multiplicative weights affect both the dispersion of variables (unless the multiplicative constants are –1 or 1) and the location of variables (unless the original mean is zero or the multiplicative constant is 1). Thus, in a best-case scenario, the function of the b weight is to make the dispersions of the Y_i and the $\hat{Y}_i$ scores equal, while the a and the b weights together make the means of the Y_i and the $\hat{Y}_i$ scores equal.

Computation of the Regression Weights

The previously described form of the regression equation presumed that we were working in the unstandardized score world. An alternative form of the prediction equation involves first converting both variables into z-score form (i.e., scores transformed to have a mean of 0.0 and an SD of 1.0 via the algorithm $z_i = (X_i - M_X) / SD_X$) and working instead in the standardized score world.

When all the variables are in z-score form, the a weight is still present, but is always zero. Therefore, the regression equation for standardized measured variables simplifies to the form

$$Z_Y \longleftarrow \hat{Y} = +\beta(Z_X)$$

Note that the multiplicative weight for this situation is always distinguished from the multiplicative weight for the nonstandardized scores by referring to the weights for z scores as β weights (versus b weights).

Just to be confusing, the β weights are also sometimes labeled **standardized regression weights**. Unfortunately, this label is an oxymoron, because a constant cannot be standardized. What is intended is a reference to "weights applied to measured variables in their standardized forms."

Note that the a, b, and β weights are all in the score world, which is necessary for them to be applicable to the scores also located in this world. However, a and b are in the unstandardized score world, whereas the β weights are in the standardized score world.

It happens that for a two-variable regression problem, the β weight to predict z_Y with z_X is the bivariate correlation coefficient between the two variables (of course, so is the β weight to predict z_X with z_Y, because $r_{YX} = r_{XY}$).

The b and β weights can readily be transformed back and forth into each other with the equation

$$b = \beta(SD_Y / SD_X) \qquad (8.1)$$

or

$$\beta = b(SD_X / SD_Y) \qquad (8.2)$$

As the equations imply, b and β will be equal when (a) either is zero or (b) the two variables' standard deviations are equal. Of course, the equations also imply that b and β always have the same signs, because the SDs cannot be negative and so cannot influence the signs of the weights. And when two measured variables are uncorrelated, $r_{XY} = b = \beta = 0$.

In essence, as suggested by Equation 8.1, the b weight is computed to remove the standard deviation of X from $\hat{Y}$ via division, and attempts to insert the SD_Y via multiplication. We do this because we care only about the dependent variable. Any value for a predictor variable is derivative solely from the predictor's ability to predict or explain Y.

Table 8.2 presents the bivariate correlation matrix associated with the Table 8.1 heuristic data. Given these results, the equation for predicting z_Y with z_X would be

$$z_Y \longleftarrow \hat{Y}_i = +0.0878(z_X)$$

As noted in Chapter 5, it happens that regression lines (and the related planes or hyperplanes when there are three or four or more measured variables) always pass through the means of all the measured variables. Because the means of both Y and $X1$ for the Table 8.1 data are 50, the regression line pivots on the Cartesian coordinate where $M_Y = 50.0$ and $M_{X1} = 50.0$. Furthermore, because for these data both SD_Y and SD_X are equal, as reported in Table 8.1, for these data the b multiplicative weight also equals $\beta = +0.0878$.

And given the form of the prediction equation, $\hat{Y}_i = a + b(X_i)$—because

TABLE 8.2. Bivariate Correlation Matrix

| Variable | Y | Predictor variables | | | | | | |
		X1	X2	X3	X4	X5	X6	X7
Y	1.0000							
X1	0.0878	1.0000						
X2	−0.3795	0.0000	1.0000					
X3	0.2170	0.0000	0.0000	1.0000				
X4	0.4819	0.1757	−0.0053	0.1247	1.0000			
X5	0.2903	0.1426	−0.3929	−0.0795	−0.3758	1.0000		
X6	0.4392	0.1525	−0.3123	−0.1864	0.4213	0.1671	1.0000	
X7	0.1740	−0.1400	0.2691	−0.1437	0.5089	−0.6302	0.3542	1.0000

when $X_i = M_X$, then $\hat{Y}_i = M_Y$ (merely another way of saying the regression line pivots on the Cartesian coordinate of the two means)—we can solve for a as

$$a = \hat{Y}_i - b(X_i) \qquad (8.3)$$

or, equivalently, for the mean value of X, as

$$a = M_Y - b(M_X) \qquad (8.4)$$

Thus, here a equals

$$45.61 = 50.0 - 0.0878(50.0)$$

For these two variables in their standard score form, involving means of zero for both variables, and because here $\beta = b = +0.0878$, the a weight for the standardized variables would be

$$0 = 0.00 - 0.0878(0.00)$$

Indeed, for standardized variables, the a weight is *always* zero, as correctly suggested by this equation.

These various dynamics are illustrated in the Figure 8.1 plot of the

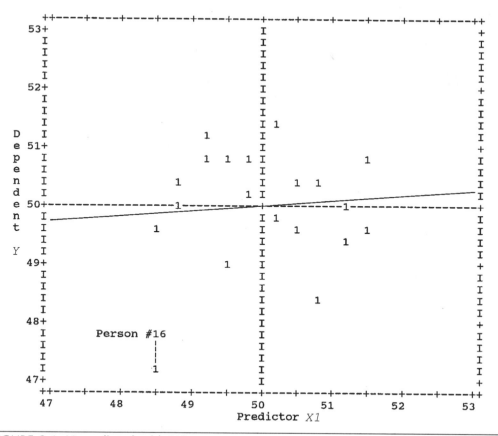

FIGURE 8.1. Y predicted with X1.

data and the regression line that best fits the data. Note that the regression line is relatively flat, because the correlation coefficient (and b and β, for these data) is nearly zero.

Table 8.3 presents related concepts from the perspective of the individual scores of the 20 participants. Because we select the regression equation to yield the best possible prediction of Y for the group as a whole, on the average, then it is no surprise that the mean e score is *always* zero. This is part of an operational definition of a "best-fit" position for the regression line.

The sum of squares of the $\hat{Y}$ scores (0.147, i.e., the explained dispersion or variability in Y) plus the sum of squares of the e scores (18.857,

TABLE 8.3. Observed and Synthetic Variable Scores Predicting Y with X1

| | Measured variables | | | | | | | Latent variables | | | | | | |
Case/statistic	Y	$-$	M_Y	$=$	y	y^2	$X1$	$\hat{Y}$	$-$	M	$=$	$\hat{y}$	$\hat{y}^2$	e	e^2
1	49.553		50.0		-0.449	0.201	48.473	49.866		50.0		-0.134	0.018	-0.313	0.098
2	50.094		50.0		0.093	0.009	48.812	49.896		50.0		-0.104	0.011	0.198	0.039
3	50.799		50.0		0.797	0.635	49.152	49.926		50.0		-0.074	0.006	0.873	0.763
4	50.778		50.0		0.776	0.603	49.491	49.955		50.0		-0.045	0.002	0.823	0.677
5	50.296		50.0		0.294	0.087	49.830	49.985		50.0		-0.015	0.000	0.311	0.097
6	51.420		50.0		1.419	2.012	50.170	50.015		50.0		0.015	0.000	1.405	1.974
7	49.582		50.0		-0.419	0.176	50.509	50.045		50.0		0.045	0.002	-0.463	0.214
8	50.345		50.0		0.343	0.118	50.848	50.075		50.0		0.074	0.006	0.270	0.073
9	49.988		50.0		-0.014	0.000	51.138	50.104		50.0		0.104	0.011	-0.116	0.014
10	50.860		50.0		0.858	0.737	51.527	50.134		50.0		0.134	0.018	0.726	0.527
11	49.753		50.0		-0.248	0.062	50.170	50.015		50.0		0.015	0.000	-0.262	0.069
12	50.491		50.0		0.489	0.240	50.509	50.045		50.0		0.045	0.002	0.446	0.199
13	48.415		50.0		-1.587	2.517	50.848	50.075		50.0		0.074	0.006	-1.660	2.754
14	49.474		50.0		-0.528	0.278	51.188	50.104		50.0		0.104	0.011	-0.630	0.398
15	49.506		50.0		-0.495	0.246	51.527	50.134		50.0		0.134	0.018	-0.628	0.395
16	47.166		50.0		-2.836	8.040	48.473	49.866		50.0		-0.134	0.018	-2.700	7.290
17	50.480		50.0		0.478	0.229	48.812	49.896		50.0		-0.104	0.011	0.584	0.341
18	51.158		50.0		1.157	1.337	49.152	49.926		50.0		-0.074	0.006	1.232	1.519
19	49.067		50.0		-0.935	0.873	49.491	49.955		50.0		-0.045	0.002	-0.888	0.789
20	50.778		50.0		0.776	0.603	49.830	49.985		50.0		-0.015	0.000	0.793	0.629
Total	1000.00					19.00	1000.00	1000.00					0.147	0.000	18.857
Mean	50.00						50.00	50.00						0.000	

229

i.e., the unexplained variability in Y) exactly (within rounding error) equals the sum of squares total ($SOS_Y = 19.000$). We can even look at the e scores to find the person who most deviates from the regression line (person #16). In Figure 8.1, the e scores are the distance, *always in vertical units of Y* (because Y is what we care about; the focus of the entire analysis is on Y units), of a given Y_i score from the $\hat{Y}$ regression line.

The sum of squares explained divided by the sum of squares of Y tells us the proportion of the variability of individual differences in Y that we can explain with the predictors. Therefore, for the simple linear regression situation,

$$r^2_{YX} = SOS_{\hat{Y}} / SOS_Y \qquad (8.5)$$

We are dividing an area-world statistic by another area-world statistic, thereby obtaining an area-world result.

In the multiple regression case, we can compute the squared multiple correlation coefficient in a corresponding manner, using the equation

$$R^2 = SOS_{\hat{Y}} / SOS_Y \qquad (8.6)$$

Conversely, given the r^2_{YX} (or the R^2), we can compute the SOS of the $\hat{Y}$ scores, called the $SOS_{\text{EXPLAINED}}$ (or, synonymously, the SOS_{MODEL}, $SOS_{\text{REGRESSION}}$, or SOS_{BETWEEN}), using the formula

$$SOS_{\text{EXPLAINED}} = r^2_{YX}(SOS_Y) \qquad (8.7)$$

for the simple linear regression situation, or

$$SOS_{\text{EXPLAINED}} = R^2 (SOS_Y) \qquad (8.8)$$

for the multiple regression situation.

Table 8.4 makes these and some other important points. As expected, the r of Y with $X1$ equals the r of Y and $\hat{Y}$, because $\hat{Y}$ is all the useful parts of any and all the predictors with all the useless parts of the predictors deleted.

It is also noteworthy that predictors and e_i scores always have r (and r^2) equal to zero. This only makes sense, because the error variability is the

TABLE 8.4. Correlation Coefficients
among Two Observed and Two Synthetic Variables

Variable	SPSS Variable Names			
	Y	$\hat{Y}$	e	$X1$
Y	1.0000	0.0878	0.9961	0.0878
$\hat{Y}$	0.0878	1.0000	0.0000	1.0000
e	0.9961	0.0000	1.0000	0.0000
$X1$	0.0878	1.0000	0.0000	1.0000

Note. $r_{Y \times X} = r$ of Y with $\hat{Y}$. r_S, the structure coefficient, $= r$ of $X1$ with $\hat{Y}$. r of e with $\hat{Y}$ always $= 0$. r of e with $X1$ always $= 0$.

variability in the Y scores that the predictors *cannot* explain. Finally, the fact that the explained and the unexplained variability in the Y scores are both conceptually discrete directly suggests the truism that the r (and r^2) of the $\hat{Y}_i$ and the e_i score also *always* equals zero.

Required Assumptions

All statistical models provide accurate estimates only when model assumptions are met. Thus, to the extent that assumptions are imperfectly met, estimates of statistics such as r^2, R^2, the weights, and $p_{CALCULATED}$ will be somewhat compromised. Of course, we can never perfectly meet the assumptions of statistical methods, but we should at least do so approximately, and when interpreting our results, we must bear in mind the degree to which assumptions are met. If we deem that assumptions are not met to an acceptable degree, alternative analyses that make fewer or weaker assumptions must be considered.

Here are the primary statistical assumptions of regression:

1. *Scale.* The dependent variable is at least interval, and the independent variables are either dichotomous or at least intervally-scaled.
2. *Model specification.* We are using (a) the correct predictor variables, and (b) only the correct predictor variables, and (c) the form of relationships (e.g., only linear relationships are considered, curvilinear relationships are modeled) being modeled is correct.

3. *Error scores.* The e_i scores are normally distributed in the population.
4. *Homoscedasticity.* In the population the e_i scores have equal variances at different values of the predictor variables.
5. *Predictors imperfectly correlated.* No predictor is a perfect linear combination of (i.e., is perfectly correlated with) any linear combination of the other predictor variables.

▪▪▪ Case #1: Perfectly Uncorrelated Predictors

Regression analysis is also relatively straightforward in the situation of multiple predictors that are perfectly uncorrelated. This sounds like an improbable occurrence, but in practice it occurs quite frequently, as when we employ as predictors certain kinds of scores from factor analysis (Thompson, 2004) or when we perform certain analyses called balanced ANOVA models, as we will see in subsequent chapters.

As noted previously, the use of a single predictor is a special case of having multiple predictor variables that are uncorrelated with each other, and many of the same dynamics occur for both situations. For example, when there is a single predictor, or when multiple predictor variables are perfectly uncorrelated with each other, the r of each predictor with the dependent variable is that predictor's individual β weight. This is illustrated in the Table 8.5 results involving the prediction of Y_i with perfectly uncorrelated predictors $X1_i$, $X2_i$, and $X3_i$.

Table 8.5 also presents the structure coefficient (r_S) for each predictor variable. A regression structure coefficient (Cooley & Lohnes, 1971, p. 55; Thompson & Borrello, 1985; Thorndike, 1978) is the bivariate correlation of a measured predictor with the latent $\hat{Y}$ scores (*not* with the Y scores), and is very useful in giving us a better understanding of the structure or the nature of the synthetic variable. Understanding the structure or makeup of the latent variable scores can be very important in understanding the predictive utility of the predictor variables, as various researchers have emphasized (cf. Courville & Thompson, 2001; Dunlap & Landis, 1998). As Thompson and Borrello (1985) explained, a predictor can have a β weight of zero, but

TABLE 8.5. Regression Results for Predicting Y with X1, X2, and X3; X4, X5, and X6; or X4, X5, and X7

Case predictors	Statistics			
	β	r	Partial r	r_S
Case #1				
X1	0.0878	0.0878	0.0977	0.1970
X2	−0.3794	−0.3795	−0.3903	−0.8511
X3	0.2170	0.2170	0.2356	0.4866
Case #2				
X4	0.6418	0.4819	0.5791	0.6844
X5	0.5177	0.2903	0.5287	0.4123
X6	0.0824	0.4392	0.0865	0.6238
Case #3				
X4	0.5841	0.4819	0.5971	0.6517
X5	0.7169	0.2903	0.6359	0.3926
X7	0.3285	0.1740	0.3310	0.2354

Note. In Case #1, a given $\beta = r_{Y \text{ with } X}$. In all cases, $r_S = r_{Y \text{ with } X} / R$.

can actually be an exceptionally powerful predictor variable. One must look at *both* β and structure coefficients when evaluating the importance of a predictor, as we shall see in some detail in Chapter 9.

Table 8.6 makes clear that something else intriguing happens when the predictors are perfectly uncorrelated: the sum of the r^2s for the predictors (each representing proportionately how much of the dependent variable's variability a predictor can explain) will equal the R^2 involving all the predictors because, in this situation, the predictors do not overlap at all with each other. Thus, 0.0077 + 0.1440 + 0.0471 = the R^2 of 19.88%.

We can see these dynamics mathematically within one of the many formulas for computing the squared multiple correlation, which applies across *all* regression cases, for any number of predictors 1 through *j*:

$$R^2 = \beta_1(r_{Y \times X1}) + \beta_2(r_{Y \times X2}) + \ldots + \beta_j(r_{Y \times Xj}) \quad (8.9)$$

However, iff we are in Case #1, because each β weight equals the correlation of a given predictor with Y, we can reexpress the equation as

TABLE 8.6. Results Associated with
Table 8.1 Data and the Prediction
of Y with Variable Sets of Size k = 3

Predictor/sum	$r_{Y \text{ with } X}$	$r^2_{Y \text{ with } X}$
X1	0.0878	0.0077
X2	−0.3795	0.1440
X3	0.2170	0.0471
Sum		0.1988
X4	0.4819	0.2322
X5	0.2903	0.0843
X6	0.4392	0.1929
Sum		0.5094
X4	0.4819	0.2322
X5	0.2903	0.0843
X7	0.1740	0.0303
Sum		0.3468

$$R^2 = r_{Y \times X1}(r_{Y \times X1}) + r_{Y \times X2}(r_{Y \times X2}) + \ldots + r_{Y \times Xj}(r_{Y \times Xj}) \quad (8.10)$$

or as

$$R^2 = r_{Y \times X1}{}^2 + r_{Y \times X2}{}^2 + \ldots + r_{Y \times Xj}{}^2 \quad (8.11)$$

▪▪▪ Case #2: Correlated Predictors, No Suppressor Effects

Collinearity (or multicollinearity) refers to the extent to which the predictor variables have nonzero correlations with each other. Computations become appreciably more complicated when the predictors are collinear. The β weights for given predictors no longer equal the rs for the same predictors with the Y_i scores, as reflected in Table 8.5. And as reported in Table 8.6, the r^2s no longer sum to R^2 (i.e., the sum, 0.5094, does not equal the R^2 of 49.575%). And notice how in Table 8.5 variable X6 has a near-zero β weight (+0.082372) but an r_s of +0.6238.

The challenge when we have correlated predictors is that we must *not* allow commonly explained variability in Y_i to be multiply credited to two or more predictor variables. We can allocate predictive credit for commonly explained portions of the Y variability however we wish (e.g., all to *X1*, all to *X2*, or split in various ways between the predictors), but the credit may be given *only one time*. Otherwise, we might obtain a squared multiple correlation greater than 100%, which illogically would assert that we can explain more variability in the Y_i scores than the Y_i scores have.

For example, conceptually, if two predictors both had r^2 with Y of 100%, and both predictors were given full credit for their predictive ability, we would obtain an erroneous estimate that $R^2 = 200\%$! Logically, we require a computational formula for the β weights that (a) takes into consideration *all* the r^2 values among all the pairs of the measured variables, and (b) allocates predictive credit to predictors such that explained portions of the variability in the Y_i scores are explained only *once*.

The number of rs that must be used to compute a single β weight can grow quite large as predictors are added. For one predictor (i.e., two measured variables, one dependent, one predictor), there is only one r. For two predictors (three measured variables), according to Equation 6.2,

$$C_{PW} = [N\,(N-1)]\,/\,2 \qquad (6.2)$$

there are $[3(3-1)]\,/\,2 =$ three correlation coefficients that must be computed. For three predictors (four measured variables), there are $[4(4-1)]\,/\,2 =$ six correlation coefficients that must be considered. For four predictors, there are 10 correlation coefficients that must be considered, and for five predictors there are 15 coefficients to consider.

To simplify the discussion of how beta weights are computed, we will limit the discussion to an example involving two predictors. For two predictor variables, the two β weights for *all* cases can be computed using the equations

$$\beta_1 = [r_{Y \times X1} - \{(r_{Y \times X2})(r_{X1 \times X2})\}]\,/\,[1 - r_{X1 \times X2}{}^2] \qquad (8.12)$$

and

$$\beta_2 = [r_{Y \times X2} - \{(r_{Y \times X1})(r_{X1 \times X2})\}]\,/\,[1 - r_{X1 \times X2}{}^2] \qquad (8.13)$$

Let's say that $r_{Y \times X1} = 0.707$ and $r_{Y \times X2} = 0.577$. To be in Case #2, $r_{X1 \times X2} \neq 0$, and we will specify $r_{X1 \times X2} = 0.800$. So, based on Equation 8.12, we have

$$[0.707 - \{(0.577)(0.800)\}] / [1 - 0.800^2]$$
$$[0.707 - \{(0.577)(0.800)\}] / [1 - 0.640]$$
$$[0.707 - \{(0.577)(0.800)\}] / 0.360$$
$$[0.707 - 0.462] / 0.360$$
$$0.245 / 0.360$$
$$\beta_1 = 0.682$$

and

$$[0.577 - \{(0.707)(0.800)\}] / [1 - 0.800^2]$$
$$[0.577 - \{(0.707)(0.800)\}] / [1 - 0.640]$$
$$[0.577 - \{(0.707)(0.800)\}] / 0.360$$
$$[0.577 - 0.566] / 0.360$$
$$0.011 / 0.360$$
$$\beta_2 = 0.032$$

And, based on Equation 8.9, the squared multiple correlation can be computed as:

$$0.682(0.707) + 0.032(0.577)$$
$$0.482 + 0.018$$
$$R^2 = 0.500$$

The score-world multiple R would equal $0.500^{0.5}$, or 0.707. One implication of these calculations is that R^2, R, and the beta weights can be computed given *only* the bivariate correlation matrix. Thus, reporting the correlation matrix for related regression analyses is good practice. This allows confirmation by readers of reported results, or the fitting of alternative regression models.

Note that iff we have perfectly uncorrelated predictors, Equation 8.12

$$\beta_1 = [r_{Y \times X1} - \{(r_{Y \times X2})(r_{X1 \times X2})\}] / [1 - r_{X1 \times X2}^2] \qquad (8.12)$$

can be reexpressed as

$$\beta_1 = [r_{Y \times X1} - \{(r_{Y \times X2})(0.0)\}] / [1 - 0.0^2] \qquad (8.14)$$

which simplifies to $\beta_1 = r_{Y \times X1}$, as noted previously. In parallel fashion, for Case #1, $\beta_2 = r_{Y \times X2}$.

Case #3: Correlated Predictors, Suppressor Effects Present

However, appreciably more complicated dynamics occur when suppressor effects are present in the data. As defined by Pedhazur (1982), a *possible* "suppressor variable is a [predictor] variable that has a zero, or close to zero, correlation with the criterion but is correlated with one or more than one of the predictor variables" (p. 104). Suppressors improve prediction *indirectly* by making other predictors better, which cannot happen if the predictor variables are all perfectly uncorrelated.

To many students, "suppression" sounds like a bad thing. Perhaps suppression sounds like "repression," which is a Freudian construct not positively viewed by most psychoanalysts as healthy over the long term. But statistical suppression and psychological repression have nothing to do with each other. Suppressor variables in multiple regression (and in other analyses throughout the general linear model) make the R^2 effect size larger, even though the suppressor has little or no correlation with the criterion variable.

So, suppressor effects are *good*, though they do complicate the interpretation of results. Nevertheless, they honor the kinds of complex relationships that can occur in reality.

Variable $X7$ in variable set $X4$, $X5$, and $X7$, as predictors of Y involves a suppression dynamic, as reflected in the Table 8.2 correlation coefficients. Notice in Table 8.6 that the sum of the r^2 values is 0.3468, but the R^2 value for these data *is* 54.677%, which is *larger* than the sum of the r^2 values!

Suppressor effects are quite difficult to explain in an intuitive manner. Horst (1966) presented an actual example that is relatively accessible. He noted that during World War II the prediction of airplane pilot ability was a major problem. At the start of the war, many trainees were crashing their planes, killing their instructors, or simply failing their final checkout flights such that precious training was wasted. But lots of data were available on the trainees. Basically, scads of men in World War II upon initial admission to the armed forces were herded into auditoria, and completed huge batteries of tests wearing their army-issued boxer shorts.

So psychologists approached this regression prediction problem by using mechanical, spatial, and verbal abilities—all three predictors being measured with paper-and-pencil tests—to predict the actual checkout flight ratings of previous trainees (i.e., group 1). If the equation worked well, new potential flight trainees (i.e., group 2) could be screened into (or not into) training based on their $\hat{Y}_i$ scores.

The verbal scores had very low correlations with the dependent variable, piloting ability, because flying has no systematic relationship with verbal ability. But verbal scores had larger correlations with the other two predictors, because the predictor variables were all measured with paper-and-pencil tests (i.e., measurement artifacts confounded the mechanical and spatial ability scores). As Horst (1966) noted, "Some verbal ability was necessary in order to understand the instructions and the items used to measure the other three abilities" (p. 355).

Counterintuitively, including verbal ability scores in the regression equation actually served to remove the contaminating influence of the verbal predictor from the other predictors, which effectively increased the R^2 value from what the effect size would have been if only mechanical and spatial abilities were used as predictors. The verbal ability variable had negative b and β weights. As Horst (1966) noted

> To include the verbal score with a negative weight served to suppress or subtract irrelevant ability, and to discount the scores of those who did well on the test simply because of their verbal ability rather than because of abilities required for success in pilot training. (p. 355)

In regression, and throughout the general linear model, measured predictor variables can help predict or explain outcomes (1) directly or (2) indirectly (by improving the predictive power of other predictor variables), or both. The job of the multiplicative weights in regression (and in other

GLM analyses) is to optimize the prediction in any (and every) way they can.

Let's look at an extreme example involving two measured predictor variables, where $r_{Y \times X1} = 0.707$, $r_{Y \times X2} = 0.000$, and $r_{X1 \times X2} = -0.707$. So, based on Equation 8.12, we have

$$[0.707 - \{(0.000)(-0.707)\}] / [1 - -0.707^2]$$
$$[0.707 - \{(0.000)(-0.707)\}] / [1 - 0.500]$$
$$[0.707 - \{(0.000)(-0.707)\}] / 0.500$$
$$[0.707 - 0.000] / 0.500$$
$$0.707 / 0.500$$
$$\beta_1 = 1.414$$

and

$$[0.000 - \{(0.707)(0.707)\}] / [1 - -0.707^?]$$
$$[0.000 - \{(0.707)(-0.707)\}] / [1 - 0.500]$$
$$[0.000 - \{(0.707)(0.707)\}] / 0.500$$
$$[0.000 - -0.500] / 0.500$$
$$0.500 / 0.500$$
$$\beta_2 - 1.000$$

And, based on Equation 8.9, the squared multiple correlation can be computed as

$$1.414(0.707) + 1.000(0.000)$$
$$0.999 + 0.000$$
$$R^2 = 0.999$$

In this example, the presence of the $X2$ suppressor variables allows β_1 to escape its upper mathematical limit of $+1.0$ because the β weights are no longer bivariate correlation coefficients.

The β weights are *only* Pearson correlation coefficients in Case #1. In Cases #2 and #3, the β weights are *not* correlation coefficients. So, in cases #2 and #3, the words "correlation" and "correlated" should *never* be used when discussing β weights. Instead, in Cases #2 and #3 the β weights *must* be interpreted as reflecting a number of fractional units (e.g., -1.571) of change in the $\hat{Y}$ scores predicted for a corresponding 1 *SD* of change in a given predictor variable, with scores on the other predictors all held constant. Unfortunately, in published research this admonition for correct practice is honored hugely more in the breach than in compliance (Courville & Thompson, 2001).

This last example also makes another very important point: *The latent or synthetic variables analyzed in all parametric methods are always more than the sum of their constituent parts.* If we only look at observed variables, by only examining a series of bivariate *r*s, we can easily under- or overestimate the actual effects that are embedded within our data. We must use analytic methods that honor the complexities of the reality that we purportedly wish to study—a reality in which measured variables can interact in all sorts of complex and counterintuitive ways.

■ ■ ■ β Weights versus Structure Coefficients

Debate over the relative merit of emphasizing β weights rather than structure coefficients during result interpretation has been fairly heated (H. R. Harris, 1989, 1992). The position taken here is that the thoughtful researcher should always interpret either (a) both the beta weights and the structure coefficients *or* (b) both the β weights and the bivariate correlations of the predictors with Y.

As noted previously, a regression structure coefficient (Cooley & Lohnes, 1971, p. 55; Thompson & Borrello, 1985) is the bivariate Pearson *r* of a measured predictor with the latent $\hat{Y}$ scores (*not* with the Y scores, unless $R^2 = 1.0$). There are two ways to obtain the structure coefficient for a given predictor variable. First, the $\hat{Y}$ scores can be computed and then correlated with the predictor variables. In SPSS, the $\hat{Y}$ scores can be obtained either by using the SAVE=PRED subcommand within the REGRESSION procedure, or by invoking a series of COMPUTE commands. Then the CORRELATIONS procedure is used to obtain the Pearson product–moment correlations of all the predictors with the $\hat{Y}$ scores.

Alternatively, for a given predictor variable, the structure coefficient (r_S) can be computed using the formula

$$r_S = r_{X \text{ with } Y} / R \qquad\qquad (8.15)$$

This computation is easily accomplished on a hand-held calculator or in Excel. The equation makes clear that structure coefficients are score-world results, because both values to the right side of the equal sign are score-world, and no squaring operations have been invoked in the equation.

It has been noted by Pedhazur (1982) that structure coefficients "are simply zero-order correlations of independent variables with the dependent variable divided by a constant, namely, the multiple correlation coefficient. Hence, the zero-order correlations provide the same information" (p. 691). Thus, the structure rs and the predictor-dependent variable rs will lead to identical interpretations, because they are merely expressed in a different metric. Because $r_S = r_{X \text{ with } \hat{Y}} = [r_{X \text{ with } Y} / R]$, structure rs and predictor-dependent variable rs will always have the same sign, because R cannot be negative, and will equal each other only when $R = 1.0$.

Although the interpretation of predictor-dependent variable correlations will lead to the same conclusions as interpretations of r_Ss, some researchers have a stylistic preference for structure coefficients. As Thompson and Borrello (1985) argued,

> it must be noted that interpretation of only the bivariate correlations seems counterintuitive. It appears inconsistent to first declare interest in an omnibus system of variables and then to consult values that consider the variables taken only two at a time. (p. 208)

The squared predictor-dependent variable correlation coefficients inform the researcher about the proportion of Y variance explained by the predictors. Squared structure coefficients inform the researcher about the proportion of $\hat{Y}$ (i.e., only the explained portion of Y) variance explained by the predictors.

Some researchers object to interpreting structure coefficients, because r_Ss are not affected by the collinearity (i.e., the correlations) among predictor variables. Beta weights, on the other hand, are affected by correlations among the predictors, and therefore may change if these correlations change, or if *any* variables in a study are added or deleted. That is, β weights are *context-specific* to a particular set of measured predictor variables.

However, the insensitivity of r_S is not an intrinsic weakness. Because science is about the business of generalizing relationships across participants, across variables and measures of variables, and across time, in some respects it is desirable that structure coefficients are not impacted by collinearity. This insensitivity honors a reality in which measured predictor variables are correlated, and r_S is unaffected by this collinearity, which is instead duly considered when computing the β weights.

On the other hand, when the measured variables in a study are the only variables of interest for the researcher's purposes in a fixed context, then one is less concerned by the impacts of collinearity among a fixed set of predictors. Here the context specificity of the β weights is less troubling. Obviously, the utility of statistics, including structure coefficients, varies somewhat from problem to problem or situation to situation.

Other researchers are troubled by the fact that structure rs are inherently bivariate. One response is that *all* conventional parametric methods are correlational (e.g., Knapp, 1978), and that even a multivariate method such as canonical correlation analysis can be conceptualized as a bivariate statistic (Thompson, 1991a). Indeed, R itself is a bivariate statistic, albeit one involving a synthetic variable, because

$$R_{Y \text{ with } X1, X2, \ldots, Xj} = r_{Y \text{ with } \hat{Y}} \qquad (8.16)$$

and

$$R_{Y \text{ with } X1, X2, \ldots, Xj}{}^2 = r_{Y \text{ with } \hat{Y}}{}^2 \qquad (8.17)$$

It should also be noted that r_S is not really completely bivariate, in that r_S is a correlation involving $\hat{Y}$ (*not* the measured variable, Y), and $\hat{Y}$ is itself a synthetic or latent variable involving all the predictor variables.

Interpreting only β weights is not sufficient (Courville & Thompson, 2001), except in Case #1, or in the one-variable situation, because given only one predictor then $r = \beta$, and $r_S^2 = 1.0$ (unless $R = 0.0$, in which case r_S is undefined). Together, through their stereoscopic representations of data dynamics, the β weights and the structure coefficients tell the researcher which situation applies to the data. Three possibilities exist. In these situations, a predictor variable with both $\beta = 0$ and $r_S = 0$ is *always* clearly and definitely useless, but otherwise the predictor is not definitively useless, and should not be interpreted as being useless.

Possibility 1

When the β weights of multiple predictors each equal the predictors' respective rs with Y (and each $r_S = r_{Y \text{ with } X} / R = \beta / R$), then the researcher knows that the predictors are uncorrelated. In this situation, interpreting β, *or* structure coefficients, *or* predictor-dependent variable correlations will all lead to identical conclusions about the importance of predictor variables.

Possibility 2

When predictors have nonzero βs, some of which do *not* equal the predictors' respective rs with Y, then predictor variables are correlated with each other (i.e., are *collinear* or *multicollinear*). Assuming no suppression, the R^2 will be less than the sum of the rs. Both β weights and structure coefficients must be interpreted. And a predictor with a zero or near-zero β weight may have the largest $|r_S|$, and be the best single predictor, albeit being denied credit in the context-specific dynamics of the β weights.

Possibility 3

Iff a predictor has, at the extreme, a zero structure coefficient (and a zero correlation with Y), the predictor may be a suppressor variable. There are two ways to distinguish whether the predictor is merely useless, or instead is a suppressor variable. First, if this predictor has a nonzero β weight, then suppressor effects are present. Second, if the R^2 with the possible suppressor included in the analysis is greater than the R^2 with the possible suppressor *not* included in the analysis, then this predictor variable is a suppressor. Either of the two strategies will *always* lead to the same conclusion about suppression for a given data set.

The importance of understanding suppressor effects is not to suggest that such predictors should necessarily be sought out when the measured variables are selected. Anticipating what predictors may be suppressors in forthcoming research can be difficult. However, suppression effects are not uncommon throughout the general linear model, and correct result interpretation may turn upon an awareness that these effects can occur even when the dynamics were not anticipated (Tzelgov & Henik, 1991).

A Final Comment on Collinearity

As noted previously, collinearity (or multicollinearity) simply refers to the fact that the measured predictor variables have nonzero bivariate correlation coefficients with each other. Traditionally, researchers sought predictor variable sets in which the predictors had as little bivariate correlation with each other as possible. This was accomplished in various ways, such as dropping some predictors that were highly correlated with other predictors, or combining highly correlated subsets of predictors into single scores by averaging or summing the predictors in a given subset, or by other methods. This objective was pursued for several reasons, some of which are no longer relevant.

First, as suggested by Equations 8.12 and 8.13, when predictors are very highly correlated, precision in the calculation of the β weights may become problematic. For example, the denominator in the calculation (e.g., $[1 - r_{X1 \times X2}^2]$) may become quite small. However, this consideration is trivial in the presence of modern computers and software, which accurately perform calculations to many more decimal places than was possible when computations were performed by humans using calculators.

Second, investigators sought research situations in which result interpretation was simple and straightforward. This is accomplished when working in Case #1, because, here, interpreting βs, *or* structure coefficients, *or* predictor-dependent variable correlations will all three lead to the same conclusions about the importance of the predictor variables. However, most researchers posit living in a reality in which measured variables are rarely, if ever, perfectly uncorrelated. Accomplishing simplified interpretation at the expense of creating sets of variables that do not honor reality may seem too high a price to pay for easier result interpretation.

Third, as predictor variables are more correlated, the standard errors of the *b* weights are inflated. Either large correlations among a few predictors, or small correlations among a large set of predictors, can be potentially problematic. The resulting $t_{CALCULATED}$ (or Wald, or critical ratio) test statistics for evaluating the nil null hypothesis that a given weight is zero becomes smaller. And for a given *b* weight, the same *t* value applies to the related β weight. The implication is that with highly correlated predictors, the possibility arises that fewer (and perhaps none) of the weights will be deemed statistically significantly different from zero.

This problem is less troubling if the weights are instead evaluated by direct comparison with the values in related prior studies. Interpreting the weights via direct comparison with related results in prior studies also avoids the problem that NHSST results in different studies are not comparable when studies involve different sample sizes (Ziliak & McCloskey, 2004). However, the problem of inflated standard errors is a factor that warrants some consideration when researchers are selecting predictor variables, and again when researchers are interpreting results involving correlated predictors.

The take-home message is that the explicit, direct comparison of results with those in related studies is always very useful (if not vital). No one study means very much in isolation, at least as regards the particular values of the statistical estimates themselves.

Some Key Concepts

Iff the predictors are all completely useless, the *b* and the β weights will all be zero, and *a* will equal M_Y. Also, given that universally

$$R^2 = \beta_1(r_{Y \times X1}) + \beta_2(r_{Y \times X2}) + \ldots + \beta_i(r_{Y \times Xi}) \qquad (8.9)$$

for this situation, R^2 will equal zero. Iff $R^2 = 0$, because the *b* and the β weights are all zero, the $\hat{Y}_i$ scores will all equal *a* and M_Y, and not constitute a variable. Iff $R^2 = 1$, the e_i scores will all equal zero and not constitute a variable.

The Y_i and the $\hat{Y}_i$ scores *always* have the same mean. The minimum *SD* and *SOS* of the $\hat{Y}_i$ scores is zero, which occurs iff $R^2 = 0$. The maximum *SD* of the $\hat{Y}_i$ scores is SD_Y, and the maximum *SOS* of the $\hat{Y}_i$ scores is SOS_Y. The maximum dispersion of the $\hat{Y}_i$ scores is reached iff $R^2 = 1$. The β weights are correlation coefficients iff we are in Case #1.

The R^2 is an "on the average" characterization of how closely the Y_i and the $\hat{Y}_i$ scores match for different participants. Thus, if R^2 is 50%, this does *not* mean that the e_i scores are equal for each person, and instead some e_i may be zero while others are relatively large. Only when $R^2 = 1$ can we apply the characterization of this effect size both to the dataset generically and across all individuals.

▨▨▨ Reflection Problems ▨▨▨

1. Given the use of z scores for all measured variables, when are $\hat{Y}_i$ scores also z scores? Given the use of z scores for all measured variables, when are e_i scores also z scores?

2. A researcher tells you *only* one result from her study: a $\beta = -2.5$. List *everything* that can be deduced about the design and the study's results.

3. β weights are correlation coefficients iff we are in Case #1. However, in *all* cases, β weights indicate how many units of change will occur in $\hat{Y}_i$ for one unit of change in a given predictor variable, holding all other predictors constant. In Chapter 5 it was asserted that r is not itself intervally scaled. However, in Case #1, if $\beta_1 = +0.50$ and $\beta_2 = +0.25$, 1 *SD* of change in X_1 does yield twice as much predicted change in $\hat{Y}_i$ than does one unit of change in X_2. Does this mean that in the metric of scores, and not in the metric of the *SOS*, r is an intervally-scaled indicator of the relative leverage of predictors in Case #1?

A GLM
Interpretation Rubric

esult interpretation strategies must be governed by the researcher's purpose. The research purpose impacts what coefficients are relevant, or what benchmarks are used to evaluate sample results, or both. For example, in an explanation or theory-testing study, perhaps the only judgment will be whether the detected effect size (e.g., R^2) is comparable to a theoretically-predicted value, regardless of which predictor variables may contribute to the effect. Conversely, in another theory focused study, perhaps the overall effect size is well established across studies, and will not be of primary interest.

Model specification error occurs when (a) predictor variables that should not be used are included in the model, *or* (b) necessary predictor variables are omitted, *or* (c) the incorrect analysis is used (e.g., a linear form of relationships is modeled when relationships are curvilinear or logistic). If the researcher believes that model specification error is not at issue, then the β weights may be of more interest in interpretation, because the *context specificity* of the weights is not a limitation if the analytic context is deemed correctly-specified.

But as Pedhazur (1982) has noted, "The rub, however, is that the true model is seldom, if ever, known" (p. 229). And as Duncan (1975) has noted, "Indeed it would require no elaborate sophistry to show that we will never have the 'right' model in any absolute sense" (p. 101).

Here a generic interpretation rubric, one with wide utility, is offered. Because multiple regression is the univariate general linear model (Cohen, 1968), and is a subcomponent within the multivariate general linear model (Knapp, 1978), this interpretation rubric has wide applicability across various analyses.

The proposed rubric involves two hierarchical steps. First, the researcher asks, "Do I have anything?" Second, if and only if (iff) the answer to the first question is yes, only then does the researcher ask, "Where does my something come from?" It is not logical to obtain nothing, and then ask, "From where does my nothing originate?"

Do I Have Anything?

Researchers can interpret any combination of three pieces of evidence to address the question, "Do I have anything?" Different researchers will make different choices about what evidence to consider, or differentially emphasize different evidence.

Statistical Significance

Some researchers begin interpretation by evaluating the nil null hypothesis that H_0: $R^2 = 0$ (or, equivalently, H_0: $R = 0$). Table 9.1 presents the requisite calculations. The first step involves computing the SOS of the Y_i scores, using Equation 3.1, or an algebraically equivalent formula. This sum of squares is sometimes called the SOS_{TOTAL}. This is the variability (i.e., the information about the amount and origins of individual differences) that we are trying to explain using the predictor variables.

Next, the $SOS_{EXPLAINED}$ (SOS_{MODEL}, $SOS_{REGRESSION}$, $SOS_{BETWEEN}$) is computed. As noted in Chapter 8, once the regression weights are derived, the $\hat{Y}$ scores can be computed. Applying Equation 3.1 (or an algebraically equivalent formula) to the $\hat{Y}_i$ scores yields the $SOS_{EXPLAINED}$.

TABLE 9.1. Variance Partitions Summary Table

Source	SOS	df	MS	$F_{\text{CALCULATED}}$	Effect size
Between groups	d	f	h	j	k
Within groups	e	g	i		
Total	a	b	c		

Note. $a = d + e$.
      $b = n - 1$.
      f = the number of predictor variables in the regression analysis.
      $g = n - 1$ – the number of predictors in the regression analysis.
      $b = f + g$.
      $h = d / f$.
      $i = e / g$.
      $c = a / c = SD_Y^2$.
      $c \neq h + i$.
      $j = h / i$, assuming $i \neq 0$.
      $k = d / a = (a - e) / a$.

Then, the $SOS_{\text{UNEXPLAINED}}$ (SOS_{ERROR}, SOS_{RESIDUAL}, SOS_{WITHIN}) can be computed. Because the $\hat{Y}_i$ scores and the e_i scores are always perfectly uncorrelated, $SOS_{\text{EXPLAINED}} + SOS_{\text{UNEXPLAINED}} = SOS_{\text{TOTAL}}$ (SOS_Y), and the $SOS_{\text{UNEXPLAINED}}$ can be computed by subtraction ($SOS_{\text{TOTAL}} - SOS_{\text{EXPLAINED}}$). Alternatively, Equation 3.1 can be applied to the e_i scores to obtain the $SOS_{\text{UNEXPLAINED}}$.

The regression effect size (R^2) can be computed using Equation 8.6 ($R^2 = SOS_{\hat{Y}} / SOS_Y$). If a "corrected" effect size is desired, the regression analog of the Ezekiel (1930) correction can be applied to obtain the "adjusted R^2":

$$1 - ((n - 1) / (n - v - 1))(1 - R^2) \tag{9.1}$$

where n is the sample size and v is the number of predictor variables. The formula can be equivalently expressed as

$$R^2 - ((1 - R^2)(v / (n - v - 1))) \tag{9.2}$$

Next, the degrees of freedom (df) must be computed. The df_{TOTAL} equals $n - 1$. For multiple regression analysis, the $df_{\text{EXPLAINED}}$ (df_{MODEL},

$df_{\text{REGRESSION}}$, df_{BETWEEN}) equals the number of predictor variables. The $df_{\text{UNEXPLAINED}}$ (df_{ERROR}, df_{RESIDUAL}, df_{WITHIN}) can be computed by substraction ($df_{\text{TOTAL}} - df_{\text{EXPLAINED}}$). Alternatively, the $df_{\text{UNEXPLAINED}}$ can be computed as $n - 1 - v$, where v is the number of predictor variables.

At this point, we can compute the variance of the Y_i scores by dividing the SOS_Y by df_{TOTAL}. However, because the test statistic used for this NHSST application is the F ratio, an area-world statistic, we also need two additional variances to compute $F_{\text{CALCULATED}}$.

We compute the mean square explained ($MS_{\text{EXPLAINED}}$, or MS_{MODEL}, $MS_{\text{REGRESSION}}$, MS_{BETWEEN}) by dividing $SOS_{\text{EXPLAINED}}$ by $df_{\text{EXPLAINED}}$. Note that this is also a variance estimate, even though the label used is "mean square." We compute the $MS_{\text{UNEXPLAINED}}$ (MS_{ERROR}, MS_{RESIDUAL}, MS_{WITHIN}) by dividing $SOS_{\text{UNEXPLAINED}}$ by $df_{\text{UNEXPLAINED}}$. Again, the mean square unexplained is a type of variance, and is an area-world statistic.

Then, when possible, we compute the $F_{\text{CALCULATED}}$ by dividing the $MS_{\text{EXPLAINED}}$ by the $MS_{\text{UNEXPLAINED}}$. However, if the R^2 is 100% (and the $SOS_{\text{EXPLAINED}} = SOS_{\text{TOTAL}}$, and $SOS_{\text{UNEXPLAINED}} = 0$), the $MS_{\text{UNEXPLAINED}}$ equals zero, and the $F_{\text{CALCULATED}}$ is undefined (i.e., cannot be computed). This means that, *ironically, we cannot perform NHSST whenever we can perfectly predict or explain an outcome variable.*

Given α, we perform the statistical significance test by comparing the $F_{\text{CALCULATED}}$ with $df_{\text{EXPLAINED}}$ and $df_{\text{UNEXPLAINED}}$ with the F_{CRITICAL} with $df_{\text{EXPLAINED}}$ and $df_{\text{UNEXPLAINED}}$. As noted in Chapter 3, we can obtain the F_{CRITICAL} for any α and any degrees of freedom by invoking the Excel FINV statistical function. Alternatively, we can determine the $p_{\text{CALCULATED}}$ value by invoking the Excel FDIST statistical function, and then compare $p_{\text{CALCULATED}}$ with p_{CRITICAL} to determine whether or not to reject H_0: $R^2 = 0$.

Of course, SPSS and other statistical packages automate all these calculations. If we wish, we may augment these results by performing "what-if" analyses using the Figure 6.3 spreadsheet. Or we can use the "what-if" spreadsheet proposed by Thompson and Kieffer (2000) instead invoking "corrected R^2."

Effect Size

The regression effect size is R^2, or the "corrected" or "adjusted" R^2. The effect size is an index of the practical significance of results (Kirk, 1996).

As strongly emphasized in Chapter 7, the correct interpretation of effect sizes does *not* invoke Cohen's benchmarks for "small," "medium," and "large" effects, except perhaps when research is being conducted in a ground-breaking venue. Instead, the correct interpretation of results focuses on *direct, explicit* comparison of effects with those in the related prior literature (Thompson, 2002b, in press).

The effect size statistics inform the researcher's subjective value judgment about the noteworthiness of the results. This value judgment turns on the researcher's personal valuing of the outcome variable. Two researchers studying the same outcome and realizing identical effect sizes may reasonably reach different judgments about result noteworthiness, if they differ in their valuing of the outcome variable.

The process of evaluating effect sizes is not totally objective. No form of research, including quantitative research, is completely objective. Judgment cannot be avoided. And, as noted in Chapter 6, NHSST provides only an illusory escape from the atavistic desire to avoid making judgments, because NHSST is not without limitations.

One of the most potent ways of thinking about effect sizes is to think of *effects as statistics that quantify* **model fit**, *or as the obverse of model specification error.* As noted in Chapter 8, *every* statistical analysis fits a model to data. As the effect size (e.g., R^2) approaches mathematical limits, or takes on large values, there is evidence that the correct variables and the correct analysis have been used, and that the model is *one* plausible model that fits the data.

Of course, using effect sizes as indices of model fit presumes that the model is "falsifiable" given the research situation (Popper, 1961, 1965). Some analyses inevitably generate perfect (or near perfect) fit if the degrees of freedom error is (or approaches) zero. *Every* model with $df_{ERROR} = 0$ will perfectly fit the data, and yield an R^2 of 100%, *regardless* of what the measured variables are. Thus, large effect sizes provide stronger evidence of model fit when the degrees of freedom error is larger.

One way to think of df_{ERROR} is as a measure of how many more predictor variables might potentially be added to the analysis. Large effect sizes are potentially more impressive when relatively few predictor variables are used, and additional predictors that could have been added are deemed unnecessary.

To see that models with zero degrees of freedom error inevitably yield $R^2 = 100\%$, consider an example involving bivariate correlation. If we have

$n = 2$ paired scores on X_i and Y_i, and both X_i and Y_i are variables, then r^2 can only be 100%. Think of the bivariate scattergram. The two asterisks within the scatterplot will define a straight line and, inevitably, will be captured by the regression line. For this problem, $df_{TOTAL} = 1$, $df_{EXPLAINED} = 1$, and $df_{ERROR} = 0$.

The same dynamic occurs as we add predictor variables. For $n = 3$, and scores on Y_i and *any* other two variables used as predictor variables, R^2 can only be 100%. For $n = 4$, and scores on Y_i and *any* other three variables used as predictor variables, R^2 can only be 100%. So, large effect sizes are more impressive when degrees of freedom error are large, and the effect size was not inevitably large.

It is important to be thoughtful when interpreting effect sizes, because the metrics of standardized differences and variance-accounted-for effect sizes can be slippery (Olejnik & Algina, 2000). Medical researchers do not confront these problems, because they conventionally use unstandardized effect sizes, as noted in Chapter 7. A comparison of deaths per thousand for a new medication versus deaths per thousand for a control condition is straightforward, even if the value judgment inherent in the interpretation remains difficult.

For example, let's say a researcher is trying to predict body temperature differences in a group of 100 healthy adults, and that three predictor variables yield a huge R^2 of 75%. Perhaps $SOS_{TOTAL} = 9.0$ ($SD_Y^2 = 0.09$; $SD_Y = 0.30$). This huge effect size is not compelling if the sum of squares does not contain any clinically meaningful information about the amount of individual differences, because explaining a lot of something about which we don't care is uninteresting.

Conversely, very small effect sizes for outcome about which we care deeply may be noteworthy. For example, the variance-accounted-for effect size for predicting heart attack incidence based on taking a daily aspirin or a placebo is only 0.11%, as explained in Chapter 5. Yet during the study, those taking aspirin were half as likely as the placebo group to have had an infarct (Rosenthal, 1994)!

Replicability Analyses

The classical view is that science is the business of discovering laws (relationships) about effects that occur (and reoccur) under stated conditions.

And because statistical significance does *not* evaluate result replicability, we need to do other analyses.

Researchers do sometimes discover important effects that others have difficulty replicating. For example, in 1989, Pons and Fleischmann, two scholars working at the University of Utah, held a press conference announcing that they had created "cold fusion" by passing an electrical current through palladium electrodes immersed in so-called heavy water (i.e., water in which the hydrogen was replaced with its isotope, deuterium). This raised the prospect that cold fusion at room temperature could produce essentially unlimited, low-cost, clean energy.

This discovery produced excitement worldwide, as well as a flurry of research activity. Unfortunately, most researchers were unable to replicate the original findings. Today, scientists are still working to understand related phenomena. Nevertheless, a view emerged that cold fusion was not a panacea for the world's energy and pollution problems.

Discovering important relationships that few, if any, other scholars can replicate may yield intense adulation for a very brief 15 minutes of fame, followed by a life of considerable disdain and skepticism. Therefore, most scholars eschew making such discoveries (except, perhaps, when they are nearing retirement).

Traditionally, social scientists have attempted (incorrectly) to use NHSST as a vehicle to evaluate result replicability. Unfortunately, NHSST is *not* a useful tool for this purpose, as explained in previous chapters. How can researchers evaluate the replicability of their results, given that NHSST does not do so?

A critical protection against overinterpretation of serendipitous results is "meta-analytic thinking" (Cumming & Finch, 2001). Thompson (2002b) defined meta-analytic thinking as

> both (a) the prospective formulation of study expectations and design by explicitly invoking prior effect sizes and (b) the retrospective interpretation of new results, once they are in hand, via *explicit, direct* comparison with the prior effect sizes in the related literature. (p. 28; emphasis added)

According to Kline (2004), meta-analytic thinking has four features:

1. An accurate appreciation of the results of previous studies is seen as essential.

2. A researcher should view his or her own study as a modest contribution to that body of previous research.

3. A researcher should report results so that they can be easily incorporated into a future meta-analysis. This includes the reporting of effect sizes and confidence intervals.

4. Retrospective interpretations of new results, once collected, are called for via direct comparison with previous effect sizes. (p. 12)

As regards empirical replicability evidence, Thompson (1996) drew a distinction between two types: external and internal. **External replicability analysis** requires completely replicating the study in an independent sample. **Internal replicability analysis** attempts to mimic true replication without requiring a new sample by invoking one or more of three statistical logics: the bootstrap, the jackknife, or cross-validation (see Thompson, 1994b).

Only external, true replication provides direct evidence about whether study results will replicate. The challenge is that external replication is expensive and time-consuming. For example, folk wisdom holds that some doctoral students graduate only after their partner declares, "Honey, you will defend this dissertation next semester, or I am out of here." The marital consequences of expecting all doctoral students to replicate results would be unspeakable. Similarly, the employment consequences of expecting all junior faculty to replicate results prior to publishing, given only a 5- or 6-year pretenure stream, are also unimaginable.

An important challenge to replicability in the social sciences is that people are individually so idiosyncratic. Physical scientists do not have to confront these differences, which in many respects make *social science the hardest science of all* (Berliner, 2002). For example, a physicist who is observing the interaction patterns of atomic particles does not have to make generalizations such as, "Quarks and neutrinos repel each other, unless the quarks in gestation had poor nutrition or in childhood received poor education."

Internal replicability analyses seek partially to overcome these challenges by mixing up the participants in different ways in an effort to evaluate whether results are *robust across the combinations of different idiosyncrasies*. Internal replicability analyses are *never* as persuasive as external replication. But internal methods are far superior to what many researchers do to evaluate result replicability (i.e., nothing, or NHSST).

Bootstrap

The **bootstrap** (sometimes called "resampling") is the first of two "computer-intensive" internal replicability analyses (i.e., the bootstrap and the jackknife). These methods, articulated by Efron and his colleagues (e.g., Efron, 1979; Efron & Tibshirani, 1993), are called computer intensive because they are logistically difficult (or impossible) without the use of modern computers and specialized software (e.g., Thompson, 1988b, 1992a).

Bootstrap methods are only briefly considered here, given their computer-intensive character. Diaconis and Efron (1983) and Robertson (1991) provide intuitive but conceptually elegant summaries of these methods. The methods are discussed in more technical detail elsewhere (e.g., Lunneborg, 1999, 2001).

Given a sample, and no access to the population (or the sample study would not be conducted), one challenge is to estimate the sampling distribution. The bootstrapped sampling distribution can be used for either inferential or descriptive purposes (Thompson, 1993).

In *inferential applications*, the bootstrapped sampling distribution is used (a) to obtain the $p_{CALCULATED}$ for inferential purposes, or (b) to compute a t (or Wald or critical ratio) statistic (i.e., statistic / $SE_{STATISTIC}$) to perform NHSST using the nil null that a given parameter equals zero. In some cases the sampling distribution or a test statistic distribution can be mathematically derived when certain assumptions can be met (e.g., that regression e_i scores are normally and independently distributed). The bootstrap can be used for *inferential* NHSST purposes when (a) the statistical assumptions of mathematical estimates cannot be met, or (b) mathematically derived sampling distribution estimation procedures have not yet been developed. We do not have a sampling or a test distribution for every possible statistic and research situation, so the bootstrap can be used to fill these gaps.

In *descriptive applications*, the bootstrapped sampling distribution is used (a) to characterize the amount of sampling error variance in the sample data as regards a particular statistic, or (b) to inform professional judgment about the likely stability of a given estimate. The bootstrap grounds *SE* and other estimates in features of the sample data rather than on theoretical assumptions that certain statistical conditions hold for estimating an *SE* with a generic formula (e.g., Equation 6.6 for the SE_M).

When we employ the bootstrap for inferential purposes (i.e., to estimate the probability of the sample statistics), focus shifts to the *extreme tails* of the sampling distribution—where the less likely (and less frequent) statistics are located—because we typically invoke small values of *p* in statistical tests. These are exactly the locations where the estimated distribution densities are most unstable, because there are relatively few statistics here (presuming the sampling distribution does not have an extraordinarily small *SE*). Thus, when we invoke the bootstrap to conduct statistical significance tests, extremely large numbers of resamples are required (e.g., 2,000, 5,000).

However, when our application is descriptive, we are primarily interested in the mean (or median) value in the bootstrapped sampling distribution, and the standard deviation from the bootstrapped sampling distribution. The standard deviation of the statistics in the bootstrapped sampling distribution is an *empirically-estimated standard error of the statistic*. These values (*M* or *Mdn*, and the *SE*) are less dependent on large numbers of resamples. This is said not to discourage using large numbers of resamples (which are essentially free, given modern microcomputers), but is noted instead to emphasize that these two uses of the bootstrap have distinct purposes.

To make the conceptual discussion of the bootstrap concrete, consider a situation in which a researcher has scores of 100 students on a statistics exam. The researcher's primary interest might be the statistic median (e.g., $Mdn_X = 72.0$), and some descriptive estimate of the SE_{Mdn} for this particular statistic.

The initial step in the bootstrap is to create a pseudo-population from which repeated samples can be drawn, statistics are computed in each, and thus the bootstrapped sampling distribution is estimated across these resamples. One way to think about this is to suggest concatenating all the 100 rows of our dataset (i.e., appending a copy of the datafile on the back of the file) such that we now have 200 rows of data. Then we concatenate the data again, creating 300 rows of data. This is done repeatedly, a huge number of times.

We can then draw a large number of resamples from this pseudo-population, computing the statistic of interest (here Mdn_X). We draw *every* resample at exactly our original sample size, here $n = 100$, because sample size impacts sampling error variance, and it is exactly this feature of sampling that we are attempting to model.

In our first resample, Geri, say, might be drawn three times, while Murray is drawn once, and Wendy is not drawn at all. In our second resample, Geri might be drawn once, while Murray is drawn twice, and Wendy is drawn five times. We are modeling how different combinations of idiosyncratic people impact our statistic. The bootstrap is so powerful, because the bootstrap mixes the cases in the original sample up in so many different ways. This may be the closest we can come to external replication, if we limit ourself only to manipulating our original sample data, rather than collecting new data.

For each sample, we compute the median, and compile the sampling distribution, let's say over 5,000 resamples. With a modern microcomputer and the correct software, this will require only a few moments. We then compute the mean (or median) and the standard deviation of the 5,000 bootstrapped statistics (i.e., the empirically—*not* theoretically—estimated SE_{Mdn}).

In actuality, the resamples are drawn by randomly selecting cases *with replacement*. This is logistically easier than concatenating the original dataset, and is more precise because sampling with replacement is equivalent to resampling from a concatenated pseudo-population in which the dataset was concatenated infinitely many times.

Jackknife

A second "computer-intensive" internal replicability analysis is the jackknife, articulated by John Tukey and his colleagues. The jackknife involves first computing results for the sample. Then subsets of cases in the dataset are successively dropped, and the analysis is repeated in turn using each subset. The subsets are created by dropping some one number of cases, k, in each jackknife resample, subject to the restriction that k is evenly divisible into n.

A common set size for dropping cases is $k = 1$. The sample size, n, is always evenly divisible by $k = 1$. For example, if $n = 300$ for a regression analysis with four predictors, the analysis would be performed with all 300 cases, and then 300 times dropping 1 case in turn so that each resample involved 299 cases of data.

Dropping one case at a time has the advantage that cases with a disproportionate influence on the results (i.e., potential outliers) can be detected. Once all the analyses (e.g., 301 regression analyses) are completed, some additional computations are usually performed to build jackknifed confidence intervals about the parameter estimates and thereby to evaluate whether the sample statistics fall within their respective confidence intervals.

However, the bootstrap combines participants in more ways than does the jackknife. Because both the bootstrap and the jackknife require specialized software (or considerable time and patience), both analyses are typically done with specialized software that makes these analyses painless. Given an automated computer-intensive analysis and the elegance of the bootstrap, most researchers choosing between the two computer-intensive methods will opt for the bootstrap (unless they are primarily interested in outlier detection).

Cross-Validation

Cross-validation involves randomly splitting the sample into two subsets, and then replicating the primary analysis in both subgroups (Huck, Cormier, & Bounds, 1974, pp. 159–160; Thompson, 1989a). Advocacy for these methods is not new (Mosier, 1951). These analyses can be conducted with commonly available statistical software.

For purposes of clarity (things get confusing if both subgroups have the same sample size), usually the sample is randomly split into two subgroups of almost equal, but not equal sizes. When more rigorous evaluations of internal replicability are desired, the subgroups may be disparate in size (e.g., 75% of n and 25% of n, or 90% of n and 10% of n). The evidence is more compelling when the results from the smaller subgroup (e.g.,

10% of *n*) replicate well in the larger subgroup (e.g., 90% of *n*). The use of disparate subgroup sizes may be more reasonable when *n* itself is quite large.

If the replicability of subgroup 1's results in subgroup 2 is evaluated, and the replicability of subgroup 2's results in subgroup 1 is also evaluated, the internal replicability analysis is called **double cross-validation**. Because the marginal increase in work over cross-validation is minimal, and the replicability evidence is more compelling when the evidence is consistent across both subgroups, researchers using this strategy invariably conduct double cross-validation.

Table 9.2 presents a small (*n* = 15) dataset that will be used to illustrate the application. The sample size is ridiculously small but sufficient for the reader to easily replicate the analysis without having to type a large datafile.

The example presumes a multiple regression problem with two predictor variables. The dataset also includes a variable (INV_GRP), reflecting random assignment to the two subgroups by coin flip, subject here to the restriction that $n_1 = 8$ and $n_2 = 7$.

Figure 9.1 presents the SPSS syntax required for the analysis. The

TABLE 9.2. Heuristic Data for
Regression Double Cross-Validation Example

Case	Y	X1	X2	INV_GRP
1	2.0	0	9	1
2	2.0	2	6	1
3	2.2	4	3	2
4	2.6	6	1	1
5	3.2	8	0	2
6	4.0	10	0	1
7	5.0	12	1	2
8	6.2	14	3	1
9	9.8	16	6	2
10	7.6	18	13	1
11	6.3	11	4	1
12	8.9	17	5	2
13	7.7	15	6	2
14	2.7	16	7	1
15	3.3	9	7	2

FIGURE 9.1. SPSS syntax for regression double cross-validation

```
set printback=listing .
data list file='c:\stat_bk2\cross.dat' records=1 /1
  y 4-6 (1) x1 8-9 x2 11-12 inv_grp 14 .
list variables=y x1 x2 inv_grp/cases=99/format=numbered .
descriptives variables=all .
correlations variables=y x1 x2/
  statistics=all .
regression variables=y x1 x2/
  dependent=y/enter x1 x2 .

select if (inv_grp eq 1) .
compute x1_1000=x1 * 1000. .
compute x2_1000=x2 * 1000. .
descriptives variables=x1 x2 x1_1000 x2_1000 .
regression variables=y x1 x2/
  dependent=y/enter x1 x2 .

data list file='c:\stat_bk2\cross.dat' records=1 /1
  case 1-2 y 4-6 (1) x1 8-9 x2 11-12 inv_grp 14 .
select if (inv_grp eq 2) .
compute x1_1000=x1 * 1000. .
compute x2_1000=x2 * 1000. .
descriptives variables=x1 x2 x1_1000 x2_1000 .
regression variables=y x1 x2/
  dependent=y/enter x1 x2 .

DATA LIST FILE='C:\STAT_BK2\CROSS.DAT' RECORDS=1 /1
  CASE 1-2 Y 4-6 (1) X1 8-9 X2 11-12 INV_GRP 14 .
IF (INV_GRP EQ 1)ZX1_1 = (X1 - 9.62500) / 6.50137 .
IF (INV_GRP EQ 1)ZX2_1 = (X2 - 5.37500) / 4.30739 .
IF (INV_GRP EQ 2)ZX1_2 = (X1 - 11.57143) / 4.79086 .
IF (INV_GRP EQ 2)ZX2_2 = (X2 - 4.00000) / 2.70801 .
VARIABLE LABELS
  ZX1_1 'z score version of X1, subgroup 1'
  ZX2_1 'z score version of X2, subgroup 1'
  ZX1_2 'z score version of X1, subgroup 2'
  ZX2_2 'z score version of X2, subgroup 2' .
DESCRIPTIVES VARIABLES=ZX1_1 ZX2_1 ZX1_2 ZX2_2 .
COMPUTE YHAT11=(.719003 * ZX1_1) + (.085253 * ZX2_1) .
COMPUTE YHAT22=(.920505 * ZX1_2) + (.078289 * ZX2_2) .
COMPUTE YHAT21=(.719003 * ZX1_2) + (.085253 * ZX2_2) .
COMPUTE YHAT12=(.920505 * ZX1_1) + (.078289 * ZX2_1) .
VARIABLE LABELS
  YHAT11 'Subgroup 1^s data, subgroup 1^s weights'
  YHAT22 'Subgroup 2^s data, subgroup 2^s weights'
  YHAT21 'Subgroup 2^s data, subgroup 1^s weights'
  YHAT12 'Subgroup 1^s data, subgroup 2^s weights' .
CORRELATIONS VARIABLES=Y YHAT11 YHAT22 YHAT21 YHAT12/
  STATISTICS=ALL .
```

Note. The analysis in conducted in two phases. First, the analysis using the lowercase syntax is completed. The output contains statistics necessary (e.g., predictor variable means and standard deviations, and the β weights) for completing and executing the second portion of the syntax, presented in capital letters. SPSS syntax commands are *not* case sensitive.

analysis is conducted in two phases. First, the analysis using the lowercase syntax is completed. The resultant output contains statistics (e.g., predictor variable means and standard deviations, and the β weights) necessary for completing and executing the second portion of the syntax, presented in capital letters. The SPSS syntax commands are *not* case sensitive.

The first step in the analyses is to compute in both subgroups the descriptive statistics for the predictor variables and the regression β weights. The syntax tricks SPSS into presenting descriptive statistics to more decimal places by creating new variables (*X1_1000* and *X2_1000*) by multiplying the predictors (*X1* and *X2*) by 1,000. Given the impact of multiplicative constants on *M* and *SD*, explicated in the exercises for Chapters 2 and 3, the means and standard deviation of *X1* and *X2* to more decimal places can be computed by dividing the means and *SD*s of *X1_1000* and *X2_1000* by 1,000.

These means and standard deviations are then used in COMPUTE statements to create *z* scores on the predictors for both subgroups (respectively named *ZX1_1* and *ZX2_1* in subgroup 1 and *ZX1_2* and *ZX2_2* in subgroup 2). The Table 9.3 results confirm that these scores are indeed in *z*-score form (i.e., means = 0.0; *SD*s = variances − 1.0). We compute these descriptive statistics to confirm that the *z* scores were correctly calculated.

Table 9.4 presents the regression results output by SPSS for both subgroups. If the R^2 values across the two subgroups differ widely from each other and/or from the R^2 value in the full sample, then the effect size appears to be unstable, and the results are deemed to replicate poorly. Conversely, if the R^2 values and the β weights for given variables match across the two subgroups, then clearly both the effect sizes and their origins appear to replicate internally.

TABLE 9.3. SPSS Output of Descriptive Statistics
for *z* Scores in Both Subgroups

Variable	Mean	SD	Valid N	Variable label
ZX1_1	0.00	1.00	8	'z-score version of *X1*, subgroup 1'
ZX2_1	0.00	1.00	8	'z-score version of *X2*, subgroup 1'
ZX1_2	0.00	1.00	7	'z-score version of *X1*, subgroup 2'
ZX2_2	0.00	1.00	7	'z-score version of *X2*, subgroup 2'

TABLE 9.4. SPSS Subgroup Regression Coefficients
for the Figure 9.1 Syntax

Statistic	Subgroup	
	$n_1 = 8$	$n_1 = 7$
Multiple R	0.73948	0.95729
R Square	0.54683	0.91641
Adjusted R Square	0.36556	0.87462
β_1	0.719003	0.920505
β_2	0.085253	0.078289

However, if the R^2 values are comparable, but the β weights differ across the subgroups, our work is not yet done. We *must* conduct further empirical analyses to investigate whether the β weights are different, but still yield reasonably comparable $\hat{Y}$ scores across the two subgroups.

Cliff (1987, pp. 177–178) suggested that such cases involve "insensitivity" of the weights. For example, if all the predictors were highly, positively correlated with each other and with the dependent variable, any one predictor could arbitrarily be given a β weight of roughly 1, while the other variables would arbitrarily be given weights of roughly 0. All of the various possible combinations of a single β weight of 1 with several weights of 0 might appear different in the subjective judgment of the researcher, but would yield essentially equivalent $\hat{Y}$ scores.

So, what is the same is the same. But what appears to be different *may* be the same (i.e., still yield roughly equivalent prediction). In the latter case, empirical analysis informs judgment as to whether apparent differences in the β weights are meaningless, or they are noteworthy.

As reflected in the Figure 9.1 SPSS syntax, the empirical analysis is conducted as follows:

1. The predicted outcome scores for subgroup 1 are computed using subgroup 1's data (the first number in the variable name) and β weights (the second number in the variable name; here YHAT11 with $n_1 = 8$).
2. The predicted outcome scores for subgroup 2 are computed using subgroup 2's data and β weights (here YHAT22 with $n_2 = 7$).

3. The predicted outcome scores for subgroup 1 are computed using subgroup 1's data and subgroup 2's β weights (here YHAT12 with $n_1 = 8$).

4. The predicted outcome scores for subgroup 2 are computed using subgroup 2's data and subgroup 1's β weights (here YHAT21 with $n_2 = 7$).

The 10 Pearson product–moment correlations of these four variables and the Y_i scores are then computed, as reported in Table 9.5.

Note that we are invoking β weights from the standardized score world, but we are using Y scores from the *un*standardized score world. In the present application, this is inconsequential. The $\hat{Y}$ scores from the standardized and the unstandardized worlds are always perfectly correlated, because additive and multiplicative weights do not affect r, as we learned in the Reflection Problems of Chapter 5. For the same reason, the r of the Y_i scores and the $\hat{Y}$ scores from the unstandardized score world always

TABLE 9.5. SPSS Output of Pearson r Coefficients

	Y	YHAT11	YHAT22	YHAT21	YHAT12
Y	1.0000 (15)				
YHAT11	.7395[a] (0)	1.0000 (8)			
YHAT22	.9573[a] (7)	. (0)	1.0000 (7)		
YHAT21	.9569[b] (7)	. (0)	.9996[c] (7)	1.0000 (7)	
YHAT12	.7391[b] (8)	.9995[c] (8)	. (0)	. (0)	1.0000 (8)

Note. The ns are presented in parentheses.

[a]These are the multiple correlation coefficients (R) in the two subgroups.

[b]These are the "shrunken" multiple correlation coefficients (R) in the two subgroups (e.g., 0.9573 to 0.9569). The shrinkage equals the difference in the R^2 versus the shrunken R^2 (e.g., $0.9573^2 - 0.9569^2 = 0.9164 - 0.9156 = 0.0008$). The proportion of the shrinkage can be expressed as $0.0008 / 0.9164 = 0.0009 = 0.09\%$.

[c]These are the invariance coefficients in the two subgroups, correlating the true $\hat{Y}$ scores in a given subgroup with the $\hat{Y}$ scores computed using the weights from the opposite subgroup.

equals the r of the z_Y scores and the $\hat{Y}$ scores from the standardized score world.

Two of these rs in Table 9.5 are actually multiple correlation coefficients (Rs). First, the $r_{Y \times \text{YHAT11}}$ in subgroup 1 ($n_1 = 8$) equals subgroup 1's $R_{Y \text{ with } X1, X2}$ ($n_1 = 8$); as reported in Table 9.5, $r_{Y \times \text{YHAT11}} = 0.7395$, and in Table 9.4, $R_{Y \text{ with } X1, X2} = 0.73948$, respectively. Second, the $r_{Y \times \text{YHAT22}}$ in subgroup 2 ($n_2 = 7$) equals subgroup 2's $R_{Y \text{ with } X1, X2}$ ($n_2 = 7$); as reported in Table 9.5, $r_{Y \times \text{YHAT22}} = 0.9573$, and in Table 9.4, $R_{Y \text{ with } X1, X2} = 0.95729$, respectively. These comparisons are important from both a conceptual and a practical point of view.

Conceptually, the recognition that a bivariate

$$r_{Y \times \hat{Y}} = R_{Y \times X1, X2 \ldots} \tag{9.3}$$

and equivalently that

$$r_{Y \times \hat{Y}^2} = R_{Y \times X1, X2 \ldots}{}^2 \tag{9.4}$$

suggests the very important concept that analyses really focus on latent variables, and so the structure of the $\hat{Y}$ scores must be an important element in result interpretation. The equality also suggests another way of thinking about the $\hat{Y}$ scores. The $\hat{Y}$ scores are the useful information (i.e., SOS) in the predictor variables, discarding all of and only the useless portion of the predictors that are not helpful in predicting Y_i. Because the analysis focuses on the criterion variable, and predicting information about the amount and origins of differences on Y, predictors are noteworthy *only* to the derivative extent that the predictors in some way explain or predict the Y_i scores, and SOS_Y.

Practically, the comparisons of these two pairs of r and R coefficients are important in testing whether the analysis has been properly conducted. If these two sets of coefficients do not match, we have made an error in our syntax, and must fix the error before proceeding further.

Next, we can compare in subgroup 1 ($n_1 = 8$) the $r_{Y \times \text{YHAT11}} = 0.7395$ (the real $R_{Y \text{ with } X1, X2}$ in subgroup 1) with the $r_{Y \times \text{YHAT12}} = 0.7391$ (the empirically-estimated "shrunken" R when we use subgroup 2's weights with subgroup 1's data). Of course, if we want to calculate the exact shrinkage, we must "square, before you compare" (i.e., shrinkage = 0.7395^2 − 0.7391^2 = $0.54686 − 0.54627 = 0.00059$). We can perform analogous comparisons with subgroup 2's results (i.e., $n_2 = 7$, $r_{Y \times YHAT11} = 0.9573$, and $r_{Y \times YHAT12} = 0.9569$).

These two comparisons allow judgment about the internal replicability evidence. When the amount of shrinkage in both subgroups is small, as is the case here, some evidence is produced that results may be replicable. This evaluation does not invoke a statistical significance test.

However, there is one complication. A small amount of shrinkage when the original effect size is small may be devastating, whereas a fairly large shrinkage in the presence of a huge initial effect size may still be tolerable.

A context-free evaluation of replicability can be estimated by computing an **invariance coefficient** to quantify the degree to which the $\hat{Y}$ scores are stable across resampling. We compute $r_{YHAT11 \times YHAT12} = 0.9995$ and $r_{YHAT22 \times YHAT21} = 0.9996$. We evaluate these coefficients against the hope that the invariance coefficients will both approach +1.0. This is our desired value for the invariance coefficients regardless of the initial effect size estimate.

However, three precepts must be considered in conducting cross-validation analyses. First, the subgroup analyses are conducted only to derive some empirical estimate of result stability, and are not used to estimate either the effect size or from where the effect originates. The full sample results are *always* used as the basis for these interpretations, because the full sample has the largest n and therefore should yield the most accurate statistics.

Second, our expectations are that (a) the invariance coefficients will both be large and (b) the invariance coefficients will be consistent across the double cross-validation. Of course, these evaluations are more rigorous when the df_{ERROR} is larger in both subgroups, because the models are more falsifiable in such situations.

Third, bear in mind that the number of possible random sample splits can be quite large, when n is reasonably large. And different sample splits may yield divergent invariance coefficients for the same data. Thus, cross-validation methods must be interpreted cautiously. The methods have the advantage that specialized software is not required (and that performing these calculations also heuristically leads to greater understanding of latent variables and of multiple correlation). And although the methods are limited, they are considerably more useful than incorrectly NHSST as some kind of internal replicability evidence.

Where Does My Something Originate?

If our answer to our first question, "Do I have anything?" is no, then our result interpretation obligations have been met, and we are done with examining the statistical results. Only a fool would ask, "From where does my nothing originate?" or "Which predictors contribute most to predicting nothing?" Conversely, iff we answer yes, based on whatever combination of the three facets of evidence we decide to evaluate, then we must address the question, "From where does my noteworthy effect originate?"

Logically, the b or the β weights might be consulted to address this second question. After all, the b and the β weights are used to compute the $\hat{Y}$ scores, which are a primary focus of the analysis. And the structure coefficients (r_S) provide insight into the nature of the $\hat{Y}$ scores, so these coefficients also seem important in addressing this second question.

As noted in Chapter 8, in Case #1, we can formulate our answer by evaluating (a) the β weights, *or* (b) the r between the Y_i scores and each predictor, *or* (c) the r between the $\hat{Y}_i$ scores and each predictor (i.e., each r_S). In Case #1, for a given predictor $\beta = r_{Y \times X}$. Also, in a given analysis, the r_S values will *always* be proportional to the corresponding β weights (and the corresponding r of Y with a given predictor) because

$$r_S = r_{X \text{ with } Y} / R \qquad (8.14)$$

The rs between predictors and the Y_i scores are simply scaled in a different metric than the rs between predictors and the $\hat{Y}_i$ scores, by a factor of R. And in Case #1, iff $R = 1.0$, for a given predictor $\beta = r_{X \text{ with } Y} = r_S$.

So, in Case #1, only one set of coefficients must be consulted to complete result interpretation. In Cases #2 or #3, two sets of coefficients must be simultaneously considered.

β Weights

Given that multiplicative weights ought to be consulted in addressing the origins of detected effects, why are the *b* weights *usually* not used as the basis for interpretation? As explained in Chapter 8, a given *b* weight is jointly influenced by (a) the uniquely credited power of *X* scores in the given research context to help predict, either directly or indirectly, the Y_i scores, and (b) the standard deviations of the predictor variable in relation to the SD_Y.

Because the *b* weights are a *confounded* function of these two dynamics, five predictors could all have *b* weights of +2.5, but each differ in their predictive contributions in the context of these five predictors. Or the predictor with the *b* weight closest to zero may actually be the best predictor in the context of the predictor variable set.

The β weights are applied to the predictors in *z*-score form in the standardized score world. Because the standard deviations of the predictors have been removed by division when computing the *z* scores, the β weights are *only* influenced by the uniquely credited power of z_X scores in the given research context to help predict, either directly or indirectly, the z_Y scores. Thus, in a given research context the β weights can be compared to each other apples to apples.

However, because

$$b = \beta(SD_Y / SD_X) \qquad\qquad (8.1)$$

if all the predictors have the same *SD*, then the set of *b* and the set of β weights will be *proportional* to each other. And when *all* the measured variables, including the *Y* variable, have the same *SD*, then the *b* and the β for given predictors will be *equal*.

Therefore, *b* weights can be used in result interpretation when the predictor variables all have the same *SD*. For example, in their study Glaser, Hojat, Veloski, Blacklow, and Goepp (1992) correctly interpreted *b* weights rather than β weights, noting that,

> As the MCAT subtests are all reported on the same standardized scale (Mean = 8, *SD* = 2) one may use the magnitude of the obtained (non-standardized) regression coefficients (*b*-values reported in the table) to deter-

mine the relative importance of the contribution of each predictor in the regression models. (p. 399)

But equality of predictor SDs occurs rarely, and so β weights are usually one focus in evaluating result origins. The a and b weights are primarily useful in predictive applications of regression, where we focus on the $\hat{Y}_i$ scores in the unstandardized score world (e.g., predicted height of children in inches once adult) rather than estimates of standardized z-score height, because z scores are seen as being less friendly by the nonstatisticians usually involved in predictive situations.

Four precepts should govern the interpretation of the β weights. First, typically, the signs of the β weights are irrelevant, except that the context of a given scaling decision must be considered. The signs of the β weights are usually arbitrary because in the social sciences the scaling direction of our measures is usually arbitrary. We can score an academic test by counting the number of right answers, or the number of wrong answers. In either case, we are measuring the same construct.

Second, remember that β are *only* bivariate correlation coefficients in Case #1. So do *not* use the word "correlation" in the context of the β weights unless you are in Case #1. But in *all* cases, a β weight indicates the predicted number of SD units of change in the $\hat{Y}_i$ scores for 1 standard deviation of change on a given predictor, given the context of a particular set of predictors. For example, if the predictor is the number of right answers on an academic test, and $\beta = +2.5$, this means that for 1 SD_X of improvement on scores on the test, the $\hat{Y}_i$ scores are predicted to improve by 2.5 SD_Ys, holding all other scores constant, and in the context of a given set of predictors.

Third, as repeatedly emphasized in Chapter 8, remember that β weights are *context specific*. If you add a single predictor to the model, or remove a single predictor, *all* the β weights could fluctuate wildly, unless you are in Case #1. In Cases #2 and #3, this implies that caution must be exercised when interpreting the β weights, unless you are somehow certain the model is correctly specified.

Fourth, use caution when interpreting NHSST for the multiplicative weights. The $p_{\text{CALCULATED}}$ values for a given pair of b and β weights in a given study are identical. But remember that all tests of statistical significance, including the test of H_0: b (or β) = 0, are driven by sample size (see

Ziliak & McCloskey, 2004). This means that an identical set of β weights may all be statistically significant in one study with a large n, whereas none are statistically significant in another study with a smaller n.

Structure Coefficients

When $b = 0.0$, $\beta = 0.0$, and vice versa, and the multiplicative weight obliterates the predictor variable. In Case #1, a predictor with β (and b) = 0.0 is definitively useless. The predictor cannot help, either directly (by predicting variability in the Y_i scores) or indirectly (by making one or more other predictors better predictors of the Y_i scores), to explain the SOS_Y.

But in Case #2, a predictor with a zero β weight might, in fact, be the single best predictor in the predictor variable set. The predictor may simply be denied any predictive credit for commonly explained Y_i score variability also explained by other correlated predictors. In such a case, the predictor would have a large r_S^2.

And in Case #3, a predictor might have r_S^2 (and r_S) of zero, but also a β weight largest in absolute magnitude among the weights for the predictor set. In such a situation, we know definitively that the predictor is a suppressor variable.

Across all cases, only when a given predictor has both $\beta = 0.0$ and $r_S = 0.0$ is the predictor completely useless, at least in the context of a given set of predictors. Clearly, as Courville and Thompson (2001) and others (e.g., Dunlap & Landis, 1998; Thompson & Borrello, 1985) have argued, "β is [often] not enough."

Of course, as noted previously, because the rs between the predictors and the Y_i scores are proportional to the corresponding rs between the predictors and the $\hat{Y}_i$ scores, the same interpretations across all three regression cases would be realized by consulting the rs between the predictors and the Y_i scores. The selection of a supplement to the interpretation of the β weights across the two choices is entirely stylistic.

Unhappily, empirical studies (e.g., Courville & Thompson, 2001) of published regression research show that researchers invariably interpret only β weights. The consequence is gross misinterpretation of results in much of the literature.

An emphasis on regression structure coefficients is also consistent with the emphasis on r_S throughout the general linear model, where for some reason the r_Ss (unlike the weights) are always called the same thing (i.e., structure coefficients). For example, structure coefficients are deemed critical to result interpretation in both exploratory (cf. Gorsuch, 1983, p. 207; Thompson, 2004) and confirmatory (cf. Graham, Guthrie, & Thompson, 2003) factor analysis.

The same is true in descriptive discriminant analysis (cf. Huberty, 1994, p. 206) and canonical correlation analysis (cf. Levine, 1977, p. 20). Thus, Meredith (1964, p. 55) suggested, "If the variables within each set are moderately intercorrelated the possibility of interpreting the canonical variates by inspection of [only] the appropriate regression weights [function coefficients] is practically nil."

Stepwise Methods

In some predictive applications, researchers have access to a large number of predictor variables, and conduct a specification search (i.e., change the model specification) by looking for a more parsimonious, smaller subset of predictors that may be almost as effective as the full set of predictors in yielding accurate $\hat{Y}_i$ scores. Some researchers attempt to invoke what are called stepwise methods for this purpose. Huberty (1994) has noted, "It is quite common to find the use of 'stepwise analyses' reported in empirically based journal articles" (p. 261).

Stepwise analysis is a forward or a backward progression in which predictor variables are added or deleted from the model one variable at a time, based atheoretically on empirical analyses of the sample data. The forward progression is more commonly encountered than is backward analysis.

In forward stepwise regression, software first computes the bivariate r^2 values between each predictor variable and the Y_i scores. The predictor with the largest r^2 with Y is entered in the first step. The selection by stepwise of the best single predictor is correct.

In the second step, the remaining predictors are evaluated to determine which one predictor, when added to the model, will yield the largest increase in R^2, in the context of the first predictor's presence in the model.

Thus, a predictor that is very highly correlated with the first-entered predictor may never be entered into the model, even if this predictor is the second-best single predictor in the predictor variable set.

In the third step, the remaining predictors are evaluated to determine which one predictor, when added to the model, will yield the largest increase in R^2, in the context of the first two predictors' presence in the model. The process continues by considering the addition of remaining predictors.

However, next and after all the remaining steps, the removal of previously-entered predictors is also considered. For example, in the presence of three predictors, if the first predictor's explanatory power is present in the second and third predictors selected, then the first predictor will be removed from the model.

As programmed in commonly-used statistical packages, the forward selection procedure continues until the change in R^2 from one step versus the R^2 in the immediately previous step is no longer statistically significantly different from zero. In any context, including stepwise, we can test the null that H_0: $R_{LARGER}^2 = R_{SMALLER}^2$ (or H_0: $R_{LARGER}^2 R_{SMALLER}^2 - 0$) using the generic equation:

$$F_{CALCULATED} - [(R_{LARGER}^2 - R_{SMALLER}^2) / (k_L - h_S)] / \qquad (9.5)$$
$$[(1 - R_{LARGER}^2) / (n - k_L - 1)]$$

where k_L is the number of predictors used to obtain R_{LARGER}^2, and k_S is the number of predictors used to obtain $R_{SMALLER}^2$. The df are $(k_L - k_0)$ for the numerator, and $(n - k_L - 1)$ for the denominator.

In stepwise, $k_L - k_S$ equals 1 at each successive step, so Equation 9.5 simplifies in this application to

$$F_{CALCULATED} = [R_{LARGER}^2 - R_{SMALLER}^2] / [(1 - R_{LARGER}^2) / (n - 2)] \quad (9.6)$$

In this application, the degrees of freedom are 1 for the numerator and $(n - k_L - 1)$ for the denominator. Of course, this means that 100 researchers evaluating the same ΔR^2 (i.e., $R_{LARGER}^2 - R_{SMALLER}^2$) for the same number of steps, but with 100 different sample sizes, will each obtain different $p_{CALCULATED}$ values, and some may make different decisions, even at a fixed α about when to discontinue the stepwise analysis.

Three Problems

There are three primary problems with stepwise analyses (Thompson, 1995). Various scholars have noted these problems (e.g., Huberty, 1989; Snyder, 1991; Thompson, 2001) and suggested that stepwise methods should **never** be used. Indeed, one article in this venue was entitled "Why Won't Stepwise Methods Die?" (Thompson, 1989b).

Wrong Degrees of Freedom

Commonly-used statistical packages incorrectly compute the $F_{CALCULATED}$ and $p_{CALCULATED}$ used to test the final R^2 evaluated at the conclusion of the stepwise analysis, because the wrong degrees of freedom are used. The df_{TOTAL} is correctly computed as $n - 1$. However, the $df_{REGRESSION}$ is computed as the number of variables that stepwise has entered, and the $df_{RESIDUAL}$ is computed as df_{TOTAL} minus this $df_{REGRESSION}$. Instead, the $df_{REGRESSION}$ *should be* the number of predictor variables in the study.

The $df_{REGRESSION}$ are the coins we spend to ask questions of our data. We can enter into a model no more than df_{TOTAL} predictor variables (and should enter considerably fewer predictors, so that $df_{RESIDUAL} \neq 0$, and the model remains falsifiable).

Software should charge us for 1 degree of freedom for every predictor "tasted," regardless of how many predictors are ultimately retained in the analysis. As Thompson (2001) observed,

> This is bad behavior. The movie I show my students to teach them that this is bad behavior is "Animal House" when John Belushi is in the student cafeteria. He tastes all the entries on the buffet line, but doesn't pay for the items he tasted and put back (or stuffed in his pockets). My students, who include some serious cafeteria experts, assure me that this behavior would not be tolerated at many of your finer cafeterias. Nor should such [bad] behavior be tolerated in statistics. (p. 87)

Note that if 5 out of 50 predictors were selected randomly, or based on prior findings, or theory, and all 50 predictors were not tasted by stepwise, then $df_{REGRESSION} = 5$ would indeed be entirely correct.

Table 9.6 illustrates the impacts for a hypothetical situation involving

TABLE 9.6. Stepwise NHSST for Hypothetical Example

Analysis/source	SOS	df	MS	$F_{CALCULATED}$	$p_{CALCULATED}$	R^2
Incorrect						
Regression	10.0	5	2.00	2.667	0.025	10.00%
Residual	90.0	120	0.75			
Total	100.0	125	0.80			
Correct						
Regression	10.0	50	0.20	0.167	1.000	10.00%
Residual	90.0	75	1.20			
Total	100.0	125	0.80			

$n = 126$, 5 steps of forward stepwise with a pool of 50 predictor variables, and an R^2 of 10.00%. For the incorrect degrees of freedom, $p_{CALCULATED}$ is 0.025, and so the result is statistically significant at $\alpha = 0.05$. But when the correct degrees of freedom are computed, $F_{CALCULATED}$ is less than 1 and so cannot be statistically significant even at infinite degrees of freedom. Here, for the correct degrees of freedom, the Excel =FDIST statistical function calculates that $p_{CALCULATED} = 1.00$, and the result is not statistically significant.

Of course, this problem is not inherent in stepwise methods, but instead is a flaw in the statistical software implementations of these methods. The consequence of using a deflated $df_{REGRESSION}$ along with an inflated $df_{RESIDUAL}$ is typically a "double whammy" inflation of $F_{CALCULATED}$ and a corresponding "double whammy" deflation of $p_{CALCULATED}$. Thus, Cliff (1987, p. 185) noted that "most computer programs for [stepwise] multiple regression are positively satanic in their temptations toward Type I errors."

The problem may be less acute when sample size is (a) extraordinarily large and the number of predictor variables is very small or (b) the final R^2 is small. In these cases, the differences in the correct and incorrect $p_{CALCULATED}$ values will not be as large, as could be seen by modeling variations on the Table 9.6 results for various ns, numbers of predictors, and effect sizes. Nevertheless, in all cases, the computer packages use the incorrect degrees of freedom, and the only question is how wrong the incorrect results are.

Capitalization on Sampling Error

All samples include variance that mirrors true variance in the population, as well as idiosyncratic variance unique to the sample (i.e., sampling error variance). Unfortunately, in stepwise even a very small amount of sampling error variance can result in an incorrect predictor selection decision (i.e., a decision that would not occur if stepwise for the same variables was performed in the population).

Furthermore, stepwise makes a linear sequence of entry decisions. A mistake at any step impacts and potentially compromises *all* subsequent entry decisions. Because in stepwise an infinitesimal competitive advantage for entering a predictor will result in that variable's selection, and that infinitesimal advantage may be due to sampling error, and also prejudice subsequent decisions, "a large proportion of the published results using this method probably present conclusions that are not supported by the data" (Cliff, 1987, pp. 120–121).

For example, if for an analysis involving 50 predictors, the best single predictor $r_{Y \times X}^2 = 10.0001\%$, and for a second predictor $r_{Y \times X}^2 = 10.0000\%$, the first predictor will be entered before the second variable, and the second variable may never get entered. Of course, this problem is partly a function of collinearity, and is less severe as the research approaches Case #1. On the other hand, in Case #1, the stepwise predictor variable entry order will exactly correspond to the squared correlations of the predictors with the Y_i scores, so stepwise in Case #1 represents an uninteresting situation in which no researcher would use stepwise.

Freedman (1983) conducted a Monte Carlo simulation study demonstrating that even if we sample from a population in which the predictors each have no relationship with Y, a large sample R^2 will result. He reported:

> To focus on an extreme case, suppose that in fact there is *no relationship* between the dependent variable and the explanatory variables. Even so, if there are many explanatory variables, the R^2 [from a stepwise analysis] will be high. . . . This is demonstrated [here] by simulation and by asymptotic calculation. (p. 152)

R^2 Not Optimized

Some researchers erroneously believe that stepwise methods identify the set of predictors of size k that will yield the largest R^2 given the use of k predictors with the dataset (Huberty, 1989, p. 45). To the contrary, (a) another combination of k predictors may yield a larger R^2 than the R^2 for the k predictors picked by stepwise, and furthermore (b) the best set of k predictors might not include *any* of the k predictors selected by stepwise (see Thompson, 1995)!

Equating stepwise with finding the optimal set of k predictors is illogical, because stepwise and finding the best set of k predictors involve two different questions. In an analogy to selecting five players on a basketball team, stepwise *sequentially* asks, "In a given selection, which one player should I add to the team, given the previous players selected?"

Conversely, the correct selection method would ask, "For all possible teams of five players, which team plays the best?" The best team of five may not be the team identified via a sequence of selections, because asking a question about team quality does *not* raise any issues of incremental selection, and incremental selection issues are completely *irrelevant* to selecting the best team.

The *only* way to select the best possible team of basketball players from a pool of 50 players is to evaluate all possible teams of 5. The best team might not include the players picked in a stepwise algorithm. And the best team of 5 might not even include the single best player, when the best player does not play well with others. By the same token, the only time that stepwise picks the best predictor variable set of size k is in Case #1, which is not a situation in which stepwise is likely to be used, because here in the presence of all the $r_{Y \times X}^2$ values, no value is added by conducting the stepwise analysis.

Alternative Models

Two alternative models to stepwise, unlike stepwise, may be very useful in research. The two models involve hierarchical and all-possible-subsets analyses, respectively.

However, it is important to realize that regardless of the model (e.g., stepwise, hierarchical, all-possible subsets) used, once a given set of k predictors is identified, the β weights and the structure coefficients for these predictors *will be the same no matter how the k predictors are identified*. So, with a given set of $k = 5$ predictors, if $\beta_1 = -2.80$, and r_S for the first predictor is -0.75, β_1 will equal -2.80 and r_S will equal -0.75 if stepwise was used, or the five predictors were selected using darts, or tarot cards, or all-possible-subsets analyses, or *any* method.

Hierarchical Entry

Hierarchical predictor variable entry involves entering predictors in predetermined blocks (e.g., using a series of ENTER subcommands within the SPSS REGRESSION procedure) based on theory or previous research. Thus, the data are *not* consulted in selecting the blocks or their order entries.

For example, if a researcher had variables measured at birth (i.e., *X1*, *X2*, and *X3*), variables measured in first grade (e.g., *F1*, and *F2*), and variables measured in sixth grade (e.g., *S1*, *S2*, and *S3*), the variables might logically be entered in three blocks reflecting the chronology of measurement. This could be accomplished in SPSS by invoking the subcommand syntax within REGRESSION:

```
ENTER x1 x2 x3/ENTER f1 f2/enter s1 s2 s3
```

At each block of variable entry, an R^2 will be printed. For a given dataset with a fixed n, the uncorrected R^2 can never become smaller as more measured predictors are used. Of course, the uncorrected R^2 could theoretically remain unchanged as more predictors are added, and the corrected R^2 could get smaller. Also, if desired, the statistical significance of the differences in the sequential R^2 values could be evaluated with Equation 9.5.

Hierarchical entry is *theory-driven*, and can be used to address interesting theoretical propositions, such as developmental models. For example, in the illustrative situation described here, we may use these models to test whether education after first grade has any impacts beyond those present in first grade.

All-Possible-Subsets Analysis

In predictive applications, the researcher may seek a more parsimonious (smaller) set of predictors that may still yield an acceptable R^2, or even an R^2 that is roughly comparable to the effect size obtained from using the full pool of predictors. However, as suggested previously, stepwise is *not* suitable for this (or any other) purpose.

The correct selection method begins by computing the R^2 for each and every combination of predictors for each and every variable set size. The computations sound daunting but, actually, can be painlessly performed by some software in only moments.

Figure 9.2 presents a line plot of the maximum R^2 values for a given number of k predictors. This plot can be consulted to inform the researcher's subjective judgment regarding the optimal number of predictors to retain. In this example, the plot seems to level off after the predictor variable set size is $k = 5$ ($R^2 = 57.1\%$ with $k = 5$, versus $R^2 = 58.1\%$ with $k = 6$).

If the ~57.1% effect size is deemed sufficient, given the researcher's predictive application, the focus then turns to which five predictors should be retained for future use. Thoughtful researchers will look at several R^2 values for $k = 5$, and then thoughtfully select the predictor variable set at $k = 5$ with variables that can be most easily or most cheaply measured. A $k = 5$ variable set with a slightly less than optimal effect size might be preferred for practical reasons.

A variant on this **all-possible-subsets analysis** would instead plot "adjusted R^2" values. This alternative will be most appealing when sam-

---

FIGURE 9.2. Line plot of successive R values

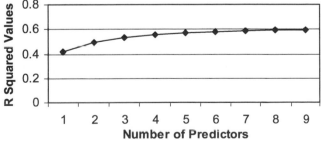

pling error variance is likely to be larger, as when sample size is relatively small.

■■■ Invoking Some Alternative Models

Various interesting alternative or complementary regression models may be helpful in some research situations. Four particularly noteworthy models are considered here: (a) commonality analysis, (b) path analysis, (c) curvilinear regression invoking predictors taken to various exponential powers to model curvilinear relationships, and (d) testing interaction effects.

Commonality Analysis

Commonality analysis (Beaton, 1973; Mood, 1969; Seibold & McPhee, 1979; Thompson, 1985) can be used to decompose either the R^2 or the $SOS_{EXPLAINED}$ into constituent, nonoverlapping parts that involve the unique and the common explanatory powers of the predictors (or sets of predictors) in all their possible combinations. For example, in the context of two predictors (or two sets of predictors, each involving one or more variables), we could ask, (a) How much explanatory power is *unique* to the first predictor (or predictor set)? (b) How much explanatory power is *unique* to the second predictor (or predictor set)? and (c) How much explanatory power is *common* to both predictors (or predictor sets) and could be derived from either predictor (or predictor set)?

Rowell (1996) presented an accessible treatment of these methods. Table 9.7 presents the formulas that can be used to derive these estimates for either two, three, or four predictor variables (or predictor variable sets). Formulas for more predictors can be found elsewhere (e.g., Rowell, 1996).

Commonality analysis is only of potential interest in either Case #2 or Case #3. In Case #1, because all the predictor variables are uncorrelated, (a) there is no common explanatory power of the predictors acting in concert in sets of two or more, and (b) all the unique explanatory power of a given predictor is quantified by the r^2 of the given predictor with the Y_i scores.

TABLE 9.7. Formulas for Unique
and Commonality Components of Shared Variance

```
Two Independent Variables
  U1 = R²(12) - R²(2)
  U2 = R²(12) - R²(1)
  C12 = R²(1) + R²(2) - R²(12)

Three Independent Variables
  U1 = R²(123) - R²(23)
  U2 = R²(123) - R²(13)
  U3 = R²(123) - R²(12)
  C12 = R²(13) + R²(23) - R²(3) - R²(123)
  C13 = R²(12) + R²(23) - R²(2) - R²(123)
  C23 = R²(12) + R²(13) - R²(1) - R²(123)
  C123 = R²(123) + R²(1) + R²(2) + R²(3) - R²(12) - R²(13) - R²(23)

Four Independent Variables
  U1 = R²(1234) - R²(234)
  U2 = R²(1234) - R²(134)
  U3 = R²(1234) - R²(124)
  U4 = R²(1234) - R²(123)
  C12 = R²(134) + R²(234) - R²(34) - R²(1234)
  C13 = R²(124) + R²(234) - R²(24) - R²(1234)
  C14 = R²(123) + R²(234) - R²(23) - R²(1234)
  C23 = R²(124) + R²(134) - R²(14) - R²(1234)
  C24 = R²(123) + R²(134) - R²(13) - R²(1234)
  C34 = R²(123) + R²(124) - R²(12) - R²(1234)
  C123 = R²(1234) + R²(14) + R²(24) + R²(34)
         - R²(4) - R²(124) - R²(134) - R²(234)
  C124 = R²(1234) + R²(13) + R²(23) + R²(34)
         - R²(3) - R²(123) - R²(134) - R²(234)
  C134 = R²(1234) + R²(12) + R²(23) + R²(24)
         - R²(2) - R²(123) - R²(124) - R²(234)
  C234 = R²(1234) + R²(12) + R²(13) + R²(14)
         - R²(1) - R²(123) - R²(124) - R²(134)
  C1234 = R²(1) + R²(2) + R²(3) + R²(4)
          + R²(123) + R²(124) + R²(134) + R²(234)
          - R²(12) - R²(13) - R²(14) - R²(23) - R²(24) - R²(34)
          - R²(1234)
```

To make this discussion concrete, let's consider the prediction of library users' ratings ($n = 69,358$) of library service quality using the LibQUAL+™ protocol (Thompson, Cook, & Heath, 2003a, 2003b), predicted by (a) global library satisfaction scores, (b) global scores on academic outcomes facilitated by the library, and (c) frequency of library use scores. The necessary results to apply the Table 9.7 equations are presented in Table 9.8.

The Table 9.8 results can easily be plugged into a spreadsheet program to produce the output reported in Table 9.9. Note that the unique

TABLE 9.8. Coefficients Required for the Table 9.7 Computations

Predictors	r^2 or R^2
Satisfaction	56.996%
Outcomes	39.280%
Use	0.117%
Satisfaction, Outcomes	58.666%
Satisfaction, Use	57.014%
Outcomes, Use	39.289%
Satisfaction, Outcomes, Use	58.698%

and the common explanatory partitions of the R^2 (i.e., 58.698%) for a given variable sum together to equal the r^2 of a given predictor with the Y_i scores (e.g., Unique_SATISFACTION + Common_SATISFACTION with OUTCOMES and USE = $r_{\text{SATISFACTION with LibQUAL+(TM)}}$ = 19.409% + 37.587% = 56.996%).

It is also noteworthy that the sum of all seven nonoverlapping partitions of R^2 equals the R^2 of the three predictors with the LibQUAL+™ scores. Thus, 19.409% + 1.684% + 0.032% + 37.488% + –0.023% + –0.014% + 0.122% = 58.698%. This merely reiterates the truism that commonality here is being used to partition the R^2 into (seven) constituent, nonoverlapping parts.

Some comment on the negative variance partitions is necessary. Clearly, negative variances are troubling because, as area-world statistics, variances theoretically have a minimum value of zero. Traditionally, near-zero values in commonality analyses are treated as zeroes. If some negative values are large, the possibilities of model misspecification, or of suppressor effects, are suggested, and the results would be deemed not reasonable.

Commonality analysis can also be used to partition the $SOS_{\text{EXPLAINED}}$ (here 56,983.94). The analysis is performed by multiplying the Table 9.9 results by the $SOS_{\text{EXPLAINED}}$ of 56,983.94, again using a spreadsheet. The result is presented in Table 9.10.

In the present example, the commonality analysis can be used to help us understand what the LibQUAL+™ scores measure. Several conclusions are suggested.

First, the LibQUAL+™ scores appear insensitive to frequency of

TABLE 9.9. Unique and Common Components of Shared Variance (R^2)

Predictors/partitions	Predictors		
	Satisfaction	Outcomes	Use
Satisfaction	19.409%		
Outcomes		1.684%	
Use			0.032%
Satisfaction, Outcomes	37.488%	37.488%	
Satisfaction, Use	−0.023%		−0.023%
Outcomes, Use		−0.014%	−0.014%
Satisfaction, Outcomes, Use	0.122%	0.122%	0.122%
Unique	19.409%	1.684%	0.032%
Common	37.587%	37.596%	0.085%
Total	56.996%	39.280%	0.117%

library use. Frequency of library use either alone ($\text{Unique}_{\text{USE}} = 0.032\%$) or in concert with either or both of the other predictors ($\text{Common}_{\text{USE}} = 0.085\%$) contributes little to defining $R^2 = 56.996\%$.

Second, academic outcomes explain about two-thirds of the $R^2 = 58.698\%$ (i.e., $r^2_{\text{LibQUAL+(TM) with OUTCOMES}} = 39.280\% / 58.698\% = 0.669$), but given that most of this overlaps with the other two predictors (i.e., $\text{Common}_{\text{OUTCOMES}} = 37.596\% / 39.280\% = 0.957$), the outcomes scores

TABLE 9.10. Sum-of-Squares (SOS) Explained by Predictor Sets

Predictors	Predictors			Cumulation
	Satisfaction	Outcomes	Use	
Satisfaction	18842.23			18842.23
Outcomes		1634.82		1634.82
Use			31.07	31.07
Satisfaction, Outcomes	36393.30	36393.30		36393.30
Satisfaction, Use	−22.33		−22.33	−22.33
Outcomes, Use		−13.59	−13.59	−13.59
Satisfaction, Outcomes, Use	118.44	118.44	118.44	118.44
Total				56983.94

contribute little to predicting the LibQUAL+™ scores in the presence of the other scores.

The satisfaction scores uniquely contribute about one-third of the R^2 = 58.698% (i.e., 19.409% / 58.698% = 0.331). And the satisfaction and outcomes scores as a predictor pair have in common the capacity to explain about two-thirds of the R^2 = 58.698% (i.e., 37.488% / 58.698% = 0.639). The remaining five variance partitions are all quite small, the largest being only Unique$_{OUTCOMES}$ = 1.684%. Clearly, in the context of this predictor variable set, the LibQUAL+™ scores must be considered basically a global measure of patron satisfaction with libraries.

Path Analysis

Path analysis was conceptualized by Sewall Wright (1921, 1934) as a way of studying the direct and indirect impacts of measured variables on other measured variables considered to be effects. A brief treatment here is warranted for three reasons. First, like commonality analysis, path analysis can be conceptualized as another way to decompose correlations. This process is fundamental to all data analysis, and so is important conceptually to an understanding of what statistical analyses do. Second, the methods can be substantively important in their own right.

Third, path analysis, when married with a multivariate technique called confirmatory factor analysis (see Thompson, 2004), creates a method called structural equation modeling (SEM). SEM is a very powerful multivariate analysis, which is beyond the scope of the present book (see Thompson, 2000b, for an introductory explanation). Nevertheless, some understanding of path analysis will facilitate subsequent understanding of SEM, and path analysis is an important analytic method in its own right.

The purpose of this brief discussion is *not* to make you an expert on path analysis. The purpose is only to make you aware of additional analytic possibilities, expose you to a few key concepts, and perhaps excite you to do some further reading.

To make this discussion concrete, consider the hypothetical data presented in Table 9.11, which represent a variation on an example provided by Kerlinger and Pedhazur (1973, pp. 305–326). The example involves

TABLE 9.11. Pearson *r* Matrix for Predicting GPA				
Variable	*SES*	*nAch*	*IQ*	*GPA*
SES	1.000	0.250	0.510	0.351
nAch	0.250	1.000	0.190	0.590
IQ	0.510	0.190	1.000	0.510
GPA	0.351	0.590	0.510	1.000

prediction of GPA with socio-economic status (SES), psychological need for achievement (nAch), and IQ scores (IQ).

The path model we will test is presented in Figure 9.3. In a real analysis, a critical feature of the investigation would involve laying out an empirical and/or theoretical justification for the model. Also, real analyses usually should test multiple rival models, because the fit of a preferred model to our data is more persuasive when the preferred model fits better than plausible rival models (Thompson, 2000b). Our model has been drawn under the assumptions that (a) all relationships are linear, (b) all causal flows are one way (i.e., there are no two variables linked by reciprocal causation, or in other words, no two variables are linked by a pair of one-headed arrows going in opposite directions), and (c) the measured variables are intervally-scaled.

We will analyze the measured variables in their *z*-score forms, and thus be estimating β weights, so that the weights can be compared with each other apples-to-apples. In a path analysis diagram involving measured variables in their *z*-score forms, two-headed arrows represent corre-

FIGURE 9.3. Path analysis model

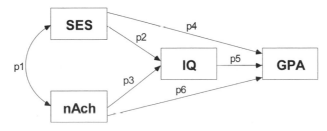

lation coefficients. One-headed arrows involve estimates of path coefficients. We require an estimate of the coefficient implied by each of the six arrows in Figure 9.3.

Path Coefficient Estimation

The coefficient for the $r_{SES \times nAch}$ two-headed arrow can be derived by inserting into the diagram the appropriate entry from Table 9.11 (i.e., $r = 0.250 = p_1$). To find the path coefficients for predicting IQ from SES, and IQ from nAch, we conduct a regression predicting IQ with only SES and nACH. The resulting β weights provide these two path coefficients.

We can compute these β weights using Equations 8.12 and 8.13. For SES predicting IQ within this model, we have

$$\beta_{SES} = [r_{SES \times IQ} - \{(r_{nAch \times IQ})(r_{SES \times nAch})\}] / [1.0 - r_{SES \times nAch}^2]$$
$$[0.510 - \{(0.190)(0.250)\}] / [1.000 - 0.250^2]$$
$$[0.510 - \{(0.190)(0.250)\}] / [1.000 - 0.063]$$
$$[0.510 - \{(0.190)(0.250)\}] / 0.938$$
$$[0.510 - 0.048] / 0.938$$
$$0.463 / 0.938$$
$$= 0.493$$

Thus, $p_2 = \beta_{SES} = 0.493$.

For nAch predicting IQ within this model, we have

$$\beta_{nAch} = [r_{nAch \times IQ} - \{(r_{SES \times IQ})(r_{SES \times nAch})\}] / [1.0 - r_{SES \times nAch}^2]$$
$$[0.190 - \{(0.510)(0.250)\}] / [1.000 - 0.250^2]$$
$$[0.190 - \{(0.510)(0.250)\}] / [1.000 - 0.063]$$
$$[0.190 - \{(0.510)(0.250)\}] / 0.938$$
$$[0.190 - 0.128] / 0.938$$
$$0.063 / 0.938$$
$$= 0.067$$

Thus, $p_3 = \beta_{nAch} = 0.067$.

Finally, to compute the p_4, p_5, and p_6 coefficients, we perform a regression predicting GPA with SES, nAch, and IQ. We could do this simply by running the necessary regression in SPSS or another package. Alternatively, we could obtain the same result by requiring SPSS to do the necessary calculations step by step, using the following syntax. In either case, when predicting GPA, we would obtain $p_4 = \beta_{SES} = 0.018$, $p_5 = \beta_{IQ} = 0.404$, and $p_6 = \beta_{nAch} = 0.509$.

```
SET PRINTBACK=LISTING .
MATRIX .
comment  R is the r matrix involving the 3 predictors .
COMPUTE R =
{1.000,   .250,   .510 ;
  .250, 1.000,   .190 ;
  .510,   .190, 1.000 } .
PRINT R /
  FORMAT='F7.3' /
  TITLE='Predictor r Matrix' /
  SPACE=4 /
  RLABELS=SES, nAch, IQ /
  CLABELS=SES, nAch, IQ / .
comment  R2 is the correlation of each predictor with Y .
COMPUTE R2 =
{ .351 ;
  .590 ;
  .510 } .
PRINT R2 /
  FORMAT='F7.3' /
  TITLE='r each Predictor with Y' /
  SPACE=4 /
  RLABELS=SES, nAch, IQ / .
COMPUTE RINV = INV (R) .
PRINT RINV /
  FORMAT='F7.3' /
  TITLE='R Matrix inverted' /
  SPACE=4 /
  RLABELS=SES, nAch, IQ /
  CLABELS=SES, nAch, IQ / .
COMPUTE BETA = RINV * R2 .
PRINT BETA /
  FORMAT='F9.6' /
  TITLE='Beta weights for each Predictor' /
  SPACE=4 /
  RLABELS=SES, nAch, IQ / .
END MATRIX .
```

Partitioning Direct and Indirect Effects

One way to interpret our results is by conceptualizing the model as predicting changes in measured variables as a cumulation of direct and indi-

rect effects from changes in predictor variable scores. For our model, we
have

$$z_{SES} = e_{SES},$$
$$z_{nAch} = e_{nAch},$$
$$z_{IQ} = p_2[z_{SES}] + p_3[z_{nAch}] + e_{IQ},$$
$$z_{GPA} = p_4[z_{SES}] + p_6[z_{nAch}] + p_2[z_{SES}][p_5] + p_3[z_{nAch}][p_5] + e_{GPA}$$

where es are the error terms resulting whenever our model does not perfectly fit our data.

The model can be used to estimate changes in an outcome associated
with change in a predictor by a given number of standard deviation units,
holding other measured variables constant. For example, if a given person's nAch increased by 1 SD, the predicted change in IQ would be solely
due to direct effects of the change in nAch, and would be

$$z_{IQ} = p_2[z_{SES}] + p_3[z_{nAch}]$$

or

$$z_{IQ} = 0.493[0] + 0.067[1]$$

or an increase of 0.067.

However, if a given person's nAch increased by 1 SD, the predicted
change in GPA would be impacted both directly and indirectly by this
change. The predicted change in GPA would be

$$z_{GPA} = p_4[z_{SES}] + p_6[z_{nAch}] + p_2[z_{SES}][p_5] + p_3[z_{nAch}][p_5]$$

or

$$z_{GPA} = 0.018[0] + 0.509[1] + 0.493[0][0.404] + 0.067[1][0.404]$$

or an increase of 0.509 (i.e., 0.509[1]) from the direct effects of the change
in nAch, as well as an additional increase of 0.027 (i.e., 0.067[1][0.404])
from the indirect effects of the change in nAch working through IQ.

Partitioning r²s and Evaluating Model Fit

The path coefficients can also be used to estimate the bivariate rs among the measured variables, or can be viewed as a decomposition of the *estimated* bivariate rs among the measured variables (see Loehlin, 2004, Ch. 1). This insight yields the conceptual understanding that *the path model is attempting to yield a matrix of estimated correlations that will approximate the actual values* in Table 9.11. Beyond the heuristic value of comparing estimated with actual r values, to emphasize that the model is an alternative representation of the correlations, from a practical standpoint we compare the reproduced or estimated correlations with our actual correlations to help *evaluate whether our model fits our data*, and the model seems reasonable. Here we can decompose the six unique correlation coefficients presented in Table 9.11.

First, given our coefficients, the $r_{\text{GPA} \times \text{SES}}$ is estimated as

$$r_{\text{GPA} \times \text{SES}} = p_4 + [(p_6)(r_{\text{SES} \times \text{nACH}})] + [(p_5)(r_{\text{IQ} \times \text{SES}})]$$
$$0.017579 + [(0.508775)(0.250)] + [(0.404368)(0.510)]$$
$$0.017579 + 0.127193 + [(0.404368)(0.510)]$$
$$0.017579 + 0.127193 + 0.206227$$
$$0.017579 + 0.333421$$
$$r_{\text{GPA} \times \text{SES}} = 0.351000$$

Alternatively, we can decompose the correlation using *only* the path coefficients from the path analysis. Now we have

$$r_{\text{GPA} \times \text{SES}} = [(p_1)(p_6)] + [(p_1)(p_3)(p_5)] + [(p_2)(p_5)] + p_4$$
$$[(0.250)(0.508775)] + [(0.250)(0.066667)(0.404368)] +$$
$$[(0.493333)(0.404368) + 0.017579$$
$$0.127194 + 0.006740 + 0.199488 + 0.017579$$
$$r_{\text{GPA} \times \text{SES}} = 0.351000$$

Second, $r_{\text{GPA} \times \text{nACH}}$ is estimated as

$$r_{\text{GPA} \times \text{nACH}} = [(p_4)(r_{\text{SES} \times \text{nACH}})] + p_6 + [(p_5)(r_{\text{IQ} \times \text{nACH}})]$$
$$[(0.017579)(0.250)] + 0.508775 + [(0.404368)(0.190)]$$
$$0.004394 + 0.508775 + [(0.404368)(0.19)]$$
$$0.004394 + 0.508775 + 0.076829$$
$$0.004394 + 0.585604$$
$$r_{\text{GPA} \times \text{nACH}} = 0.589999$$

Alternatively, using only the path coefficients, we have

$$r_{GPA \times nACH} = [(p_1)(p_4)] + [(p_1)(p_2)(p_5)] + [(p_3)(p_5)] + p_6$$
$$[(0.250)(0.017579)] + [(0.250)(0.493333)(0.404368)] +$$
$$[(0.066667)(0.404368)] + 0.508775$$
$$0.004395 + 0.049872 + 0.026958 + 0.508775$$
$$r_{GPA \times nACH} = 0.590000$$

Third, $r_{GPA \times IQ}$ can be decomposed as

$$r_{GPA \times IQ} = [(p_4)(r_{IQ \times SES})] + [(p_6)(r_{IQ \times nACH})] + p_5$$
$$[(0.017579)(0.510)] + [(0.508775)(0.190)] + 0.404368$$
$$0.008965 + [(0.508775)(0.190)] + 0.404368$$
$$0.008965 + 0.096667 + 0.404368$$
$$0.008965 + 0.501035$$
$$r_{GPA \times IQ} = 0.510000$$

Using only the path coefficients from the path model, we have

$$r_{GPA \times IQ} = [(p_2)(p_1)(p_6)] + [(p_3)(p_1)(p_4)] + [(p_3)(p_6)] + [(p_2)(p_4)] + p_5$$
$$[(0.493333)(0.250)(0.508775)] + [(0.066667)(0.250)(0.017579)] +$$
$$[(0.066667)(0.508775)] + [(0.493333)(0.017579)] + 0.404368$$
$$0.062749 + 0.000292 + 0.033919 + 0.008672 + 0.404368$$
$$r_{GPA \times IQ} = 0.510000$$

Fourth, $r_{IQ \times SES}$ can be decomposed as

$$r_{IQ \times SES} = p_2 + [(p_3)(r_{SES \times nACH})]$$
$$0.493333 + [(0.066667)(0.250)]$$
$$0.493333 + 0.016666$$
$$r_{IQ \times SES} = 0.509999$$

Using only path coefficients yields:

$$r_{IQ \times SES} = [(p_1)(p_3)] + p_2$$
$$[(0.250)(0.066667)] + 0.493333$$
$$0.016667 + 0.493333$$
$$r_{IQ \times SES} = 0.510000$$

Fifth, we can compute $r_{IQ \times nACH}$ as

$$r_{IQ \times nACH} = [(p_2)(r_{SES \times nACH})] + p_3$$
$$[(0.493333)(0.250)] + 0.066667$$
$$0.123333 + 0.066667$$
$$r_{IQ \times nACH} = 0.190000$$

Using only path coefficients, we have

$$r_{IQ \times nACH} = [(p_1)(p_2)] + p_3$$
$$[(0.250)(0.493333)] + 0.066667$$
$$0.123333 + 0.066667$$
$$r_{IQ \times nACH} = 0.190000$$

Sixth, we can estimate $r_{nACH \times SES}$. However, in our path model involving measured variables in z-score form, this path is a correlation, represented in our path diagram as a two-headed arrow. Thus, $r_{nACH \times SES} = p_1 = 0.250$.

Note that our six estimated Pearson r values *exactly* match the actual values reported in Table 9.11. This means that our model perfectly fit our data. This will *not* typically occur with real path analysis problems! The matches here are an artifact of the fact that our model required estimation of six path coefficients, and we had a correlation matrix with six unique entries.

Think about the recomposition of the correlations using the path coefficients. Logically, if we had fewer path coefficients, then the path coefficient recompositions of the correlations might not (and probably would not) exactly reproduce the correlations. So, if our path model had estimated fewer than six path coefficients, our path model doubtless would not have perfectly fit our data (see Thompson, 2000b). But in such situations the near fit of a model to data is more persuasive, because models estimating fewer parameters are "falsifiable," and do not fit data merely because we are estimating a number of path coefficients equal to the number of unique entries in the correlation matrix. For an example of a related falsifiable path model, see Kerlinger and Pedhazur (1973). In actual research, only falsifiable models that do not inherently fit the data, but nevertheless do so reasonably well, are of real interest.

Regression Invoking Exponentiated Predictors

Both Chapters 8 and 9 have emphasized that the matrix of all possible pairwise Pearson product–moment correlation coefficients (rs) is the basis for the remaining multiple regression computations, including the computation of R^2. However, as emphasized in Chapter 5, the Pearson r asks two questions, and is sensitive *only* to *linear* patterns of relationship.

An important implication is that because R^2 is a function of statistics measuring only linear relationship, R^2 is itself also only a measure of linear relationship. How can classical multiple regression procedures be modified so that the analysis is *sensitive to curvilinear relationships* of the predictors with the Y_i scores?

The required analyses can be performed quite simply by taking some or all of the predictor variables to various exponential (or polynomial) powers. Table 9.12 presents a hypothetical dataset ($n = 9$) that can be used to illustrate the calculations.

As reported in Table 9.13, the linear relationship between the X_i and the Y_i scores is trivially small (i.e., $r^2 = 0.0761^2 = 0.6\%$) and not statistically significant ($p_{\text{CALCULATED}} = 0.846$), at least at commonly used values of α (e.g., 0.05, 0.01). When we square the predictor variable to create X_i^2, that variable also has a small relationship with the Y_i scores (i.e., $r^2 = $

TABLE 9.12. Hypothetical Data for Polynomial Prediction

Y	Predictors	
	X	X^2
1	1	1
4	2	4
6	3	9
7	4	16
8	5	25
7	6	36
6	7	49
4	8	64
2	9	81

TABLE 9.13. Computer Output
of Pearson r Correlation Matrix for the Table 9.11 Data

Variables	Predictors		
	Y	X	X^2
Y	1.0000		
	$p = .$		
X	0.0761	1.0000	
	$p = 0.846$	$p = .$	
X^2	−0.1448	0.9753	1.0000
	$p = 0.710$	$p = 0.000$	$p = .$

Note. Even though computer packages report "$p = 0.000$," because $p_{CALCULATED}$ can **never** be exactly zero, convert such values to "$p < 0.001$" in your articles or dissertation. Alternatively, use the appropriate Excel spreadsheet function to report the exact p value.

−0.1448^2 = 2.1%) and is not statistically significant ($p_{CALCULATED} = 0.710$) as a single predictor.

However, when we use both the X_i and the X_i^2 scores to predict Y, the $R^2 = 98.8\%$ ($F_{CALCULATED} = 259.59$; $df = 2, 6$; $p_{CALCULATED} < 0.0001$). Of course, one very important implication of these results is that we *cannot* anticipate the predictive power of a system of predictors merely by examining *only* each bivariate r of the predictors with the Y_i scores. The comparison is apples-to-oranges, because the regression analyses *simultaneously* consider *all* the relationships among all the measured variables.

We can visually see the curvilinear dynamics within the data if we run the SPSS procedure GRAPH, INTERACTIVE, and SCATTERGRAM and request the plotting of the regression line within the scatterplot. The regression line is quite flat, and the a weight approximates the M_Y, reflecting the fact that the $r_{Y \text{ with } X^2}$ is only 0.0761^2 = 0.6%. However, the curvilinear relationship between the two measured variables is obvious in the scatterplot.

For the full regression model, $a = -2.357$, $b_X = 3.898$, and $b_{X\ SQUARED} = -0.383$. We can use this equation to estimate the $\hat{Y}_i$ scores for the nine cases. However, the regression equation can be used to estimate $\hat{Y}_i$ scores corresponding to all conceivable values of X_i, subject to the constraint that we believe these other cases are reasonably comparable to our original sample.

Figure 9.4 uses the equation with a range of values of X_i, including scores *not* in the original dataset, to estimate the corresponding $\hat{Y}_i$ scores. The regression line, or now the *regression curve* or parabola, consists of infinitely many $\hat{Y}_i$ scores. Nevertheless, Figure 9.4 makes obvious that we are *no longer estimating linear relationships* once we take some or all of our predictor variables to exponential powers.

When we square predictors, we are estimating a regression curve or parabola, as we did in Figure 9.4. If we cubed one of more predictors, we would be estimating a regression curve with two possible bends. If we took predictors to the fourth power, we would be estimating a regression curve with three possible bends.

Researchers rarely elect to use exponential powers higher than three. And often using the original predictors and the predictors squared provides a reasonable fit in many datasets involving curvilinear dynamics.

If the R^2 is 100% when the predictors are not taken to exponential powers (i.e., the implicit exponent of 1 is used for each predictor), then curvilinear relationship is excluded as a possibility. Linear relationships perfectly fit the data, and curvilinear relationships are not present. Conversely, if R^2 is zero or near-zero, as in the present example, it is possible that curvilinear relationship is also not present in large measure or, at the other extreme, may be present in huge amounts.

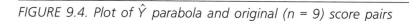

FIGURE 9.4. Plot of $\hat{Y}$ parabola and original (n = 9) score pairs

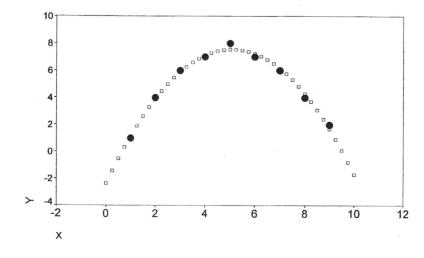

Testing Interaction Effects

Fairly early in their history, social scientists shifted their focus from an effort to discover interventions or predictions that work well for everyone, to efforts to discover interventions or predictions that work well or best for some people, but may not work well or best for other people. A major impetus for this shift was provided by Cronbach (1957, also see 1975) in his American Psychological Association (APA) presidential address.

Interaction effects quantify the degree to which predictors or independent variables perform differently in the presence of other predictors, thereby creating unique additional effects through their joint functioning. Obviously, the investigation of interaction effects requires the use of more than one predictor variable. Interaction can be studied using predictors in variable pairs, variable triplets, and so forth.

Interaction is a difficult statistical concept to master. A major counterintuitive aspect of interaction is that (a) interaction effects are independent of the effects of the measured variables used to study the interaction, and (b) knowledge of effects for predictors acting alone cannot be used to test or quantify interaction effects.

Interactions in medicine provide useful metaphors for better understanding interaction dynamics. As you may be aware, some antibiotics lose effectiveness in the presence of milk, and some other drugs lose effectiveness in the presence of such foods as spinach.

Some interactions are harmful. For example, in recent years two drugs colloquially labeled "fen" and "phen" were combined into a single cocktail to treat obesity. There was considerable evidence that each drug taken alone was reasonably safe. But, when taken together, the cocktail induced an increased risk of serious heart damage. Again, the *only* way to confirm interaction effects is to use the variables together in a single study.

Drug–alcohol interactions are another example. For most of us, taking or not taking an over-the-counter antihistamine does not seriously compromise our abilities to drive or to think. Similarly, drinking or not drinking one or two glasses of cabernet sauvignon does not seriously compromise our abilities to drive or to think. But the combination of one antihistamine pill and two glasses of wine for many of us may be another matter entirely.

Three Common Measured Variable Transformations

For various reasons, in some situations researchers elect to convert their measured variables into new forms. Three combinations are seen most often.

First, researchers may compute **centered/standardized scores**. A common form of centered/standardized scores involves the z scores ($M_z = 0.0$; $SD = SD^2 = 1.0$) discussed in Chapter 3. These z scores have several useful features. For example, if I know my test grade was $z_i = +1.00$, because z scores are themselves deviation scores (and thus symbolized with a lower-case letter), I know that my score was 1 SD higher than the mean, regardless of the shape of the distribution. And if I know that the scores were normally distributed, from the discussion in Chapter 4 I know that I scored higher than roughly 84% of my classmates.

The use of z scores in computing grade averages has the useful feature of adjusting for the differences in test difficulties across the semester. And, perversely, presenting students their grades by announcing only z scores inevitably ensures that students at least understand z scores.

The z scores can also be used to compute other centered/standardized scores (e.g., IQ scores: $M = 100.0$, $SD = 15.0$; McCall's T scores: $M = 50.0$, $SD = 10.0$; or GRE scores: $M = 500.0$, $SD = 100.0$). To compute these centered/standardized scores, we do two steps of calculations.

First, we multiply the z scores by the desired standard deviation (e.g., $SD = 100$). The mean of the new scores remains 0.0, because the old mean of 0.0 times the multiplicative constant of 100.0 yields a mean of the new scores that is still zero. But the scores now have a new SD of 100.0, because $1.0 \times 100.0 = 100.0$. Second, we add to each new score the desired mean (e.g., 500.0). This yields centered/standardized scores with $M = 500.0$ and $SD = 100.0$.

A second type of transformed scores involves **noncentered/standardized scores**. These can be computed in various ways. One way is to convert the scores into z scores and then add the original mean. This yields a set of scores with $SD = SD^2 = 1.0$, but a mean equal to the original mean.

A third alternative involves **centered/nonstandardized scores**. We simply subtract the original mean from each score (not z scores). We are left with scores with a new mean of zero, but their original, unaltered SD.

Centered/nonstandardized scores can be used for various purposes. Sometimes the predictor variables in regression are centered, especially if a score of zero on each predictor is *not* psychologically meaningful. For example, an IQ of zero for a live person seems implausible, but centering the IQ scores at their mean is reasonable, because average IQ has meaning.

Conversely, drinking zero glasses of wine and taking zero antihistamine pills both represent plausible occurrences involving the possibility that participants have had, or might have had, no wine or drugs. We would usually not center these two variables.

One benefit of centering in the regression context is that centering makes the *a* weight statistically more meaningful (not just used to estimate the $\hat{Y}_i$ scores). The *a* weight can be thought of as the predicted value of the $\hat{Y}_i$ scores when the predictors all equal scores of zero. For centered predictors, then, once the predictors are centered so that values of zero equal the predictor means, the *a* weight now reflects *the predicted outcome score when all the predictor variables are at their means*. And the *a* weight = $M_Y - M_Y$.

Another useful function of centered/nonstandardized scores in regression is to model interaction effects (see Aiken & West, 1991; Cohen, Cohen, West, & Aiken, 2003). As Cohen et al. (2003) noted,

> Doing so yields two straightforward, meaningful interpretations of each first-order regression coefficient of predictors entered into the regression equation: (1) effects of individual predictors at the mean of the sample, and (2) average effects of each individual predictors [*sic*] across the range of the other variables. Doing so *also eliminates the nonessential multicollinearity* [emphasis added] between first-order predictors and predictors that carry their interaction with other predictors. (p. 266)

Heuristic Example

As noted in Chapter 5, mediator variables "speak to *how or why* . . . effects occur," and "moderator variables specify *when* certain effects will hold" (Baron & Kenny, 1986, p. 1176; emphasis added). One way to model moderator effects is through interaction terms.

Our heuristic example involves the blood alcohol levels of $n = 32$ cases. The predictors are body weight in pounds and number of cocktails consumed. Table 9.14 presents the three initial measured variables, as well as the two predictor variables transformed into centered/nonstandardized scores. The interaction term (LBSxDRIN) is computed simply by multiplying these centered predictor variables by each other. Table 9.15 presents the bivariate correlation matrix for the data.

The R^2 value reported in Table 9.16 (91.841%) suggests that one can get a very accurate prediction of blood alcohol using only weight and number of drinks, assuming these data generalize. As reported in Table 9.16, the prediction for unstandardized, uncentered variables is $\hat{Y}_i =$ 0.09941 + (–0.00058 × weight in pounds) + (0.02388 × number of drinks).

However, as reported in Table 9.16, the R^2 is even higher (i.e., 98.135%) when we add the interaction term to the regression model. To understand the origins of this effect, the Table 9.16 β weights can be interpreted apples to apples, because the β weights are the multiplicative weights in the regression model for the measured variables in their standardized forms, with standard deviations all set to 1. As noted previously, unlike a given β weight, a given b weight is jointly confounded by (a) the explanatory utility of a measured predictor, (b) SD_Y, and (c) SD_{X_j}.

Within the context of exactly these measured variables, and not considering how much time was spent drinking, or whether food was consumed, the number of drinks is the single most influential factor, with intoxication increasing as drinks increase (β = +0.85779). However, other factors held constant, intoxication differed with heaviness, with heavier people tending to be less intoxicated for a given amount of nonzero consumption (β = –0.42732).

But the interaction effect of the number of drinks with weight is not zero, reflected in the fact that the β for the interaction (i.e., –0.25089) is nonzero. Thus, there is a unique predictive contribution of the various *different combinations* of drinks and weight not explained by considering drinks and weight each acting in their own right.

The b weights can also be interpreted more concretely in terms of anticipated changes in the $\hat{Y}_i$ scores. For example, the b weight for drinks (i.e., +0.02388) indicates that, other factors held constant and

				SPSS Computed Variables		
Case/Statistics	Blood alcohol	Weight	Drinks	D_LBS	D_DRINKS	LBSxDRIN
1	0.04	100	1	−70.0	−3.0	210.0
2	0.11	100	3	−70.0	−1.0	70.0
3	0.19	100	5	−70.0	1.0	−70.0
4	0.26	100	7	−70.0	3.0	−210.0
5	0.03	120	1	−50.0	−3.0	150.0
6	0.09	120	3	−50.0	−1.0	50.0
7	0.16	120	5	−50.0	1.0	−50.0
8	0.22	120	7	−50.0	3.0	−150.0
9	0.03	140	1	−30.0	−3.0	90.0
10	0.08	140	3	−30.0	−1.0	30.0
11	0.13	140	5	−30.0	1.0	−30.0
12	0.19	140	7	−30.0	3.0	−90.0
13	0.02	160	1	−10.0	−3.0	30.0
14	0.07	160	3	−10.0	−1.0	10.0
15	0.12	160	5	−10.0	1.0	−10.0
16	0.16	160	7	−10.0	3.0	−30.0
17	0.02	180	1	10.0	−3.0	−30.0
18	0.06	180	3	10.0	−1.0	−10.0
19	0.11	180	5	10.0	1.0	10.0
20	0.15	180	7	10.0	3.0	30.0
21	0.02	200	1	30.0	−3.0	−90.0
22	0.06	200	3	30.0	−1.0	−30.0
23	0.09	200	5	30.0	1.0	30.0
24	0.13	200	7	30.0	3.0	90.0
25	0.02	220	1	50.0	−3.0	−150.0
26	0.05	220	3	50.0	−1.0	−50.0
27	0.09	220	5	50.0	1.0	50.0
28	0.12	220	7	50.0	3.0	150.0
29	0.02	240	1	70.0	−3.0	−210.0
30	0.05	240	3	70.0	−1.0	−70.0
31	0.08	240	5	70.0	1.0	70.0
32	0.11	240	7	70.0	3.0	210.0
M	0.096	170.00	4.00	0.00	0.00	0.00
SD	0.063	46.56	2.27	46.56	2.27	104.11

TABLE 9.14. Drinks-by-Pounds Interaction Example

limited to the context of these measured variables, consuming one more cocktail yields a predicted increase in blood alcohol level of about 0.024. Similarly, holding the number of drinks constant (but assuming some consumption), in the context of these measured variables, an

TABLE 9.15. Pearson r Matrix for the Measured and the Centered Variables

SPSS Variable	SPSS Variables					
	BLOOD	LBS	DRINKS	D_LBS	D_DRINKS	LBSxDRIN
BLOOD	1.0000					
LBS	–0.4273	1.0000				
DRINKS	0.8578	0.0000	1.0000			
D_LBS	–0.4273	1.0000	0.0000	1.0000		
D_DRINKS	0.8578	0.0000	1.0000	0.0000	1.0000	
LBSxDRIN	–0.2509	0.0000	0.0000	0.0000	0.0000	1.0000

Note. The correlations of the two original and the two centered predictor variables with the outcome variable are equal. Also note that the interaction term is perfectly uncorrelated with the other two predictors in both their uncentered and centered forms.

increase of weight by 1 pound yields a predicted decrease in blood alcohol level of –0.00058.

The β weights can be used to make similar statements, but we are now predicting the z-score values of the measured outcome variable. As explained in Chapter 8, in *all* situations, from worst case to best case, the mean of the $\hat{Y}_i$ scores equals the mean of the outcome variable (i.e., either Y or z_Y). Thus, for the measured variables in their standardized form, $M_{zY} = M_{\hat{Y}} = 0$.

The SOSs of the Y_i scores and the $\hat{Y}_i$ scores will *only* be equal iff we are at the best-case extreme, when $R^2 = 100\%$, and $SOS_{\text{EXPLAINED}} = SOS_Y$. Therefore, when we are predicting the z_Y scores, only when $R^2 = 100\%$ will the $\hat{Y}_i$ scores have $SOS = n - 1$ (so that $SOS / [n - 1] = SD^2 = 1.0$), and $SD = SD^2 = 1.0$, and the $\hat{Y}_i$ scores will be in z-score form. In all other cases, for the measured variables in standardized form, the $\hat{Y}_i$ scores are *not z* scores.

In the current example, we can say that an increase in the number of drinks by 1 standard deviation yields a predicted increase in the $\hat{Y}_i$ scores of +0.85779. Or we can say that an increase in weight by 1 standard deviation yields a predicted change in the $\hat{Y}_i$ scores of –0.42732 (i.e., a decrease). Such statements, using metrics of SDs, are more useful when the standard deviations of the predictors are familiar, meaningful, and well established.

Some Key Concepts

Throughout the general linear model, result interpretation should be approached using a two-stage, hierarchical strategy. First, address the question "Do I have anything?" by consulting some combination of (a) statistical significance, (b) effect sizes, and (c) external or internal replicability evidence. Do *not* interpret NHSST results as tests of replicability. Iff the answer to the first question is yes, then and only then address the question: "From where do my detected effects originate?" For most regression cases, both standardized weights and structure coefficients must be consulted to understand fully data dynamics.

However, it is important to note that when you have nothing statistically (i.e., a zero effect size), you may nevertheless have something huge scientifically. For example, if you are doing an equivalence study of the side effects of a new chemotherapy drug versus a placebo, a zero effect size might be unprecedented and hugely important.

Stepwise methods should *not* be used. Instead, when the selection

TABLE 9.16. Regression Coefficients for Various Models

Variable/Statistic	Statistics			
	b	SE_b	β	t
Uncentered predictors				
LBS	−5.80E-04	7.20E-05	0.42732	8.056
DRINKS	0.02388	0.00148	0.85779	16.171
a	0.09941	0.01399		7.105
R^2	91.841%			
Centered predictors				
D_LBS	−5.80E-04	7.20E-05	−0.42732	−8.056
D_DRINKS	0.02388	0.00148	0.85779	16.171
a	0.09625	0.00330		29.156
R^2	91.841%			
Full model				
D_LBS	−5.80E-04	3.50E-05	−0.42732	−16.558
D_DRINKS	0.02388	7.18E-04	0.85779	33.237
LBSxDRIN	−1.52E-04	1.57E-05	−0.25089	−9.721
a	0.09625	0.00161		59.923
R^2	98.135%			

Note. The a weight in analyses involving the centered variables equals the M_Y reported in Table 9.14, and also equals $M_{\hat{Y}}$.

of a more parsimonious set of variables is necessary in predictive applications, use all-possible-subsets analyses. However, replicability analyses are especially important when any variable selection strategies are used, because these decisions may especially be impacted by sampling error.

Complementary regression methods can be used to supplement primary results. Both commonality analysis and path analysis offer alternative decompositions of the actual or the estimated correlations. Path analysis may be used to explore both the direct and the indirect effects of predictors.

Taking predictors to exponential powers other than 1 to explore curvilinear relations may be useful when initial effect sizes not invoking exponentiated predictors are appreciably smaller than $R^2 = 100\%$. Interaction effects can be explored in regression by using product variables involving the measured predictors in centered/nonstandardized form. Interaction models may be useful in testing moderator effects (Baron & Kenny, 1986).

■■■ Reflection Problems ■■■

1. Venn diagrams can be heuristically powerful in understanding regression dynamics, notwithstanding the limitation that two-dimensional graphics cannot capture all the influences operating in more complex spaces (Craeger, 1969). Consider an example in which we have 200 units of information regarding the amount and origins of individual differences on the variable, Y. Let's say Y is predicted by three measured variables, $X1$, $X2$, and $X3$. There are potentially seven commonality partitions of the $SOS_{EXPLAINED}$ (i.e., $U1$, $C12$, $C13$, $C123$, $U2$, $C23$, and $U3$).

    On graph paper, draw a rectangle that is 20 wide × 10 high. Now draw the areas of information explained or predicted by the three predictors in their various combinations, where the area for $X1$ is in the lower right corner of the Y and is 5 wide by 7 high (i.e., $U1 + C12 + C13 = 35$). Draw the useful $X2$ information such that this area is 5 wide × 4 high, and the rightmost portion of $X2$ (1 wide by 4 high) overlaps with the useful information in $X1$.

    Draw the useful information of $X3$ as 5 wide × 7 high at the top of the rectangle, but not to the far right, subject to the restriction that a

2-wide-x-4-high portion overlaps with the information explained by $X1$, and a 4-wide-x-1-high portion overlaps with the information explained by $X2$.

We now have $U1 = 24$, $C12 = 3$, $C123 = 1$, $C13 = 7$, $U2 = 13$, $C23 = 3$, and $U3 = 27$. What is the $SOS_{EXPLAINED}$, the $SOS_{UNEXPLAINED}$, and the R^2? What is the r^2 of each predictor with the Y_i scores? What is the r^2 of each predictor with the e_i scores? What is the $r_{Y \text{ with } \hat{Y}^2}$? What is the r^2 of each predictor with the $\hat{Y}_i$ scores (i.e., each squared structure coefficient)?

2. Find a real dataset, such as one of the datasets built into computer statistics packages. Pick a problem with 10 to 15 measured variables, and perform a stepwise regression. Then conduct all-possible-subsets analyses for the same data. Do the results agree as to the best predictor set size, and the best predictors? Rerun the stepwise analysis, using only the first 15 cases. How do the stepwise results change?

3. Draw a path diagram in which variable Y is predicted by variable X. Insert the path coefficient 0.5 on the path. Now draw a second diagram incorporating the first diagram, but adding a new variable, M, with a path from X to M with a path coefficient of 0.7, and a path from M to Y also with a path coefficient of 0.7. In the new diagram, the path from X to Y now has a path coefficient of 0.0. What does the comparison of the two path models tell you about how X predicts Y, and the role that M plays in the prediction? In addition to Baron and Kenny (1986), look first at Frazier, Tix, and Baron (2004), and then at Shrout and Bolger (2002).

4. Interpret these results, making up a specific context for the study:
$R^2 = 4\%$
"Adjusted" $R^2 = -16\%$
Invariance "double cross-validation" coefficients

$r_{\hat{Y} \text{ using group 1's } \beta \text{ weights and group 1's data with } \hat{Y} \text{ using group 1's data and group 2's } \beta \text{ weights}} = 0.05$

$r_{\hat{Y} \text{ using group 2's } \beta \text{ weights and group 2's data with } \hat{Y} \text{ using group 2's data but group 1's } \beta \text{ weights}} = -0.15$

$\beta_1 = 0.25$; r_s for $X1 = 0.75$
$\beta_2 = 0.20$; r_s for $X2 = 0.50$
$\beta_3 = -0.20$; r_s for $X3 = 0.00$

5. Interpret these results, making up a specific context for the study:

    $R^2 = 50\%$

    "Adjusted" $R^2 = 47\%$

    $p_{CALCULATED} = 0.11$

    Invariance "double cross-validation" coefficients

    $r_{\hat{Y} \text{ using group 1's } \beta \text{ weights and group 1's data with } \hat{Y} \text{ using group 1's data and group 2's } \beta \text{ weights}} = 0.95$

    $r_{\hat{Y} \text{ using group 2's } \beta \text{ weights and group 2's data with } \hat{Y} \text{ using group 2's data but group 1's } \beta \text{ weights}} = 0.85$

    $\beta_1 = 0.6$; r_S for $X1 = 0.9$

    $\beta_2 = 0.0$; r_S for $X2 = -0.7$

    $\beta_3 = 0.4$; r_S for $X3 = 0.9$

10

One-Way Analysis of Variance (ANOVA)

nalysis of variance (ANOVA) is a statistical analysis for evaluating the equality of means (i.e., mean differences, or differences of means) on a single, at least intervally-scaled outcome variable across two or more groups. The outcome variable must at least be intervally-scaled, or the means cannot reasonably be computed, much less compared.

Many of the ideas underlying ANOVA concepts were formulated by Sir Ronald Fisher, beginning in 1918, as noted by Huberty (1999) in his brief history of statistics. Fisher popularized these and related methods in his hugely influential books, including those published in 1925 and 1935. ANOVA procedures were greatly facilitated by Snedecor's (1934) development of a relevant test statistic, which he suggested be named F in Fisher's honor.

The purpose of this chapter is to present ANOVA terminology and the ANOVA computational process, with an emphasis on explaining the "homogeneity of variance" assumption that ANOVA presumes, and why this assumption is required. The chapter addresses what should be an

obvious paradox: When location and dispersion are two separate characterizations of data, how can the analysis of *variance* test whether group
dependent variable *means* are equal? Dispersion may be a useful characterization of how well a mean represents a set of scores, once we have the
mean. But dispersion is not used in calculating central tendency, and being
told *only* about the dispersion of a set of scores tells us *nothing* about
what will be the numerical value for the mean.

When the means of only two groups are being compared, ANOVA
and the two-sample t test yield *identical* $p_{CALCULATED}$ values for a given
dataset, and the ANOVA $F_{CALCULATED}$ equals $t_{CALCULATED}^2$ (because t is a
score-world test statistic, and F is an area-world test statistic). However,
when testing the equality of means with more than two groups, ANOVA
has several advantages, *only one* of which involves control of the
experimentwise Type I error rate.

Experimentwise Type I Error

In Chapter 6, a Type I error was defined as rejecting H_0 when in reality the
null hypothesis is true in the population. We limit the likelihood of making
this error on a given hypothesis test by selecting a small value for $p_{CRITICAL}$
(or α) for a given test. What was actually being defined in Chapter 6 was
$\alpha_{TESTWISE}$, which is the probability of making a Type I error for a *given, single hypothesis test*.

Experimentwise error rate ($\alpha_{EXPERIMENTWISE}$) refers to the probability of
having made one or more Type I errors *anywhere within the study*. When
only one hypothesis is tested for a given group of participants in a study,
the experimentwise error rate will exactly equal the testwise error rate. But
when more than one hypothesis is tested in a given study, the two error
rates *may* not be equal.

Given the presence of multiple hypothesis tests (e.g., two or more
pairs of means are being compared, two or more dependent variables are
tested) in a single study, the testwise and the experimentwise error rates
will still be equal iff the hypotheses (or the dependent variables) are perfectly correlated. Logically, the correlation of the dependent variables will
impact the experimentwise error rate because, for example, when one has

perfectly correlated hypotheses, in actuality one is still only testing a single hypothesis.

Thus, $\alpha_{\text{EXPERIMENTWISE}} = \alpha_{\text{TESTWISE}}$ iff (a) only one hypothesis is tested in a given study, *or* (b) the hypotheses (or the dependent variables) being tested are perfectly correlated. Otherwise, $\alpha_{\text{EXPERIMENTWISE}}$ will be greater than α_{TESTWISE}. Two factors impact the degree of inflation of Type I error probability reflected in $\alpha_{\text{EXPERIMENTWISE}}$: (a) the number of hypotheses tested and (b) the degree of correlation among the dependent variables or the hypotheses being tested.

When the dependent variables or hypotheses tested are perfectly *un*correlated, the experimentwise error rate ($\alpha_{\text{EXPERIMENTWISE}}$) can be calculated. This is done using the formula related to work by Bonferroni (see Howell, 2002, pp. 384–386):

$$\alpha_{\text{EXPERIMENTWISE}} = 1 - (1 - \alpha_{\text{TESTWISE}})^K \qquad (10.1)$$

where K is the number of perfectly uncorrelated hypotheses being tested at a given testwise α level (α_{TESTWISE}). Love (1988) presented a mathematical proof of the formula.

For example, if three perfectly uncorrelated hypotheses (or dependent variables) are tested, each at the $\alpha_{\text{TESTWISE}} = 0.05$ level of statistical significance, the experimentwise Type I error rate will be

$$
\begin{aligned}
\alpha_{\text{EXPERIMENTWISE}} &= 1 - (1 - \alpha_{\text{TESTWISE}})^K \\
&= 1 - (1 - 0.05)^3 \\
&= 1 - (0.95)^3 \\
&= 1 - (0.95(0.95)(0.95)) \\
&= 1 - (0.9025\ (0.95)) \\
&= 1 - 0.8574 \\
\alpha_{\text{EXPERIMENTWISE}} &= 0.1426
\end{aligned}
$$

Thus, for a study testing the equality of means across two groups on each of three perfectly uncorrelated dependent variables—using the two-sample t test, each at the $\alpha_{\text{TESTWISE}} = 0.05$ level of statistical significance—the probability is 0.1426 (or 14.26%) that one or more null hypotheses will be incorrectly rejected. Most unfortunately, knowing this will *not* inform the researcher as to (a) how many Type I errors (e.g., one, two, three) are being made, *or* (b) which one or more of the statistically significant hypotheses is, in fact, a Type I error.

Table 10.1 presents these calculations for several conventional $\alpha_{TESTWISE}$ levels and for various numbers of perfectly uncorrelated dependent variables or hypotheses. Clearly, because exponential functions are at work, experimentwise Type I error rates can inflate quite rapidly as we test more hypotheses. Experimentwise error rate inflation also occurs when we test multiple hypotheses in a study, even when the hypotheses or the dependent variables are not perfectly uncorrelated, although the inflation is *less* severe as the dependent variables or the hypotheses are *more* highly correlated.

TABLE 10.1. Experimentwise Type I Error Inflation When Hypotheses Are Perfectly Uncorrelated

Testwise α	Tests	Experimentwise α
$1 - (1 - 0.05)$ ^	$1 =$	
$1 - (\quad 0.95)$ ^	$1 =$	
$1 - \quad 0.95$	$=$	0.05000^a
Range over $\alpha_{TESTWISE} = 0.01$		
$1 - (1 - 0.01)$ ^	$5 =$	0.04901
$1 - (1 - 0.01)$ ^	$10 =$	0.09562
$1 - (1 - 0.01)$ ^	$20 =$	0.18209
Range over $\alpha_{TESTWISE} = 0.05$		
$1 - (1 - 0.05)$ ^	$5 =$	0.22622
$1 - (1 - 0.05)$ ^	$10 =$	0.40126
$1 - (1 - 0.05)$ ^	$20 =$	0.64151
Range over $\alpha_{TESTWISE} = 0.10$		
$1 - (1 - 0.10)$ ^	$5 =$	0.40951
$1 - (1 - 0.10)$ ^	$10 =$	0.65132
$1 - (1 - 0.10)$ ^	$20 =$	0.87842

Note. "^" = "raise to the power of."

[a]The first set of calculations demonstrates that when only one test is conducted, the experimentwise error rate equals the testwise error rate, as should be expected if the formula behaves properly.

Heuristic Explanation

However, these concepts are too abstract to be readily grasped. Happily, the two error rates can be explained using an intuitively appealing example involving coin tosses (cf. Witte, 1985, p. 236). If the toss of heads is equated with a Type I error, and if a coin is tossed only once, then the probability of a head on the one toss ($\alpha_{TESTWISE}$), and of at least one head within the set ($\alpha_{EXPERIMENTWISE}$) consisting of one toss, will both equal 50%.

If the coin is tossed three times, rather than only once, the testwise probability of a head on each toss is still exactly 50% (i.e., $\alpha_{TESTWISE} = 0.50$, *not* 0.05). Now Equation 10.1 is a perfect fit to this situation (i.e., is a literal analogy rather than merely a figurative analogy), because the coin's behavior on each flip is literally uncorrelated with the coin's behavior on previous flips. That is, a coin is not aware of its behavior on previous flips, and does not alter its behavior on any single flip, given some awareness of its previous behavior.

Thus, the experimentwise probability ($\alpha_{EXPERIMENTWISE}$) that there will be at least one head in the whole set of three flips will be exactly

$$\alpha_{EXPERIMENTWISE} = 1 - (1 - \alpha_{TESTWISE})^K$$
$$= 1 - (1 - 0.50)^3$$
$$= 1 - (0.50)^3$$
$$= 1 - ((0.50)(0.50)(0.50))$$
$$= 1 - (0.2500(0.50))$$
$$= 1 - 0.125$$
$$\alpha_{EXPERIMENTWISE} = 0.875$$

Figure 10.1 illustrates these concepts in a more concrete fashion. There are eight *equally likely* outcomes for sets of three coin flips. These are all listed in the table. Seven of the eight equally-likely sets of three flips involves one or more Type I errors, defined in this example as a head. And $7 / 8 = 0.875$, as expected, according to Equation 10.1.

Controlling Experimentwise Error Rates

Researchers can use either of two strategies to control the inflation of the experimentwise error rate. Note that "experimentwise error rate" *always* means the "experimentwise Type I error rate."

```
          Flip #
          1   2   3
   1.     T : T : T  __
   2.     H : T : T  |    p of 1 or more heads (i.e.,
   3.     T : H : T  |    testwise error analog)
   4.     T : T : H  |    in set of 3 Flips = 7/8 = 87.5%
   5.     H : H : T  |                  or
   6.     H : T : H  |    where testwise error analog = .50,
   7.     T : H : H  |    experimentwise p = 1 - (1 - .5)³
   8.     H : H : H  |__  = 1 - (.5)³
                          = 1 - .125 = .875
p of H on
each Flip       50% 50% 50%
```

Note. The probability of one *or more* occurrences of a given outcome in a set of events is $1 - (1 - p)^K$, where p is the probability of the given occurrence on each trial and K is the number of trials in a set of perfectly independent events.

FIGURE 10.1. All possible families of outcomes for a fair coin flipped three times

First, because $\alpha_{\text{EXPERIMENTWISE}}$ is partially a function of α_{TESTWISE}, as suggested by Equation 10.1, $\alpha_{\text{EXPERIMENTWISE}}$ can be controlled by lowering our initial α_{TESTWISE}. The **Bonferroni correction** involves using a new testwise α level, $\alpha_{\text{TESTWISE}}{}^*$, computed by dividing α_{TESTWISE} by the number of K hypotheses in the study:

$$\alpha_{\text{TESTWISE}}{}^* = \alpha_{\text{TESTWISE}} / K \qquad (10.2)$$

For example, if we are testing five hypotheses, and the initial $\alpha_{\text{TESTWISE}} = 0.05$, our new $\alpha_{\text{TESTWISE}}{}^*$ would be revised to be $0.05 / 5 = 0.01$.

Table 10.1 can be consulted to establish that this correction does roughly achieve the desired effect. As reported in Table 10.1, testing five hypotheses at $\alpha^* = 0.01$ results in an $\alpha_{\text{EXPERIMENTWISE}}$ of 0.049, which is less than our original α of 0.05.

However, there are some problems with using this correction. First, unless the hypotheses (or dependent variables) are perfectly uncorrelated, the correction will be too severe or conservative. The correction is too severe because Equation 10.1 is correct iff the hypotheses (or dependent variables) are perfectly uncorrelated and, in other situations, the inflation of experimentwise error rates is smaller.

Second, even when the hypotheses (or dependent variables) are perfectly uncorrelated, there is a big problem with using the Bonferroni correction. As explained in Chapter 6, assuming the effect size and the sample size are fixed, if we lower α, we are going to raise β, and thus lower our power against Type II error. So, as a device to control $\alpha_{EXPERIMENTWISE}$, the Bonferroni correction is not very useful unless we have (a) a very large sample size, or we (b) expect large effect sizes, in which cases power will still remain sufficiently high following the Bonferroni adjustment.

We can instead control $\alpha_{EXPERIMENTWISE}$ by testing fewer hypotheses, without altering at all our initial $\alpha_{TESTWISE}$. This may achieve our objective of controlling $\alpha_{EXPERIMENTWISE}$ without reducing power.

An **omnibus hypothesis** is a test of differences in means across groups that simultaneously considers *all* group means. For example, if we test H_0: $M_{MALES} = M_{FEMALES}$, when we consider that these are the only categories constituting gender, then the hypothesis is an omnibus hypothesis. If we test H_0: $M_{FRESHMEN} - M_{SOPHOMORES} = M_{JUNIORS} = M_{SENIORS} = M_{GRADUATE\ STUDENTS}$, when we are concerned with only these five groups of students, then this null is an omnibus hypothesis.

In this second example, if a researcher wanted to compare five means prior to the invention of ANOVA, there was no recourse except to perform *t* tests on all possible pairs of means. According to Equation 6.2, this would require performing 10 *t* tests (i.e., [5 (5 − 1)] / 2). These 10 *t* tests are not completely uncorrelated (e.g., knowledge of whether $M_{FRESHMEN} = M_{SOPHOMORES}$ and $M_{FRESHMEN} = M_{JUNIORS}$ may presage a finding with regard to $M_{SOPHOMORES} = M_{JUNIORS}$). Nevertheless, some inflation in experimentwise error would result from performing the 10 *t* tests.

ANOVA would directly test the omnibus null hypothesis that H_0: $M_{FRESHMEN} = M_{SOPHOMORES} = M_{JUNIORS} = M_{SENIORS} = M_{GRADUATE\ STUDENTS}$, thus avoiding both the inflation of the experimentwise error rate, and a Bonferroni correction that would lessen power. And, as will be explained in Chapter 11, ANOVA has some other positive features in addition to the capacity to test omnibus nulls about mean differences.

ANOVA Terminology

ANOVA has some of its own technical terminology, mainly to confuse graduate students about concepts that they would otherwise find quite understandable. A way or factor is an independent or grouping variable in

ANOVA. In this book, the term "way" is used throughout, mainly to avoid confusing the ANOVA "factor" with the concept of "factor" used in a different, multivariate methodology called factor analysis (Thompson, 2004).

Ways are always grouping variables (e.g., experimental group, gender) and therefore are treated as being nominally-scaled. These variables may have started out as other than nominally-scaled (e.g., IQ pretest scores), but in such cases must be converted to nominal/categorical scale in order to implement ANOVA.

An ANOVA study must involve at least one way, because science focuses on relationships among variables. A scientific study is never conducted using an outcome or dependent variable, but no independent or predictor variables. It may be worthwhile for descriptive purposes to examine a single outcome variable and no predictors, but such descriptive analyses do not explore the origins of individual differences in different participants' scores on the outcome, and therefore are not scientific, although descriptions can in themselves be quite valuable.

One-way studies are ANOVA studies involving a single grouping variable (e.g., gender). **Multiway** studies involve more than one way. When studies are multiway, researchers often specify the number of ways within their descriptions (e.g., "two-way," "three-way").

Because each way is a grouping variable, rather than a constant, each must consist of two or more groups, called **levels**. For example, if a researcher is exploring the effects of two teaching methods on posttest reading achievement scores, the one way has two levels.

Researchers often describe their studies by citing the number of levels in each way. For example, a researcher may say, "I did a 5 × 3 × 2 ANOVA." Here the number of numbers (i.e., three) is the number of ways in the study. Of course, the number of outcome variables is necessarily one, because ANOVA *always* involves a single intervally-scaled outcome variable, so a 5 × 4 × 3 design implies consideration of a total of four variables.

The numbers themselves specify the levels in each way. In this example, the three ways have five levels (e.g., freshman, sophomore, junior, senior, graduate students), three levels (e.g., left-handed, right-handed, ambidextrous), and two levels (e.g., male and female), respectively. Because nominally-scaled variables, such as ways, have no intrinsic order, the ways may be specified in any order (e.g., 5 × 3 × 2, 2 × 3 × 5, 3 × 5 × 2).

However, some researchers prefer to name the ways by progressing downward from ways having the most to the fewest levels.

If one multiplies the number of levels times each other (e.g., $5 \times 3 \times 2 = 30$), the number of groups, or **cells**, is obtained. For example, in a $5 \times 3 \times 2$ design, there may be (1) freshman, left-handed males; (2) freshman, left-handed females; (3) freshman, right-handed males; . . . (30) graduate student, ambidextrous females.

A design is **balanced** if there are equal numbers of participants in each group. If the numbers of participants in each group are not exactly equal, the design is **unbalanced**. Balanced designs necessarily involve total sample sizes that are some multiple of the number of cells in the design (e.g., for a $5 \times 3 \times 2$ design, $n = 30$, $n = 60$, $n = 90$).

▨▨▨ The Logic of Analysis of Variance

ANOVA can be implemented to estimate the effect sizes associated with group mean differences, or to test the statistical significance of differences in group means, or for both these purposes. The first focus is on practical significance, whereas the second focus involves NHSST. Here we treat the analysis for a balanced, one-way design.

Several steps are involved in calculating the analysis of variance. The building blocks of ANOVA are the total sum of squares (SOS_{TOTAL}), the sum of squares between ($SOS_{BETWEEN}$), and the sum of squares within (SOS_{WITHIN}). The $SOS_{BETWEEN}$ and SOS_{WITHIN} are the constituent parts of SOS_{TOTAL}, so together they always sum exactly to the SOS_{TOTAL}. Thus, $SOS_{BETWEEN}$ and SOS_{WITHIN} are the partitioned, nonoverlapping (and uncorrelated) portions of the SOS_{TOTAL}, and with any two of these three sums of squares we could compute the missing term by addition or subtraction.

Table 10.2 presents data for balanced ($n_k = 9$; $n = 18$) two-level one-way ANOVAs for four different outcome variables (i.e., *Y1*, *Y2*, *Y3*, and *Y4*). Notice that the outcome variables' dispersions are exactly equal across the two groups for all four variables (e.g., for *Y1*, $SD_1 = SD_2 = 1.22$; for *Y2*, $SD_1 = SD_2 = 1.22$; for *Y3*, $SD_1 = SD_2 = 0.71$; for *Y2*, $SD_1 = SD_2 = 0.71$). Also, the mean differences (1.0) are smaller for *Y1* and *Y3* (means

	TABLE 10.2. Four Outcome Variables Scores for a Two-Level One-Way ANOVA				
	SPSS Variable				
Case/ statistic	$Y1$	$Y2$	$Y3$	$Y4$	Level
1	1	1	2	2	1
2	2	2	2	2	1
3	2	2	3	3	1
4	3	3	3	3	1
5	3	3	3	3	1
6	3	3	3	3	1
7	4	4	3	3	1
8	4	4	4	4	1
9	5	5	4	4	1
Group 1 (n_1 = 9)					
M	3.00	3.00	3.00	3.00	
SOS	12.00	12.00	4.00	4.00	
SD^2	1.50	1.50	0.50	0.50	
SD	1.22	1.22	0.71	0.71	
10	2	3	3	4	2
11	3	4	3	4	2
12	3	4	4	5	2
13	4	5	4	5	2
14	4	5	4	5	2
15	4	5	4	5	2
16	5	6	4	5	2
17	5	6	5	6	2
18	6	7	5	6	2
Group 2 (n_2 = 9)					
M	4.00	5.00	4.00	5.00	
SOS	12.00	12.00	4.00	4.00	
SD^2	1.50	1.50	0.50	0.50	
SD	1.22	1.22	0.71	0.71	
Total sample (n = 18)					
M	3.50	4.00	3.50	4.00	
SOS	28.50	42.00	12.50	26.00	
SD^2	1.68	2.47	0.74	1.53	
SD	1.29	1.57	0.86	1.24	

Note. The dispersion of the Y_i scores is *exactly* equal across the two groups for all four outcome variables.

of 3.00 and 4.00) than the mean differences (2.0) for *Y2* and *Y4* (means of 3.00 and 5.00).

However, the outcome variables' dispersions are larger for *Y1* and *Y2* ($SD_1 = SD_2 = 1.22$) than the dispersion for *Y3* and *Y4* ($SD_1 = SD_2 = 0.71$). Thus, *Y1* involves (a) the smaller mean difference (i.e., 1.0) coupled with (b) the larger within-group score dispersion ($SD_1 = SD_2 = 1.22$), while *Y4* involves (a) the larger mean difference (i.e., 2.0) coupled with (b) the smaller within-group score dispersion ($SD_1 = SD_2 = 1.22$). The ANOVA calculations are illustrated here using the *Y1* scores.

The SOS_{TOTAL} is the sum of squares of the scores on the dependent variable, which is *always* the focus in any univariate parametric method. As always, SOS_{TOTAL} is computed by finding the mean of the *Y1* scores, and subtracting this mean from each person's *Y1*$_i$ score to get a deviation ($y1_i$) of each person's score from the grand mean ($M_{Y1.}$). The **grand mean** is simply the mean computed ignoring group membership, or what previously has simply been called the mean. But because several means are computed in ANOVA, calling the overall mean the grand mean distinguishes this mean from the means computed separately for each group. As always, these deviation scores are then squared and summed, yielding the SOS_{TOTAL}.

The SOS_{TOTAL} is computed as a measure of *variability of the dependent variable scores around the mean of the total sample, ignoring the fact that the ANOVA groups even exist*. If the outcome scores are all the same, SOS_{TOTAL} is zero, indicating that the scores do not constitute a variable. In this situation, ANOVA calculations cannot be performed for either statistical or practical significance evaluation purposes. We simply have no information about the origins of individual differences in Y_i scores when the Y_i scores do not constitute a variable.

Table 10.3 illustrates these calculations for the *Y1* variable. Here we have $SOS_{Y1} = 28.50$ units of squared information about the amount and origins of individual differences. Not everyone contributed equally to creating this information. For example, cases #1 and #18 contributed disproportionately large amounts of information. At any rate, because $SOS_{Y1} \neq 0$, we can proceed to partition this information, to determine how much of this information could be predicted or explained solely with knowledge of to which group the 18 participants belonged.

TABLE 10.3. Calculation of SOS_{TOTAL} as the Sum of Squared Deviations of $n = 18$ *Individual Scores about the Grand Mean* ($M_{Y1.}$)

Case	$Y1 - M_{Y1.}$	=	$y1$	$y1^2$
1	1 − 3.50	=	−2.5	6.25
2	2 − 3.50	=	−1.5	2.25
3	2 − 3.50	=	−1.5	2.25
4	3 − 3.50	=	−0.5	0.25
5	3 − 3.50	=	−0.5	0.25
6	3 − 3.50	=	−0.5	0.25
7	4 − 3.50	=	0.5	0.25
8	4 − 3.50	=	0.5	0.25
9	5 − 3.50	=	1.5	2.25
10	2 − 3.50	=	−1.5	2.25
11	3 − 3.50	=	−0.5	0.25
12	3 − 3.50	=	−0.5	0.25
13	4 − 3.50	=	0.5	0.25
14	4 − 3.50	=	0.5	0.25
15	4 − 3.50	=	0.5	0.25
16	5 − 3.50	=	1.5	2.25
17	5 − 3.50	=	1.5	2.25
18	6 − 3.50	=	2.5	6.25
SOS_Y				28.50

Next, we compute the $SOS_{BETWEEN}$. As always with an SOS, the $SOS_{BETWEEN}$ is also a measure of variability of data about means, but $SOS_{BETWEEN}$ is a measure of the variability or spreadoutness of *k group means (**not** individual scores) about the grand mean*. Table 10.4 illustrates the calculation of $SOS_{BETWEEN}$ as a squared deviation of the two means about the grand mean.

Iff the group means are all the same, they will all equal the grand mean, and the $SOS_{BETWEEN}$ will be zero. As the group means differ more from each other, they will also increasingly differ from the grand mean, and $SOS_{BETWEEN}$ will become larger. Conversely, if you know only that the $SOS_{BETWEEN}$ is zero, you do not know what the group means were, but you know that they were identical. And if you know only that the $SOS_{BETWEEN}$ is not zero, you do not know what the group means were, but you know that they were not identical.

Thus we begin to resolve the paradox of how the analysis of *variance* can test whether group dependent variable *means* are equal, given that location and dispersion are two separate characterizations of data. The dispersion of the Y_i scores, measured in the SOS_Y, tells us *nothing* about what will be the numerical value for M_Y. But the SOS_Y and the $SOS_{BETWEEN}$ are two different characters, and the $SOS_{BETWEEN}$ (unlike the SOS_{TOTAL}) directly *quantifies the magnitude of mean differences*.

Finally, we compute the SOS_{WITHIN}. We could do so by subtraction (i.e., $SOS_{TOTAL} - SOS_{BETWEEN}$), but then the meaning and relevance of SOS_{WITHIN} would be lost to us. SOS_{WITHIN} *is the sum of the k SOS values within the various groups, calculated separately as squared deviations of scores within each group about each group's own individual kth group mean, ignoring both all other groups and the grand mean, and then* <u>*pooled*</u> *together.*

We shall soon see that this pooling is reasonable iff certain circumstances are met. And if the pooling used to compute the SOS_{WITHIN} is unreasonable, then the ANOVA process and both its statistical and practical significance results may be fatally compromised. Table 10.5 illustrates these calculations for the heuristic data.

Conceptually, what is SOS_{WITHIN}, and why is SOS_{WITHIN} used in ANOVA computations? In Chapter 3, we learned that all means do not do equally well at representing a set of scores. For example, for a given data set, if SD is zero, the mean does a spectacular job of representing the scores. But if SD is huge, the mean serves poorly, and indeed may serve so poorly at characterizing central tendency as to be nonsensical. Just because we can compute a statistic does not mean that the statistic is always sensible!

The SOS_{WITHIN} computes the outcome variable dispersion separately in

TABLE 10.4. $SOS_{BETWEEN}$ as the Weighted (by n_k) Sum of Squared Deviations of $k = 2$ *Group Means about the Grand Mean* ($M_{Y1.}$)

Group	$M_k - M_{Y1.} = y1_k$	$y1_k^2 \times n_k = SOS_k$
1	3.00 − 3.50 = −0.5	0.25 × 9 = 2.25
2	4.00 − 3.50 = 0.5	0.25 × 9 = 2.25
$SOS_{BETWEEN}$		4.50

TABLE 10.5. SOS_{WITHIN} as the *Pooling of the SOS's*
Computed Separately Within Each k Group,
Ignoring Both the Other Group and the Grand Mean

Case	$Y1 - M_k = y1$	$y1^2$
1	$1 - 3.00 = -2.0$	4.00
2	$2 - 3.00 = -1.0$	1.00
3	$2 - 3.00 = -1.0$	1.00
4	$3 - 3.00 = 0.0$	0.00
5	$3 - 3.00 = 0.0$	0.00
6	$3 - 3.00 = 0.0$	0.00
7	$4 - 3.00 = 1.0$	1.00
8	$4 - 3.00 = 1.0$	1.00
9	$5 - 3.00 = 2.0$	4.00
Subtotal		12.00
10	$2 - 4.00 = -2.0$	4.00
11	$3 - 4.00 = -1.0$	1.00
12	$3 - 4.00 = -1.0$	1.00
13	$4 - 4.00 = 0.0$	0.00
14	$4 - 4.00 = 0.0$	0.00
15	$4 - 4.00 = 0.0$	0.00
16	$5 - 4.00 = 1.0$	1.00
17	$5 - 4.00 = 1.0$	1.00
18	$6 - 4.00 = 2.0$	4.00
Subtotal		12.00
SOS_{WITHIN}		**24.00**

each group, and then pools these estimates. The separate estimates quantify how well each group mean does at representing the scores in a given group. The pooled estimate *quantifies for the means as a set how well these means do at representing the scores in the respective groups.*

Based on these considerations, would the mean differences on *Y1* and *Y3* be equally noteworthy, given that the mean difference in both cases equals 1.0? Would the mean differences on *Y2* and *Y4* be equally noteworthy, given that the mean difference in both cases equals 2.0? Which combination of (a) means and (b) within-group dispersions *least* contradicts a null hypothesis assumption that the two means are equal? Which combination of (a) means and (b) within-group dispersions *most* contradicts a null hypothesis assumption that the two means are equal?

■■■ Practical and Statistical Significance

The sums of squares partitions can be employed to estimate the effect size associated with group differences, in a metric like that of r^2. This estimate is called η^2, or synonymously, the correlation ratio:

$$\eta^2 = SOS_{\text{BETWEEN}} / SOS_{\text{TOTAL}} \qquad (10.3)$$

The correlation coefficient and the correlation ratio are two distinct concepts, even though the first word of the their two-word names is the same. The r is a score-world statistic, and η^2 is an area-world statistic.

Note that Equation 10.3 is remarkably similar to Equations 8.5 and 8.6, which are formulas for estimating the r^2 and the R^2 effect sizes! Thus, key elements of the general linear model are beginning to emerge.

Nevertheless, also recognize that r^2 is a measure of linear relationship between two intervally-scaled variables. The η^2 quantifies how much of the variability in the Y_i scores, measured as SOS_Y, we can explain or predict with knowledge only about the group membership of each participant. Thus, η^2 involves one intervally-scaled variable, and one nominally-scaled variable, and not two intervally-scaled variables. And it makes no sense to talk about linear relationship in the context of one of two nominally-scaled variables because the concept of linearity itself only makes sense in a context, such as a scattergram, in which *both* axes are demarcated by intervals for continuous variables.

So, η^2 is a measure of relationship sensitive to *all* sorts of relationship, and not just linear relationship. For the Table 10.2 data, the η^2 values are 15.8% (i.e., 4.50 / 28.50), 42.8%, 36.0%, and 69.2%, respectively.

Just as the uncorrected effect size r^2 / R^2 can be "corrected" (e.g., Ezechiel, 1930), the η^2 can be adjusted to remove estimated capitalization on sampling error. One such correction is Hays' (1981) ω^2.

The starting point in the calculation of ω^2 requires the entries in the variance partitions summary table, such as that presented for regression in Table 9.1. Given the general linear model, the basic computations are similar in ANOVA. One difference is that the sums of squares are computed differently, but once in hand, we manipulate these in parallel fashion. And in regression the $df_{\text{EXPLAINED}}$ equals the number of predictor variables, whereas in one-way ANOVA, the df_{BETWEEN} is $k - 1$. Using the sums of squares computed in Tables 10.3, 10.4, and 10.5, Table 10.6 presents the summary table for the tests of mean differences on *Y1*.

Hays' ω^2 can be computed as

$$\omega^2 = [SOS_{\text{BETWEEN}} - (k - 1)MS_{\text{WITHIN}}] / [SOS_Y + MS_{\text{WITHIN}}] \quad (10.4)$$

where k is the number of levels in the ANOVA way. For our data we have

$$[4.50 - (2 - 1)1.50] / [28.50 + 1.50]$$
$$[4.50 - (1)1.50] / [28.50 + 1.50]$$
$$[4.50 - (1)1.50] / 30.00$$
$$[4.50 - 1.50] / 30.00$$
$$3.00 / 30.00$$
$$\omega^2 = 10.0\%$$

As explained in Chapter 7, and illustrated in Table 7.1, corrected effect sizes are equal to or smaller than their uncorrected counterparts. The difference (i.e., "shrinkage") is greater when (a) sample size is small, (b) the number of measured variables is larger, or (c) the population effect size is smaller. Here we had an $n = 18$ for our $\eta^2 = 15.8\%$, so shrinkage to $\omega^2 = 10.0\%$ is not an undue surprise.

One can also use the sums of squares variance partitions to test the statistical significance of the differences in the group means. When either the levels of the way exhaust all possible values of the way (e.g., gender in humans is measured at two levels), or the levels being used are the only ones of interest to the researcher (e.g., we collect data only from freshmen and seniors, because we only care about freshmen and seniors for a given

TABLE 10.6. Variance Partitions for the M_{Y1} Comparisons							
Source	SOS	df	MS	$F_{\text{CALCULATED}}$	$p_{\text{CALCULATED}}$	η^2	ω^2
Between	4.50	1	4.50	3.00	0.102	15.8%	10.0%
Within	24.00	16	1.50				
Total	28.50	17	1.68				

Note. For ANOVA, the df_{BETWEEN} = the numbers of groups minus 1 (i.e., $df_{\text{BETWEEN}} = k - 1$).

purpose), the NHSST *TS* using the *F* distribution is calculated by dividing the MS_{BETWEEN} by the MS_{WITHIN}. This $F_{\text{CALCULATED}}$ can be reexpressed as $p_{\text{CALCULATED}}$ by invoking the Excel spreadsheet function

$$\texttt{=FDIST}(F_{\text{CALCULATED}}, df_{\text{BETWEEN}}, df_{\text{WITHIN}})$$

■■■ The "Homogeneity of Variance" Assumption

As explained previously, the SOS_{WITHIN} is computed by calculating separately the sums of the squared deviations from the group mean within each group, ignoring both all other groups and the grand mean. Then the cell sums of squares are "pooled" by adding them together, yielding SOS_{WITHIN}. *This pooling process is legitimate iff (if, and only if) the variabilities of the scores in each group are roughly the same.* This is the so-called **homogeneity (equality) of variance** assumption required in ANOVA.

When we pool, we are invoking a kind of averaging process, or at least a summation similar to that which we use in computing the numerator for the mean. It is *not* reasonable to lump things together when they are wildly disparate.

This homogeneity of variance assumption is necessary both for statistical significance testing and for effect size interpretation. The consequences of meeting or not meeting this assumption can be concretely demonstrated using some small hypothetical datasets.

Equal Group Means, Equal Group Variances

Figure 10.2 presents hypothetical data for a three-group one-way ANOVA with five people in each cell. The five scores in each cell are exactly equally "spread out" (i.e., the homogeneity of variance assumption is exactly met in all three groups). The group means are also equal (i.e., all 3.0), and the grand mean is 3.0, too. As noted earlier, because SOS_{BETWEEN} is the sum of the squared deviations of the group means from the grand mean, when the group means are all the same, the SOS_{BETWEEN} will be zero.

Figure 10.2 presents the computations confirming that the expected

```
Statistic       Grp 1      Grp 2      Grp 3      Sum
                  1          1          1
                  2          2          2
                  3          3          3
                  4          4          4
                  5          5          5
Mean              3          3          3
Sum (Σ)          15         15         15         45
(Σ) squared     225        225        225        2025
Yᵢ squared,
   then summed   55         55         55        165
n                 5          5          5          15
```

$SOS_{\text{BETWEEN}} = ((\Sigma)_1{}^2)/n_1 + ((\Sigma)_2{}^2)/n_2 + ((\Sigma)_3{}^2)/n_3 - \Sigma_{\text{TOT}}{}^2 / n$

```
         225  / 5 + 225   / 5 +  225   / 5 - 2025  /15
              45 +            45 +          45 -      135
                             90 +          45 -      135
                                          135 -      135
                                                    0.00
```

$SOS_{\text{TOTAL}} = Y_i$ squared, then summed $- \Sigma\text{TOT}^2 / n$

```
              165 - 2025 /15
              165 - 135
              30.00
```

$SOS_{\text{WITHIN}} = SOS_{\text{TOTAL}} - SOS_{\text{BETWEEN}} = 30 - 0 = \mathbf{30.00}$

Source	SOS	df	MS	$F_{\text{CALCULATED}}$	η^2
Between groups	0	2	0	0	0%
Within groups	30	12	2.5		
Total	30	14	2.14		

FIGURE 10.2. ANOVA example (n = 15, k = 3) with equal means, equal variances

outcome is realized. The SOS_{BETWEEN} and the η^2 equal zero when the group means are equal. The figure uses different computational procedures than those illustrated in Tables 10.3, 10.4, and 10.5, but the procedures are algebraically equivalent. Because we have perfectly met the homogeneity of variance assumption, at least as regards this assumption we can fully trust both the ANOVA practical and NHSST results.

Equal Group Means, Unequal Group Variances

Figure 10.3 presents hypothetical data for a three-group one-way ANOVA with five people in each cell. Here the five scores in each cell vary in their "spreadoutness" (i.e., the scores in group 1 are the least spread out, and the scores in group 3 are the most spread out). However, the group means are all equal (i.e., all group means equal 3.0, and the grand mean is 3.0, too).

FIGURE 10.3. ANOVA example ($n = 15$, $k = 3$) with equal means, unequal variances

Statistic	Grp 1	Grp 2	Grp 3	Sum
	2	1	0	
	2	2	1	
	3	3	3	
	4	4	5	
	4	5	6	
Mean	3	3	3	
Sum Σ	15	15	15	45
(Σ) squared	225	225	225	2025
Y_i squared, then summed	49	55	71	175
n	5	5	5	15

$$SOS_{BETWEEN} = ((\Sigma)_1{}^2)/n_1 + ((\Sigma)_2{}^2)/n_2 + ((\Sigma)_3{}^2)/n_3 - \Sigma_{TOT}{}^2 / n$$

```
          225  /  5 + 225   / 5 +  225   / 5 - 2025  /15
                45 +         45 +         45 -        135
                             90 +         45 -        135
                                         135 -        135
                                                     0.00
```

$$SOS_{TOTAL} = Y_i \text{ squared, then summed} - \Sigma TOT^2 / n$$

```
              175 - 2025 / 15
              175 - 135
              40.00
```

$$SOS_{WITHIN} = SOS_{TOTAL} - SOS_{BETWEEN} = 40 - 0 = \mathbf{40.00}$$

Source	SOS	df	MS	$F_{CALCULATED}$	η^2
Between groups	0	2	0	0	0%
Within groups	40	12	3.33		
Total	40	14	2.86		

Even though the homogeneity of variance assumption is no longer met perfectly, because the three means are all identical, the effect size and statistical significance results remain unchanged. Thus, *if there are no group mean differences, ANOVA results will not be distorted even if the homogeneity of variance assumption is violated.*

Unequal Group Means, Equal Group Variances

Figure 10.4 presents hypothetical data for a three-group one-way ANOVA with five people in each cell. The five scores in each cell have exactly the same amount of "spreadoutness." However, the group means are now different (i.e., 2.0, 3.0, and 4.0, respectively, while the grand mean is still 3.0). Now the η^2 effect size ($SOS_{BETWEEN} / SOS_{TOTAL}$) is 25%, and $F_{CALCULATED}$ is 2.00. The results honor the differences in the means, and because the homogeneity of variance assumption is met perfectly, we can vest confidence in a conclusion that the result is not an artifact of violating a statistical assumption.

Unequal Group Means, Unequal Group Variances

Figure 10.5 presents hypothetical data for a three-level one-way ANOVA with five people in each cell. The five scores in each cell no longer have exactly the same amount of spreadoutness. However, the group means are still different (i.e., 2.0, 3.0, and 4.0, respectively, while the grand mean is still 3.0). Now the effect size ($SOS_{BETWEEN} / SOS_{TOTAL}$) is 20%, and $F_{CALCULATED}$ is 1.50.

Even though the magnitude of the mean differences is identical to those in the previous example, both effect size and statistical significance results in this example have been attenuated, because the homogeneity of variance assumption has been violated to some degree. It is important to note that such violations can lead to degrees of distortion causing the unwary researcher to make *entirely unjustified interpretations.*

Testing Homogeneity of Variance Using NHSST

The homogeneity assumption requires an assertion that the population variances of the dependent variable scores for each group are the same

Statistic	Grp 1	Grp 2	Grp 3	Sum
	0	1	2	
	1	2	3	
	2	3	4	
	3	4	5	
	4	5	6	
Mean	2	3	4	
Sum (Σ)	10	15	20	45
(Σ) squared	100	225	400	2025
Y_i squared, then summed	30	55	90	175
n	5	5	5	15

$$SOS_{BETWEEN} = ((\Sigma)_1^2)/n_1 + ((\Sigma)_2^2)/n_2 + ((\Sigma)_3^2)/n_3 - \Sigma_{TOT}^2 / n$$

```
        100  /  5 + 225    /  5 +   400   /  5 - 2025  /15
               20 +           45 +          80 -         135
                              65 ⌐          80          135
                                           145 -         135
                                                       10.00
```

$$SOS_{TOTAL} = Y_i \text{ squared, then summed} - \Sigma TOT^2 / n$$

```
        175 - 2025 / 15
        175 - 135
            40.00
```

$$SOS_{WITHIN} = SOS_{TOTAL} - SOS_{BETWEEN} = 40 - 10 = \textbf{30.00}$$

Source	SOS	df	MS	$F_{CALCULATED}$	η^2
Between groups	10	2	5.00	2.00	25%
Within groups	30	12	2.50		
Total	40	14	2.86		

FIGURE 10.4. ANOVA example (n = 15, k = 3) with unequal means, equal variances

(e.g., $SD_1^2 = SD_2^2 = SD_3^2$). This, of course, is the null hypotheses that the dependent variable score variances are equal across the groups. Some researchers elect to evaluate the homogeneity of variance assumption by using the statistical significance tests available within software ANOVA procedures. For the two-group situation, for either the two-sample t test or one-way, two-level ANOVA, NHSST results may be obtained by invok-

Statistic	Grp 1	Grp 2	Grp 3	Sum
	1	1	1	
	1	2	2	
	2	3	4	
	3	4	6	
	3	5	7	
Mean	2	3	4	
Sum (Σ)	10	15	20	45
(Σ) squared	100	225	400	2025
Y_i squared, then summed	24	55	106	185
n	5	5	5	15

$$SOS_{\text{BETWEEN}} = ((\Sigma)_1{}^2)/n_1 + ((\Sigma)_2{}^2)/n_2 + ((\Sigma)_3{}^2)/n_3 - \Sigma_{\text{TOT}}{}^2 / n$$

$$100 \ / \ 5 + 225 \ / \ 5 + 400 \ / \ 5 - 2025 \ /15$$
$$20 + \qquad 45 + \qquad 80 - \qquad 135$$
$$65 + \qquad 80 - \qquad 135$$
$$145 - \qquad 135$$
$$\mathbf{10.00}$$

$$SOS_{\text{TOTAL}} = Y_i \text{ squared, then summed} - \Sigma\text{TOT}^2 / n$$
$$185 - 2025 \ / \ 15$$
$$185 - 135$$
$$\mathbf{50.00}$$

$$SOS_{\text{WITHIN}} = SOS_{\text{TOTAL}} - SOS_{\text{BETWEEN}} = 50 - 10 = \mathbf{40.00}$$

Source	SOS	df	MS	$F_{\text{CALCULATED}}$	η^2
Between groups	10	2	5.00	1.50	20%
Within groups	40	12	3.33		
Total	50	14	3.57		

FIGURE 10.5. ANOVA example (n = 15, k = 3) with unequal means, unequal variances

ing Equation 6.3. For three or more groups, a test proposed by Levene (1960) may be used.

Using NHSST to evaluate whether methodological assumptions are met (and thus the researcher hopes that the test of this H_0 is *not* statistically significant) can suggest a paradox. As Thompson (1994c) noted,

The researcher desirous of statistically significant effects for substantive main and interaction effects will quite reasonably employ the largest sample possible so as to achieve the hoped-for results. Regrettably, large samples that tend to yield significance for substantive tests also tend to yield statistically significant results leading to rejection of method assumption null hypotheses, as in the test of equality of dependent variable variances across groups required by the ANOVA homogencity of variance assumption. (p. 13)

The implication is that common sense (and effect sizes), and not just NHSST, must be used to evaluate whether the homogeneity of variance assumption has been reasonably well met.

Unfortunately, empirical studies of published research show that researchers too often ignore the assumptions of their statistical methods (Keselman et al., 1998). These assumptions are more important than many researchers realize, as suggested by Wilcox (1998) in his article titled "How many discoveries have been lost by ignoring modern statistical methods?"

Post Hoc Tests

If the omnibus null hypothesis is not rejected, the researcher's analytic tasks are completed. On the other hand, iff both (a) the omnibus null is rejected, and (b) the way has more than two levels, further analyses are required to determine which group means differ. Perhaps every mean differs to a statistically significant degree from every other mean. Or, at the other extreme, perhaps only one mean differs from all the other means, none of which, in turn, differ from each other.

Some have argued that some post hoc tests may be invoked in the presence of three or more groups, even if the omnibus hypothesis is not tested or rejected. However, what are described here are the most common practices as of this date.

Post hoc tests are analyses conducted following the rejection of an omnibus null involving three or more levels to investigate more specifically which group means differ. There are many names for these analyses, some of which are summarized in Table 10.7. The alternative names are constructed by selecting one entry from the first column of the table and pair-

TABLE 10.7. Synonymous Names
for ANOVA Post Hoc Tests

Phrase elements	
First	Second
post hoc	contrast
a posteriori	comparison
unfocused	test
unplanned	
follow-up	

ing the selection with one entry chosen from the second column of the table (e.g., post hoc contract, a posteriori comparison).

Post hoc analysis can be conceptualized in converse, but equally appropriate, terms as detecting how many homogeneous subsets there are within the means. For example, given a six-level way, if one mean differed from the remaining five, none of which differed to a statistically significant degree from each other, there would be two homogeneous subsets. Or, if all six means differed to a statistically significant degree each from every other, there would be six homogeneous subsets of means.

Or, among the ordered means, the first two means might not differ from each other, but the first mean might differ from means three through six, and the second mean might not differ from the third mean, but might differ to a statistically significant degree from means four through six, and so forth. Figure 10.6 presents a graphic representation of such an analysis, yielding five homogeneous subsets among the six means.

One among several alternative reporting formats uses superscripts. For example, the researcher may report the results of these analyses by

FIGURE 10.6. Graphic representation of results from a post hoc analysis

k	1	2	3	4	5	6
M	10.5	15.2	19.8	24.9	30.2	35.1

saying, "The group means were $M_1 = 10.5^a$, $M_2 = 15.2^{a,b}$, $M_3 = 19.8^{b,c}$, $M_4 = 24.9^{c,d}$, $M_5 = 30.2^{d,e}$, and $M_6 = 35.1^e$," where means with common superscripts do not differ to a statistically significant degree.

Researchers using ANOVA soon realized the importance of conducting post hoc analyses for statistically significant omnibus hypotheses involving three or more levels. Of course, if a way has exactly two levels (e.g., boys versus girls), post hoc methods are unnecessary even if the omnibus null is rejected, because we know exactly where such differences arise (i.e., boys and girls must differ, "duh"—or if you are Australian, "der").

Post hoc contrasts compare *two* means. **Simple contrasts** compare the outcome variable mean of one level of the way with the outcome variable mean of another level of the way (e.g., H_0: $M_{FRESHMEN} = M_{SOPHOMORES}$, or "the dependent variable mean of the 10 freshmen equals the dependent variable mean of the 10 sophomores"). *No levels are combined* to create either (or both) of the two means being compared using simple contrasts. **Complex contrasts** compare two means, either one or both of which are computed by creating means from *combining levels* of the way (e.g., H_0: $M_{FRESHMEN} = M_{SOPHOMORES, JUNIORS}$; H_0: $M_{FRESHMEN} = M_{SOPHOMORES, JUNIORS, SENIORS}$; H_0: $M_{FRESHMEN, SOPHOMORES} = M_{JUNIORS, SENIORS}$, or "the dependent variable mean of the 20 students who are either freshmen or sophomores equals the dependent variable mean of the 20 students who are either juniors or seniors").

At first pale the use of conventional t tests to conduct post hoc analyses might have some appeal, because post hoc tests evaluate whether two means are equal, and two sample t tests can be used to evaluate the equality of two means. But one reason we are using ANOVA in the first place is to avoid the inflation of the experimentwise error rate. Of course, an argument might be made that the experimentwise error rate would be inflated less severely if we only conducted t tests following the rejection of an omnibus null, rather than using t tests straightaway and without testing the omnibus. Indeed, this "protected" t testing would be less problematic than the unprotected counterpart.

However, there are serious difficulties with using conventional t tests for post hoc analyses. For example, even using protected t tests post hoc when evaluating means results in some experimentwise error rate inflation. Also, we would not be taking into account how many means are being compared. For example, the error rate inflation from using protected t tests would not be equal in one study involving 3 levels versus another study involving 10 levels.

In addition, using conventional t tests would not take into account the number of contrasts we are conducting, even across situations involving the same number of means. For example, given a three-level way, according to Equation 6.2 ([3 (3 − 1)] / 2), three simple contrasts are possible. Three complex contrasts are also possible: {1 vs. 2,3}, {2 vs. 1,3}, and {3 vs. 1,2}. Thus, for a three-level way, there are three post hoc tests if only simple contrasts are being conducted, but there are six post hoc tests if both simple and complex contrasts are being conducted.

If we have a four-level way, there are six possible simple contrasts ([4(4 − 1)] / 2). But there are 19 complex contrasts for this design:

{1 vs. 2,3}	{1 vs. 2,4}	{1 vs. 3,4}	
{2 vs. 1,3}	{2 vs. 1,4}	{2 vs. 3,4}	
{3 vs. 1,2}	{3 vs. 1,4}	{3 vs. 2,4}	
{4 vs. 1,2}	{4 vs. 1,3}	{4 vs. 2,3}	
{1,2 vs. 3,4}	{1,3 vs. 2,4}	{1,4 vs. 2,3}	
{1 vs. 2,3,4}	{2 vs. 1,3,4}	{3 vs. 1,2,4}	{4 vs. 1,2,3}

Clearly, as we have more levels, (a) the number of possible contrasts expands quite rapidly, and (b) the discrepancy between the number of *only* simple contrasts versus the number of *both* simple and complex contrasts expands as well.

Beginning in the 1950s, statisticians began to propose dozens of modified t test procedures that take into account (a) how many group means or levels and (b) how many contrasts (i.e., only simple, or both simple and complex) are being considered. Conceptually, these post hoc methods can be thought of as *being special t tests that invoke a Bonferroni-type correction* taking into account the number of post hoc hypothesis tests. Actually, the methods adjust the critical value of the test statistic to take these issues into consideration.

Commonly used post hoc tests do either (a) only simple or (b) both simple and complex contrasts, and they do *all* the contrasts available for a given situation. Thus, for a three-level way, a post hoc method that evaluates only simple contrasts tests all three of the possible simple contrasts, and a post hoc method that does both simple and complex contrasts does all six of the possible contrasts.

An important implication of this is that (a) post hoc tests might evaluate contrasts not of interest to you and (b) force you to pay for testing uninteresting hypotheses as part of the Bonferroni-type correction. As we shall see in Chapter 12, we can escape this potentially unsavory situation by using planned contrasts instead.

Two of the most commonly used of the myriad post hoc tests are the Tukey and the Scheffé tests. **Tukey post hoc tests** evaluate all (and only) the simple contrasts available for a given design. Thus, the correction considers only simple contrasts, but will nevertheless differ for designs with $k = 3$, versus $k = 4$, versus $k = 5$ levels. **Scheffé post hoc tests** evaluate all the both simple and complex contrasts that are available for a given design. Thus, the Scheffé corrections for a $k = 3$ design are more severe than are the Tukey corrections for a $k = 3$ design. And the gaps between the amounts of correction between Tukey and Scheffé methods grow rapidly as more levels are involved in the design. One consequence of these adjustment dynamics is that Scheffé tests have considerably less power than Tukey tests, especially as the number of levels increases.

Clearly, if only simple contrasts are of interest, of the two choices discussed here Tukey tests are the correct choice. If complex contrasts are of interest, especially when the ways have many levels, Scheffé methods will be more appealing when the sample size is very large, so that power will remain reasonable even with these tests. Note that with some post hoc tests, including choices not considered here, it is possible to reject the null omnibus hypothesis and then find none of the post hoc tests statistically significant.

Some Key Concepts

ANOVA (a) **tests the equality of group means on the outcome variable, (b) taking into account the quality of the means.** As emphasized in Chapter 3, dispersion statistics characterize how well the mean does at representing a given group of scores. The $SOS_{BETWEEN}$ quantifies how similar or dissimilar the group means are from each other, and equals zero iff the group means are all equal. The SOS_{WITHIN}

quantifies how well each group mean does at representing the scores in each group, and equals zero iff within each group every score equals the group mean, regardless of whether or not the group means are equal. The $F_{CALCULATED}$ and $p_{CALCULATED}$ use both these sums of squares, and therefore are influenced by both considerations. The η^2 does not explicitly use the SOS_{WITHIN}, but the SOS_{WITHIN} is part of the SOS_{TOTAL}, and therefore the ANOVA uncorrected variance-accounted-for effect also takes into consideration both dynamics.

For a two-level one-way design, the two-sample t test and one-way ANOVA of the same data yield identical $p_{CALCULATED}$ and effect size statistics. For one-way designs involving more than two levels, the use of all possible pairwise two-sample t tests will result in inflated experimentwise error rates. To avoid this problem, and for other reasons explained in Chapter 11, ANOVA is used only to test mean differences for three or more groups, and can be used to test mean differences involving only two groups. ANOVA can be used to test only the statistical significance of mean differences, or only the practical significance of these differences, or both.

ANOVA requires an assumption that in the population the dispersions of the dependent variable scores are equal across the groups. The failure to meet this homogeneity of variance assumption may compromise the accuracy of both NHSST and effect size statistics.

When an omnibus null hypothesis is rejected and the way has three or more levels, post hoc tests are necessary to determine where the mean differences lie. Post hoc tests evaluate either simple (e.g., Tukey tests) or both simple and complex contrasts (e.g., Scheffé tests). Because for a given design Scheffé tests evaluate more hypotheses, and therefore invoke a stronger Bonferroni-type correction, Scheffé tests have less power against Type II error.

▦▦▦ Reflection Problems ▦▦▦

1. Consider the outcome variable scores for three studies involving balanced one-way two-level ANOVAs.

    Study A

    　　　Group 1: 8, 9, 10; $M = 9$; Group 2: 10, 11, 12; $M = 11$

    Study B

    　　　Group 1: 7, 8, 9; $M = 8$; Group 2: 11, 12, 13; $M = 12$

Study C

> Group 1: 7, 9, 11; *M* = 9; Group 2: 9, 11, 13; *M* = 11

Effect sizes are zero when sample statistics exactly match the expectations specified in the null hypothesis. For each of the three studies, what is the effect size for the homogeneity of variance hypothesis? Is the effect size zero for the null hypothesis tested by ANOVA in any of the three studies?

In Study A versus Study B, which, if any, of the three sums of squares (i.e., total, between, within) will be equal? In Study A versus Study C, which, if any, of the three sums of squares (i.e., total, between, within) will be equal? The mean difference (M_1 = 9; M_2 = 11) is the same for Study A and Study C, the homogeneity of variance assumption is perfectly met in both studies, and the *n*s are the same across the two studies. Will the $p_{CALCULATED}$ be equal for these two studies?

What is the rank ordering of the $p_{CALCULATED}$ values for the three studies? Are the three η^2 values equal across any of the studies?

2. Run omnibus ANOVA tests for each of the four outcome variables presented in Table 10.2. Compare and contrast the ANOVA results for (1) *Y1* versus *Y2*, (2) *Y1* versus *Y3*, (3) *Y4* versus *Y2*, and (4) *Y4* versus *Y3*. What explains the dynamics reflected in these comparisons? What two issues drive ANOVA tests? Why is it (perfectly) reasonable that both these factors drive ANOVA results?

3. Limiting the discussion to *n* – 8, and with possible scores of only { 1, 2, 3, 4, 5}, what 8 scores would yield the mathematically maximum values of dispersion *for this context*? What are the mathematically maximum values of (a) the sum of squares, (b) the variance, and (c) the *SD*, for this context? Draw the histogram of these data.

Next, let's now assume that the data involve a two-level one-way ANOVA problem, with two groups of scores. We have already computed the SOS_{TOTAL}. Compute (a) the $SOS_{BETWEEN}$ and (b) the SOS_{WITHIN}. Why does the SOS_{WITHIN} yield this result for these data?

In Chapter 3, I emphasized that every report of a mean should include a report of the related *SD*, and that the *SD* quantifies how well a given mean does at representing all the scores. In ANOVA, the $SOS_{BETWEEN}$ quantifies the degree of mean differences. What will $SOS_{BETWEEN}$ be for a two-level one-way ANOVA if the two dependent variable means are equal? What will $SOS_{BETWEEN}$ be for a four-level one-way ANOVA if the four dependent variable means are equal?

In descriptive statistics, the SD for the dataset quantifies how well the group mean does at representing all the scores in the dataset. In ANOVA, does the SOS_{WITHIN} perform an analogous function of quantifying how noteworthy the groups' mean differences are, *by taking into account as part of the mean comparison how well each mean does at representing the scores in each group*?

4. The effect sizes for a given design are context-driven. For example, if we explore the effects on myocardial infarcts of being randomly assigned to take 81, 325, or 750 milligrams of aspirin daily, we cannot conclusively extrapolate findings to cover taking 2,500 milligrams of aspirin daily. So, too, if studies cover similar but different dosages, the effect sizes cannot be directly compared exactly apples-to-apples. But can the effects be rescaled to take design differences into account? Consult Fowler (1987), Olejnik and Algina (2003), and Ronis (1981) to help clarify your views.

Multiway and Other Alternative ANOVA Models

n Chapter 10, only one-way designs were considered. In this chapter, multiway designs are introduced. The use of nonfactorial models is discussed. And the possibilities of fixed-, random-, and mixed-effects models are considered.

Multiway Models

One-way ANOVA for k greater than two levels represented an important advance over the alternative of conducting all possible pairwise t tests, thus avoiding the associated experimentwise Type I error rate inflation. However, multiway ANOVA designs afford two additional advantages over alternative analyses.

First, design efficiencies can be realized by evaluating two or more omnibus hypotheses within a single study rather than across separate studies. For example, if we wish to evaluate the effects of three dosages of drug

A on blood pressure and four alternative dosages of drug B on blood pressure, we can conduct a single two-way 3 × 4 ANOVA, rather than two independent one-way ANOVAs. We will theoretically obtain equivalent results across these alternatives, if sample sizes are compared apples-to-apples. So, we can answer more questions in fewer studies by using multiway ANOVA.

Second, and perhaps more importantly, as noted in Chapter 9, researchers are often keenly interested in testing interaction effects, and multiway ANOVA can be used to investigate these effects, just as interaction effects can be tested in regression. Investigating which educational or therapy intervention works best for everybody may be interesting, but also may be quixotic. Investigating in the same study which treatment works best for whom is important, and usually essential. In reality, few treatments work best (or worst) for every conceivable group of people (Cronbach, 1957).

Terminology

A **main effect** is an omnibus effect that evaluates differences in dependent variable means across all the levels of a given way, ignoring all the levels of all the remaining ways. An **interaction effect** evaluates the joint impacts of the combinations of the levels from two or more ways on the differences in the dependent variable means, ignoring all the levels of all the ways not involved in the interaction.

For example, in the previously described 3 × 4 design, if the design was balanced with 10 people in each cell, the total sample size would be 120. Two main effect null hypotheses may be tested:

(a) The mean blood pressure of the 40 people taking dose 1 of drug A equals the mean blood pressure of the 40 people taking dose 2 of drug A equals the mean blood pressure of the 40 people taking dose 3 of drug A, and

(b) the mean blood pressure of the 30 people taking dose 1 of drug B equals the mean blood pressure of the 30 people taking dose 2 of drug B equals the mean blood pressure of the 30 people taking dose 3 of drug B equals the mean blood pressure of the 30 people taking dose 4 of drug B.

Note that ANOVA, unlike the conventional *t* test, which *cannot* evaluate interaction effects, readily handles tests of interaction hypotheses. For this design, only one interaction hypothesis, the two-way A × B interaction effect, may be tested. However, designs with more ways accommodate more main and interaction effect tests. For example, all three-way designs can involve testing three main effects, three two-way interaction effects, and one three-way interaction effect. A four-way design can involve testing four main effects, six two-way interaction effects, four three-way interaction effects, and one four-way interaction effect.

Mathematically, it can be proven that for any balanced design, *all* pairs of all main and interaction hypotheses are *perfectly uncorrelated* (see Hester, 2000, pp. 22–27). Consequently, the sums of squares for all effects in a balanced design are unique for a given effect and, together with the SOS_{ERROR}, sum to equal the SOS_Y exactly.

This property, that omnibus hypotheses are *perfectly uncorrelated* for all *balanced* ANOVA designs, was noteworthy for two reasons. First, a balanced ANOVA can be effectively thought of as a Case #1 regression situation. And, as we saw in Chapter 9, all the computations necessary for an analysis in this situation are vastly simplified. The computational simplicity accomplished through the magic of the ANOVA logic, which yields perfectly uncorrelated, nonoverlapping effects for balanced designs, was *hugely* important in the decades when all computations had to be performed (repeatedly, to check for calculation errors) on calculators.

Second, obtaining nonoverlapping or unique effects for each omnibus test also hugely simplifies result interpretation, just as regression result interpretation is simplified in Case #1. If 10% of the SOS_Y is predicted or explained by information about to which levels of way A the participants belonged, and if that 10% has no commonality with any other effect, there is no debate about allocating nonexistent common predictive credit.

Computational Example

We will reuse the Table 9.14 blood alcohol data to illustrate the computations for a factorial 2 × 2 analysis. Here, again, we are partitioning the information regarding the amount and origins of individual differences quantified by the SOS_{TOTAL} of 0.124. The small number even for $n = 32$

participants suggests that blood alcohol levels do not vary much, on average, even when people have had up to seven drinks. Of course, on this variable, small score differences can yield huge differences in motor skills, such as those required to operate an automobile. Clearly, what makes a given *SOS* large or small depends on what variable we are measuring.

For the purposes of this analysis, because ANOVA requires nominally-scaled data on the independent variables, we have mutilated the intervally-scaled scores on the two predictors to yield dichotomies. You should find this troubling. When, if ever, would one be willing to mutilate interval independent variables simply so that ANOVA could be used?

However, the mutilation does afford us the heuristic opportunity to compare apples-to-apples effects for the nonmutilated and the mutilated data. And remember that this comparison is made within the context of a single study.

When such mutilations are made across the studies in a literature, the consequences may be quite dire. If all researchers mutilated their interval predictors by using sample-specific medians, the medians may well differ in each sample, and then, when the ANOVA results are inconsistent across studies, we do not know whether (a) the inconsistencies across studies occurred because results were unstable across samples, or (b) the variations in median cutpoints used to create groups made consistency unattainable, and the findings irreconcilable.

More will be said later on the question of mutilation of intervally-scaled data. Table 11.1 presents the Table 9.3 data after the intervally-scaled predictors have been converted into nominal scale.

First, we will compute the two main effect sums of squares. We could use the same procedures described in detail in Chapter 10, but will instead use algebraically-equivalent formulas that yield identical results. These formulas involve the outcome scores squared, and then summed (i.e., *not* the *SOS*, because *SOS* is instead the sum of the squared *deviations from the mean*). Here, as reported in Table 11.1, the outcome scores squared and then summed equal 0.4204. The formulas also require the sums of the scores in the four cells: $\Sigma_{1,1}$, $\Sigma_{1,2}$, $\Sigma_{2,1}$, and $\Sigma_{2,2}$. Last, the formulas require the sum of all the outcome scores, which is 3.08, as reported in Table 11.1.

TABLE 11.1. Conversion of Table 9.14 Data into ANOVA Form

Group/case	W_GRP	DR_GRP	BLOOD	Cell total	BLOOD^2
	SPSS Variables				
Low weight, low drinks					
1	1	1	0.04		0.0016
2	1	1	0.11		0.0121
5	1	1	0.03		0.0009
6	1	1	0.09		0.0081
9	1	1	0.03		0.0009
10	1	1	0.08		0.0064
13	1	1	0.02		0.0004
14	1	1	0.07	0.47	0.0049
Low weight, high drinks					
3	1	2	0.19		0.0361
4	1	2	0.26		0.0676
7	1	2	0.16		0.0256
8	1	2	0.22		0.0484
11	1	2	0.13		0.0169
12	1	2	0.19		0.0361
15	1	2	0.12		0.0144
16	1	2	0.16	1.43	0.0256
High weight, low drinks					
17	2	1	0.02		0.0004
18	2	1	0.06		0.0036
21	2	1	0.02		0.0004
22	2	1	0.06		0.0036
25	2	1	0.02		0.0004
26	2	1	0.05		0.0025
29	2	1	0.02		0.0004
30	2	1	0.05	0.30	0.0025
High weight, high drinks					
19	2	2	0.11		0.0121
20	2	2	0.15		0.0225
23	2	2	0.09		0.0081
24	2	2	0.13		0.0169
27	2	2	0.09		0.0081
28	2	2	0.12		0.0144
31	2	2	0.08		0.0064
32	2	2	0.11	0.88	0.0121
Sum			3.08	3.08	0.4204

The SOS_{WEIGHT}, or the main effect SOS for weight, is computed as

$$SOS_A = \{[(\Sigma_{1,1} + \Sigma_{1,2})^2 + (\Sigma_{2,1} + \Sigma_{2,2})^2] / [j(n)]\} - \{\Sigma^2 / [i(j)(n)]\} \quad (11.1)$$

where i is the number of levels in the A way, j is the number of levels in the B way, and n is the number of participants in each cell. For our data we have

$$\{[(0.47 + 1.43)^2 + (0.30 + 0.88)^2] / [2(8)]\} - \{3.08^2 / [2(2)(8)]\}$$
$$\{[1.90^2 + 1.18^2] / [2(8)]\} - \{3.08^2 / [2(2)(8)]\}$$
$$\{[3.6100 + 1.3924] / [2(8)]\} - \{9.4864 / [2(2)(8)]\}$$
$$\{5.0024 / [2(8)]\} - \{9.4864 / [2(2)(8)]\}$$
$$\{5.0024 / 16\} - \{9.4864 / 32\}$$
$$0.3127 - 0.2965$$
$$SOS_{\text{WEIGHT}} = 0.0162$$

The SOS_{DRINKS}, or the main effect SOS for drinks, is computed as

$$SOS_B = \{[(\Sigma_{1,1} + \Sigma_{2,1})^2 + (\Sigma_{1,2} + \Sigma_{2,2})^2] / [i(n)]\} - \{\Sigma^2 / [i(j)(n)]\} \quad (11.2)$$

For our data we have

$$\{[(0.47 + 0.30)^2 + (1.43 + 0.88)^2] / [2(8)]\} - \{3.08^2 / [2(2)(8)]\}$$
$$\{[0.77^2 + 2.31^2] / [2(8)]\} - \{3.08^2 / [2(2)(8)]\}$$
$$\{[0.5929 + 5.3361] / [2(8)]\} - \{9.4864 / [2(2)(8)]\}$$
$$\{5.9290 / [2(8)]\} - \{9.4864 / [2(2)(8)]\}$$
$$\{5.9290 / 16\} - \{9.4864 / 32\}$$
$$0.3706 - 0.2965$$
$$SOS_{\text{DRINKS}} = 0.0741$$

The $SOS_{\text{WEIGHT} \times \text{DRINKS}}$ is computed as

$$SOS_{A \times B} = \{[\Sigma_{1,1}^2 + \Sigma_{2,1}^2 + \Sigma_{1,2}^2 + \Sigma_{2,2}^2] / n\} \quad (11.3)$$
$$- SOS_A - SOS_B - \{\Sigma^2 / [i(j)(n)]\}$$

For our data we have

$$\{[0.47^2 + 1.43^2 + 0.30^2 + 0.88^2] / 8\} - 0.0162 - 0.0741 - \{3.08^2 / [2(2)(8)]\}$$
$$\{[0.2209 + 2.0449 + 0.0900 + 0.7744] / 8\}$$
$$- 0.0162 - 0.0741 - \{9.4864 / [2(2)(8)]\}$$
$$\{3.1302 / 8\} - 0.0162 - 0.0741 - \{9.4864 / [2(2)(8)]\}$$
$$\{3.1302 / 8\} - 0.0162 - 0.0741 - \{9.4864 / 32\}$$
$$0.3913 - 0.0162 - 0.0741 - 0.2965$$
$$SOS_{A \times B} = 0.0045$$

Notice that we subtract out of $SOS_{A \times B}$ the main effect SOS that reflects the differences of the two outcome variable means on both the A way and the B way. This reflects the reality that the differences in the four cell means are jointly influenced by the interaction effect and both main effects. One implication, as we will see momentarily, is that *plotting the cell means to understand interaction effects can be misleading* because, as the title of Rosnow and Rosenthal's (1991) article implies, "If you're looking at the cell means, you're not looking at only the interaction (unless all main effects are zero)."

The SOS_{WITHIN} is computed as

$$SOS_{WITHIN} = \Sigma(Y_i^2) - \{[\Sigma_{1,1}^2 + \Sigma_{2,1}^2 + \Sigma_{1,2}^2 + \Sigma_{2,2}^2] / n\} \quad (11.4)$$

For our data we have

$$0.4204 - \{[0.47^2 + 1.43^2 + 0.30^2 + 0.88^2] / 8\}$$
$$0.4204 - \{[0.2209 + 2.0449 + 0.0900 + 0.7744] / 8\}$$
$$0.4204 - \{3.1302 / 8\}$$
$$0.4204 - 0.3913$$
$$SOS_{WITHIN} = 0.0291$$

These values can then be arrayed into the summary table reported in Table 11.2.

The degrees of freedom for main effects equal the number of levels in a given way minus 1. This reflects the computation of $SOS_{BETWEEN}$ as involving all group means in the presence of the estimated grand mean (i.e., $M_{Y.}$). Given M_Y, only $k - 1$ of the group means are free to vary.

TABLE 11.2. Summary Table for 2 × 2 Factorial Analysis

Source	SOS	df	MS	$F_{\text{CALCULATED}}$	$p_{\text{CALCULATED}}$	η^2
Weight	0.0162	1	0.0162	15.5742	<0.001	13.1%
Drinks	0.0741	1	0.0741	71.2498	<0.001	59.8%
WeightXD	0.0045	1	0.0045	4.3382	0.047	3.6%
Within	0.0291	28	0.0010			
Total	0.1240	31	0.0040			

The degrees of freedom for interaction effects equal the degrees of freedom for the main effects named in a given interaction term times each other. For example, for a 5 × 4 × 3 design, $df_{A \times B} = 12$, $df_{A \times C} = 8$, $df_{B \times C} = 6$, and $df_{A \times B \times C} = 24$.

Interpreting Interaction Effects

The presence of a noteworthy interaction effect implies that the main effects named in the interaction cannot be interpreted without taking into account the interaction. For example, if there is an interaction effect for drug A with drug B, we cannot interpret the main effect for drug A outside the context of interaction, because we have learned that drug A works differently in the presence of different levels of drug B. So, the focus in such cases turns to the interaction effect. The main effects in a multiway design will be the basis for interpretation *only* when all interaction effects are deemed trivial, based on their $p_{\text{CALCULATED}}$ values or their effect sizes.

As noted in Chapter 9, the recognition of the importance of interaction effects in the social sciences was hugely advanced by Cronbach's (1957) American Psychological Association (APA) presidential address. Cronbach (1957, 1975) noted that a study may involve a way of defining treatment conditions, called a **treatment way**, and a pretest measure in the same domain as the outcome variable (e.g., academic ability) used to define an **aptitude way**. The **aptitude–treatment interaction** (ATI) effect can be very informative about for whom different treatments work best.

The ATI designs are useful, because the search for the elusive treatment that is best for everyone may be unrealistic.

Unfortunately, the interpretation of interaction effects is not as straightforward as the procedures recommended in many statistics textbooks. Researchers have defined a **Type IV error** as occurring when an hypothesis is correctly rejected but the basis for the rejection is incorrectly interpreted (Levin & Marascuilo, 1972; Marascuilo & Levin, 1970). In a related vein, Rosnow and Rosenthal (1989b) noted that interaction effects are "probably the universally most misinterpreted empirical results in psychology" (p. 1282).

Many textbooks recommend the plotting of cell means to explore interaction effects, especially for two-way interaction effects. The vertical axis is used (as always) to represent the outcome variable. Usually the horizontal axis is demarcated by the levels of the aptitude way (e.g., low, medium, and high IQ). Then symbols (e.g., circles and triangles) are used to represent cell means across the treatment conditions (e.g., lecture versus discovery instruction, "talk" therapy versus behavior modification therapy). Like symbols are then linked by like continua (e.g., the three means for lecture are linked by a continuous line, while the three means for discovery methods are linked by a dashed line).

If a given treatment has higher means across the three IQ levels, then arguably that treatment is best for all IQ groups, or at least the groups represented within the study. If the plotted lines cross, then one treatment may be best for some people, but the other treatments may be best for other people.

These ATI (or other interaction) plots do reflect real differences in the cell means. This information can be quite important from a practical point of view. However, plots of the cell means do *not* reflect only interaction effect dynamics.

Instead, the cell means used in these plots are impacted by the confounded joint influences of a variety of factors. As noted by Rosnow and Rosenthal (1989a), the cell means "are the combined effects of the interaction, the row effects [a main effect], the column effects [a second main effect], and the grand mean" (p. 144). By the same token, simple post hoc tests of the cell means also do not yield insight about the origins of interaction effects, because the interaction effects are *not* uniquely a function of the cell means (Boik, 1979).

Figure 11.1 presents the cell means, the margin means, and the grand

		Low Drinks	High Drinks	
W a y A	Low Weight	$M_{1,1} = 0.058$	$M_{1,2} = 0.179$	$M_{1,j} = 0.118$
	High Weight	$M_{2,1} = 0.038$	$M_{2,2} = 0.110$	$M_{2,j} = 0.074$
		$M_{i,1} = 0.048$	$M_{i,2} = 0.144$	$M. = 0.096$

FIGURE 11.1. Cell and margin means and grand mean

means for the heuristic Table 11.1 data. Figure 11.2 presents a plot of these four cell means, which is *incorrect* iff the researcher's sole focus is on interpreting the interaction effects.

Interaction effects can *correctly* be explored by plotting (or analyzing) *corrected or adjusted cell means*, rather than the actual cell means (e.g., Harwell, 1998). For our data, these values are

$$\text{Corrected } M_{1,1} = M_{1,1} - M_{1,j} - M_{i,1} + M.$$
$$0.058 - 0.118 - 0.048 + 0.096 = -0.012$$

$$\text{Corrected } M_{1,2} = M_{1,2} - M_{1,j} - M_{i,2} + M.$$
$$0.179 - 0.118 - 0.144 + 0.096 = +0.013$$

$$\text{Corrected } M_{2,1} = M_{2,1} - M_{2,j} - M_{i,1} + M.$$
$$0.038 - 0.074 - 0.048 + 0.096 = +0.012$$

$$\text{Corrected } M_{2,2} = M_{2,2} - M_{2,j} - M_{i,2} + M.$$
$$0.110 - 0.074 - 0.144 + 0.096 = -0.012$$

Marascuilo and Levin (1970) provided various examples of how Scheffé post hoc methods can be applied to explore these dynamics analytically.

FIGURE 11.2. Plot of cell means

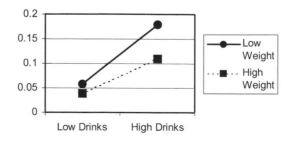

The take-home message is *not* that plots of cell means are unimportant from a practical point of view, but instead is that such plots involve more than interaction dynamics, and plots of adjusted means are of interest if the focus is on understanding interaction effects.

Factorial versus Nonfactorial Analyses

Factorial analyses test all possible main and interaction effects. **Nonfactorial designs** test at least one effect but fewer than all the possible main and interaction effects. One-way designs are inherently factorial. For our illustrative 3 × 4 design, if we test all three possible omnibus hypotheses, the design is factorial. If we do not conduct any one or more of the possible omnibus tests, the analysis is no longer factorial.

At first impression one might think that conducting a nonfactorial analysis is illogical. If the ways are thoughtfully selected, does this not imply interest in all possible main and interaction effects? However, there are two possible situations in which nonfactorial designs have appeal, although the decision in favor of a nonfactorial over a factorial design of course turns upon thoughtful personal judgment of what is best in a given situation.

First, in multiway designs with many ways, researchers might reasonably forgo the testing of very high-order interaction effects. Even second-order effects can be complicated to interpret. Think of a five-way design in which the interpretation of the five-way interaction effect would require consideration of all the possible combinations of all levels conditioned upon each other in their effects on the outcome variable. Furthermore, the means at the highest order involve the fewest participants per estimate, and so these effects theoretically are least stable.

Second, some researchers forgo testing main effects for ways that are not malleable. For example, a researcher might conduct a 3 × 2 study involving a treatment way with three levels, and a gender way. If we find as a main effect that women learn more than men, how can we apply our knowledge? Many men will resist having their gender altered in service of improved outcome variable scores, no matter how persuasive an argument is presented!

But if the researcher is not interested in gender as a main effect, why include gender as a way in the first place? The answer may be that the researcher only used gender to be able to explore the treatment-by-gender two-way interaction effect. Perhaps we cannot force a new gender on the men, but we may be able to teach males one way, and females another way, if the empirical evidence in favor of doing so is quite compelling.

Note that neither factorial nor nonfactorial analyses always enjoy a statistical power advantage over each other. Table 11.3 presents hypothetical data involving a three-level treatment way and a two-level gender way. The factorial analysis is presented in the top of the table. If we decide not to test the gender omnibus main effect *before we analyze any data*, when we conduct the analysis we pool the SOS_{GENDER} and df_{GENDER} into the error SOS and df, respectively. The nonfactorial results are presented in the bottom of Table 11.3 and, for this example, show loss of statistical significance ($\alpha = 0.05$) for the remaining effects in the nonfactorial analysis.

Table 11.4 presents a counterexample for a 2×2 design involving two treatment conditions and participants' handedness (i.e., left or right dominant). For these data, testing the nonfactorial model results in statistically significant effects ($\alpha = 0.05$) that would not otherwise occur.

Some statistical packages allow the researcher to declare which omni-

TABLE 11.3. Example of a Nonfactorial Analysis *Hurting* Power

Source	SOS	df	MS	$F_{CALCULATED}$	$p_{CALCULATED}$	η^2
Factorial						
Treatment	45.0	2	22.50	5.40	0.021	22.5%
Gender	**55.0**	**1**	55.00	13.20	0.003	27.5%
T × G	50.0	2	25.00	6.00	0.016	25.0%
Error	50.0	12	4.17			
Total	200.0	17	11.76			
Nonfactorial						
Treatment	45.0	2	22.50	*2.79*	*0.098*	22.5%
T × G	50.0	2	25.00	*3.10*	*0.080*	25.0%
Error	*105.0*	*13*	*8.08*			
Total	200.0	17	11.76			

Note. Values pooled into error *SOS* and *df* are in **bold**. Entries altered in the conversion to the nonfactorial analyses are in *italics*.

TABLE 11.4. Example of a Nonfactorial Analysis *Helping* Power

Source	SOS	df	MS	$F_{\text{CALCULATED}}$	$p_{\text{CALCULATED}}$	η^2
Factorial						
Treatment	55.0	1	55.00	6.47	0.064	36.7%
Handed	**1.0**	**1**	1.00	0.12	0.749	0.7%
T × H	60.0	1	60.00	7.06	0.057	40.0%
Error	34.0	4	8.50			
Total	150.0	7	21.43			
Nonfactorial						
Treatment	55.0	1	55.00	*7.86*	*0.038*	36.7%
T × H	60.0	1	60.00	*8.57*	*0.033*	40.0%
Error	*35.0*	*5*	*7.00*			
Total	150.0	7	21.43			

Note. Values pooled into error SOS and *df* are in **bold**. Entries altered in the conversion to the nonfactorial analyses are in *italics*.

bus hypotheses are to be tested. Even if the software package does not afford this choice, a nonfactorial analysis can be conducted simply by taking the sums of squares and the *df* from the effects not being tested, pooling these into the error SOS and *df*, as illustrated in Tables 11.3 and 11.4, and then recomputing the mean squares, $F_{\text{CALCULATED}}$ and $p_{\text{CALCULATED}}$ values.

Fixed-, Random-, and Mixed-Effects Models

The notion of randomly sampling participants drawn from the population of all possible participants is familiar. The power of random samples to produce representative results (e.g., 2,000 voters randomly sampled out of 160 million eligible voters) is demonstrated on a quadrennial election cycle in the United States. Logically, if the random sampling of participants generates data that support generalization to a larger field of participants, why could we not randomly sample levels for a way from a wider population of potential levels, and thereby achieve generalization beyond the levels of the way actually used in the study?

A **fixed effect** in ANOVA occurs when (a) we use all the conceivable levels of a way, or (b) we do not want to generalize beyond the levels we actually employ. For example, if we use male and female as the levels for a gender way in a study of people, most of us would presume that we have exhausted the commonly-recognized levels of this way, and treat the gender way as a fixed-effect omnibus. Or, if we include only high school juniors and seniors as two grade levels in a grade-level way, and we declare interest in only these two levels, then this way would also be a fixed-effects way. A **fixed-effects ANOVA model** occurs when all the omnibus hypotheses in the analysis are treated as fixed effects.

A **random effect** presumes a representative sample of levels from the more numerous potential levels on the way, along with interest in generalizing from the sampled levels to the population of all possible levels. For example, a researcher might be interested in studying the efficacy of all potential lengths of therapy sessions, ranging from 45 minutes to 120 minutes, in 5-minute increments: {45, 50, 55, 60, 65 . . . 110, 115, 120}. A six-level way might be created by randomly sampling the levels: {45, 80, 90, 100, 105, 115}.

A **random-effects ANOVA model** occurs when all the omnibus hypotheses in the analysis are treated as random effects. Any interaction effect involving one or more ways treated as random effects are also considered random effects. For example, two therapy methods might be levels deemed to constitute a fixed-effects way. But if the two-way interaction involves the six-level therapy duration random effect, the 2 × 6 two-way interaction is considered a random effect. A **mixed-effects model** occurs when at least one omnibus hypothesis is treated as a fixed effect, and at least one omnibus hypothesis is treated as a random effect.

All of the calculations of the (a) sums of squares, (b) degrees of freedom, and (c) mean squares are *identical* for fixed-, random-, and mixed-effects models. What differs across the models is the *denominator* used in computing the $F_{CALCULATED}$ values. In a fixed-effects model, the MS_{WITHIN} is used as the denominator in computing *all* the $F_{CALCULATED}$ values. This computation reflects the fact that in a fixed-effects model only the sampling error variance involved in sampling participants is expected to impact estimates (Kennedy & Bush, 1985).

However, in random-effects and mixed-effects models, some estimates are impacted by both (a) sampling error variance involving sampling participants and (b) sampling error associated with sampling levels. Thus, in these models some denominators for calculating F values will be mean squares *other than* the MS_{WITHIN}.

The correct denominators for computing $F_{\text{CALCULATED}}$ values can be mathematically derived by solving for various statistics called "expected mean squares" (i.e., E(MS)). But these calculations are extraordinarily tedious. An alternative solution invokes a rubric presented in various locations (e.g., Frederick, 1999; C. R. Hicks, 1973; Ott, 1984).

E(MS) Derivation Rubric

The rubric is illustrated here presuming a factorial model in which the A way is a random effect for six therapy session lengths, and the B way involves a comparison of psychoanalytic therapy versus behavioral therapy. We will presume a balanced design of $n = 3$ in each of the 12 cells. The rubric involves six steps.

First, create a two-way layout with an empty header and rows that list the variance partitions, and the subscripts to be used for each partition.

	E(MS)
Main A_i	
Main B_j	
Interaction $A \times B_{ij}$	
Error $e_{n(ij)}$	

Second, complete the header to characterize the omnibus effects. In the middle row of the header, put F for any fixed effect, and R for any random effect. Remember that any interaction involving one or more random effects is itself random. In the bottom row of the header, place the subscript being used for given effects. In the top row, place the maximum value for the subscript for a given effect.

	6 R i	2 F j	3 R n	E(MS)
Main A_i				
Main B_j				
Interaction $A \times B_{ij}$				
Error $e_{n(ij)}$				

Third, copy the number in the top row of the header to each of the rows in that column *only* for rows in which the header subscript does *not* appear in the row label.

	6 R i	2 F j	3 R n	E(MS)
Main A_i		2	3	
Main B_j	6		3	
Interaction $A \times B_{ij}$			3	
Error $e_{n(ij)}$				

Fourth, for any row with subscripts that are in parentheses, place a 1 in the cell in the columns that are headed by a letter in the parentheses.

	6 R i	2 F j	3 R n	E(MS)
Main A_i		2	3	
Main B_j	6		3	
Interaction $A \times B_{ij}$			3	
Error $e_{n(ij)}$	1	1		

Fifth, fill in the remaining empty cells of the layout. Put zeroes in empty cells for a fixed effect. Put 1s in empty cells for a random effect.

	6 R i	2 F j	3 R n	E(MS)
Main A_i	1	2	3	
Main B_j	6	0	3	
Interaction $A \times B_{ij}$	1	0	3	
Error $e_{n(ij)}$	1	1	1	

Sixth, use the σ^2 symbol for random-effects variance, and ϕ^2 for fixed-effects variance. Enter σ_E^2 for the E(MS) for error. Next, for a given row, use a pencil, thumb, or finger to cover all columns with the row's subscript in the bottom row of the header only for row subscripts not in parentheses (e.g., for the A_i row, cover the first column, which has the subscript i; for the $e_{n(ij)}$ row, cover only the third column, which has the subscript n). So, for the A-way main effect, cover only the first of the three columns. Then enter the uncovered weights for rows containing the i subscript and the associated variance terms in the rightmost column. Of course, if any uncovered column has a zero entry, the zero cancels out the variance from that source.

	6 R i	2 F j	3 R n	E(MS)
Main A_i	1	2	3	$(2)(3)\sigma_A^2 + (1)(1)\sigma_E^2$
Main B_j	6	0	3	
Interaction $A \times B_{ij}$	1	0	3	
Error $e_{n(ij)}$	1	1	1	σ_E^2

For the B-way main effect, cover only the middle column. Then enter the uncovered weights and the associated variance terms in the rightmost column for the B main-effect row. Ignore σ_A^2 because there is not a j subscript for the A-way main effect.

	6	2	3	
	R	F	R	E(MS)
	i	j	n	
Main A_i	1	2	3	$(2)(3)\sigma_A^2 + (1)(1)\sigma_E^2$
Main B_j	6	0	3	$(6)(3)\phi_B^2 + (1)(3)\sigma_{A \times B}^2 + (1)(1)\sigma_E^2$
Interaction $A \times B_{ij}$	1	0	3	
Error $e_{n(ij)}$	1	1	1	σ_E^2

For the two-way interaction effect, cover the two left columns. Then enter the uncovered weights and the associated variance terms in the rightmost column for the A × B interaction effect row. Ignore σ_A^2 and ϕ_B^2 because they do not have an ij subscript.

	6	2	3	
	R	F	R	E(MS)
	i	j	n	
Main A_i	1	2	3	$(2)(3)\sigma_A^2 + (1)(1)\sigma_E^2$
Main B_j	6	0	3	$(6)(3)\phi_B^2 + (1)(3)\sigma_{A \times B}^2 + (1)(1)\sigma_E^2$
Interaction $A \times B_{ij}$	1	0	3	$(3)\sigma_{A \times B}^2 + (1)\sigma_E^2$
Error $e_{n(ij)}$	1	1	1	σ_E^2

We now know what the *MS* is expected to be for each of the four variance partitions. Logically, when we compute ANOVA $F_{\text{CALCULATED}}$ values, we are trying to evaluate whether the variance source *uniquely* due to an effect makes a noteworthy contribution over and above other variance sources for a given effect. So the correct denominator for these computations uses all the mean squares contributing to a given effect, *except the* variability uniquely due to the tested effect itself, as reflected in the E(MS)s.

For the A-way main effect, the E(MS) is $6\sigma_A^2 + \sigma_E^2$. To test the effect of variance contributed *only* from A, we are looking for a variance that contains *all* these variances *except* $6\sigma_A^2$. The variance with this property is σ_E^2, the E(MS) for the error source. This means that when we are testing the random-effect A way, we will compute the F by dividing MS_A by the MS_{ERROR}.

For the B-way main effect, the E(MS) is $18\phi_B^2 + 3\sigma_{A \times B}^2 + \sigma_E^2$. Again, to test this main effect, we are looking for an E(MS) that contains *all* these terms *except* $18\phi_B^2$. The E(MS) for the interaction term is $3\sigma_{A \times B}^2 + \sigma_E^2$. This means that we will compute the $F_{CALCULATED}$ for the B main effect by dividing MS_B by the $MS_{A \times B}$, instead of by the MS_{ERROR}.

For the interaction effect, the expected mean square is $3\sigma_{A \times B}^2 + \sigma_E^2$. Because the only variance source in addition to the $A \times B$ interaction is the error variance, we will compute the F test for this $A \times B$ interaction random effect by dividing $MS_{A \times B}$ by the MS_{ERROR}.

Power versus Generality

To make this discussion concrete, Table 11.5 presents an hypothetical dataset for our 6×2 mixed-effects model, in which the B way is treated as the only fixed effect. Table 11.6 presents the ANOVA summary for the mixed-effects model. Notice that the A-way main effect and the two-way interaction effects are both statistically significant, but that the B-way main effect is not statistically significant.

For *pedagogical purposes only*—*not* as a model for the flexible and incorrect analytic practice of treating the same data by invoking contradictory models—Table 11.6 also presents a fixed-effects summary table for the same data. As noted previously, the model employed does not change the sums of squares, the degrees of freedom, or the mean squares. However, the model selection does impact the denominator used in computing the $F_{CALCULATED}$ values, and these changes in turn impact the corresponding $p_{CALCULATED}$ values. For our heuristic data, for the fixed-effects model reported in Table 11.6, the $p_{CALCULATED}$ for the B way is 6E 8, but for the mixed-effects model, the $p_{CALCULATED}$ for the B way is 0.301.

To summarize for the two-way case only, a fixed-effects model uses

TABLE 11.5. Illustrative Data for the Mixed-Effects Model

Case	SPSS variable		
	DV	A	B
1	42	1	1
2	44	1	1
3	40	1	1
4	47	2	1
5	43	2	1
6	45	2	1
7	46	3	1
8	48	3	1
9	47	3	1
10	51	4	1
11	53	4	1
12	54	4	1
13	56	5	1
14	58	5	1
15	59	5	1
16	61	6	1
17	62	6	1
18	64	6	1
19	47	1	2
20	49	1	2
21	48	1	2
22	52	2	2
23	54	2	2
24	55	2	2
25	57	3	2
26	59	3	2
27	58	3	2
28	63	4	2
29	64	4	2
30	66	4	2
31	49	5	2
32	51	5	2
33	52	5	2
34	54	6	2
35	56	6	2
36	58	6	2

TABLE 11.6. Summary Tables for Fixed- versus Mixed-Effects Models

Source	SOS	df	MS	$F_{CALCULATED}$	$P_{CALCULATED}$
Fixed-effects model					
A	883.56	5	176.71	73.122	9.9156E-14
B	144.00	1	144.00	**59.586**	**0.00000006**
A × B	542.00	5	108.40	44.855	2.0986E-11
Error	58.00	24	2.42		
Total	1627.56	35	46.50		
Mixed-effects model					
A	883.56	5	176.71	73.122	9.9156E-14
B	144.00	1	144.00	**1.328**	**0.301**
A × B	542.00	5	108.40	44.855	2.0986E-11
Error	58.00	24	2.42		
Total	1627.56	35	46.50		

Note. The differences in entries for the two models are highlighted in **bold**.

the MS_{WITHIN} as the denominator for all three computations of the $F_{CALCULATED}$ values. For a random-effects model, the MS_{WITHIN} is used as the denominator only for the test of the two-way interaction effect, and the $MS_{A \times B}$ is used as the denominator for both main effect tests. For a mixed-effects model the $MS_{A \times B}$ is used to test the fixed-effect main effect, while the MS_{WITHIN} is used to test both the random-effects main effect and the interaction effect.

What impact does using a model other than the fixed effects model have? As suggested by the heuristic comparisons in Table 11.6, the presence of random effects within a model can reduce power against Type II error. So, the capacity to generalize beyond the levels actually used in random-effects ways may come at a cost.

None of this is to argue against treating effects as random. Indeed, some research problems almost cry out for this treatment (see Clark, 1973). But the take-home message is to be thoughtful when making these decisions, because their consequences can be dramatic. Finally, it should be noted that some modern statistical packages do *not* correctly perform these calculations, so carefully review your computer results for mixed-effects models.

▦▦▦ Brief Comment on ANCOVA

In 1963, Campbell and Stanley wrote an influential chapter on experimental and quasi-experimental design published in the *Handbook of Research on Teaching*. The paperback reprint of this single chapter continues to be widely used as a design textbook. In their chapter, Campbell and Stanley (1963, p. 193) recommended the use of a model called the analysis of covariance (ANCOVA), suggesting that "the use of this more precise analysis [i.e., ANCOVA] would seem highly desirable." They also argued that "covariance analysis and blocking on 'subject variables' such as prior grades, test scores, parental occupation, etc., can be used, thus increasing the power of the significance test" (p. 196).

ANCOVA can be roughly thought of as "in effect, an analysis of variance performed [not on the Y scores, but] on the $(Y - \hat{Y})$'s [or e_i scores], where the $\hat{Y}$'s are predicted in the usual $b_1X + b_0$ [regression] way" (Glass & Stanley, 1970, p. 499), described in Chapter 8. Or, in Cliff's (1987) words, "We could say that we are fitting a single regression equation to the data for all the groups and then doing an anova of the deviation from the regression line [i.e., the e_i scores]" (p. 275). Huitema (1980) and Loftin and Madison (1991) presented more detailed treatments of ANCOVA.

These linkages are intimated by the layout of the variance partitions in an ANCOVA summary table. Each main effect has degrees of freedom equal to the number of levels in a given way minus 1. In a factorial layout, each interaction effect is presented in a given row, with degrees of freedom equal to the product of the degrees of freedom for the relevant main effects. And in the first row of the summary table, the covariates effect is presented, with degrees of freedom equal to the number of covariates, just as would be the case in a regression summary table. The degrees of freedom for covariates do *not* take into account group membership, because grouping is not considered within the covariance residualization portion of the analysis.

Some brief comments on using ANCOVA are warranted here, because as Keppel and Zedeck (1989) suggested,

> It is somewhat depressing to note that while all statistical methodology books continue to stress the conclusion that ANCOVA should not be used in quasi-

experimental designs [i.e., intact groups not randomly assigned], mis-applications of the procedure are still committed and reported in the literature. (p. 482)

Three cautions about ANCOVA applications are presented here, with a particular emphasis on the first concern (Thompson, 1992b).

Homogeneity of Regression Assumption Must Be Met

What ANCOVA actually does is to create a *single* regression equation, *ignoring groups*, to predict dependent variable (Y_i) scores using the covariate(s) (e.g., $X1_i$, $X2_i$, $X3_i$). Then, in essence, an ANOVA, not ignoring groups, is performed using the residualized scores (e_i) of each person computed by subtracting each person's predicted score ($\hat{Y}$), based on the single equation, from the participants' actual scores (Y_i).

These computations are legitimate iff the regression equations that predict the Y_i scores, computed *separately* in the ANOVA groups, have parallel slopes. This is the so called **homogeneity of regression assumption**, which requires that the b weights applied to the covariate(s) are reasonably equal across each group. If this assumption is not met, the use of a single average, or "pooled" equation, for all the participants is unreasonable, creates e scores using a single regression equation that may not fit in *any* of the groups, and thus focuses the analysis on outcome scores (i.e., e_i scores) that are *an inaccurate distortion for everybody*.

In education intervention studies, these slopes involving academic achievement pretest covariates and posttest Y scores can actually be conceptualized as "rate of learning" curves. When the ANOVA groups were not randomly created, but instead involved intact groups—especially when one group was a compensatory group being given a remedial intervention such as Head Start—the homogeneity of regression assumption may be difficult, if not outright impossible, to meet.

Using ANCOVA to study intact groups may be appealing, because when we have intact groups, especially in a compensatory intervention, we realize that the groups differed at pretest, and *something* must be done to take into account these pretest differences. Unfortunately, using ANCOVA in these situations may lead to "tragically misleading analyses" that actually "can mistakenly make compensatory education look harmful" (Campbell & Erlebacher, 1975, p. 597). Similarly, Cliff (1987) argued that, "It could be that the relationship between the dependent variable and the covariate is different under different treatments. Such occurrences tend to invalidate the interpretation of the simple partial correlations . . ." (p. 273).

Covariate(s) Data Must Be Extremely Reliable

Statistical corrections require extremely reliable measurement of the control variables. Score reliability is an important requisite for *any* statistical analysis (Thompson, 2003), but "measurement reliability becomes *crucial* [emphasis added] . . . in employing statistical partialling operations, as in the analysis of covariance . . ." (Nunnally, 1975, p. 10).

Unfortunately, too many researchers incorrectly presume that tests are reliable, and rarely check the reliabilities of the scores actually being analyzed, as Vacha-Hasse, Henson, and Caruso (2002) reported in their measurement mega-meta-analysis. As Loftin and Madison (1991) emphasized, "the covariate(s) used must be especially reliable, or one will end up potentially adjusting sampling error with measurement error, and creating a mess" (p. 145).

Residualized Dependent Variable Scores Must Be Interpretable

Some textbook authors have suggested that "adding covariates creates no real problem" (Keppel & Zedeck, 1989, p. 479). But, on the contrary, some covariance corrections may result in the analysis of a dependent variable that no longer makes any sense.

Statistical corrections remove parts of the dependent variable, and then analyze whatever is left, even if whatever is left no longer makes any sense. At some point we may no longer know what we are analyzing. As Thompson (1991b) suggested,

> Consider an actual dissertation . . . in which the posttest [reading] achievement variable was "corrected" using four pretest [reading] achievement

subtests. What was the posttest achievement variable after this correction? . . . [W]hatever it was, this student probably wasn't analyzing achievement after this nuclear weapon covariance correction. (p. 508)

As Cliff (1987) explained, because "this [statistical correction] is really a form of regression, inferences become slipperier as the variables [covariates] increase" (p. 278) in number.

Some Key Concepts

Interaction effects are of considerable importance in social science research, because few if any interventions (e.g., instructional methods, drugs) work equally well for all people (Cronbach, 1957, 1975). ATI and related designs help us to determine for whom different interventions may be most effective.

Nonfactorial analyses exclude the testing of one or more omnibus hypotheses. Researchers select nonfactorial analyses in some cases because a main effect may not be malleable, or because a higher-order interaction may not be readily interpretable. For some data, factorial analyses have more power, but for other data, nonfactorial analyses are more powerful.

Just as people may be randomly sampled to yield generalizable results, levels of ways may be randomly sampled in a random- or mixed-effects model. Such designs achieve greater generalizability beyond the sampled levels, but due so at the cost of less statistical power for a given sample size.

ANCOVA is a statistical method that may be used to adjust statistically for preintervention differences in groups. When enough participants are randomly assigned to groups in a true experiment, the law of large numbers functions efficiently, and such fine tuning will usually be unnecessary. When intact groups are used in a quasi-experiment (i.e., no random assignment to groups), adjustment for preintervention differences may be desperately needed, but ANCOVA is less likely to be appropriate in exactly these cases. ANCOVA requires that the homogeneity of regression assumption is met, otherwise invoking a single regression equation across groups may result in adjustments that are inappropriate for all groups. The assumption may be most difficult to meet when the intact groups were created using eligibility rules (e.g., intervention is available only if academic performance is at least one grade level below average) as part of compensatory or remedial efforts (Campbell & Erlebacher, 1975). Also, the use of multiple covariates is possible, but may result in the analysis of an uninterpretable outcome variable.

▪▪▪ Reflection Problems ▪▪▪

1. In a balanced three-way ANOVA, all seven omnibus hypotheses are inherently perfectly uncorrelated. This is worst-case as regards the experimentwise error rate. What will $\alpha_{EXPERIMENTWISE}$ be? What will happen to $\alpha_{EXPERIMENTWISE}$ if a nonfactorial analysis is conducted?

2. Create hypothetical data for a balanced 3×2 design. For heuristic purposes, use SPSS to analyze the data using (a) a fixed-effects model, (b) a random-effects model, (c) a mixed-effects model with the A way declared to be random and the B way declared to be fixed, and (d) a mixed-effects model with the B way declared to be random and the A way declared to be fixed. Which summary table entries are the same, and which differ across the analyses? Do all the output results use the correct error terms for the F calculations?

The General Linear Model (GLM)

ANOVA via Regression

I n one of his several seminal articles, Cohen (1968) noted that ANOVA and ANCOVA are special cases of multiple regression analysis, and argued that in these realizations "lie possibilities for more relevant and therefore more powerful exploitation of research data" (p. 426). In a book published shortly thereafter, Kerlinger and Pedhazur (1973) argued that multiple regression analysis

can be used equally well in experimental or non-experimental research. It can handle continuous and categorical variables. It can handle two, three, four, or more independent variables. . . . Finally, as we will abundantly show, multiple regression analysis can do anything the analysis of variance does—sums of squares, mean squares, F ratios—and more. (p. 3)

Indeed, Maurice Tatsuoka (1975) noted that:

In the early writing of R. A. Fisher, the originator of ANOVA, it is evident that he initially approached the problem of multi-group significance testing via the multiple linear regression method—which, as we shall soon see, is essentially what the [univariate] general linear model is. It was only (or at least mainly) because the calculations needed for the multiple-regression approach were practically infeasible for all but the simplest designs in the pre-computer days, that Fisher invented the MS_b/MS_w approach.... [A]ll conceivable designs in ANOVA and ANCOVA could be handled by a single general linear model, differing from design to design only in minute technical detail. (pp. 1–2)

The present chapter has two important foci: (a) presenting the basic concepts of the general linear model (GLM), for the *heuristic* purpose of showing the linkages among statistical analyses, so that we may understand conceptually the similarities and the dissimilarities of these analyses, and (b) describing the *practical* reasons for using regression approaches in conducting the analysis of variance. The heuristic lessons of the chapter reinforce key messages that *all* analyses (a) are correlational, (b) yield effect sizes analogous to r^2, and (c) apply weights to measured variables to yield scores on latent variables that are actually the focus of the analysis.

Two implications of the GLM are, first, that effect sizes can (and should) be presented and interpreted for all analyses. Second, although there are important differences in experimental versus nonexperimental designs (Raudenbush, 2005; Rubin, 1974), because *all* analyses are correlational and part of a single analytic family, there is no justification for unilaterally preferring ANOVA over other models. In particular, it will be suggested that *the mutilation of intervally-scaled predictor variables into nominal scale in order to perform ANOVA generally should be avoided.*

Planned Contrasts

Regression Subsumes ANOVA and the Two-Sample *t* Test

Table 12.1 presents a small one-way dataset that will be used to illustrate the fact that regression subsumes ANOVA (and by implication the two-sample *t* test) as a special case. This means that regression can be used to conduct ANOVA (or the two-sample *t* test, because for this problem $t_{\text{CALCULATED}}^2 = F_{\text{CALCULATED}}$), but not vice versa. These data are modeled on the example provided by Tucker (1991).

For the purposes of this heuristic demonstration, we will use here the

TABLE 12.1. Orthogonal Contrast Variables for a One-Way ANOVA

			SPSS variable names				
Case	DV	LEVEL	A1	A2	A3	A4	A5
1	11	1	−1	−1	−1	−1	−1
2	21	1	−1	−1	−1	−1	−1
3	10	2	1	−1	−1	−1	−1
4	20	2	1	−1	−1	−1	−1
5	10	3	0	2	−1	−1	−1
6	20	3	0	2	−1	−1	−1
7	10	4	0	0	3	−1	−1
8	20	4	0	0	3	−1	−1
9	10	5	0	0	0	4	−1
10	20	5	0	0	0	4	−1
11	31	6	0	0	0	0	5
12	41	6	0	0	0	0	5

Note. The six levels of the balanced (*n* in each cell is 2) one-way design are university academic classifications: 1 = freshmen, 2 = sophomores, 3 = juniors, 4 = seniors, 5 = masters students, and 6 = doctoral students.

five contrast variables, *A1* through *A5*, *as a set* in place of the group membership variable, LEVEL. These five variables merely reexpress exactly the same information expressed in "LEVEL." For example, saying that a participant had contrast variable scores of {−1, −1, −1, −1, −1} is merely another way of saying that a participant was in level 1 of the A way. Or, saying that a participant had contrast variable scores of {0, 0, 0, 0, 5} is merely another way of saying that the participant was in level 6 of the A way. Indeed, the R^2 (and R) of the five contrast variables with LEVEL is 100%, reflecting the fact that the five contrast variables *as a set* contain no more (and no less) information than that contained in LEVEL.

If we perform a regression analysis of these data using SPSS, we will obtain the summary table presented in Table 12.2. The relevant SPSS command syntax is

```
REGRESSION VARIABLES=dv a1 a2 a3 a4 a5/
    DEPENDENT=dv/ENTER a1 a2 a3 a4 a5 .
```

This is *exactly* the same summary table that will result from performing ANOVA using only the variables DV and LEVEL. Clearly, ANOVA can be

TABLE 12.2. One-Way ANOVA Omnibus Test Summary Table

Source	SOS	df	MS	$F_{CALCULATED}$	$p_{CALCULATED}$	η^2
H_0: $\mu_{Fr} = \mu_{So} = \mu_{Jr} = \mu_{Sr} = \mu_{Ma} = \mu_{Doc}$	722.667	5	144.533	2.891	0.114	70.66%
Within	300.000	6	50.000			
Total	1022.667	11	92.970			

Note. "Fr" = freshmen, "So" = sophomores, "Jr" = juniors, "Sr" = seniors, "Ma" = master's students, and "Doc" = doctoral students.

performed using regression, and is both (a) a special case of the univariate GLM, regression, and (b) is a correlational analysis, even though mean differences are being tested.

This does *not* mean that regression can test only mean differences, but does mean that regression can be used to test mean differences. The notion that there are two schools of analyses, experimental and correlational, died with Cohen's (1968) article, if not with Cronbach's (1957) presidential address. There clearly are different research designs (Thompson et al., 2005), but univariate parametric analyses, such as ANOVA, ANCOVA, and *t* tests, are *all* special cases of multiple regression.

Testing Planned Contrasts

Aside from the important heuristic value of understanding that *all* analyses are correlational, yield r^2-type effect sizes, and apply weights to measured variables to estimate latent variable scores, there are also important practical reasons in some cases for conducting ANOVA via regression. The Table 12.1 data will also be used to illustrate this application.

In Chapter 10, I explained the use of omnibus ANOVA tests, followed by post hoc tests when necessary. The alternative ANOVA approach eschews entirely the use of either omnibus tests, or post hoc tests. Table 12.3 presents the various synonyms used to refer to this alternative analytic strategy.

Planned nontrend contrasts are variables created to test specific hypotheses about differences in means. In applied research, planned contrasts are almost always created subject to the restriction that the contrast

TABLE 12.3. Synonymous Names
for Planned Contrasts

Phrase Elements	
First	Second
planned	contrast
a priori	comparison
focused	test

variables are perfectly uncorrelated. **Orthogonal planned contrasts** are uncorrelated variables created to test perfectly uncorrelated hypotheses. Another form of orthogonal planned contrasts, trend or polynomial orthogonal contrasts, will be explained momentarily.

Whenever *any* orthogonal planned contrasts are used, they partition the omnibus sum of squares for a main or interaction effect into nonoverlapping variance partitions. Thus, because these partitions are nonoverlapping, the sum of the *SOS* partitions created using orthogonal planned contrasts always exactly equals the omnibus *SOS* for a given effect. Thus planned contrasts provide more specific information about dynamics within ANOVA data, but *do not change the overall effect sizes for the omnibus effects.*

Because planned contrasts do *not* require an omnibus test, we may test interesting contrasts that might not be testable if an omnibus hypothesis was not rejected. And because when we use planned contrasts we do *not* test all possible simple or simple and complex contrasts, thus requiring a potentially large Bonferroni-type correction, planned contrasts can have more power than post hoc tests. Planned contrasts do not require us to test contrasts that are not of interest to us, or to lessen statistical power as the price for conducting the full suite of post hoc comparisons.

For a given omnibus *SOS*, planned contrasts will cut this *SOS* into nonoverlapping components, iff the planned contrast knives are orthogonal. Using orthogonal planned contrasts has the appealing feature that nonoverlapping sums of squares simplifies our interpretation as to where predictive credit originates.

Recall from Chapter 5 that

$$r_{XY} = COV_{XY} / (SD_X * SD_Y) \tag{5.1}$$

where COV_{XY} is also a description of bivariate relationship, and can be computed as

$$COV_{XY} = (\Sigma(X_i - M_X)(Y_i - M_Y)) / (n - 1) \tag{5.2}$$

Clearly, a necessary and sufficient condition for r_{XY} to equal zero is for COV_{XY} to equal zero, as long as SD_X and SD_Y are nonzero, such that r_{XY} is defined (i.e., can be computed). And the COV_{XY} will equal zero as long as the numerator of Equation 5.2, $(\Sigma(X_i - M_X)(Y_i - M_Y))$, equals zero.

Traditionally, contrast variables as tests of specific hypotheses are created such that their means (and sums) are zero. Thus, the contrast variables are also deviation scores (as are any scores where $M = 0$), and Equation 5.2 can be rewritten as

$$COV_{XY} = (\Sigma(x_i y_i)) / (n - 1) \tag{5.3}$$

Moreover, COV_{XY} and r_{XY} will both be zero for any two variables for which $\Sigma(x_i y_i) = 0$.

As noted in Table 12.4, the 5 contrast variables all have means (and sums) of zero. Furthermore, the sums of the crossproducts for all 10 pairwise combinations are all zero. This is illustrated in Table 12.4 for 5 of the 10 possible pairwise combinations ($[5(5 - 1)] / 2$) of the 5 orthogonal planned contrasts. All deviation score crossproducts for the tabled 5 pairs sum to zero.

Thus, all the planned contrasts in Table 12.1 are orthogonal (uncorrelated). Therefore, they will cut the omnibus SOS for the main effect with $df = 5$ into five nonoverlapping sums of squares, each with 1 degree of freedom. We can subdivide any omnibus sums of squares further, as long as the df of the omnibus effect is greater than 1. Once the degrees of freedom for a variance partition equals 1, we cannot further subdivide the SOS information about individual differences.

What are the hypotheses tested by the tabled orthogonal nontrend contrasts? In effect, we are applying the contrast variable scores to the group membership variable (e.g., LEVEL), and doing so is also equivalent to applying the contrast variable scores to the means. On a given contrast variable, whenever the score is zero, the dependent variable scores of participants in levels for which a zero is applied are *not* part of the mean difference being tested. For example, the *A1* contrast does not involve levels 3 through 6 of the A way, but does involve the outcome variable scores of the four participants in levels 1 and 2.

The nontrend contrast variables *each* involve the *two* means for participants with nonzero contrast variable scores. Each contrast variable involves two different numbers. The contrast variables test the equality of the two means defined by the two nonzero contrast variable scores. For example, the *A1* contrast tests the **simple contrast** H_0 that the outcome variable mean of the $n = 2$ participants who were freshmen equals the outcome variable mean of the $n = 2$ participants who were sophomores.

The remaining orthogonal nontrend contrasts all test complex contrasts. For example, the *A5* contrast tests the **complex contrast** H_0 that the outcome variable mean of the $n = 2$ participants who were doctoral students equals the outcome variable mean of the $n = 10$ participants who were any classification except doctoral students.

TABLE 12.4. Table 12.1 Contrast Variables and **Selected** Deviation Crossproducts

	Contrasts					Deviation cross-products				
Case	A1	A2	A3	A4	A5	a1*a2	a1*a3	a1*a4	a1*a5	a4*a5
1	-1	1	-1	-1	-1	1	1	1	1	1
2	-1	1	-1	-1	-1	1	1	1	1	1
3	1	-1	-1	-1	-1	-1	-1	-1	-1	1
4	1	-1	-1	-1	-1	-1	-1	-1	-1	1
5	0	2	-1	-1	-1	0	0	0	0	1
6	0	2	-1	-1	-1	0	0	0	0	1
7	0	0	3	-1	-1	0	0	0	0	1
8	0	0	3	-1	-1	0	0	0	0	1
9	0	0	0	4	-1	0	0	0	0	-4
10	0	0	0	4	-1	0	0	0	0	-4
11	0	0	0	0	5	0	0	0	0	0
12	0	0	0	0	5	0	0	0	0	0
Sum	0.0	0.0	0.0	0.0	0.0	0.0	0.0	0.0	0.0	0.0
Mean	0.0	0.0	0.0	0.0	0.0	0.0	0.0	0.0	0.0	0.0

The planned contrasts are tested by executing the SPSS syntax:

```
REGRESSION VARIABLES=dv a1 a2 a3 a4 a5/
DEPENDENT=dv/ENTER a1/ENTER a2/ENTER a3/
       ENTER a4/ENTER a5 .
```

Note that because the planned contrasts are perfectly uncorrelated, the order of entry into the regression model is irrelevant. The sum of squares that each contrast hypothesis will explain will be identical for any combination of entry orders. However, the contrast hypotheses must be entered one at a time, so that the unique explanatory contribution of each hypothesis can be determined.

Portions of the regression output are then consulted to use Excel, or another spreadsheet, to build an ANOVA summary table. The sources in the summary table at the outset can be listed as $A1$ (or H_0: $\mu_{FRESHMEN}$ = $\mu_{SOPHOMORES}$), $A2$ (or H_0: $\mu_{FRESHMEN \text{ or } SOPHOMORES}$ = $\mu_{JUNIORS}$), A3, A4, A5, ERROR, and TOTAL. The degrees of freedom, known from the model even before the analysis is conducted, are 1, 1, 1, 1, 1, 6, and 11, respectively.

At the entry of the first contrast variable, $A1$, the $SOS_{REGRESSION}$ is 1.000 (reflecting the fact that the means of 16.0 and 15.0 are not equal). This SOS from the SPSS output is entered in the summary table for the $A1$ contrast. At the entry of the second contrast variable, $A2$, the *cumulative* sum of squares explained is 1.333. This means that the SOS for the second contrast hypothesis alone is 0.333 (1.333 − 1.000). The sums of squares for the remaining contrast hypotheses are computed in an analogous manner, by subtraction.

After all the contrast variables are entered, the SOS_{ERROR}, the df_{ERROR}, and the MS_{ERROR} are then correct, and can be read off the printout and entered into the spreadsheet. The SOS_{TOTAL} can be computed at any entry point, because the SOS_{TOTAL} is fixed for a given dataset.

Then the SPSS output is discarded, and the remaining entries in the summary table are computed using Excel. The resulting summary table is presented in Table 12.5. Notice that all we have done is to partition the omnibus SOS (i.e., 722.667 in Table 12.2) into five nonoverlapping components. And the SOS_{ERROR} and SOS_{TOTAL} remain unaltered by the decision

TABLE 12.5. Planned Contrast Tests

Source	SOS	df	MS	$F_{\text{CALCULATED}}$	$p_{\text{CALCULATED}}$	η^2	η
A1	1.000	1	1.000	0.020	0.892	0.10%	0.03127
A2	0.333	1	0.333	0.007	0.938	0.03%	0.01805
A3	0.167	1	0.167	0.003	0.956	0.02%	0.01276
A4	0.100	1	0.100	0.002	0.966	0.01%	0.00988
A5	721.067	1	721.067	14.421	0.009	70.51%	0.83969
Error	300.000	6	50.000				
Total	1022.667	11	92.970				

Note. A1 tests $\mu_{\text{Freshmen}} = \mu_{\text{Sophomores}}$; A2 tests $\mu_{\text{Freshmen, or Sophomores}} = \mu_{\text{Juniors}}$; A3 tests $\mu_{\text{Freshmen, Sophomores,}}$ or Juniors $= \mu_{\text{Seniors}}$; A4 tests $\mu_{\text{Freshmen, Sophomores, Juniors, or Seniors}} = \mu_{\text{Masters}}$; A5 tests $\mu_{\text{Freshmen, Sophomores, Juniors,}}$ Seniors, or Masters $= \mu_{\text{Doctoral}}$.

to test planned contrasts *in place of* omnibus tests followed by post hoc tests, if needed.

However, the NHSST decisions are *not* the same across the two analytic choices. The Table 12.2 omnibus test was *not* statistically significant at $\alpha = 0.05$ ($p_{\text{CALCULATED}} = 0.114$). Furthermore, even if Tukey and Scheffé post hoc tests were inappropriately conducted, even though the omnibus hypothesis was not rejected, no mean differences are statistically significant in these post hoc tests either.

On the other hand, the last contrast null hypothesis (i.e., the H_0 that the outcome variable mean of the $n = 2$ participants who were doctoral students equals the outcome variable mean of the $n = 10$ participants who were any classification except doctoral students) was rejected ($p_{\text{CALCULATED}} = 0.009$). Indeed, this planned contrast hypothesis would be rejected even if a Bonferroni correction was invoked, and the contrast null hypothesis was tested at $p_{\text{CRITICAL}}{}^* = 0.05 / 5 = 0.01$. Clearly, *planned contrasts can have more statistical power against Type II error*, as this heuristic example so powerfully demonstrates!

However, for any design involving only two-level ways, no power advantages accrue for invoking planned contrasts. For a two-level way, the *only possible* contrast variable is {–1, 1} or {1, –1}, both of which test exactly the same null hypothesis. This contrast tests the equality of two means, or the omnibus hypothesis. So, for example, for a 2 × 2 × 2 × 2 design, invoking either omnibus or planned contrasts yields exactly identical results for every effect in a factorial analysis. For this design, there are no power advantages (or disadvantages) for using a regression model to perform the analysis. And there are no choices about what hypotheses to test for each effect.

Nevertheless, in general, for research conducted on topics for which prior research or theory, or both, can support reasonable expectations, planned contrasts may be very useful. First, if expectations pan out, planned contrasts have more power against Type II error, as illustrated in our example. Second, and perhaps more importantly, because the number of planned orthogonal contrasts is capped for a main effect at $k - 1$, researchers must thoughtfully select the hypotheses they will test. And *thoughtfulness is absolutely the most critical ingredient in conducting high-quality scholarship.*

Constructing Nontrend Planned Contrasts

We construct orthogonal planned contrasts for main effects such that the number of planned contrasts is less than or equals the number of groups minus 1. One nontrend hypothesis tests a simple contrast, the second contrast tests the mean outcome score of two groups versus the mean of a third group, and so forth.

We can create the nontrend contrasts in any order. For example, we may be most certain that one group's mean will differ from the combined mean of all other participants, and we could define this complex contrast first. If this is the fifth contrast, we assign the one group contrast scores of 5, and all other participants −1. In our example, the last contrast tested the mean of group 6 versus the mean of everyone else combined. We could instead have used this contrast to test *any* one group (e.g., freshmen) versus the remaining groups.

As we consecutively create the contrasts in any order, once we have created $k - 2$ contrasts, the last contrast is fixed. So we have no discretion in creating the last orthogonal nontrend contrast, whichever contrast we elect to create last.

Once the contrasts are selected, the contrast variables should have means (and sums) of zero, and the crossproducts of all pairs of contrasts should sum to zero. The orthogonal nontrend contrasts should also have a pattern in which the positive number equals the number of the contrast variable. If we order the contrasts, as in Table 12.1, such that the simple contrast is first, and the contrasts each successively involve one additional level, there will also be a pattern in which any participant with a nonzero contrast variable score on a given contrast has −1 contrast scores on all contrasts to the right of the given orthogonal nontrend contrast.

Logistically, there are two ways to create the contrast variable scores in an SPSS analysis. First, we can literally type the contrast variable scores into the datafile. Second, we can input only dependent variable scores and group membership information for each way, and then invoke a series of IF and COMPUTE statements to construct the contrast variable scores. This will save us a lot of work, especially if we have a lot of participants in each cell of the design.

Figure 12.1 provides the SPSS syntax used to analyze the Table 12.1 data. Note that only the outcome variable scores (DV) and the group membership information for the single way (LEVEL) are input, and that COMPUTE and IF statements are used to create the orthogonal nontrend contrasts.

Let's consider another example. A researcher is conducting a balanced, factorial 4 × 3 ANOVA using nontrend contrasts. For a 4 × 3 factorial design, there will be a total of (4 × 3) − 1 degrees of freedom for explained effects. Each contrast hypothesis requires 1 degree of freedom. So, for this model there will be 11 orthogonal nontrend contrast variables (i.e., cells minus 1, or [4 × 3] − 1).

Only the outcome scores (DEP_VAR) and cell information (WAY_A and WAY_B) are input in the dataset. The contrast variables for the A way might be created as

```
COMPUTE  A1  =  0  .
COMPUTE  A2  =  0  .
COMPUTE  A3  =  0  .
IF  (WAY_A  EQ  1)  A1  =  -1  .
IF  (WAY_A  EQ  4)  A1  =  1  .
IF  (A1  NE  0)  A2  =  -1  .
IF  (WAY_A  EQ  3)  A2  =  2  .
IF  (A2  NE  0)  A3  =  -1  .
IF  (WAY_A  EQ  2)  A3  =  3  .
```

```
set printback=listing .
data list file='c:\spsswin\tucker.dat' records=1 /1
  dv 1-2 level 4 .
compute a1 = 0 .
compute a2 = 0 .
compute a3 = 0 .
compute a4 = 0 .
compute a5 = 0 .
if (level eq 1) a1 = -1 .
if (level eq 2) a1 = 1 .
if (a1 ne 0) a2 = -1 .
if (level eq 3) a2 = 2 .
if (a2 ne 0) a3 = -1 .
if (level eq 4) a3 = 3 .
if (a3 ne 0) a4 = -1 .
if (level eq 5) a4 = 4 .
if (a4 ne 0) a5 = -1 .
if (level eq 6) a5 = 5 .
print formats a1 to a5 (F3) .
list variables=dv to a5/cases=99999/format=numbered .
correlations variables=dv a1 to a5 .
regression variables=level a1 to a5/
  dependent=level/enter a1 to a5 .
oneway dv by level(1,6)/ranges=tukey/ranges=scheffe/
  statistics=all .
regression variables=dv a1 to a5/
  dependent=dv/enter a1/enter a2/enter a3/
  enter a4/enter a5 .
descriptives variables=dv a1 to a5/save .
compute yhat=(-.031270 * za1) + (-.018054 * za2) +
  (-.012766 * za3) + (-.009889 * za4) + (.839693 * za5) .
compute e = zdv - yhat .
print formats yhat e (F8.5) .
list variables=dv zdv yhat e/cases=99999/format=numbered .
correlations variables=zdv yhat e/statistics=all .
oneway yhat by level(1,6)/statistics=all .
```

FIGURE 12.1. SPSS syntax used to analyze the Table 12.1 data

The contrast variables for the B way might be created as

```
COMPUTE  B1  =  0  .
COMPUTE  B2  =  0  .
IF  (WAY_B  EQ  2)  B1  =  -1  .
IF  (WAY_B  EQ  3)  B1  =  1  .
IF  (B1  NE  0)  B2  =  -1  .
IF  (WAY_B  EQ  1)  B2  =  2  .
```

The orthogonal contrast variables for the interaction effects, requiring a total of 6 degrees of freedom ([4 − 1][3 − 1]), can be created as

```
COMPUTE  A1_B1  =  A1  *  B1  .
COMPUTE  A2_B1  =  A2  *  B1  .
COMPUTE  A3_B1  =  A3  *  B1  .
COMPUTE  A1_B2  =  A1  *  B2  .
COMPUTE  A2_B2  =  A2  *  B2  .
COMPUTE  A3_B2  =  A3  *  B2  .
```

Are these contrasts orthogonal? What hypotheses are tested by the five main effect contrasts? You might benefit from creating hypothetical outcome variable scores for this problem, and then conducting the analysis using the REGRESSION procedure.

Selecting Nontrend Orthogonal Contrasts

The potentially greater power of planned contrasts is *not* an inherent function of *all* planned contrasts. Instead, this power is a function of our *thoughtful selection* of contrasts being informed by prior research, or theory, or both. Greater statistical power will not usually occur if planned contrasts are created randomly, or thoughtlessly.

One implication is that planned contrasts should *not* be used in new areas of inquiry where theory has not been elaborated. In such circum stances, the use of omnibus tests followed by post hoc tests, if needed, is the appropriate exploratory procedure. Thus, omnibus tests have an important role in social science, even though planned contrasts can be very useful for some research problems.

The study by Carr and Thompson (1996) provided an example of the planned contrasts model with an applied research problem. The researchers were exploring the nature of reading learning disabilities. One model posits that people with learning disabilities (LD) are not qualitatively different from non-LD persons, and that disabilities merely reflect developmental delays.

The researchers reasoned from this perspective that (a) sixth-grade LD readers should *not* differ substantially in reading proficiency from fourth-grade non-LD readers, but (b) sixth-grade non-LD readers should differ substantially in reading proficiency from both sixth-grade LD readers and fourth-grade non-LD readers. For this three-level one-way design, the researchers used the nontrend orthogonal contrasts:

A1	A2	Group
−1	−1	sixth-grade LD readers
1	−1	fourth-grade non-LD readers
0	2	sixth-grade non-LD readers

In other words, the researchers expected (and obtained) small effect sizes and large $p_{CALCULATED}$ values for the A1 planned contrast. And the researchers expected (and obtained) large effect sizes and small $p_{CALCULATED}$ values for the A2 planned contrast. The beauty of the analysis is that the researchers were able to test theoretical expectations about when effects should be small, as well as when effects should be large, all in the same study!

Using Bonferroni Corrections in a Planned Contrast Context

By tradition, researchers typically do not invoke the Bonferroni correction when using orthogonal planned contrasts, even though experimentwise error rate inflation is at its maximum whenever the hypotheses being tested are perfectly uncorrelated. The rationale for this decision involves the number of contrasts being tested.

In a six-level one-way design evaluating the omnibus hypothesis and then post hoc tests, there are a huge number of simple and complex contrasts being tested post hoc. Some correction for experimentwise error rate inflation seems essential when conducting post hoc tests, and the correction is built into the Tukey or Scheffé post hoc analyses.

However, in the alternative analysis, a maximum of only five orthogonal planned contrasts can be conducted with this design. So, when planned contrasts are tested, experimentwise error rate inflation is somewhat capped as a function of being limited to testing only a few contrasts. For a main effect, no more than $k − 1$ contrasts can be tested.

The fact that, traditionally, researchers do not invoke the Bonferroni correction when testing planned contrasts does not mean that doing so would be unreasonable. For more discussion of this issue, and on the use of *nonorthogonal* planned contrasts, see Thompson (1994c).

Using Latent Variable Scores in ANOVA

A brief comment on the implicit presence of weights and latent variables in ANOVA is also warranted to flesh out the final general linear model linkages of regression and ANOVA. The point is conceptual rather than an argument that estimating ANOVA $\hat{Y}_i$ scores usually has important practical value.

Note that when we invoke orthogonal planned contrasts, we essentially are in a Case #1 regression situation (i.e., multiple, perfectly-uncorrelated predictors). And in Case #1, the beta weights for a regression model equal the *r*s of each predictor with the Y_i scores.

Table 12.5 presents the η^2 and η values for each of the five orthogonal planned contrast variables associated with the analysis of the Table 12.1 data. As presented in the Figure 12.1 SPSS syntax, the Table 12.5 η values analogous to *r* values can be used as β weights to compute the $\hat{Y}_i$ scores.

First, we reexpress the five orthogonal planned contrasts in *z*-score form. We can do this either by using COMPUTE statements, or by invoking the SPSS command:

```
DESCRIPTIVES VARIABLES=dv a1 to a5/SAVE .
```

We then use the Table 12.5 η values as β weights in the syntax to create the two ANOVA latent variable scores:

```
COMPUTE yhat=(-.031270 * za1) + (-.018054 * za2) +
(-.012766 * za3) + (-.009889 * za4) + (.839693 * za5) .
COMPUTE e = zdv - yhat .
PRINT FORMATS yhat e (F8.5) .
```

Table 12.6 presents the latent variable scores from this ANOVA. Remember that, in regression, the bivariate

$$r_{Y \times \hat{Y}} = R_{Y \times X1,X2 \ldots} \qquad (9.3)$$

and equivalently that

$$r_{Y \times \hat{Y}}^2 = R_{Y \times X1,X2 \ldots}^2 \qquad (9.4)$$

which suggests an analogous linkage elsewhere in the general linear model. If we use the SPSS CORRELATIONS command to obtain the Pearson product–moment correlation between the ZDV (or the DV scores) and the ANOVA YHAT scores, we obtain $r = 0.8406$. As expected, the squared value of this correlation coefficient, $0.8406^2 = 70.66\%$, equals the omnibus ANOVA η^2 (i.e., $722.67 / 1022.67 = 70.66\%$), as reported in Table 12.2.

Furthermore, for regression we learned that the SOS of the $\hat{Y}_i$ scores equals the $SOS_{EXPLAINED}$. The same truism applies in ANOVA. Here we are

TABLE 12.6. Latent Variable Scores for the Table 12.1 ANOVA Data

Case/statistic	SPSS variable			
	DV	ZDV	YHAT	E
1	11	−0.795	−0.276	−0.518
2	21	0.242	−0.276	0.518
3	10	−0.899	−0.380	−0.518
4	20	0.138	−0.380	0.518
5	10	−0.899	−0.380	−0.518
6	20	0.138	−0.380	0.518
7	10	−0.899	−0.380	−0.518
8	20	0.138	−0.380	0.518
9	10	−0.899	−0.380	−0.518
10	20	0.138	−0.380	0.518
11	31	1.279	1.798	−0.518
12	41	2.316	1.798	0.518
M	18.667	0.000	0.000	0.000
SOS	1022.667	11.000	7.773	3.220
SD^2	92.970	1.000	0.707	0.293
SD	9.642	1.000	0.841	0.541

using β weights, so we are predicting z_Y rather than Y_i scores. The SOS of the $n = 12$ z_Y scores is, of course, 11.000, as reported in Table 12.6. The SOS of the ANOVA $\hat{Y}_i$ scores, reported in Table 12.6, is 7.773. The omnibus ANOVA η^2 (i.e., 70.66%) reported in Table 12.2 also equals 7.773 / 11.000, as expected.

Trend/Polynomial Planned Contrasts

In the special case in which (a) a way is quantitative and (b) the levels are equally spaced, researchers may elect to use trend or polynomial contrasts. Nontrend planned contrasts test whether two means are equal. **Trend/ polynomial planned contrasts** do *not* each test whether two means are equal but instead test whether the means across the levels form a certain pattern (e.g., a line, a parabola).

In a two-way design, if both the A way and the B way are quantitative and their levels are equally spaced, trend contrasts can be used with the A way only, with the B way only, with both, or with neither. And if trend contrasts are used for either or both ways, all the contrast variables, including those for interaction effects, will be uncorrelated as long as the design is balanced.

Table 12.7 presents orthogonal polynomial contrasts that can be used with a three-level, four-level, or five-level way. Contrasts are not presented for a two-level way, because for a two level way only one contrast is possible, and that contrast must test the omnibus hypothesis. Also, a two-level way cannot create patterns of means other than a line, even if the way is quantitative and the levels are equally spaced, because two points inherently define a line, and no nonlinear patterns can be created by only two points in a Cartesian space. The interested reader will confirm that the tabled contrasts are orthogonal.

Figure 12.2 presents a plot of the patterns being tested by the four orthogonal polynomial contrasts for a five-level way. The linear contrast, {−2, −1, 0, 1, 2}, defines a straight line in Figure 12.2. The quadratic contrast, {2, −1, −2, −1, 2}, creates a parabola with one bend, in the middle of the plot. The cubic contrast, {−1, 2, 0, −2, 1}, defines a line with two bends, both equidistant from the boundaries of the plot. The quartic con-

TABLE 12.7. Selected Polynomial/Trend Orthogonal Contrasts

Levels	Contrast	Levels				
		1	2	3	4	5
3	Linear	−1	0	1		
	Quadratic	1	−2	1		
4	Linear	−3	−1	1	3	
	Quadratic	1	−1	−1	1	
	Cubic	−1	3	−3	1	
5	Linear	−2	−1	0	1	2
	Quadratic	2	−1	−2	−1	2
	Cubic	−1	2	0	−2	1
	Quartic	1	−4	6	−4	1

trast, {1, −4, 6, −4, 1}, defines a line with three bends, or a shape resembling the letter W.

When we are fitting orthogonal trend contrasts to our data, we are testing the fit of the pattern of the contrast to the fit of the pattern in the means on the quantitative way. For example, the study might involve an outcome of psychological adjustment, with the way being five equidistant durations of therapy sessions (e.g., 40, 45, 50, 55, and 60 minutes). Or, the study might involve a drug dosage investigation with an outcome of the joint mobility of arthritis patients, each given either 500, 600, 700, 800, or 900 milligrams of aspirin. We are interested in seeing whether

FIGURE 12.2. Plots of polynomial contrast variables for a five-level way

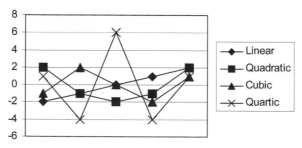

greater dosages linearly produce successively smaller or larger outcome means, or whether there are curvilinear reaction patterns across dosages.

When we use the linear contrast variable, which is an upward sloping line in Figure 12.2, we are *not* testing whether the means define an upward sloping line with a given slope, or even an upward versus a downward sloping line. Instead, we are testing whether the pattern of the means has the same basic character (not direction or orientation) as the polynomial contrast. So, the linear contrast tests whether the means *either* progressively and incrementally go up, *or* progressively and incrementally go down.

By the same token, the quadratic pattern in Figure 12.2 defines a V shape. But the quadratic contrast is *not* testing whether the pattern of the means has this particular V shape, or indeed any V shape. Instead, we are testing whether the pattern of the means either (a) goes down, and correspondingly then up, with the single pattern bend in the middle, *or* (b) goes up, and correspondingly then down, again with the single pattern bend in the middle.

Table 12.8 presents a heuristic dataset for a five-level quantitative way. For these data, the means have the pattern of {10, 20, 30, 25, 20}. Here we will test whether the means create a linear, a quadratic, or some other pattern. For heuristic purposes, we will not break the omnibus sum of squares into four subcomponents; instead we will break the omnibus $SOS_{EXPLAINED}$ only into three subcomponents, one of which will have two degrees of freedom. Of course, for comparative purposes, you are encouraged to perform an alternative analysis with all four possible orthogonal polynomial contrasts.

Table 12.9 presents the results from an omnibus ANOVA test. This table is presented only for heuristic comparative purposes. In actual research, one always uses *either* omnibus tests with post hoc tests, if needed, *or* planned contrasts. However, the Table 12.9 omnibus results will later be used to confirm that the planned contrast analysis does not impact the error or total variance partitions, and only subdivides the $SOS_{EXPLAINED}$ into nonoverlapping sums of squares associated with each tested pattern of the five means.

TABLE 12.8. Orthogonal Polynomial Data
for One-Way Five-Level ANOVA

			SPSS variable names			
Case	DV	LEVEL	LINEAR	QUADRATIC	CUBIC	QUARTIC
1	9	1	−2	2	−1	1
2	10	1	−2	2	−1	1
3	11	1	−2	2	−1	1
4	19	2	−1	−1	2	−4
5	20	2	−1	−1	2	−4
6	21	2	−1	−1	2	−4
7	29	3	0	−2	0	6
8	30	3	0	−2	0	6
9	31	3	0	−2	0	6
10	24	4	1	−1	−2	−4
11	25	4	1	−1	−2	−4
12	26	4	1	−1	−2	−4
13	19	5	2	2	1	1
14	20	5	2	2	1	1
15	21	5	2	2	1	1

We conduct the analysis the same way we conducted the analysis for the nontrend orthogonal contrasts. We can use the SPSS syntax:

```
REGRESSION VARIABLES=dv linear quadratc cubic quartic/
   ENTER linear/ENTER quadratc/ENTER cubic quartic .
```

We use the output to compute the five sums of squares of interest in our analysis. For example, the SOS_{LINEAR}, after the linear contrast variable is entered, is 187.50. After the quadratic contrast is entered second, we con-

TABLE 12.9. One-Way ANOVA Omnibus Test of Table 12.6 Data

Source	SOS	df	MS	$F_{CALCULATED}$	$p_{CALCULATED}$	η^2
Between	660.00	4	165.00	165.00	0.000000004	98.51%
Within	10.00	10	1.00			
Total	670.00	14	47.86			

sult the output and perform a subtraction of the cumulative $SOS_{EXPLAINED}$ minus the SOS_{LINEAR} to determine the $SOS_{QUADRATIC}$, which is 433.93.

After the sums of squares are computed, we then use Excel to compute the remaining elements of the required summary table. Table 12.10 presents the summary table for these data.

One heuristic digression may be worthwhile. For these data, when the outcome variable is intervally-scaled, so, too, is the quantitative way. Therefore, for this special ANOVA case, we could compute the Pearson product–moment r^2 between the outcome variable and the levels of the quantitative way, using the SPSS CORRELATIONS procedure. Doing so yields $r = 0.5290$. The r^2 value (i.e., $0.5290^2 = 27.98\%$) is remarkably similar (i.e., identical) to the η^2 value (27.98%) reported for the linear contrast in Table 12.10.

The comparison makes two heuristic points. First, the linear contrast tests for *only* linear patterns, and the Pearson r *only* measures linear relationship, so of course we expect this correspondence. Second, the omnibus η^2 (98.51%) is sensitive to *all* forms of relationship, which is why the omnibus η^2 is greater than the r^2. Linear relationship is only one form of relationship. Thus, $\eta^2 = 98.51\%$ includes the linear component (i.e., 27.98%), but *also all other* relationship forms (i.e., 27.98% + 64.77% + 5.76% = 98.51%).

For this hypothetical, small dataset, the effect sizes are huge (i.e., cumulatively, almost perfect). Nevertheless, the example illustrates the best fit of the quadratic effect. Assuming the outcome scores are scaled such that higher scores are better, such a pattern suggests an optimal dosage located near the middle treatment level used in the way. If this way involved a study of therapy session durations of 40, 45, 50, 55, and 60 minutes, the result would suggest an optimal session length of 50 minutes.

TABLE 12.10. Polynomial Trend Tests of Table 12.6 Data

Source	SOS	df	MS	$F_{CALCULATED}$	$p_{CALCULATED}$	η^2
Linear	187.50	1	187.50	187.50	0.000000083	27.98%
Quadratic	433.93	1	433.93	433.93	0.000000001	64.77%
Other	38.57	2	19.29	19.29	0.000369909	5.76%
Within	10.00	10	1.00			
Total	670.00	14	47.86			

Of course, the effect sizes we have considered are *always* on the average. (For an interesting exception, see Grissom, 1994.) Effect sizes (unless they are perfect) do not mean that the effect was consistent for all participants. A large but imperfect effect means that an intervention generally worked in a given fashion for the group as a whole, but for some participants the optimal treatment may not be as effective, and may even be least effective.

Repeated-Measures ANOVA via Regression

Repeated-measures ANOVA designs repeatedly (at least twice) measure participants on one or more outcome variables over time. For example, a drug study might be conducted to evaluate the effects of three anticholesterol drugs. In a **between-subjects** design, in which a given participant is involved in only one level of the way, 90 participants (30 per group) might be randomly assigned to take only one of the three drugs for a month, after which outcome cholesterol scores would be recorded. Alternatively, in a **within-subjects** (or repeated measures) design, 30 participants would each successively receive each drug, and have cholesterol outcome scores recorded, over the course of the study.

For example, the three drugs might be administered in a counterbalanced order to subgroups of participants. Ten participants might receive drug A during January, drug B during March, and drug C during May, having their cholesterol recorded at the end of January, March, and May. Ten other participants might receive drug B during January, drug C during March, and drug A during May, having their cholesterol recorded at the end of each month. Finally, 10 other participants might receive drug C during January, drug A during March, and drug B during May, having their cholesterol recorded at the end of each month.

Repeated measures may have two appealing features. First, we may be able to record the same number of outcome scores (e.g., 30 per drug) with a repeated-measures design that requires fewer participants than a between-subjects design (e.g., 30 versus 90 participants). Second, repeated-measures designs have the appealing feature that each participant may be exposed to each treatment. This may be important, particularly if the sample size is small and includes one or more atypical people. The influence of outliers may be minimized either by (a) washing out these influences within a large sample, or (b) including the outliers in every treatment condition so that outliers do not distort outcome means only for certain conditions to which they were assigned.

The key issue in deciding whether a repeated-measures design is appropriate in a given study involves whether or not the performances of the participants over time are reasonably independent. For example, in a cholesterol study, with drugs administered every other month over a 5-month period and with 1 month of no treatment separating the drug administrations, there is probably not much reason to expect carryover effects across drug treatments.

But what if the study was an educational intervention designed to teach first graders how to spell 10 target words? Once a child receives any instruction, and learns some of the target words, the prior learning will compromise the ability to detect new impacts when the same words are retaught. Nevertheless, for some research, repeated-measures designs can be quite useful.

Table 12.11 presents a heuristic dataset for the simplest possible repeated-measures design. A multiway repeated-measures design might involve a within-subjects effect, and one or more between-subjects effects for which people by choice are not, or simply cannot be, assigned successively to each condition (e.g., two genders). Here there is only one within-subjects effect, and no between-subjects effects. Let's say Table 12.11

TABLE 12.11. Repeated-Measures ANOVA Data

Participant/statistic	Test 1	2	3	4	Sum	Mean
1	5	7	7	8	27	6.75
2	4	5	8	9	26	6.50
3	4	4	4	8	20	5.00
4	3	3	4	8	18	4.50
5	2	2	4	5	13	3.25
Sum	18	21	27	38		
Mean	3.60	4.20	5.40	7.60		5.20

involves giving five participants therapy for four weeks, and measuring psychological adjustment at the end of each week.

We could enter the data into SPSS as a file containing five rows and four outcome variable scores, *T1*, *T2*, *T3*, and *T4*, arrayed as the data are within Table 12.11 but entering only these $5 \times 4 = 20$ data points. The required SPSS syntax to yield a repeated-measures ANOVA would be

```
MANOVA t1 t2 t3 t4
/WSFACTORS test(4)
/PRINT=SIGNIF(UNIV MULTIV AVERF HF GG EFSIZE)
PARAM(ESTIM)
/WSDESIGN=test/DESIGN .
```

Alternatively, if we wish, we can conduct the repeated-measures ANOVA using regression. And because the four measurements are quantitative (i.e., time) and equally spaced (i.e., weekly), here we can conduct the analysis using orthogonal polynomial planned contrasts. The data are entered as 20 rows, in the format presented in Table 12.12. Using the method first suggested by Pedhazur (1977), we also enter the sum of each participant's four outcome variable scores (e.g., $\Sigma_1 = 5 + 7 + 7 + 8 = 27$) in every row for a given participant.

We implement the analysis in SPSS, using the syntax

```
REGRESSION VARIABLES=dv linear quadratc cubic sum/
    DEPENDENT=dv/ENTER sum/ENTER linear/ENTER quadratc/
    ENTER cubic .
```

As before, we use elements from the output to create the summary table in Excel. The SOS_{PEOPLE} is derived from the entry of the variable "SUM" into the model. This sum of squares (33.70) reflects the variability within different people across the four measurements.

The cumulative *SOS* after "LINEAR" is entered is 77.26, which means that the *SOS* for the linear pattern in the four outcome means is 43.56 (i.e., 77.26 − 33.70). By successive subtractions, we compute $SOS_{QUADRATIC}$ to be 3.20, and SOS_{CUBIC} to be 0.04. The residual, or people × time interaction *SOS*, is 10.70. After entering these values into Excel, we discard the SPSS output, and compute the remaining entries in the sum-

TABLE 12.12. Repeated-Measures Data with Polynomial Contrasts

			SPSS variable names			
Row	CASE	TEST	LINEAR	QUADRATC	CUBIC	SUM	DV
1	1	1	−3	1	−1	27	5
2	2	1	−3	1	−1	26	4
3	3	1	−3	1	−1	20	4
4	4	1	−3	1	−1	18	3
5	5	1	−3	1	−1	13	2
6	1	2	−1	−1	3	27	7
7	2	2	−1	−1	3	26	5
8	3	2	−1	−1	3	20	4
9	4	2	−1	−1	3	18	3
10	5	2	−1	−1	3	13	2
11	1	3	1	−1	−3	27	7
12	2	3	1	−1	−3	26	8
13	3	3	1	−1	−3	20	4
14	4	3	1	−1	−3	18	4
15	5	3	1	−1	−3	13	4
16	1	4	3	1	1	27	8
17	2	4	3	1	1	26	9
18	3	4	3	1	1	20	8
19	4	4	3	1	1	18	8
20	5	4	3	1	1	13	5

mary table, yielding the results reported in Table 12.13. For a related example, see Edwards (1985, Ch. 10).

One complication is that we have not taken into account an important statistical assumption. The **sphericity** assumption requires that the variances of the differences between all possible pairs of means must be equal. The F test (and associated $p_{CALCULATED}$ values) will be inaccurate to the extent that we violate this assumption.

The initial repeated-measures ANOVA presumes that data perfectly meet the sphericity assumption. We can attempt to quantify the extent to which we are violating this assumption, and then use this estimate, called epsilon (ε), to obtain more accurate $p_{CALCULATED}$ values. One estimate of ε is the Geisser-Greenhouse correction (Geisser & Greenhouse, 1958), which is provided by SPSS upon request. For our data, $\varepsilon_{GG} = 0.721$. Another estimate was developed by Huynh and Feldt (1976). For our data, $\varepsilon_{HF} = 1.000$.

TABLE 12.13. Summary Table for Repeated-Measures
ANOVA with Planned Polynomial Contrasts

Source	SOS	df	MS	$F_{CALCULATED}$	$p_{CALCULATED}$	η^2
People	33.70	4	8.42			
Time	46.80	3	15.60			
Linear	43.56	1	43.56	48.85	0.00001	47.76%
Quadratic	3.20	1	3.20	3.59	0.08252	3.51%
Cubic	0.04	1	0.04	0.04	0.83582	0.04%
Within Time (Total – Time)	44.40					
People × Time (Within – People)	10.70	12	0.89			
Total	91.20	19				

Note. The omnibus hypothesis is *not* tested when planned contrasts are performed, but for heuristic purposes note that the omnibus $F_{CALCULATED}$ is 17.50 ($p = 0.0001$).

The ε values are used to adjust the degrees of freedom when computing $p_{CALCULATED}$ values from the $F_{CALCULATED}$ results, subject to the restriction that the adjusted $df_{NUMERATOR}$ not be less than 1 and the adjusted $df_{DENOMINATOR}$ not be less than the number of participants. For our data, the uncorrected $p_{CALCULATED}$ value for the linear effect was obtained in Excel by inputting the F of 48.85 with degrees of freedom 1 and 12:

$$=FDIST(48.85,1,12)$$

which yields a $p_{CALCULATED}$ value of 0.00001.

However, if we invoke the Geisser-Greenhouse correction, we instead input

$$=FDIST(48.85,1,.721*12)$$

or, alternatively,

$$=FDIST(48.85,1,8.652)$$

and obtain a $p_{CALCULATED}$ value of 0.00011. But for our example, invoking ε_{HF} yields the same $p_{CALCULATED}$ results as the uncorrected results, because our $\varepsilon_{HF} = 1.000$.

The ε_{GG} is generally lower than ε_{HF}, and thus results in a larger correction of degrees of freedom (i.e., fewer degrees of freedom), less power against Type II error, and larger $p_{CALCULATED}$ values. Some researchers have suggested computing ε as an average of ε_{GG} and ε_{HF} (e.g., J. Stevens, 1996). Others (cf. Girden, 1992) have suggested using ε_{HF} iff ε_{GG} is larger than 0.75. For more detail on these decisions, see Tanguma (1999).

Our results suggest a linear effect of therapy over time. Of course, our conclusions must be limited to 4 weeks of treatment. Our design will not allow us to conclude that longer durations of therapy will necessarily continue to lead to incremental improvements in mental health. Our results also suggest that individual differences due to people (i.e., SOS_{PEOPLE} = 33.70) are noteworthy. We can *only* estimate these person effects by using a repeated-measures design in which individuals are measured repeatedly.

GLM Lessons

Analysis of variance (ANOVA) has traditionally been among the most commonly used of all inferential statistical techniques in the behavioral sciences (Edgington, 1974; Wick & Dirkes, 1973), though a growing trend favoring the use of regression and general linear model methods has emerged (Kieffer, Reese, & Thompson, 2001) since Cohen's (1968) influential article.

Edgington (1974) reviewed American Psychological Association research journals and found that 71% of the articles using statistical inference had employed analysis of variance. He concluded his review by noting that ". . . every one of the journals showed an upward trend in the use of analysis of variance . . ." (p. 26). Willson (1980) proposed that there might be a change in techniques used in research articles published between 1969 and 1978, due to the expansion of educational research training in the late 1960s. He examined the articles published in *American Educational Research Journal* (*AERJ*) from 1969 to 1978, and he found little extension of the research tools used—ANOVA and ANCOVA were included in 56% of the articles.

Goodwin and Goodwin (1985) found that the total percentage of usage for ANOVA-based techniques decreased to 34.47% in the 189 articles that were published in *AERJ* from 1979 to 1983. Elmore and Woehlke (1988) found that ANOVA/ANCOVA were still the most frequent research methods utilized in all articles appearing in *AERJ*, *Educational Researcher*, and *Review of Educational Research* from 1978 to 1987.

Take-Home Messages

In this chapter, several arguments have been presented. First, regression approaches to ANOVA that invoke planned contrasts have been recommended for many designs in which one or more ways have more than two levels. Planned contrasts (a) may have more power against Type II error, iff researchers have a reasonable basis for formulating specific, nonomnibus hypotheses, and (b) tend to force researchers to thoughtfully select hypotheses as against testing every possible mean difference. Second, omnibus tests followed by post hoc tests, if needed, are perfectly appropriate for research situations in which prior research or theory is not available.

We will now turn to a major, third implication of the heuristic demonstration that ANOVA and the two-sample *t* test are special cases of the univariate general linear model (i.e., multiple regression). Because *all* analyses are correlational, ANOVA and regression are part of one GLM, so do not fall prey to the tendency to mutilate intervally-scaled predictors to nominal scale merely so that ANOVA methods can then be used.

Mutilating Intervally-Scaled Independent Variables

One reason why researchers may be prone to categorizing continuous variables (i.e., converting intervally scaled variables down to nominal scale) is that some researchers unconsciously and *erroneously* associate ANOVA with the power of experimental designs. Researchers often value the ability of experiments to provide information about causality (Thompson et al., 2005); they know that ANOVA can be useful when independent variables are inherently nominally-scaled and dependent variables are intervally-scaled; they then begin to *unconsciously* identify the analysis of ANOVA with the design of an experiment.

It is one thing to employ ANOVA when an experimental design is in fact used. However, it is something quite different to assume that causal inferences can be made just because an ANOVA is performed. This illogic, in which design and analysis are confused with each other, are all the more pernicious, because the confusion tends to arise unconsciously and thus is not readily perceived by the researcher (Cohen, 1968).

Humphreys (1978) noted that:

> The basic fact is that a measure of individual differences is not an independent variable, and it does not become one by categorizing the scores and treating the categories as if they defined a variable under experimental control in a factorially designed analysis of variance. (p. 873)

Similarly, Humphreys and Fleishman (1974) noted that categorizing variables in a nonexperimental design using an ANOVA analysis "not infrequently produces in both the investigator and his audience the illusion that he has experimental control over the independent variable. Nothing could be more wrong" (p. 468).

These sorts of confusion are especially disturbing when the researcher has some independent or predictor variables that are intervally-scaled (e.g., pretest IQ scores), and converts them to nominal scale (e.g., low IQ, high IQ), just to be able to perform some ANOVA analysis. As Cliff (1987) noted, the practice of discarding variance on intervally scaled predictor variables to perform OVA analyses creates problems in almost all cases:

> Such divisions are not infallible; think of the persons near the borders. Some who should be highs are actually classified as lows, and vice versa. In addition, the "barely highs" are classified the same as the "very highs," even though they are different. (p. 130)

Moreover, not enough researchers realize that the practice of discarding variance on an intervally-scaled predictor variable to perform OVA analyses from a score reliability or measurement point of view "makes the variable more unreliable, not less" (Cliff, 1987, p. 130), which in turn lessens statistical power against Type II error. Pedhazur (1982) made the same point, and explicitly presented the ultimate consequences of bad practice in this vein:

> Categorization of attribute variables is all too frequently resorted to in the social sciences. . . . It is possible that some of the conflicting evidence in the research literature of a given area may be attributed to the practice of categorization of continuous variables. . . . Categorization leads to a loss of information, and consequently to a less sensitive analysis. (pp. 452–453)

It is the IQ dichotomy or trichotomy in the computer, and not the intervally-scaled IQ data with a Cronbach's α reliability of 0.93 sitting and collecting dust on the shelf, that will be reflected in the ANOVA results.

Score variability is the "stuff" (i.e., information about the amount and origins of individual differences) on which all analyses are based. Discarding variance by categorizing variables amounts to "squandering of information" (Cohen, 1968, p. 441). As Kerlinger (1986) explained,

> partitioning a continuous variable into a dichotomy or trichotomy throws information away. . . . To reduce a set of values with a relatively wide range to a dichotomy is to reduce its variance and thus its possible correlation with other variables. A good rule of research data analysis, therefore, is: *Do not reduce continuous variables to partitioned variables* (dichotomies, trichotomies, etc.) unless compelled to do so by circumstances or the nature of the data (seriously skewed, bimodal, etc.). (p. 558)

The conversion of interval predictor variables into dichotomies or trichotomies distorts (a) the distribution shape of the converted variables in relation to the distribution we believe the variables have in the reality we purportedly wish to study; (b) the variability of the converted variable by discarding variance we believe exists in the reality we purportedly wish to study; and (c) the relationships among predictors by making all predictors perfectly uncorrelated when a balanced ANOVA is performed, thus dishonoring a reality in which variables are usually correlated (Hester, 2000; Thompson, 1986, 1988a). This last feature of ANOVA, as Cohen (1968) pointed out, vastly simplifies the calculation process, which was important in the 1920s, but hardly seems a worthy sacrifice when a microcomputer can perform calculations in seconds without requiring such computational simplifications.

Of course, ANOVA does remain a useful tool when the independent variables are all inherently nominal (e.g., dichotomies or trichotomies, such as assignment to experimental condition or gender). However, in many areas of inquiry, relatively few independent variables are inherently nominally-scaled, and so in many cases using ANOVA may raise questions about distorting data.

Three Possible Data Mutilation Scenarios

Three potential scenarios can be envisioned for data mutilation. First, an independent variable (e.g., pretest standardized test scores, pretest IQ scores) may be intervally-scaled with considerable variability, and perhaps even a normal distribution. In this scenario, converting the scores into a dichotomy or a trichotomy (a) discards score variability, which in turn (b) reduces score reliability, (c) distorts score shape by converting a normal distribution into a uniform/rectangular distribution, and (d) alters relationships with other variables in the analysis.

If our model of reality is that people are quite variable in IQ or academic achievement, and that these differences are noteworthy or meaningful, why would we then use an analytic model that conceptualizes the predictor as a dichotomy? Shouldn't we match the analytic model to our model of reality, so that we are studying the reality we presume exists, rather than some nonreality?

If we take IQ scores, for example, and use a sample median split of 95.0 to create two IQ levels, our ANOVA analytic model says that two people with IQ scores of 94 and 96 are different. Our ANOVA analytic model says that two people with IQ scores of 65 and 94 are identical in intelligence, as are two people with IQ scores of 96 and 175. Are any of these suppositions reasonable?

Second, an intervally-scaled independent variable may be arrayed in such a way that conversion to nominal scale represents *no* mutilation of our predictive information. For example, if all our IQ scores were clustered by happenstance as scores of 79, 80, 81; scores of 99, 100, 101; and scores of 119, 120, and 121, then expressing the scores as a trichotomy would be perfectly acceptable. We might reasonably decide that (a) the people in the three score clusters are qualitatively different from each other and (b) the people within each score cluster cannot reasonably be differentiated as regards their IQs.

Third, converting an intervally-scaled "variable" into nominal scale may create variance in a scenario where there actually is no real score variability. For example, consider an actual dissertation on childhood depression in which the depression scores had a mean of 1.18 and a standard deviation of 0.70, and a trichotomy was created using cutscores of 0.65 and 1.09. On this measure, the test manual recommended a clinical cutoff for depression of 4!

Clearly, some score mutilations take the form of creating variance where there really is not much variability. Attempting to study childhood depression with a sample of children all of whom are well-adjusted and happy creates insurmountable scientific challenges. The example reinforces the importance of obtaining large sums of squares on variables of primary interest, and especially the outcome variable, which is always our focus. The *SOS* is information about the amount and the origins of individual differences. We simply cannot understand or explain or predict a construct when we have little or no information about individual differences involving the construct.

Some Key Concepts

Multiple regression is the most general case of the univariate general linear model (GLM), and subsumes other univariate parametric analyses (i.e., two-sample *t* tests, ANOVA, ANCOVA, Pearson *r*) as special cases. This implies that *all* analyses are correlational, yield r^2-type effect sizes, and apply weights to measured variables to estimate latent variable scores.

These analytic relationships are important to understand for *heuristic* purposes. We do not really understand a given analysis unless we know what the analysis does and does not have in common with alternative analyses.

And, from a *practical* applied research point of view, the use of regression to conduct ANOVA via planned contrasts may have important benefits of (a) potentially yielding more statistical power against Type II error, and (b) forcing us to think. On the other hand, when we are conducting research for which there is limited prior research and theory, the exploratory use of omnibus tests and post hoc tests, if necessary, is perfectly sensible.

But it is important not to confuse design with analysis. Only experimental designs yield definitive conclusions about causality (Thompson et al., 2005). ANOVA may be quite useful with experimental data, but invoking ANOVA does not itself yield the capacity to make causal inferences.

The mutilation of intervally-scaled independent variables to conduct ANOVA may involve invoking an analytic model that does not match our model of reality, and in such analyses we are illogically exploring a reality that we do not believe exists. Usually, converting intervally-scaled data to nominal scale (a) discards information about the amounts and origins of individual differences, (b) lessens predictor score reliability, (c) distorts predictor distribution shapes, (d) dishonors relationships among predictors as they naturally occur, and (e) lessens power against Type II error.

▣▣▣ Reflection Problems ▣▣▣

1. For our drinks, weight, and drinks × weight regression model using the predictor variables in their unmutilated form, according to Table 9.15, the R^2 = 98.135%. If we square the r values in Table 9.14, the respective effects due to each predictor are 0.4272^2 = 18.26%, 0.8578^2 = 73.58%, and -0.2509^2 = 6.30%. For the mutilated version of the data, in the factorial ANOVA model reported in Table 11.2, we obtain respective η' values of 13.1%, 59.8%, and 3.6%, which sum to 76.5%.

    Why are the effects smaller for the predictors after they have been mutilated? Which effects involve an analytic model that honors your model of reality about how drinks and weight might best be measured?

2. **Dummy coding** is an alternative to using orthogonal nontrend contrasts. Each dummy code tests whether the mean of a single level differs from the grand mean. Analyze the Table 12.1 data with the following dummy codes created in SPSS syntax:

    ```
    compute d1 = 0 .
    compute d2 = 0 .
    compute d3 = 0 .
    compute d4 = 0 .
    compute d5 = 0 .
    if (level eq 2) d1 = 1 .
    if (level eq 3) d2 = 1 .
    ```

```
if (level eq 4) d3 = 1 .
if (level eq 5) d4 = 1 .
if (level eq 6) d5 = 1 .
```

Are the dummy-coded contrast variables orthogonal? How does the summary table from this analysis compare to the Table 12.2 and 12.5 summary tables?

13

Some Logistic Models

Model Fitting in a Logistic Context

s noted in Chapter 9, effect sizes can *quantify the degree of fit of models to data*. For example, in ANOVA, we may fit a factorial model, which by definition includes all possible main and interaction effects, or we may fit a nonfactorial model by excluding one or more effects (e.g., the gender main effect in a treatment-by-gender two-way study). In regression, we may or may not model interaction effects, or we may or may not model nonlinear relationships by using predictor variables taken to various exponential powers. Or, in path analysis, we may create models involving different path dynamics.

The analyses considered in previous chapters (excluding Spearman's ρ, ϕ, and r_{pb}) had in common the premises that (a) the single outcome variable is at least intervally-scaled, (b) the distribution shapes of either measured or latent variables are normal, and (c) the analytic weights should maximize $SOS_{\text{EXPLAINED}}$ and minimize $SOS_{\text{UNEXPLAINED}}$ (i.e., maximize r^2, R^2, or η^2). These analyses require certain statistical assumptions to be reasonably well met. For example, as noted in Chapter 8, multiple regression analyses require, among other assumptions, that e_i scores are normally distributed, and across various values of the predictor variables have equal variances (i.e., homoscedasticity). Analyses that require at least interval scale for the dependent variable and distributional assumptions are called **parametric analyses**.

Nonparametric analyses make no distributional assumptions and may be employed with outcome variables that are less than intervally-scaled. Of course, we can also apply nonparametric methods to intervally-scaled data either for substantive reasons, or because there are problems meeting distributional assumptions. Here we will consider logistic regression (Cox, 1970) and loglinear analyses. A brief discussion of these two potent nonparametric analyses will broaden your understanding of statistical analyses as model testing procedures, as well as lay the heuristic groundwork for mastering more complex statistics, such as multivariate analyses (e.g., structural equation modeling, hierarchical linear modeling, growth curve analyses). Readers seeking more in-depth, excellent treatments of these two topics are referred to Rice (1994) and Pampel (2000), or to Rice (1992), respectively.

Logistic Regression

Not infrequently, outcome variables are dichotomous. For example, people may or may not die, marry, divorce, have children, receive welfare, be unemployed, join a union, vote, be a felon, drop out, or enter college. We will use the hypothetical data presented in Table 13.1 to make this discussion concrete. The outcome variable, smoking, has been dummy-coded 1 = smoker, 0 = nonsmoker. The predictor variables are highest level of education and gender (dummy-coded 0 = male, 1 = female).

The heuristic data are crudely modeled on the reality that roughly 25% of American adults smoke, with males and less educated individuals being disproportionately more likely to smoke. Table 13.2 presents descriptive statistics for the Table 13.1 data.

TABLE 13.1. Prediction of Smoking (n = 150) Logits
Computed Separately Within Predictor Score Profiles

ID	Education level	Gender	Smoking	P	$1 - P$	$P / (1 - P)$	log of $P / (1 - P)$
Predictor profile {7,0}							
1	7	0	1	0.478	0.522	0.917	−0.087
2	7	0	1	0.478	0.522	0.917	−0.087
3	7	0	1	0.478	0.522	0.917	−0.087
4	7	0	1	0.478	0.522	0.917	−0.087
5	7	0	1	0.478	0.522	0.917	−0.087
6	7	0	1	0.478	0.522	0.917	−0.087
7	7	0	1	0.478	0.522	0.917	−0.087
8	7	0	1	0.478	0.522	0.917	−0.087
9	7	0	1	0.478	0.522	0.917	−0.087
10	7	0	1	0.478	0.522	0.917	−0.087
11	7	0	1	0.478	0.522	0.917	−0.087
12	7	0	0	0.522	0.478	1.091	0.087
13	7	0	0	0.522	0.478	1.091	0.087
14	7	0	0	0.522	0.478	1.091	0.087
15	7	0	0	0.522	0.478	1.091	0.087
16	7	0	0	0.522	0.478	1.091	0.087
17	7	0	0	0.522	0.478	1.091	0.087
18	7	0	0	0.522	0.478	1.091	0.087
19	7	0	0	0.522	0.478	1.091	0.087
20	7	0	0	0.522	0.478	1.091	0.087
21	7	0	0	0.522	0.478	1.091	0.087
22	7	0	0	0.522	0.478	1.091	0.087
23	7	0	0	0.522	0.478	1.091	0.087
Predictor profile {10,0}							
24	10	0	1	0.467	0.533	0.875	−0.134
25	10	0	1	0.467	0.533	0.875	−0.134
26	10	0	1	0.467	0.533	0.875	−0.134
27	10	0	1	0.467	0.533	0.875	−0.134
28	10	0	1	0.467	0.533	0.875	−0.134
29	10	0	1	0.467	0.533	0.875	−0.134
30	10	0	1	0.467	0.533	0.875	−0.134
31	10	0	0	0.533	0.467	1.143	0.134
32	10	0	0	0.533	0.467	1.143	0.134
33	10	0	0	0.533	0.467	1.143	0.134
34	10	0	0	0.533	0.467	1.143	0.134
35	10	0	0	0.533	0.467	1.143	0.134
36	10	0	0	0.533	0.467	1.143	0.134
37	10	0	0	0.533	0.467	1.143	0.134
38	10	0	0	0.533	0.467	1.143	0.134
Predictor profile {10,1}							
39	10	1	1	0.267	0.733	0.364	−1.012
40	10	1	1	0.267	0.733	0.364	−1.012
41	10	1	1	0.267	0.733	0.364	−1.012
42	10	1	1	0.267	0.733	0.364	−1.012
43	10	1	0	0.733	0.267	2.750	1.012

cont.

TABLE 13.1. *(cont.)*

ID	Education level	Gender	Smoking	P	$1 - P$	$P / (1 - P)$	log of $P / (1 - P)$
44	10	1	0	0.733	0.267	2.750	1.012
45	10	1	0	0.733	0.267	2.750	1.012
46	10	1	0	0.733	0.267	2.750	1.012
47	10	1	0	0.733	0.267	2.750	1.012
48	10	1	0	0.733	0.267	2.750	1.012
49	10	1	0	0.733	0.267	2.750	1.012
50	10	1	0	0.733	0.267	2.750	1.012
51	10	1	0	0.733	0.267	2.750	1.012
52	10	1	0	0.733	0.267	2.750	1.012
53	10	1	0	0.733	0.267	2.750	1.012
Predictor profile {12,0}							
54	12	0	1	0.400	0.600	0.667	−0.405
55	12	0	1	0.400	0.600	0.667	−0.405
56	12	0	1	0.400	0.600	0.667	−0.405
57	12	0	1	0.400	0.600	0.667	−0.405
58	12	0	1	0.400	0.600	0.667	−0.405
59	12	0	1	0.400	0.600	0.667	−0.405
60	12	0	0	0.600	0.400	1.500	0.405
61	12	0	0	0.600	0.400	1.500	0.405
62	12	0	0	0.600	0.400	1.500	0.405
63	12	0	0	0.600	0.400	1.500	0.405
64	12	0	0	0.600	0.400	1.500	0.405
65	12	0	0	0.600	0.400	1.500	0.405
66	12	0	0	0.600	0.400	1.500	0.405
67	12	0	0	0.600	0.400	1.500	0.405
68	12	0	0	0.600	0.400	1.500	0.405
Predictor profile {12,1}							
69	12	1	1	0.267	0.733	0.364	−1.012
70	12	1	1	0.267	0.733	0.364	−1.012
71	12	1	1	0.267	0.733	0.364	−1.012
72	12	1	1	0.267	0.733	0.364	−1.012
73	12	1	0	0.733	0.267	2.750	1.012
74	12	1	0	0.733	0.267	2.750	1.012
75	12	1	0	0.733	0.267	2.750	1.012
76	12	1	0	0.733	0.267	2.750	1.012
77	12	1	0	0.733	0.267	2.750	1.012
78	12	1	0	0.733	0.267	2.750	1.012
79	12	1	0	0.733	0.267	2.750	1.012
80	12	1	0	0.733	0.267	2.750	1.012
81	12	1	0	0.733	0.267	2.750	1.012
82	12	1	0	0.733	0.267	2.750	1.012
83	12	1	0	0.733	0.267	2.750	1.012
Predictor profile {16,0}							
84	16	0	1	0.267	0.733	0.364	−1.012
85	16	0	1	0.267	0.733	0.364	−1.012
86	16	0	1	0.267	0.733	0.364	−1.012
87	16	0	1	0.267	0.733	0.364	−1.012

cont.

	TABLE 13.1. *(cont.)*						
ID	Education level	Gender	Smoking	P	$1 - P$	$P / (1 - P)$	log of $P / (1 - P)$
88	16	0	0	0.733	0.267	2.750	1.012
89	16	0	0	0.733	0.267	2.750	1.012
90	16	0	0	0.733	0.267	2.750	1.012
91	16	0	0	0.733	0.267	2.750	1.012
92	16	0	0	0.733	0.267	2.750	1.012
93	16	0	0	0.733	0.267	2.750	1.012
94	16	0	0	0.733	0.267	2.750	1.012
95	16	0	0	0.733	0.267	2.750	1.012
96	16	0	0	0.733	0.267	2.750	1.012
97	16	0	0	0.733	0.267	2.750	1.012
98	16	0	0	0.733	0.267	2.750	1.012
Predictor profile {16,1}							
99	16	1	1	0.133	0.867	0.154	−1.872
100	16	1	1	0.133	0.867	0.154	−1.872
101	16	1	0	0.867	0.133	6.500	1.872
102	16	1	0	0.867	0.133	6.500	1.872
103	16	1	0	0.867	0.133	6.500	1.872
104	16	1	0	0.867	0.133	6.500	1.872
105	16	1	0	0.867	0.133	6.500	1.872
106	16	1	0	0.867	0.133	6.500	1.872
107	16	1	0	0.867	0.133	6.500	1.872
108	16	1	0	0.867	0.133	6.500	1.872
109	16	1	0	0.867	0.133	6.500	1.872
110	16	1	0	0.867	0.133	6.500	1.872
111	16	1	0	0.867	0.133	6.500	1.872
112	16	1	0	0.867	0.133	6.500	1.872
113	16	1	0	0.867	0.133	6.500	1.872
Predictor profile {20,0}							
114	20	0	1	0.267	0.733	0.364	−1.012
115	20	0	1	0.267	0.733	0.364	−1.012
116	20	0	1	0.267	0.733	0.364	−1.012
117	20	0	1	0.267	0.733	0.364	1.012
118	20	0	0	0.733	0.267	2.750	1.012
119	20	0	0	0.733	0.267	2.750	1.012
120	20	0	0	0.733	0.267	2.750	1.012
121	20	0	0	0.733	0.267	2.750	1.012
122	20	0	0	0.733	0.267	2.750	1.012
123	20	0	0	0.733	0.267	2.750	1.012
124	20	0	0	0.733	0.267	2.750	1.012
125	20	0	0	0.733	0.267	2.750	1.012
126	20	0	0	0.733	0.267	2.750	1.012
127	20	0	0	0.733	0.267	2.750	1.012
128	20	0	0	0.733	0.267	2.750	1.012
Predictor profile {20,1}							
129	20	1	1	0.067	0.933	0.071	−2.639
130	20	1	0	0.933	0.067	4.000	2.639
131	20	1	0	0.933	0.067	4.000	2.639

cont.

TABLE 13.1. *(cont.)*

ID	Education level	Gender	Smoking	P	$1 - P$	$P / (1 - P)$	log of $P / (1 - P)$
132	20	1	0	0.933	0.067	4.000	2.639
133	20	1	0	0.933	0.067	4.000	2.639
134	20	1	0	0.933	0.067	4.000	2.639
135	20	1	0	0.933	0.067	4.000	2.639
136	20	1	0	0.933	0.067	4.000	2.639
137	20	1	0	0.933	0.067	4.000	2.639
138	20	1	0	0.933	0.067	4.000	2.639
139	20	1	0	0.933	0.067	4.000	2.639
140	20	1	0	0.933	0.067	4.000	2.639
141	20	1	0	0.933	0.067	4.000	2.639
142	20	1	0	0.933	0.067	4.000	2.639
143	20	1	0	0.933	0.067	4.000	2.639
Predictor profile {24,1}							
144	24	1	1	0.200	0.800	0.250	−1.386
145	24	1	0	0.800	0.200	4.000	1.386
146	24	1	0	0.800	0.200	4.000	1.386
147	24	1	0	0.800	0.200	4.000	1.386
148	24	1	0	0.800	0.200	4.000	1.386
Predictor profile {33,1}							
149	33	1	1	0.500	0.500	1.000	0.000
150	33	1	0	0.500	0.500	1.000	0.000

Multiple Regression Solution

Given the Table 13.2 results, we can solve for $\beta_{\text{EDUCATION}}$ with Equation 8.12. For our data we have

$$\beta_1 = [r_{Y \times X1} - \{(r_{Y \times X2})(r_{X1 \times X2})\}] / [1 - r_{X1 \times X2}{}^2] \qquad (8.12)$$
$$[-0.183 - \{(-0.208)(0.316)\}] / [1.000 - 0.316^2]$$
$$[-0.183 - \{(-0.208)(0.316)\}] / [1.000 - 0.100]$$
$$[-0.183 - \{(-0.208)(0.316)\}] / 0.900$$
$$[-0.183 - \{-0.066\}] / 0.900$$
$$-0.117 / 0.900$$
$$\beta_{\text{EDUCATION}} = -0.130$$

For β_{GENDER} we have

$$\beta_2 = [r_{Y \times X2} - \{(r_{Y \times X1})(r_{X1 \times X2})\}] / [1 - r_{X1 \times X2}{}^2] \quad (8.13)$$
$$\beta_2 = [-0.208 - \{(-0.183)(0.316)\}] / [1.000 - 0.316^2]$$
$$[-0.208 - \{(-0.183)(0.316)\}] / [1.000 - 0.100]$$
$$[-0.208 - \{(-0.183)(0.316)\}] / 0.900$$
$$[-0.208 - \{-0.058\}] / 0.900$$
$$-0.150 / 0.900$$
$$\beta_{\text{GENDER}} = -0.167$$

For the measured variables in their unstandardized form, we can solve for the b weights by using

$$b = \beta(SD_Y / SD_X) \quad (8.1)$$

For education we have

$$-0.130(0.460 / 5.280)$$
$$-0.130(0.087)$$
$$b_{\text{EDUCATION}} = -0.011$$

For gender we have

$$-0.167(0.460 / 0.500)$$
$$-0.167(0.920)$$
$$b_{\text{GENDER}} = -0.153$$

TABLE 13.2. Descriptive Statistics for the Heuristic Table 13.1 Data

| | r of variable | | | | | Coefficient | |
SPSS variable	SMOKE	ED_LEV	GENDER	M	SD	Skewness	Kurtosis
SMOKE	1.000			0.30[a]	0.46	0.88	-1.24
ED_LEV	-0.183	1.000		13.91	5.28	0.76	0.72
GENDER	-0.208	0.316	1.000	0.45[b]	0.50	0.22	-1.98

[a]Proportion of sample who smoke.

[b]Proportion of sample who are female.

The additive constant may be computed using a generalization of

$$a = M_Y - b(M_X) \tag{8.4}$$

For our data we have

$$a = M_Y - b_{\text{EDUCATION}}(M_{\text{EDUCATION}}) - b_{\text{GENDER}}(M_{\text{GENDER}})$$
$$0.300 - -0.011(13.910) - -0.153(0.450)$$
$$0.300 - -0.158 - -0.069$$
$$a = 0.527$$

Finally, we may solve for the $R^2_{\text{SMOKING with EDUCATION,GENDER}}$ with Equation 8.9. For our data we have

$$\beta_{\text{EDUCATION}}(r_{\text{SMOKING} \times \text{EDUCATION}}) + \beta_{\text{GENDER}}(r_{\text{SMOKING} \times \text{GENDER}})$$
$$-0.130(-0.183) + -0.167(-0.208)$$
$$0.024 + 0.035$$
$$R^2_{\text{SMOKING with EDUCATION,GENDER}} = 0.059$$

At this point, we may also compute the latent variable scores. We will do so only for $\hat{Y}_i$ scores of the two hypothetical women who took multiple postgraduate degrees, including both J.D.s and English Ph.D.s that set records for duration of study. Working with somewhat more precision for these two cases, we have

$$0.5265 + -0.0114(33) + -0.1536(1)$$
$$0.5265 + -0.3762 + -0.1536$$
$$\hat{Y}_{149} = \hat{Y}_{150} = -0.0033$$

Note that these two $\hat{Y}_i$ scores fall outside the plausible range of the dichotomous outcome variable. People cannot be less of a smoker than being a nonsmoker! This mathematical conundrum is only one troubling aspect of using conventional multiple regression for this analytic problem.

Odds and Odds Ratios

Another difficulty is conceptual. In this context our analytic goal is *not* to approximate continuous Y_i scores using $\hat{Y}_i$ scores subject to a constraint that the *SOS* of the $\hat{Y}_i$ scores will be maximized, whereas, conversely, the *SOS* of the e_i scores will be minimized, and thus R^2 (i.e., $SOS_{EXPLAINED}$ / SOS_Y) will be maximized.

Instead, what we really want to do here is to develop an equation for unstandardized predictor variables that classifies people into our groups (i.e., either smoker or nonsmoker) with the greatest accuracy. As Menard (2002) explained, "The distinction between the arbitrary numerical value of Y . . . and the probability that Y has one or the other of its two possible values is problematic for . . . [classical] regression and leads us to consider alternative methods for estimating parameters to describe the relationship between Y" (p. 10) and the predictors. If our equation works well with our current sample, perhaps we will use the equation with similar new samples to decide for whom antismoking interventions should be targeted.

So, our real focus is on some function of the proportional incidence, P_j, of a targeted outcome. In the present example, P_j is the proportional incidence of smoking within a given, *j*th predictor variable profile (e.g., {7,0}, {10,0}, {10,1}, {33,1}). In any situation in which the targeted outcome (e.g., death, smoking) is coded 1 and the absence of the targeted outcome is coded 0, P_j is the portion of people in the score profile exhibiting the targeted outcome (e.g., for 1 smoker out of 10,000 people in a given predictor score profile group, P_j – 1 / 10000 = 0.0001). Thus, P_j values range between 0 and 1 and, for a dataset other than our example, might include values such as

$$P_j$$

0.0001
0.001
0.01
0.1
0.2
0.4
0.5
0.6

0.8
0.9
0.99
0.999
0.9999

However, what we really want to predict is the *odds* that the people with a given predictor score profile (e.g., 7th-grade males, 10th-grade females) exhibit the targeted outcome (e.g., smoking or its absence, or vice versa). So, the real focus of the analysis is the odds (O_j), defined for a given *j*th predictor score profile as $P_j / (1 - P_j)$. The odds corresponding to our illustrative P_j values would be

P_j	$1 - P_j$	$P_j / (1 - P_j)$
0.0001	0.9999	0.0001
0.001	0.999	0.0010
0.01	0.99	0.0101
0.1	0.9	0.1111
0.2	0.8	0.2500
0.4	0.6	0.6667
0.5	0.5	1.0000
0.6	0.4	1.5000
0.8	0.2	4.0000
0.9	0.1	9.0000
0.99	0.01	99.0000
0.999	0.001	999.0000
0.9999	0.0001	9999.0000

When the incidence of the targeted outcome is a 50% / 50% proposition in a given profile group, the odds equal 1.0. The odds are less than 1.0 when the proportion of the targeted outcome is less than a 50% / 50% proposition, and greater than 1.0 when the proportion of the targeted outcome is more than a 50% / 50% proposition.

The use of odds implies interest in a comparison using an **odds ratio** (i.e., the odds for one group or score profile versus the odds for another group or score profile). Here we are interested in the odds ratio for females versus males, or the odds ratio for less-educated versus more-educated people. And in our Table 5.8 aspirin and heart attack example, the P of a heart attack for physicians taking aspirin daily was 0.010 (i.e., 5 / 500; $O = 0.010 / 0.990 = 0.0101$), while the P of a heart attack for the physicians not taking a daily aspirin was 0.018 ($O = 0.018 / 0.982 = 0.0183$). Although the odds of myocardial infarct were small in both treatment conditions, the odds ratio ($0.0101 / 0.0183 = 0.552$) was sufficiently different from 1.0 that in the parallel real study the investigation was halted before the planned completion date, and today adult patients are routinely encouraged to take aspirin daily to minimize the risk of heart attack.

Log Odds as Outcomes

Unfortunately, there is an additional difficulty. Notice that at the larger values of P_j, the odds become huge! For example, as we move from $P_j = 0.8$ to $P_j = 0.9$, the corresponding odds move from $O_j = 4.0$ to $O_j = 9.0$. And at P_j values of 0.99, 0.999, and 0.9999, we obtain odds of 99.0, 999.0, and 9999.0, respectively.

Figure 13.1 makes clear the exact nature of the problem. The figure presents odds for our values of P_j ranging from 0.001 to 0.999. The statistical difficulty of using the odds as the dependent variable in a classical regression analysis is that odds are *not linear*. This would be less of

FIGURE 13.1. Plot of odds and corresponding logits

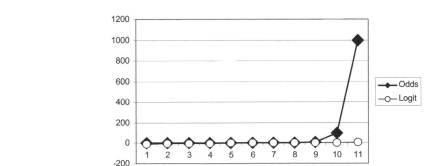

a difficulty if our data included P_j values that were less extreme, such that our odds did not reach hugely inflated values. However, we will use a transformation of the dichotomous outcome variable that will make logistic regression reasonable whether or not our data include extraordinary odds.

Classical regression requires the form of the relationship between the predictors and the outcome variable to be linear. When the relationship is not linear, sometimes we can transform the *independent* variables to model curvilinear relationship, by adding predictor variables that take predictors to various exponential powers, as illustrated in Chapter 9. In a similar vein, here we will invoke a mathematical transformation of the outcome variable (i.e., O_j) so that we can model nonlinear data dynamics within a linear model.

In conventional mathematics, we perform operations that count using an *additive* function in the base unit of 1.0. An alternative is counting instead with a *multiplicative* function using the base unit of 10, or 2.718, or any other number we wish to use as a base. **Logarithms** measure the power to which the base must be raised to obtain a given value on X.

Our visit to logarithm land will be relatively brief. However, the reader is advised that the first experience of logarithms may be facilitated by the presence of a dry gin martini, up, with a twist (No olives!!!).

Common logarithms, by definition, use a base of 10. So consider these data for X that increase in *multiples* of 10: {10, 100, 1,000, 10,000}. For these data, we now have

X	Base	Exponent	Base^{EXPONENT}
10	10	1	10^1
100	10	2	10^2
1,000	10	3	10^3
10,000	10	4	10^4

This means that, if we wish, we may reexpress our X scores in common log units as the value of the exponents:

X	log X
10	1
100	2
1,000	3
10,000	4

One feature of this reexpression is that the focus is shifted from *absolute* change to *relative* change. For example, if the X scores were dollars, the increases in worth are $90, $900, and $9,000, respectively. However, each increase reflects relative worth that grows by 10 times, or by 1,000%. A model that focuses on relative increments of income might be of interest, for example, if we felt that absolute increases in income in dollars are insensitive to those people who value fixed absolute increases less and less as they become more wealthy.

We measure the yield of hydrogen bombs in absolute or additive terms, in megatons. A 1-megaton bomb releases the energy equivalent to 1 million tons of TNT. A 2-megaton bomb releases an additional equivalent of another 1 million tons of TNT.

But we measure earthquakes using a common logarithmic (i.e., base 10) scale. On the Richter scale, an increase of 1 magnitude unit represents a multiplicative factor of a *relative* increase of 10 times in the seismic wave amplitude. The seismic waves of a magnitude-7 earthquake are 10 times greater in amplitude than those of a magnitude-6 earthquake, 100 times larger than a magnitude-5 earthquake, and 1,000 times as large as a 4-magnitude earthquake.

Logarithms are mathematically defined (i.e., can be computed) only for values of X above zero. O_i is always greater than zero, because profile groups with no incidence of the target outcome have no information available to help us understand the likelihood of the outcome, and thus are excluded. Logs are negative for values of X between 0 and 1. The log is 0 when $X = 1$, because any number raised to the power of 0 equals 1. Finally, the log is a positive number for any X greater than 1.

Natural logs, unlike common logs, count instead in multiples of a base that roughly equals 2.718. *Logistic regression uses natural logs of the odds as the focus of the analysis.* Consider the following five scores on X

expressed in natural logs. These five scores reflect a constant *relative, multiplicative* increase of 171.83%:

X	Relative % change	Base	Exponent	Base^{exp}	Natural log X
1.00000	—	2.718282	0	1.0000	0.0000
2.71828	171.828	2.718282	1	2.7183	1.0000
7.38906	171.828	2.718282	2	7.3891	2.0000
20.08554	171.828	2.718282	3	20.0855	3.0000
54.59816	171.828	2.718282	4	54.5982	4.0000
148.41320	171.828	2.718282	5	148.4132	5.0000

Natural log values can be easily computed in Excel using the LN statistical function. For example, if you type in

+LN(2.718282)

the program will return the value of 1.000. Conversely, if you type in

+EXP(1)

the program will return the value of 2.718282.

The natural logs of values of odds are called **logits**. For selected values of P_j and O_j, the *logits (i.e., the rightmost column)* are

P_j	$1 - P_j$	$P_j / (1 - P_j)$	Log $P_j / (1 - P_j)$
0.0001	0.9999	0.0001	−9.210
0.001	0.999	0.0010	−6.907
0.01	0.99	0.0101	−4.595
0.1	0.9	0.1111	−2.197
0.2	0.8	0.2500	−1.386
0.4	0.6	0.6667	−0.405
0.5	0.5	1.0000	0.000
0.6	0.4	1.5000	0.405
0.8	0.2	4.0000	1.386
0.9	0.1	9.0000	2.197

0.99	0.01	99.0000	4.595
0.999	0.001	999.0000	6.907
0.9999	0.0001	9999.0000	9.210

Table 13.1 presents the odds and logits for the smoking data, computed to help build a conceptual bridge between analyzing the dichotomous dummy-coded binary outcome data, using conventional regression, and doing the actual computations in logistic regression in a different manner. And Figure 13.1 illustrates that the *logits form a linear pattern*, even when odds have an extremely curvilinear pattern.

We can then run a classical regression to predict the Table 13.1 logit scores using education level and gender (dummy-coded as 0 = male and 1 = female) as independent variables. The R^2 is now 22.7%, versus our previous value of 5.9%, reflecting improved model fit when logits are the analytic focus. Our a, b_1, and b_2 weights are 0.46, –0.05, and –0.73, respectively, or –0.046, 0.05, and 0.73, depending on whether we want to predict smoking or nonsmoking as the target outcome. In either case, the uncorrected effect size is R^2 because, as we have previously learned, multiplicative constants applied to Y (i.e., –1) do not affect squared correlations. However, there is another complication.

Estimation Theory

All the statistical methods taught in this book to this point invoke a statistical estimation theory called **ordinary least squares** (OLS). As we have noted repeatedly, OLS estimation seeks weights that maximize $SOS_{EXPLAINED}$, minimize SOS_{ERROR}, and thus maximize uncorrected effect sizes analogous to r^2.

The OLS estimates turn on the critical premise that sample data are representative of population scores, and therefore *do not take sampling error into account*. This works reasonably well when sampling error is minimal (e.g., sample size is quite large).

However, various other statistical estimation theories also can be used! Just as cursive writing is not mentioned to primary school students first learning to print, lest they form mass suicide pacts, some intellectual withholding until now may have been justified to protect at least partially the reader's mental health.

Maximum likelihood (ML) estimation theory differs from OLS methods by focusing directly on estimating population parameters such as *b* weights (and *not* sample statistics). The OLS estimates will equal ML estimates when OLS analyses fully meet analytic assumptions. And OLS methods have the advantage that they are computationally hugely more simple. This advantage was critical in the days before the advent of modern computers and software, when all analyses were repeatedly performed by hand to confirm that computation errors had not been made.

However, various classical regression assumptions (e.g., homoscedasticity) are difficult, if not impossible, to meet in the context of a dichotomous outcome variable. Thus, logistic regression software uses maximum likelihood estimation theory to obtain statistics.

Maximum likelihood estimation does *not* use formulas to compute statistics. Instead, in a logistic regression model for given statistics estimates the probability of each case being a 1 or a 0 on the outcome variable is computed. If the persons in the dataset are independent of each other, as when people are independently sampled and the scores of given cases do not constrain other people's scores, these probabilities can be multiplied times each other across all the cases to compute a likelihood function statistic for the dataset. The parameter estimates achieve maximum likelihood when this likelihood function for a given dataset is largest.

Conceptually, the computer guesses statistical estimates of the weights, and keeps tweaking them until the likelihood function stops changing much with repeated tweaking. Thus, logistic regression invokes another form of the iteration process first described in Chapter 7. If you ask, the computer software will divulge how many iterations were performed and what the guesses were at each iteration.

Maximizing the likelihood function is equivalent to maximizing the log of the likelihood function. For our data, the log likelihood function stabilized after three iterations. The estimates at each iteration were

Iteration	Log likelihood	*a* weight	*b* Education	*b* Gender
1	−87.369	0.10616	−0.04540	−0.61442
2	−87.025	0.27554	−0.06043	−0.76257
3	−87.023	0.29094	−0.06176	−0.77368

The analyst need not fully understand the magic of this process. However, when conducting analyses that invoke iteration, it is important to confirm that the iteration "converges" (i.e., stabilizes). There is no guarantee that for a given dataset an iterative process will converge. So, to avoid "infinite loops," software has a default maximum number of iterations that is allowed. If the solution does not converge, override the default iteration limits by allowing more iterations. If you set this number ridiculously high, and the solution still will not converge, the likely culprit is insufficient sample size.

Result Interpretation

The first interpretation question, as usual, is "Do I have anything?" As in classical regression, we can evaluate some combination of (a) NHSST results, (b) effect sizes, and (c) result replicability.

First, we can look at the *statistical significance* of our results. We compute the log-likelihood ratio for a model containing no predictor variables as a baseline against which to compare results for alternative models.

The baseline is a model containing only a constant. In classical regression, a model with only the a weight, or when all the predictors are useless, sets the a weight equal to M_Y, so that all the $\hat{Y}_i$ scores equal M_Y. The analogous process in logistic regression uses only the knowledge of baseline group membership (e.g., 30% smokers; 70% nonsmokers) to make predictions.

The log likelihood for our data, using only a prediction equation additive constant, equals $[n_1\{\ln(P_1)\} + n_0\{\ln(1 - P_1)\}]$. The log likelihood can be converted to a χ^2 test statistic by multiplying the log likelihood by -2.

For our smoking data, there were 45 smokers (30%) and 105 nonsmokers (70%) out of 150 participants. So the test statistic is computed as

$$-2[n_1\{\ln(P_1)\} + n_0\{\ln(1 - P_1)\}]$$
$$-2[45\{\ln(0.3)\} + 105\{\ln(1 - 0.3)\}]$$
$$-2[45\{\ln(0.3)\} + 105\{\ln(0.7)\}]$$
$$-2[45\{-1.204\} + 105\{-0.357\}]$$
$$-2[-54.179 + -37.451]$$
$$-2[-91.6296]$$
$$\chi^2 = 183.259$$

In an analogous fashion, the χ^2 is computed for the model using the two predictors, and for our data is 174.046.

Smaller χ^2 values reflect better model fit. We want small values for χ^2 (and *larger* $p_{\text{CALCULATED}}$ values) for the models we prefer, so that we do not reject the null that the model fits the data. However, in analyses that presume large sample sizes, these test statistics are primarily useful in quantifying the differential fits of alternative models, and *not* in evaluating overall model fit, for the reasons noted in Chapters 6 and 7 (i.e., large samples tend to yield statistical significance even when effect sizes are small).

Test statistic χ^2 values and their degrees of freedom are both additive. This means that we can use these χ^2 values to compute the statistical significance of model fit using a constant and two predictors versus using only the constant. For our data, we have 183.259 – 174.046 = 9.213. The estimation of each additional model parameter costs $df = 1$. So, the df spent to obtain the 9.213 improvement (i.e., decrease) in the χ^2 was 2. If we enter into Excel

$$+\text{CHIDIST}(9.213,2)$$

the program will return the $p_{\text{CALCULATED}}$ value of 0.010. Thus, using our two predictor variables results in a statistically significant improvement over the baseline model that uses only an additive constant.

Second, we can look at various *effect sizes* for our results. In classical regression, the R^2 can be computed as the ratio of the SOS_{MODEL} to the SOS_Y. In logistic regression, there is the difficulty that "the model predicts the logged odds, a transformation which represents a dependent variable without bounds and with an arbitrarily defined variance" (Pampel, 2000, p. 32) and thus a nonfixed and arbitrary SOS. However, a variety of pseudo-R^2 statistics has been suggested.

SPSS provides an estimate ($R_{\text{C\&S}}^2$) suggested by Cox and Snell (1989). For our data this estimate is 6.0%. However, Nagelkerke (1991) noted that $R_{\text{C\&S}}^2$ cannot mathematically attain a limit of 1.0 for most datasets, and proposed computing the pseudo-R_{MAX}^2 and dividing $R_{\text{C\&S}}^2$ by this R_{MAX}^2 to estimate the corrected value, $R_{\text{C\&S}}^{2*}$. SPSS also presents this corrected value, and for our data $R_{\text{C\&S}}^{2*} = 8.4\%$.

Another alternative is the proportional improvement in χ^2, computed as

$$R_{\text{PROPORTIONAL}}^2 = (\chi_{\text{NULL}}^2 - \chi_{\text{MODEL}}^2) / \chi_{\text{NULL}}^2 \qquad (13.1)$$

For our data we have

$$(183.259 - 174.046) / 183.259$$
$$9.213 / 183.259$$
$$R_{\text{PROPORTIONAL}}^2 = 5.03\%$$

Aldrich and Nelson (1984) proposed an alternative computed as

$$R_{\text{A\&S}}^2 = (\chi_{\text{NULL}}^2 - \chi_{\text{MODEL}}^2) / [(\chi_{\text{NULL}}^2 - \chi_{\text{MODEL}}^2 + n) \qquad (13.2)$$

For our data we have

$$(183.259 - 174.046) / (183.259 - 174.046 + 150)$$
$$9.213 / (9.213 + 150)$$
$$9.213 / 159.213$$
$$R_{\text{A\&S}}^2 = 5.79\%$$

Hagle and Mitchell (1992) noted that $R_{\text{A\&S}}^2$ is attenuated, depending on the distribution of the binary outcome scores, and they presented tables for correcting $R_{\text{A\&S}}^2$ to obtain $R_{\text{A\&S}}^{2*}$ by taking into account the percentage of cases in the modal group. For our data, the modal group is nonsmokers, with 70% of the cases in this group. The corresponding tabled correction factor is 1.82. So, for our data we have

$$5.79\%(1.82)$$
$$R_{\text{A\&S}}^{2*} = 10.53\%$$

Finally, given Equation 8.16

$$R_{Y \text{ with } X1, X2, \ldots, Xj} = r_{Y \text{ with } \hat{Y}} \qquad (8.16)$$

and Equation 8.17,

$$R_{Y \text{ with } X1, X2, \ldots, Xj}^{2} = r_{Y \text{ with } \hat{Y}}^{2} \qquad (8.17)$$

a parallel procedure must be reasonable in logistical regression. In logistic regression, predicted membership in the outcome group dummy-coded as 1 (here smoking) can be computed as

$$P_1 = \exp^{(b0 + b1 \times 1 + \ldots + bp \times p)} / [1 + \exp^{(b0 + b1 \times 1 + \ldots + bp \times p)}] \quad (13.3)$$

This equation can be used in future samples to predict group membership, invoking whatever baseline for the cutscore probability (e.g., 50%) the researcher deems reasonable. But in the context of the present discussion, Pampel (2000, p. 53) suggested saving the predicted probabilities in SPSS using the SAVE subcommand within the LOGISTIC REGRESSION procedure, and then using the CORRELATIONS procedure to correlate these probabilities with the observed outcome variable scores. For our data, this Pearson r equals 0.2552, so the estimated $R^2 = 0.2552^2 = 6.5\%$.

Caution must be exercised when evaluating the logistic regression effect sizes. As Hosmer and Lemeshow (2000) noted, "Unfortunately low R^2 values in logistic regression are the norm and this presents a problem when reporting their values to an audience accustomed to seeing [classical] linear regression values" (p. 167).

Third, we can evaluate model *invariance* by replicating results with an independent sample, or invoking cross-validation, or any of the previously described external and internal replicability analytic strategies. These analyses may be more feasible in logistic regression. In classical regression, researchers often seek a minimum sample size greater than the number of measured variables times 10 (or 15 or 20). However, in logistic regression, researchers may require a sample size in the lower incidence outcome group (here $n_{\text{SMOKERS}} < n_{\text{NONSMOKERS}}$, $n_{\text{SMOKERS}} = 45$) that is at least 10 times the number of predictor variables (Hosmer & Lemeshow, 2000). Thus, researchers may have larger sample sizes when invoking logistic regression analyses.

Several results may be consulted to answer the question "If I have something, from where does my noteworthy effect originate?" First, the equation weights may be examined. However, as output in conventional software, these are not standardized weights, and so cannot be compared with each other apples-to-apples. One solution is to obtain semistandardized weights by standardizing *only* the predictor variables before running the logistic regression analysis (Pampel, 2000, pp. 32–33).

Second, structure coefficients may be computed in logistic regression. In the context of estimating R^2 by squaring the correlation of predicted probabilities with the dichotomous outcome variable (e.g., for our data, $R^2 = 0.2552^2 = 6.5\%$), we could analogously compute r_S by correlating the predictor variables with the predicted probabilities. For our data, these structure coefficients are –0.7496 and –0.8517, respectively.

Loglinear Analysis

As noted in the previous discussion of logistic regression, sometimes outcome variables are dichotomous. However, sometimes *all* the variables in an analysis are categorical. **Loglinear analyses** are powerful methods for modeling dynamics within categorical data. However, before presenting loglinear analysis, an historical precursor for loglinear analysis will first be presented. This presentation will allow the comparative advantages of loglinear analyses to be emphasized.

Pearson Contingency Table χ^2

Halpin et al. (1982) presented real data in *The Journal of the American Medical Association* on Reye's syndrome. The syndrome is a rare but quite serious illness that usually occurs following influenza or chicken pox. The researchers were interested in exploring linkages between the syndrome and taking aspirin to treat these illnesses. Janet Rice (1992), a collaborator in the research, used a related example in her thoughtful exposition of loglinear analyses. Table 13.3 presents a related hypothetical dataset modeled on this research. Our example presumes that the data came from retrospective searches of clinical records, rather than from a randomized clinical trial.

The classical Pearson χ^2 test evaluates whether the proportional distribution of cases within the contingency table is random (i.e., the cases

TABLE 13.3. Hypothetical Reye's Syndrome Data

Case	Reye's Syndrome	Aspirin	Gender
1	1	1	0
2	1	1	0
3	1	1	0
4	1	1	0
5	1	1	0
6	1	1	0
7	1	1	0
8	1	1	0
9	1	1	0
10	1	1	0
11	1	1	0
12	1	1	0
13	1	1	0
14	1	1	0
15	1	1	0
16	1	1	0
17	1	1	0
18	1	1	0
19	1	1	0
20	1	1	0
21	1	1	0
22	1	1	0
23	1	1	0
24	1	1	0
25	1	1	1
26	1	1	1
27	1	1	1
28	1	1	1
29	1	1	1
30	1	1	1
31	1	1	1
32	1	1	1
33	1	1	1
34	1	1	1
35	1	1	1
36	1	1	1
37	1	1	1
38	1	1	1
39	1	1	1
40	1	1	1
41	1	1	1
42	1	1	1
43	1	1	1
44	1	1	1
45	1	1	1
46	1	1	1
47	1	1	1
48	1	1	1
49	1	0	0
50	1	0	1
51	0	1	0

TABLE 13.3. *(cont.)*

| | Variable | | |
| | Reye's Syndrome | Aspirin | Gender |
Case			
52	0	1	0
53	0	1	0
54	0	1	0
55	0	1	0
56	0	1	0
57	0	1	0
58	0	1	0
59	0	1	0
60	0	1	0
61	0	1	0
62	0	1	0
63	0	1	0
64	0	1	0
65	0	1	0
66	0	1	0
67	0	1	0
68	0	1	0
69	0	1	0
70	0	1	0
71	0	1	0
72	0	1	0
73	0	1	0
74	0	1	0
75	0	1	1
76	0	1	1
77	0	1	1
78	0	1	1
79	0	1	1
80	0	1	1
81	0	1	1
82	0	1	1
83	0	1	1
84	0	1	1
85	0	1	1
86	0	1	1
87	0	0	0
88	0	0	0
89	0	0	0
90	0	0	0
91	0	0	0
92	0	0	0
93	0	0	0
94	0	0	0
95	0	0	0
96	0	0	1
97	0	0	1
98	0	0	1
99	0	0	1
100	0	0	1

are distributed independently) against the alternative hypothesis that the variables are associated. Table 13.4 presents a subset of the Table 13.3 data using only two variables that we will use to illustrate these computations.

For a rows-by-columns (*r*-by-*c*) contingency table, the test statistic can be computed using observed and expected cell frequencies:

$$\chi^2 = \sum_{i=1}^{r} \sum_{j=1}^{c} (O_{ij} - E_{ij})^2 / E_{ij} \qquad (13.4)$$

The expected cell frequencies are computed by multiplying the cell margin subtotals and then dividing this product by *n*. For example, for the Reye's-syndrome-no, aspirin-no cell, the expected cell frequency is (50 * 16) / 100 = 800 / 100 = 8.00.

For our data, the Pearson χ^2 is

$$[\{14 - ((50 * 16) / 100)\}^2 / ((50 * 16) / 100)] +$$
$$[\{36 - ((50 * 84) / 100)\}^2 / ((50 * 84) / 100)] +$$
$$[\{2 - ((50 * 16) / 100)\}^2 / ((50 * 16) / 100)] +$$
$$[\{48 - ((50 * 84) / 100)\}^2 / ((50 * 84) / 100$$

$$[\{14 - (800 / 100)\}^2 / (800 / 100)] +$$
$$[\{36 - (4200 / 100)\}^2 / (4200 / 100)] +$$
$$[\{2 - (800 / 100)\}^2 / (800 / 100)] +$$
$$[\{48 - (4200 / 100)\}^2 / (4200 / 100)]$$

$$[\{14 - 8.00\}^2 / 8.00] +$$
$$[\{36 - 42.00\}^2 / 42.00] +$$
$$[\{2 - 8.00\}^2 / 8.00] +$$
$$[\{48 - 42.00\}^2 / 42.00]$$

$$[6.00^2 / 8.00] + [-6.00^2 / 42.00] + [-6.00^2 / 8.00] + [6.00^2 / 42.00]$$
$$[36.00 / 8.00] + [36.00 / 42.00] + [36.00 / 8.00] + [36.00 / 42.00]$$
$$4.500 + 0.857 + 4.500 + 0.857$$
$$\chi^2 = 10.714$$

TABLE 13.4. Contingency Table Layout of the Table 13.3 Data for Reye's Syndrome and Aspirin Variables

	Aspirin		
Reye's Syndrome	No	Yes	Total
No	14	36	50
Yes	2	48	50
Total	16	84	100

The Pearson contingency table χ^2 test statistic has degrees of freedom equal to (rows minus 1) times (columns minus 1), which for our data equal $(2 - 1)(2 - 1)$, or 1. The $p_{CALCULATED}$ for this test (i.e., $\chi^2 = 10.714$; $df = 1$) for our data is 0.00106. So we reject the null hypothesis that there is no relationship between the two variables reflected in the Table 13.4 cell counts or proportions.

Now, what does this widely used statistic tell us? This crude result suggests that Reye's syndrome, *or* aspirin, *or* the relationship of these two variables, *or* some combination of these produces a nonzero association. But the *specific* origins of the effect are *not* elucidated by the Pearson χ^2 analysis as it is classically conducted. As Ramsey and Schafer (1997) noted so succinctly, "Although the [Pearson contingency table] chi-squared test is *one of the most widely used* of statistical tools, it is also *one of the least informative*" (p. 548; emphasis added).

Logistic Alternative

In classical ANOVA, we could conduct a multiway study, pool together all the explained sums of squares and their degrees of freedom, and then test a single, superomnibus null hypothesis of no difference among all the various main effect and cell means. For example, in a 4×3 factorial design, we could crudely lump together SOS_A plus SOS_B plus $SOS_{A \times B}$ and then test this superordinate $SOS_{EXPLAINED}$ with degrees of freedom equal to cells − 1 (i.e., $[4 \times 3] - 1 = 11 = df_A = 3 + df_B = 2 + df_{A \times B} = 6$). However, testing of such superomnibus ANOVA hypotheses in a multiway study makes no sense! We want to know *where* differences or relationships do or do not occur.

In exactly the same vein, when analyzing multiway contingency table data, we also want to test separately the effects of the variables acting singly and in various combinations with each other. Loglinear analysis has the compelling appeal that for a given design all possible models can be tested. Thus, loglinear models have the capacity to help researchers isolate *the origins of detected relationships*.

Loglinear analyses invoke the likelihood ratio χ^2 test statistic, L^2. For a two-dimensional *r*-by-*c* contingency table,

$$L^2 = \sum_{i=1}^{r} \sum_{j=1}^{c} 2[O_{ij}][\ln(O_{ij} / E_{ij})] \quad (13.5)$$

Equation 13.5 makes explicit that a logistic function is being invoked.

For the Table 13.4 data we have

$$2(14)[\ln(14 / 8.00)] + 2(36)[\ln(36 / 42.00)]$$
$$+ 2(2)[\ln(2 / 8.00)] + 2(48)[\ln(48 / 42.00)]$$
$$2(14)[\ln(1.750)] + 2(36)[\ln(0.857)]$$
$$+ 2(2)[\ln(0.250)] + 2(48)[\ln(1.142)]$$
$$2(14)[0.560] + 2(36)[-0.154] + 2(2)[-1.386] + 2(48)[0.133]$$
$$2(7.835) + 2(-5.549) + 2(-2.772) + 2(6.409)$$
$$15.669 + -11.098 + -5.545 + 12.818$$
$$L^2 = 11.844$$

The L^2 is distributed as a χ^2 and again has $(r - 1)(c - 1)$ degrees of freedom, or for our data, $df = 1$. The $p_{CALCULATED}$ for this test for our data is 0.00058. Note that this $p_{CALCULATED}$ does *not* equal the $p_{CALCULATED}$ from the Pearson χ^2 for the same data (i.e., 0.00106).

The L^2 and the Pearson χ^2 will approach each other for the same data as the sample size is larger. Nevertheless, the L^2 test statistic is preferred in loglinear analyses. Unlike the Pearson χ^2, the L^2 test statistic has the *critical* feature that for two nested models in which one model contains a subset of the terms in the other model, the model with the subset of terms will *always* have a larger L^2 test statistic than the other model. This critical feature allows the quantification of differential fits of alternative models, and statistical significance testing of differential fit, which is precisely what loglinear analysis is all about.

In addition to the commonality that logistic regression and loglinear analyses both invoke natural logarithms, some loglinear analyses, like logistic regression, also require iteration and maximum likelihood estimation of the expected values used in computing the likelihood function. For more detailed comparisons of loglinear analysis and logistic regression, see Rice (1994).

Figure 13.2 presents the SPSS syntax used to perform all possible model tests for our data. Table 13.5 presents the test statistics for each of the 19 models.

Interpretation Issues

When we are testing the fit of loglinear models to data, the null hypothesis is that the data are compatible with a given model. So we are seeking models that are *not* statistically significant.

One complication is that more complex models have fewer degrees of freedom, and so become less and less falsifiable. And models with different degrees of freedom are difficult to compare apples-to-apples. One alternative is to compute L^2 / df as another comparative interpretation aid.

Finally, when a subset of alternative models fits reasonably well, among these we will tend to prefer simpler models. This is in keeping with the admonitions of William of Occam, a sultan who, centuries ago, argued that when two explanations fit a set of facts, the more parsimonious explanation is more likely to be true. We prefer more parsimonious models, because *true findings are most likely to replicate.*

When a particular variable is of interest, we can also conduct further computations using the Table 13.5 test statistics to better understand the dynamics within our data. For example, presume that we are interested in exploring correlates of Reye's syndrome. We test given relationships by computing χ^2 difference test between models containing the effect of interest and models containing all the terms *except* the effect of interest. Thus, Table 13.6 tests the effect of the association for ill people between Reye's and taking aspirin.

```
set printback=listing .
data list file='c:\stat_bk2\reye.dat' records=1/1
  id 1-3 reye_s 5 aspirin 7 gender 9 .
value labels
  reye_s 0 'no' 1 'yes'/aspirin 0 'no' 1 'yes'/
  gender 0 'female' 1 'male' .
list variables=all/cases=999 .
frequencies variables=reye_s to gender .
crosstabs tables=reye_s by aspirin/
  reye_s by aspirin by gender/statistics=all .
COMMENT  Test the equiprobability model by creating a
  constant, used as a covariate .
compute constant = reye_s .
loglinear reye_s (0,1) aspirin (0,1) gender (0,1)
  WITH constant/print=all/
  design=constant .
loglinear reye_s (0,1) aspirin (0,1) gender (0,1)/
  print=all/
  design=reye_s /
  design=aspirin /
  design=gender /
  design=reye_s, aspirin /
  design=reye_s, gender /
  design=aspirin, gender /
  design=reye_s, aspirin, gender /
  design=reye_s, aspirin, reye_s by aspirin /
  design=reye_s, gender, reye_s by gender /
  design=aspirin, gender, aspirin by gender /
  design=gender, reye_s, aspirin, reye_s by aspirin /
  design=aspirin, reye_s, gender, reye_s by gender /
  design=reye_s, aspirin, gender, aspirin by gender /
  design=reye_s, aspirin, gender,
    reye_s by aspirin, reye_s by gender /
  design=reye_s, aspirin, gender,
    reye_s by aspirin, aspirin by gender /
  design=reye_s, aspirin, gender,
    reye_s by gender, aspirin by gender /
  design=reye_s, aspirin, gender,
    reye_s by aspirin, reye_s by gender,
    aspirin by gender /
  design=reye_s, aspirin, gender,
   reye_s by aspirin, reye_s by gender, aspirin by gender,
   reye_s by aspirin by gender .
```

FIGURE 13.2. SPSS syntax for all possible loglinear models

The effect due to the relationship of Reye's and taking aspirin is statistically significant ($L^2 / \chi^2 = 11.8442$, $df = 1$, $p_{\text{CALCULATED}} = 0.00058$). Of course, a definitive causal conclusion cannot be reached on the basis of these nonexperimental data, as emphasized in Chapter 1. Nevertheless, the result is suggestive.

TABLE 13.5. Model Fit Statistics for All 19 Possible Loglinear Models

Model family/model	Statistic			
	$p_{\text{CALCULATED}}$	L^2	df	L^2 / df
Baseline				
Null, equiprobability model	1.E-12	67.7762	7	9.682
Single Margins				
Reye's	1.E-12	67.7762	6	11.296
Aspirin	0.009	17.0807	6	2.847
Gender	4.E-12	65.2052	6	10.868
Two Margins				
Reye's, Aspirin	0.004	17.0807	5	3.416
Reye's, Gender	1.E-12	65.2052	5	13.041
Aspirin, Gender	0.013	14.5097	5	2.902
Three Margins				
Reye's, Aspirin, Gender	0.006	14.5097	4	3.627
Relationship Between Two Variables				
Reye's, Aspirin, Reye's by Aspirin	0.264	5.2365	4	1.309
Reye's, Gender, Reye's by Gender	8.E-12	62.5650	4	15.641
Aspirin, Gender, Aspirin by Gender	0.006	14.3499	4	3.587
Relationship and One Omitted Margin				
Gender, Reye's, Aspirin, Reye's By Aspirin	0.446	2.6655	3	0.888
Aspirin, Reye's, Gender, Reye's By Gender	0.008	11.8696	3	3.957
Reye's, Aspirin, Gender, Aspirin By Gender	0.002	14.3499	3	4.783
Two Relationships Among Predictors				
Reye's, Aspirin, Gender, Reye's By Aspirin, Reye's By Gender	0.987	0.0253	2	0.013
Reye's, Aspirin, Gender, Reye's By Aspirin, Aspirin By Gender	0.286	2.5057	2	1.253
Reye's, Aspirin, Gender, Reye's By Gender, Aspirin By Gender	0.003	11.7098	2	5.855
Three Sets of Relationships				
Reye's, Aspirin, Gender, Reye's By Aspirin, Reye's By Gender, Aspirin By Gender	0.947	0.0044	1	0.004
Saturated (df = 0) Model				
Reye's, Aspirin, Gender, Reye's By Aspirin, Reye's By Gender, Aspirin By Gender, Reye's By Aspirin By Gender	1.000	0.0000	0	—

Note. The saturated model, which uses all possible table margins and relationships, like any model with zero degrees of freedom, always fits the data perfectly, and thus is not falsifiable.

TABLE 13.6. Test of the Effect of the Reye's By Aspirin Relationship Alone

Model/effect	Statistic		
	$\chi^2 (L^2)$	df	$p_{CALCULATED}$
Reye's, Aspirin, Gender, Aspirin By Gender	14.3499	3	
Reye's, Aspirin, Gender, **REYE'S BY ASPIRIN**, Aspirin By Gender	2.5057	2	
Due to Reye's By Aspirin Relationship	11.8442	1	0.00058

Note. The effect of the Reye's By Aspirin relationship is evaluated by computing the differences in the χ^2 / L^2 values for the nested models, and then the $p_{CALCULATED}$ value for this L^2 difference. The $p_{CALCULATED}$ can be found using the Excel CHIDIST statistical function.

We can also test the main and interaction effects on an outcome of interest. Again, we test given effects by computing the χ^2 difference test between models containing the effect of interest and models containing all the terms *except* the effect of interest. Thus, Table 13.7 tests (a) the main effect of aspirin on Reye's for participants with either influenza or chicken

TABLE 13.7. Tests of the Effects of Aspirin and Gender, Controlling for Each Other

Model/effect	Statistic		
	$\chi^2 (L^2)$	df	$p_{CALCULATED}$
Reye's, Aspirin, Gender, Reye's By Gender, Aspirin By Gender	11.7098	2	
Reye's, Aspirin, Gender, **REYE'S BY ASPIRIN**, Reye's By Gender, Aspirin By Gender	0.0044	1	
Aspirin main effect controlling for Gender	11.7054	1	0.00062
Reye's, Aspirin, Gender, Reye's By Aspirin, Aspirin By Gender	2.5057	2	
Reye's, Aspirin, Gender, Reye's By Aspirin, **REYE'S BY GENDER**, Aspirin By Gender	0.0044	1	
Gender main effect controlling for Aspirin	2.5013	1	0.11375

Note. The main effects on Reye's syndrome are evaluated by computing the differences in the χ^2 / L^2 values for the nested models and then the $p_{CALCULATED}$ values for these L^2 differences. The $p_{CALCULATED}$ values can be found using the Excel CHIDIST statistical function.

pox, controlling for gender, and (b) the main effect of gender on Reye's for participants with either influenza or chicken pox, controlling for aspirin.

The aspirin main effect is statistically significant ($p_{CALCULATED}$ = 0.00062), whereas the gender main effect is not ($p_{CALCULATED}$ = 0.11375). Again, however, we recall that the aspirin regimen in the hypothetical data was not randomly assigned in a clinical trial, so strong causal conclusions may not be drawn. For example, perhaps the families more aggressively treating illness-related fever with aspirin may have had different diets, or differed in their genotypes.

We test the aspirin by gender two-way interaction effect on Reye's syndrome by computing the L^2 / χ^2 difference between the model containing all terms *except* the three-relationship term (L^2 / χ^2 = 0.0044, df = 1), and the saturated model containing all the possible terms (L^2 / χ^2 = 0.0, df = 0). This interaction effect (L^2 / χ^2 = 0.0044, df = 1) is not statistically significant ($p_{CALCULATED}$ = 0.94711).

However, interaction effects must be interpreted cautiously in loglinear analyses, just as in ANOVA. In a balanced 3 × 5 ANOVA with 10 people per cell (n = 3 × 5 × 10 = 150), for example, the A-way main effect means are each based on an n of 50, the B way main effect means are each based on an n of 30, and the interaction effects involve 15 means each with an n of 10. We estimate more parameters for higher order interactions, and we pay the price for doing so, by spending more degrees of freedom. Lower ns for interaction estimates, and the associated greater expenditure of degrees of freedom, reduce power against Type II error for higher-order ANOVA interaction effects versus lower-order effects. Exactly the same dynamics occur within the loglinear context.

Thus, from a variety of perspectives, these hypothetical data (modeled on real data) tell the story that people sick with influenza or chicken pox possibly should avoid taking aspirin. No medication, or an alternative medication, may represent the more prudent course of treatment.

Some Key Concepts

Logarithms focus on *relative*, multiplicative score changes rather than absolute, additive changes. Logarithmic transformation may be sensible for substantive reasons, as when we believe that increments to income have meaning only in the context of previous baselines for given people. Logarithmic transformations can also be useful for statistical reasons, when data dynamics involve nonlinear patterns. Thus, these transformations are used in both logistic regression and loglinear analyses. Logistic regression and loglinear analyses also have in common the use of iteration and maximum likelihood estimation.

Logistic regression is used with a dichotomous outcome and predictors that are some combination of interval or categorical. Polytomous logistic regression methods useful with outcomes involving three or more categories have also been developed, but are beyond the scope of the present treatment.

Predictive discriminant analysis (PDA) is an alternative to logistic regression (Huberty, 1994). PDA is a multivariate method not covered in the present treatment. However, it will be noted that several Monte Carlo simulation studies have compared the two methods (e.g., Halperin, Blackwelder, & Verter, 1971; Hosmer, Hosmer, & Fisher, 1983). In Monte Carlo studies, researchers create known populations, and then examine the capacity of alternative analyses to recover known parameters. Efron (1975) found that PDA is more statistically efficient iff the assumptions of PDA are met.

▦▦▦ Reflection Problems ▦▦▦

1. For the various effect sizes considered in Chapters 1–12 (e.g., Cohen's d, η^2, ω^2, r^2, adjusted R^2), what were the effect sizes if the sample statistics exactly matched the expectations of the nil null hypothesis? The odds ratio is also an effect size. However, for odds ratios, what will the odds ratio be if the odds are exactly equal in two groups (e.g., odds of infarct among people taking a daily aspirin versus among people not taking a daily aspirin)?

2. Create a dataset by computing odds ($P_j / (1 - P_j)$) for P_j ranging from 0.2 to 0.8 inclusive, incrementing by values of 0.01. Compute the corresponding log odds values for the odds. First, plot the odds and logit data pairs in a scattergram. Second, compute the Pearson r between the two variables. What do these graphical and statistical analyses suggest about the necessity to use the logarithmic transform when values of P_j are not extreme?

3. Compute the Pearson contingency table χ^2 test for the variable pairs A and B, and then C and D. Note that for both contingency tables, the omnibus test $\chi^2 = 9.0$, $df = 4$, $p_{CALCULATED} = 0.06$, and $\phi = 0.50$. Then use the SPSS LOGLINEAR command to test various models for both variable pairs, and compare the model fit results. What do these comparisons suggest about the appropriateness for multiway contingency tables of using the omnibus χ^2 test as the only analysis?

	SPSS variables			
Case	A	B	C	D
1	1	1	1	1
2	1	1	1	1
3	1	1	1	1
4	1	1	1	1
5	1	1	1	1
6	1	1	1	2
7	1	1	1	2
8	1	2	1	3
9	1	2	1	3
10	1	2	1	3
11	1	2	1	3
12	1	3	1	3
13	2	1	2	1
14	2	1	2	1
15	2	1	2	2
16	2	1	2	2
17	2	2	2	2
18	2	2	2	2
19	2	2	2	2
20	2	2	2	2
21	2	3	2	2
22	2	3	2	2
23	2	3	2	3
24	2	3	2	3
25	3	1	3	1

26	3	2	3	1
27	3	2	3	1
28	3	2	3	1
29	3	2	3	1
30	3	3	3	2
31	3	3	3	2
32	3	3	3	3
33	3	3	3	3
34	3	3	3	3
35	3	3	3	3
36	3	3	3	3

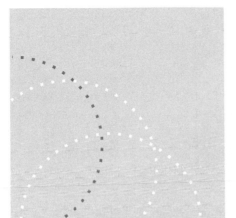

Scores (n = 100) with Near Normal Distributions

Case/statistic	Score form			
	~z	~T	~IQ	~GRE
1	−2.5	25	62.5	250
2	−2.2	28	67.0	280
3	−2.0	30	70.0	300
4	−1.8	32	73.0	320
5	−1.7	33	74.5	330
6	−1.6	34	76.0	340
7	−1.5	35	77.5	350
8	−1.4	36	79.0	360
9	−1.4	36	79.0	360
10	−1.3	37	80.5	370
11	−1.3	37	80.5	370
12	−1.2	38	82.0	380
13	−1.2	38	82.0	380
14	−1.1	39	83.5	390
15	−1.1	39	83.5	390
16	−1.0	40	85.0	400
17	−1.0	40	85.0	400
18	−0.9	41	86.5	410

19	−0.9	41	86.5	410
20	−0.9	41	86.5	410
21	−0.8	42	88.0	420
22	−0.8	42	88.0	420
23	−0.8	42	88.0	420
24	−0.7	43	89.5	430
25	−0.7	43	89.5	430
26	−0.7	43	89.5	430
27	−0.6	44	91.0	440
28	−0.6	44	91.0	440
29	−0.6	44	91.0	440
30	−0.5	45	92.5	450
31	−0.5	45	92.5	450
32	−0.5	45	92.5	450
33	−0.4	46	94.0	460
34	−0.4	46	94.0	460
35	−0.4	46	94.0	460
36	−0.4	46	94.0	460
37	−0.3	47	95.5	470
38	−0.3	47	95.5	470
39	−0.3	47	95.5	470
40	−0.3	47	95.5	470
41	−0.2	48	97.0	480
42	−0.2	48	97.0	480
43	−0.2	48	97.0	480
44	−0.2	48	97.0	480
45	−0.1	49	98.5	490
46	−0.1	49	98.5	490
47	−0.1	49	98.5	490
48	−0.1	49	98.5	490
49	0.0	50	100.0	500
50	0.0	50	100.0	500
51	0.0	50	100.0	500
52	0.0	50	100.0	500
53	0.1	51	101.5	510
54	0.1	51	101.5	510
55	0.1	51	101.5	510
56	0.1	51	101.5	510
57	0.2	52	103.0	520
58	0.2	52	103.0	520
59	0.2	52	103.0	520
60	0.2	52	103.0	520
61	0.3	53	104.5	530
62	0.3	53	104.5	530

63	0.3	53	104.5	530
64	0.3	53	104.5	530
65	0.4	54	106.0	540
66	0.4	54	106.0	540
67	0.4	54	106.0	540
68	0.4	54	106.0	540
69	0.5	55	107.5	550
70	0.5	55	107.5	550
71	0.5	55	107.5	550
72	0.6	56	109.0	560
73	0.6	56	109.0	560
74	0.6	56	109.0	560
75	0.7	57	110.5	570
76	0.7	57	110.5	570
77	0.7	57	110.5	570
78	0.8	58	112.0	580
79	0.8	58	112.0	580
80	0.8	58	112.0	580
81	0.9	59	113.5	590
82	0.9	59	113.5	590
83	0.9	59	113.5	590
84	1.0	60	115.0	600
85	1.0	60	115.0	600
86	1.1	61	116.5	610
87	1.1	61	116.5	610
88	1.2	62	118.0	620
89	1.2	62	118.0	620
90	1.3	63	119.5	630
91	1.3	63	119.5	630
92	1.4	64	121.0	640
93	1.4	64	121.0	640
94	1.5	65	122.5	650
95	1.6	66	124.0	660
96	1.7	67	125.5	670
97	1.8	68	127.0	680
98	2.0	70	130.0	700
99	2.2	72	133.0	720
100	2.5	75	137.5	750
M	0.000	50.000	100.000	500.000
SD	1.005	10.048	15.073	100.483
Skewness	0.000	0.000	0.000	0.000
Kurtosis	−0.170	−0.170	−0.170	−0.170

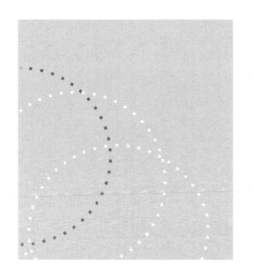

References

Aaron, B., Kromrey, J. D., & Ferron, J. M. (1998, November). *Equating r-based and d-based effect size indices: Problems with a commonly recommended formula*. Paper presented at the annual meeting of the Florida Educational Research Association, Orlando, FL. (ERIC Document Reproduction Service No. ED 433 353)

Abelson, R. P. (1997). A retrospective on the significance test ban of 1999 (If there were no significance tests, they would be invented). In L. L. Harlow, S. A. Mulaik, & J. H. Steiger (Eds.), *What if there were no significance tests?* (pp. 117–141). Mahwah, NJ: Erlbaum.

Aiken, L. S., & West, S. G. (1991). *Multiple regression: Testing and interpreting interactions*. Newbury Park, CA: Sage.

Aldrich, J. H., & Nelson, F. D. (1984). *Linear, probability, logit, and probit models*. Thousand Oaks, CA: Sage.

Algina, J., & Keselman, H. J. (2003). Approximate confidence intervals for effect sizes. *Educational and Psychological Measurement, 63*, 537–553.

Algina, J., Keselman, H. J., & Penfield, R. D. (2005). Effect sizes and their intervals: The two-level repeated measures case. *Educational and Psychological Measurement, 65*, 241–258.

Altman, D. G., Machin, D., Bryant, T. N., & Gardner, M. J. (2000). *Statistics with confidence: Confidence intervals and statistical guidelines* (2nd ed.). London: British Medical Journal Books.

American Psychological Association. (2001). *Publication manual of the American Psychological Association* (5th ed.). Washington, DC: Author.

Anderson, D. R., Burnham, K. P., & Thompson, W. (2000). Null hypothesis testing: Problems, prevalence, and an alternative. *Journal of Wildlife Management, 64,* 912–923.

Bagozzi, R. P., Fornell, C., & Larcker, D. F. (1981). Canonical correlation analysis as a special case of a structural relations model. *Multivariate Behavioral Research, 16,* 437–454.

Baron, R. M., & Kenny, D. A. (1986). The moderator-mediator variable distinction in social psychological research: Conceptual, strategic, and statistical considerations. *Journal of Personality and Social Psychology, 51,* 1173–1182.

Beaton, A. E. (1973). *Commonality.* Princeton, NJ: Educational Testing Service. (ERIC Document Reproduction Service No. ED 111 829)

Berkson, J. (1938). Some difficulties of interpretation encountered in the application of the chi-square test. *Journal of the American Statistical Association, 33,* 526–536.

Berliner, D. C. (2002). Educational research: The hardest science of all. *Educational Researcher, 31*(8), 18–20.

Boik, R. J. (1979). Interactions, partial interactions, and interaction contrasts in the analysis of variance. *Psychological Bulletin, 86,* 1084–1089.

Boring, E. G. (1919). Mathematical vs. scientific importance. *Psychological Bulletin, 16,* 335–338.

Breaugh, J. A. (2003). Effect size estimation: Factors to consider and mistakes to avoid. *Journal of Management, 29,* 79–97.

Campbell, D. T. (1957). Factors relevant to the validity of experiments in social settings. *Psychological Bulletin, 54,* 297–312.

Campbell, D. T., & Erlebacher, A. (1975). How regression artifacts in quasi-experimental evaluations can mistakenly make compensatory education look harmful. In M. Guttentag & E. L. Struening (Eds.), *Handbook of evaluation research* (Vol. 1, pp. 597–617). Beverly Hills: Sage.

Campbell, D. T., & Stanley, J. C. (1963). Experimental and quasi-experimental designs for research on teaching. In N. L. Gage (Ed.), *Handbook of research on teaching* (pp. 171–246). Chicago: Rand McNally.

Campbell, T. C. (2005). An introduction to clinical significance: An alternative index of intervention effect for group experimental design. *Journal of Early Intervention, 27,* 210–227.

Caparro, R. M., & Capraro, M. (2002). Treatments of effect sizes and statistical significance tests in textbooks. *Educational and Psychological Measurement, 62,* 771–782.

Carr, S. C., & Thompson, B. (1996). The effects of prior knowledge and schema activation strategies on the inferential reading comprehension of learning disabled and nonlearning disabled children. *Learning Disabilities Quarterly, 19,* 48–61.

Carter, D. S. (1979). Comparison of different shrinkage formulas in estimating population multiple correlation coefficients. *Educational and Psychological Measurement, 39,* 261–266.

Carver, R. (1978). The case against statistical significance testing. *Harvard Educational Review, 48,* 378–399.

Cattell, R. B. (1944). Psychological measurement: Normative, ipsative, interactive. *Psychological Review, 51,* 292–303.

Chambless, D. (1998). Defining empirically supported therapies. *Journal of Consulting and Clinical Psychology, 66,* 7–18.

Clark, H. H. (1973). The language-as-fixed-effect fallacy: A critique of language statistics in psychological research. *Journal of Verbal Learning and Verbal Behavior, 12,* 335–359.

Cliff, N. (1987). *Analyzing multivariate data.* San Diego: Harcourt Brace Jovanovich.

Cohen, J. (1968). Multiple regression as a general data-analytic system. *Psychological Bulletin, 70,* 426–443.

Cohen, J. (1969). *Statistical power analysis for the behavioral sciences.* New York: Academic Press.

Cohen, J. (1977). *Statistical power analysis for the behavioral sciences* (rev. ed.). Hillsdale, NJ: Erlbaum.

Cohen, J. (1988). *Statistical power analysis for the behavioral sciences* (2nd ed.). Hillsdale, NJ: Erlbaum.

Cohen, J. (1994). The earth is round ($p < .05$). *American Psychologist, 49,* 997–1003.

Cohen, J., Cohen, P., West, S. G., & Aiken, L. S. (2003). *Applied multiple regression/correlation analysis for the behavioral sciences* (3rd ed.). Mahwah, NJ: Erlbaum.

Cooley, W. W., & Lohnes, P. R. (1971). *Multivariate data analysis.* New York: Wiley.

Courville, T., & Thompson, B. (2001). Use of structure coefficients in published multiple regression articles: β is not enough. *Educational and Psychological Measurement, 61,* 229–248.

Cox, D. R. (1970). *The analysis of binary data.* London: Methuen.

Cox, D. R., & Snell, E. J. (1989). *Analysis of binary data* (2nd ed.). London: Chapman & Hall.

Craeger, J. (1969). The interpretation of multiple regression via overlapping rings. *American Educational Research Journal, 6,* 706–709.

Cronbach, L. J. (1957). The two disciplines of scientific psychology. *American Psychologist, 12,* 671–684.

Cronbach, L. J. (1975). Beyond the two disciplines of psychology. *American Psychologist, 30,* 116–127.

Cumming, G., & Finch, S. (2001). A primer on the understanding, use and calculation of confidence intervals that are based on central and noncentral distributions. *Educational and Psychological Measurement, 61,* 532–575.

Cumming, G., & Finch, S. (2005). Inference by eye: Confidence intervals, and how to read pictures of data. *American Psychologist, 60,* 170–180.

Dawson, T. E. (1999). Relating variance partitioning in measurement analyses to the exact same process in substantive analyses. In B. Thompson (Ed.), *Advances in social science methodology* (Vol. 5, pp. 101–110). Stamford, CT: JAI Press.

Diaconis, P., & Efron, B. (1983). Computer-intensive methods in statistics. *Scientific American, 248*(5), 116–130.

Duncan, O. D. (1975). *Introduction to structural equation models.* New York: Academic Press.

Duncan, T. E., & Duncan, S. C. (1995). Modeling the process of development via latent growth curve methodology. *Structural Equation Modeling, 2,* 187–213.

Duncan, T. E., Duncan, S. C., Strycker, L. A., Li, F., & Anthony, A. (1999). *An introduction to latent variable growth curve modeling: Concepts, issues, and applications.* Mahwah, NJ: Erlbaum.

Dunlap, W. P., & Landis, R. S. (1998). Interpretations of multiple regression borrowed from factor analysis and canonical correlation. *Journal of General Psychology, 125,* 397–407.

Edgington, E. S. (1974). A new tabulation of statistical procedures used in APA journals. *American Psychologist, 29,* 25–26.

Edwards, A. E. (1985). *Multiple regression and the analysis of variance and covariance* (2nd ed.). New York: Freeman.

Efron, B. (1975). The efficiency of logistic regression compared to normal discriminant analysis. *Journal of the American Statistical Association, 70,* 892–898.

Efron, B. (1979). Bootstrap methods: Another look at the jackknife. *Annals of Statistics, 7,* 1–26.

Efron, B., & Tibshirani, R. J. (1993). *An introduction to the bootstrap.* New York: Chapman & Hall.

Elmore, P. B., & Woehlke, P. L. (1988). Statistical methods employed in *American Educational Research Journal, Educational Researcher,* and *Review of Educational Research* from 1978 to 1987. *Educational Researcher, 17*(9), 19–20.

Erlenmeyer-Kimling, L., & Jarvik, L. (1963). Genetics and intelligence: A review. *Science, 142,* 1477–1479.

Ezekiel, M. (1930). *Methods of correlational analysis.* New York: Wiley.

Fan, X. (1996). Canonical correlation analysis as a general analytic model. In B. Thompson (Ed.), *Advances in social science methodology* (Vol. 4, pp. 71–94). Greenwich, CT: JAI Press.

Fidler, F. (2002). The fifth edition of the APA *Publication Manual*: Why its statistics recommendations are so controversial. *Educational and Psychological Measurement, 62,* 749–770.

Finch, S., Cumming, G., & Thomason, N. (2001). Reporting of statistical inference in the *Journal of Applied Psychology*: Little evidence of reform. *Educational and Psychological Measurement, 61,* 181–210.

Fisher, R. A. (1925). *Statistical methods for research workers.* Edinburgh: Oliver & Boyd.

Fisher, R. A. (1935). *The design of experiments.* Edinburgh: Oliver & Boyd.

Fowler, R. L. (1987). A general method for comparing effect magnitudes in ANOVA designs. *Educational and Psychological Methods, 47,* 361–367.

Frazier, P. A., Tix, A.P., & Baron, K. E. (2004). Testing of moderator and mediator effects in counseling psychology research. *Journal of Counseling Psychology, 51,* 115–134.

Frederick, B. N. (1999). Fixed-, random-, and mixed-effects ANOVA models: A user-friendly guide for increasing the generalizability of ANOVA results. In B. Thompson, *Advances in social science methodology* (Vol. 5, pp. 111–122). Stamford, CT: JAI Press.

Freedman, D. A. (1983). A note on screening regression equations. *American Statistician, 37,* 152–155.

Friedman, H. (1968). Magnitude of experimental effect and a table for its rapid estimation. *Psychological Bulletin, 70,* 245–251.

Gage, N. L. (1978). *The scientific basis of the art of teaching.* New York: Teachers College Press.

Galton, F. (1886). Regression towards mediocrity in hereditary stature. *Journal of the Anthropological Institute, 15,* 246–263.

Geisser, S., & Greenhouse, S. W. (1958). An extension of Box's results on the use of the F distribution in multivariate analysis. *Annals of Mathematical Statistics, 29,* 885–891.

Girden, E. R. (1992). *ANOVA: Repeated measures.* Newbury Park, CA: Sage.

Glaser, K., Hojat, M., Veloski, J. J., Blacklow, R. S., & Goepp, C. E. (1992). Science, verbal, or qualitative skills: Which is the most important predictor of physician competence? *Educational and Psychological Measurement, 52,* 395–406.

Glass, G. V (1976). Primary, secondary, and meta-analysis of research. *Educational Researcher, 5*(10), 3–8.

Glass, G. V, McGaw, B., & Smith, M. L. (1981). *Meta-analysis in social research.* Beverly Hills, CA: Sage.

Glass, G. V, & Stanley, J. C. (1970). *Statistical methods in education and psychology*. Englewood Cliffs, NJ: Prentice-Hall.

Good, P. I., & Hardin, J. W. (2003). *Common errors in statistics (and how to avoid them)*. New York: Wiley.

Goodwin, L. D., & Goodwin, W. L. (1985). Statistical techniques in *AERJ* articles, 1979–1983: The preparation of graduate students to read the educational research literature. *Educational Researcher, 14*(2), 5–11.

Gorsuch, R. L. (1983). *Factor analysis* (2nd ed.). Hillsdale, NJ: Erlbaum.

Graham, J. M., Guthrie, A. C., & Thompson, B. (2003). Consequences of not interpreting structure coefficients in published CFA research: A reminder. *Structural Equation Modeling, 10*, 142–153.

Greenwald, A. G. (1975). Consequences of prejudice against the null hypothesis. *Psychological Bulletin, 82*, 1–20.

Grissom, R. J. (1994). Probability of the superior outcome of one treatment over another. *Journal of Applied Psychology, 79*, 314–316.

Grissom, R. J., & Kim, J. J. (2005). *Effect sizes for research: A broad practical approach*. Mahwah, NJ: Erlbaum.

Guilford, J. (1954). *Psychometric methods* (2nd ed.). New York: McGraw-Hill.

Hagle, T. M., & Mitchell II, G. E. (1992). Goodness-of-fit measures for probit and logit. *American Journal of Political Science, 36*, 762–784.

Halperin, W., Blackwelder, C., & Verter, J. (1971). Estimation of multivariate logistic risk function: A comparison of the discriminant function and maximum likelihood approaches. *Journal of Chronic Diseases, 24*, 125–158.

Halpin, T., Holtzhauer, F., Campbell, R., Hall, L., Correa-Villaseñor, A., Lanese, R., Rice, J., & Hurwitz, E. (1982). Reye's syndrome and drug use. *Journal of the American Medical Association, 248*, 687–691.

Harlow, L. L., Mulaik, S. A., & Steiger, J. H. (Eds.). (1997). *What if there were no significance tests?*. Mahwah, NJ: Erlbaum.

Harris, K. (2003). Instructions for authors. *Journal of Educational Psychology, 95*, 201.

Harris, R. J. (1989). A canonical cautionary. *Multivariate Behavioral Research, 24*, 17–39.

Harris, R. J. (1992, April). *Structure coefficients versus scoring coefficients as bases for interpreting emergent variables in multiple regression and related techniques*. Paper presented at the annual meeting of the American Educational Research Association, San Francisco.

Harwell, M. (1998). Misinterpreting interaction effects in analysis of variance. *Measurement and Evaluation in Counseling and Development, 31*, 125–136.

Hays, W. L. (1981). *Statistics* (3rd ed.). New York: Holt, Rinehart & Winston.

Hedges, L. V. (1981). Distribution theory for Glass's estimator of effect size and related estimators. *Journal of Educational Statistics*, 6, 107–128.

Hedges, L. V., & Olkin, I. (1985). *Statistical methods for meta-analysis*. San Diego: Academic Press.

Henson, R. K. (1999). Multivariate normality: What is it and how is it assessed? In B. Thompson (Ed.), *Advances in social science methodology* (Vol. 5, pp. 193–212). Stamford, CT: JAI Press.

Herzberg, P. A. (1969). The parameters of cross-validation. *Psychometrika Monograph Supplement*, 16, 1–67.

Hess, B., Olejnik, S., & Huberty, C. J (2001). The efficacy of two Improvement-over-chance effect sizes for two-group univariate comparisons under variance heterogeneity and nonnormality. *Educational and Psychological Measurement*, 61, 909–936.

Hester, Y. C. (2000). An analysis of the use and misuse of ANOVA. (Doctoral dissertation, Texas A&M University.) *Dissertation Abstracts International*, 61, 4332A. (University Microfilms No. AAT9994257)

Hicks, C. R. (1973). *Fundamental concepts in the design of experiments* (2nd ed.). New York: Holt, Rinehart & Winston.

Hicks, L. (1970). Some properties of ipsative, normative, and forced-choice normative measures. *Psychological Bulletin*, 74, 167–184.

Horst, P. (1931). A proof that the point from which the sum of the absolute deviations is a minimum is the median. *Journal of Educational Psychology*, 22(3), 25–26.

Horst, P. (1966). *Psychological measurement and prediction*. Belmont, CA: Wadsworth.

Hosmer, D. W., & Lemeshow, S. (2000). *Applied logistic regression* (2nd ed.). New York: Wiley.

Hosmer, T., Hosmer, D., & Fisher, L. (1983). A comparison of the maximum likelihood and discriminant function estimators of the coefficients of the logistic regression model for mixed continuous and discrete variables. *Communications in Science*, B12, 577–593.

Howell, D. C. (2002). *Statistical methods for psychology* (6th ed.). Pacific Grove, CA: Duxbury.

Hubbard, R., & Ryan, P. A. (2000). The historical growth of statistical significance testing in psychology—and its future prospects. *Educational and Psychological Measurement*, 60, 661–681.

Huber, P. J. (1981). *Robust statistics*. New York: Wiley.

Huberty, C. J (1989). Problems with stepwise methods—better alternatives. In B. Thompson (Ed.), *Advances in social science methodology* (Vol. 1, pp. 43–70). Greenwich, CT: JAI Press.

Huberty, C. J (1994). *Applied discriminant analysis*. New York: Wiley.

Huberty, C. J (1999). On some history regarding statistical testing. In B. Thompson (Ed.), *Advances in social science methodology* (Vol. 5, pp. 1–23). Stamford, CT: JAI Press.

Huberty, C. J (2002). A history of effect size indices. *Educational and Psychological Measurement, 62,* 227–240.

Huberty, C. J, & Holmes, S. E. (1983). Two-group comparisons and univariate classification. *Educational and Psychological Measurement, 43,* 15–26.

Huberty, C. J, & Lowman, L. L. (2000). Group overlap as a basis for effect size. *Educational and Psychological Measurement, 60,* 543–563.

Huberty, C. J, & Morris, J. D. (1988). A single contrast test procedure. *Educational and Psychological Measurement, 48,* 567–578.

Huck, S. W. (1992). Group heterogeneity and Pearson's *r*. *Educational and Psychological Measurement, 52,* 253–260.

Huck, S. W., Cormier, W. H., & Bounds, W. G., Jr. (1974). *Reading statistics and research*. New York: Harper & Row.

Huck, S. W., Wright, S. P., & Park, S. (1992). Pearson's *r* and spread: A classroom demonstration. *Teaching of Psychology, 19*(1), 45–47.

Huitema, B. E. (1980). *The analysis of covariance and alternatives*. New York: Wiley.

Humphreys, L. G. (1978). Doing research the hard way: Substituting analysis of variance for a problem in correlational analysis. *Journal of Educational Psychology, 70,* 873–876.

Humphreys, L. G., & Fleishman, A. (1974). Pseudo-orthogonal and other analysis of variance designs involving individual-differences variables. *Journal of Educational Psychology, 66,* 464–472.

Huynh, H., & Feldt, L. S. (1976). Estimation of the Box correction for degrees of freedom from sample data in randomized block and split-plot designs. *Journal of Educational Statistics, 1,* 69–82.

International Committee of Medical Journal Editors. (1997). Uniform requirements for manuscripts submitted to biomedical journals. *Annals of Internal Medicine, 126,* 36–47.

Johnson, H. G. (1985). Beneath the technological fix: Outliers and probability statements. *Journal of Chronic Diseases, 38,* 957–961.

Jones, L. V. (1955). Statistics and research design. *Annual Review of Psychology, 6,* 405–430.

Kendall, P. C. (1999). Clinical significance. *Journal of Consulting and Clinical Psychology, 67,* 283–284.

Kendall, P. C., Marrs-Garcia, A., Nath, S. R., & Sheldrick, R. C. (1999). Normative comparisons for the evaluation of clinical significance. *Journal of Counseling and Consulting Psychology, 67,* 285–299.

Kennedy, J. J., & Bush, A. J. (1985). *An introduction to the design and analysis of experiments in behavioral research*. Lanham, MD: University Press of America.

Keppel, G., & Zedeck, S. (1989). *Data analysis for research designs*. New York: Freeman.

Kerlinger, F. N. (1977). The influence of research on educational practice. *Educational Researcher, 6*(8), 5–12.

Kerlinger, F. N. (1986). *Foundations of behavioral research* (3rd ed.). New York: Holt, Rinehart & Winston.

Kerlinger, F. N., & Pedhazur, E. J. (1973). *Multiple regression in behavioral research.* New York: Holt, Rinehart & Winston.

Keselman, H. J., Huberty, C. J, Lix, L. M., Olejnik, S., Cribbie, R., Donahue, B., Kowalchuk, R. K., Lowman, L. L., Petoskey, M. D., Keselman, J. C., & Levin, J. R. (1998). Statistical practices of educational researchers: An analysis of their ANOVA, MANOVA and ANCOVA analyses. *Review of Educational Research, 68,* 350–386.

Keselman, H. J., Kowalchuk, R. K., & Lix, L. M. (1998). Robust nonorthogonal analyses revisited: An update based on trimmed means. *Psychometrika, 63,* 145–163.

Keselman, H. J., Lix, L. M., & Kowalchuk, R. K. (1998). Multiple comparison procedures for trimmed means. *Psychological Methods, 3,* 123–141.

Kieffer, K. M., Reese, R. J., & Thompson, B. (2001). Statistical techniques employed in *AERJ* and *JCP* articles from 1988 to 1997: A methodological review. *Journal of Experimental Education, 69,* 280–309.

Kimbell, A. (2001, February). *The basic concepts of the General Linear Model (GLM): Canonical correlation analysis (CCA) as a GLM.* Paper presented at the annual meeting of the Southwest Educational Research Association, New Orleans. (ERIC Document Reproduction Service No. ED 450 147)

Kirk, R. E. (Ed.). (1972). *Statistical issues: A reader for the behavioral sciences.* Monterey, CA: Brooks/Cole.

Kirk, R. E. (1996). Practical significance: A concept whose time has come. *Educational and Psychological Measurement, 56,* 746–759.

Kirk, R. E. (2003). The importance of effect magnitude. In S. F. Davis (Ed.), *Handbook of research methods in experimental psychology* (pp. 83–105). Oxford, UK: Blackwell.

Kline, R. (2004). *Beyond significance testing: Reforming data analysis methods in behavioral research.* Washington, DC: American Psychological Association.

Knapp, T. R. (1978). Canonical correlation analysis: A general parametric significance testing system. *Psychological Bulletin, 85,* 410–416.

Knapp, T., & Sawilowsky, S. (2001). Constructive criticisms of methodological and editorial practices. *Journal of Experimental Education, 70,* 65–79.

Kulik, J., & Kulik, C-L. (1992). Meta-analysis: Historical origins and contemporary practice. In B. Thompson (Ed.), *Advances in social science methodology* (Vol. 2, pp. 53–80). Greenwich, CT: JAI Press.

Levene, H. (1960). Robust tests for equality of variances. In I. Olkin, S. G.

Ghurye, W. Hoeffding, W. G. Madow, & H. B. Mann (Eds.), *Contributions to probability and statistics: Essays in honor of Harold Hotelling* (pp. 278–292). Stanford, CA: Stanford University Press.

Levin, J. R., & Marascuilo, L. A. (1972). Type IV errors and interactions. *Psychological Bulletin, 78,* 368–374.

Levine, M. S. (1977). *Canonical analysis and factor comparison.* Beverly Hills, CA: Sage.

Likert, R. (1932). A technique for the measurement of attitudes. *Archives of Psychology,* no. 32.

Little, R. J. A., & Rubin, D. R. (1987). *Statistical analysis with missing data.* New York: Wiley.

Loehlin, J. C. (2004). *Latent variable models: An introduction to factor, path, and structural equation analysis* (4th ed.). Mahwah, NJ: Erlbaum.

Loftin, L., & Madison, S. (1991). The extreme dangers of covariance corrections. In B. Thompson (Ed.), *Advances in educational research: Substantive findings, methodological developments* (Vol. 1, pp. 133–147). Greenwich, CT: JAI Press.

Love, G. (1988, November). *Understanding experimentwise error probability.* Paper presented at the annual meeting of the Mid-South Educational Research Association, Louisville, KY. (ERIC Document Reproduction Service No. ED 304 451)

Lunneborg, C. E. (1999). *Data analysis by resampling: Concepts and applications.* Pacific Grove, CA: Duxbury.

Lunneborg, C. E. (2001). Random assignment of available cases: Bootstrap standard errors and confidence intervals. *Psychological Methods, 6,* 402–412.

McCartney, K., & Rosenthal, R. (2000). Effect size, practical importance, and social policy for children. *Child Development, 71,* 173–180.

Mangel, M., & Samaniego, F. J. (1984). Abraham Wald's work on aircraft survivability. *Journal of the American Statistical Association, 79,* 259–267.

Marascuilo, L. A., & Levin, J. R. (1970). Appropriate post hoc comparisons for interaction and nested hypotheses in analysis of variance designs: The elimination of Type IV errors. *American Educational Research Journal, 7,* 397–421.

Maxwell, S. E., & Delaney, H. D. (2004). *Designing experiments and analyzing data* (2nd ed.). Mahwah, NJ: Erlbaum.

Menard, S. (2002). *Applied logistic regression* (2nd ed.). Thousand Oaks, CA: Sage.

Meredith, W. (1964). Canonical correlations with fallible data. *Psychometrika, 29,* 55–65.

Mittag, K. C., & Thompson, B. (2000). A national survey of AERA members' perceptions of statistical significance tests and other statistical issues. *Educational Researcher, 29*(4), 14–20.

Mood, A. R. (1969). Macro-analysis of the American educational system. *Operations Research, 17,* 770–784.

Mosier, C. I. (1951). The need and means of cross-validation, I: Problems and design of cross-validation. *Educational and Psychological Measurement, 11,* 5–11.

Mosteller, F., & Boruch, R. (Eds.). (2002). *Evidence matters: Randomized trials in education research.* Washington, DC: Brookings Institution Press.

Mulaik, S. A., Raju, N. S., & Harshman, R. A. (1997). There is a time and place for significance testing. In L. L. Harlow, S. A. Mulaik, & J. H. Steiger (Eds.), *What if there were no significance tests?* (pp. 65–115). Mahwah, NJ: Erlbaum.

Nagelkerke, N. J. D. (1991). A note on a general definition of the coefficient of determination. *Biometrika, 78,* 691–692.

Nelson, N., Rosenthal, R., & Rosnow, R. L. (1986). Interpretation of significance levels and effect sizes by psychological researchers. *American Psychologist, 41,* 1299–1301.

Nunnally, J. C. (1975). Psychometric theory—25 years ago and now. *Educational Researcher, 4*(10), 7–14, 19–20.

Nunnally, J. C. (1978). *Psychometric methods* (2nd ed.). New York: McGraw-Hill.

Oakes, M. (1986). *Statistical inference: A commentary for the social and behavioral sciences.* New York: Wiley.

Odom, S. L., Brantlinger, E., Gersten, R., Horner, R. H., & Thompson, B. (2005). Research in special education: Scientific methods and evidence-based practices. *Exceptional Children, 71,* 137–148.

Olejnik, S., & Algina, J. (2000). Measures of effect size for comparative studies: Applications, interpretations, and limitations. *Contemporary Educational Psychology, 25,* 241–286.

Olejnik, S., & Algina, J. (2003). Generalized eta and omega squared statistics: Measures of effect size for some common research designs. *Psychological Methods, 8,* 434–437.

Ott, L. (1984). *Introduction to statistical methods and data analysis.* Boston: Prindle, Weber, & Schmidt.

Pampel, F. C. (2000). *Logistic regression: A primer.* Thousand Oaks, CA: Sage.

Pedhazur, E. J. (1977). Coding subjects in repeated measures designs. *Psychological Bulletin, 34,* 298–305.

Pedhazur, E. J. (1982). *Multiple regression in behavioral research: Explanation and prediction* (2nd ed.). New York: Holt, Rinehart & Winston.

Pedhazur, E. J., & Schmelkin, L. P. (1991). *Measurement, design, and analysis: An integrated approach*. Hillsdale, NJ: Erlbaum.

Popper, K. R. (1961). *The logic of scientific discovery*. New York: Science Editions.

Popper, K. R. (1965). *Conjectures and refutations* (2nd ed.). New York: Harper Torchbooks.

Ramsey, F. L., & Schafer, D. W. (1997). *The statistical sleuth: A course in methods of data analysis*. Belmont, CA: Duxbury.

Raudenbush, S. W. (2005). Learning from attempts to improve schooling: The contribution of methodological diversity. *Educational Researcher, 34*(5), 25–31.

Rencher, A. C., & Pun, F-C. (1980). Inflation of R^2 in best subset regression. *Technometrics, 22,* 49–53.

Rice, J. (1992). Loglinear analysis: Analysis of categorical variables in the logit setting. In B. Thompson (Ed.), *Advances in social science methodology* (Vol. 2, pp. 1–52). Greenwich, CT: JAI Press.

Rice, J. (1994). Logistic regression: An introduction. In B. Thompson (Ed.), *Advances in social science methodology* (Vol. 3, pp. 191–245). Greenwich, CT: JAI Press.

Robertson, C. (1991). Computationally intensive statistics. In P. Lovie & A. Lovie (Eds.), *New developments in statistics for psychology and the social sciences* (Vol. 2, pp. 49–80). Leicester, UK: British Psychological Society.

Robinson, D. H., & Wainer, H. (2002). On the past and future of null hypothesis significance testing. *Journal of Wildlife Management, 66,* 263–271.

Robinson, W. S. (1950). Ecological correlations and the behavior of individuals. *American Sociological Review, 15,* 351–357.

Rokeach, M. (1973). *The nature of human values*. New York: Free Press.

Ronis, D. L. (1981). Comparing the magnitude of effects in ANOVA designs. *Educational and Psychological Measurement, 41,* 993–1000.

Rosenthal, R. (1979). The "file drawer problem" and tolerance for null results. *Psychological Bulletin, 86,* 638–641.

Rosenthal, R. (1994). Parametric measures of effect size. In H. Cooper & L. V. Hedges (Eds.), *The handbook of research synthesis* (pp. 231–244). New York: Russell Sage Foundation.

Rosenthal, R., & Gaito, J. (1963). The interpretation of level of significance by psychological researchers. *Journal of Psychology, 55,* 33–38.

Rosenthal, R., & Rubin, D. (1979). A note on percent variance explained as a measure of the importance of effects. *Journal of Applied Social Psychology, 9,* 395–396.

Rosnow, R. L., & Rosenthal, R. (1989a). Definition and interpretation of interaction effects. *Psychological Bulletin, 105,* 143–146.

Rosnow, R. L., & Rosenthal, R. (1989b). Statistical procedures and the justification of knowledge in psychological science. *American Psychologist, 44,* 1276–1284.

Rosnow, R. L., & Rosenthal, R. (1991). If you're looking at the cell means, you're not looking at only the interaction (unless all main effects are zero). *Psychological Bulletin, 110,* 574–576.

Rowell, R. K. (1996). Partitioning predicted variance into constituent parts: How to conduct commonality analysis. In B. Thompson (Ed.), *Advances in social science methodology* (Vol. 4, pp. 33–44). Greenwich, CT: JAI Press.

Rozeboom, W. W. (1997). Good science is abductive, not hypothetico-deductive. In L. L. Harlow, S. A. Mulaik, & J. H. Steiger (Eds.), *What if there were no significance tests?* (pp. 335–392). Mahwah, NJ: Erlbaum.

Rubin, D. B. (1974). Estimating causal effects of treatments in randomized and nonrandomized studies. *Journal of Educational Psychology, 66,* 688–701.

Sackett, D. L., Straus, S. E., Richardson, W. S., Rosenberg, W., & Haynes, R. B. (2000). *Evidence-based medicine: How to practice and teach EBM* (2nd ed.). New York: Churchill Livingstone.

Satterthwaite, F. W. (1946). An approximate distribution of estimates of variance components. *Biometrics Bulletin, 2,* 110–114.

Schmidt, F. L. (1996). Statistical significance testing and cumulative knowledge in psychology: Implications for the training of researchers. *Psychological Methods, 1,* 115–129.

Schmidt, F. L., & Hunter, J. E. (1997). Eight common but false objections to the discontinuation of significance testing in the analysis of research data. In L. L. Harlow, S. A. Mulaik, & J. H. Steiger (Eds.), *What if there were no significance tests?* (pp. 37–64). Mahwah, NJ: Erlbaum.

Schulzer, M., & Mancini, G. B. J. (1996). "Unqualified success" and "unmitigated" failure: Number needed-to-treat related concepts for assessing treatment efficacy in the presence of treatment induced adverse effects. *International Journal of Epidemiology, 25,* 704–712.

Seibold, D. R., & McPhee, R. D. (1979). Commonality analysis: A method for decomposing explained variance in multiple regression analyses. *Human Communication Research, 5,* 355–365.

Shavelson, R. J., & Towne, L. (Eds.). (2002). *Scientific research in education.* Washington, DC: National Academy Press.

Shaver, J. (1985). Chance and nonsense. *Phi Delta Kappan, 67*(1), 57–60.

Shrout, P. E., & Bolger, N. (2002). Mediation in experimental and non-experimental studies: New procedures and recommendations. *Psychological Methods, 7,* 422–445.

Siegel, S. (1956). *Nonparametric statistics for the behavioral sciences.* New York: McGraw-Hill.

Simpson, C. (1951). The interpretation of interaction in contingency tables. *Journal of the Royal Statistical Society, 13,* 238–241.

Smithson, M. (2000). *Statistics with confidence.* London: Sage.

Smithson, M. (2001). Correct confidence intervals for various regression effect sizes and parameters: The importance of noncentral distributions in computing intervals. *Educational and Psychological Measurement, 61,* 605–632.

Smithson, M. (2002). *Confidence intervals.* Thousand Oaks, CA: Sage.

Snedecor, G. W. (1934). *Calculation and interpretation of analysis of variance and covariance.* Ames, IA: Collegiate Press.

Snyder, P. (1991). Three reasons why stepwise regression methods should not be used by researchers. In B. Thompson (Ed.), *Advances in educational research: Substantive findings, methodological developments* (Vol. 1, pp. 99–105). Greenwich, CT: JAI Press.

Snyder, P. (2000). Guidelines for reporting results of group quantitative investigations. *Journal of Early Intervention, 23,* 145–150.

Snyder, P., & Lawson, S. (1993). Evaluating results using corrected and uncorrected effect size estimates. *Journal of Experimental Education, 61,* 334–349.

Steering Committee of the Physicians' Health Study Research Group. (1988). Preliminary report: Findings from the aspirin component of the ongoing physicians' health study. *New England Journal of Medicine, 318,* 262–264.

Steiger, J. H., & Fouladi, R. T. (1992). R^2: A computer program for interval estimation, power calculation, and hypothesis testing for the squared multiple correlation. *Behavior Research Methods, Instruments, and Computers, 4,* 581–582.

Stevens, J. (1996). *Applied multivariate statistics for the social sciences* (3rd ed.). Mahwah, NJ: Erlbaum.

Stevens, S. (1946). On the theory of scales of measurement. *Science, 103,* 677–680.

Stevens, S. (1951). Mathematics, measurement, and psychophysics. In S. Stevens (Ed.), *Handbook of experimental psychology* (pp. 1–49). New York: Wiley.

Stevens, S. (1968). Measurement, statistics, and the schemapiric view. *Science, 161,* 849–856.

"Student." [W. S. Gosset] (1908). The probable error of a mean. *Biometrika, 6,* 1–25.

Tanguma, J. (1999). Analyzing repeated measures designs using univariate and multivariate methods: A primer. In B. Thompson (Ed.), *Advances in social science methodology* (Vol. 5, pp. 233–250). Stamford, CT: JAI Press.

Tashakkori, A., & Teddlie, C. (Eds.). (2002). *Handbook of mixed methods social and behavioral research*. Thousand Oaks, CA: Sage.

Tatsuoka, M. M. (1975). *The general linear model: A "new" trend in analysis of variance* (Selected topics in advanced statistics: An elementary approach, no. 7). Champaign, IL: Institute for Personality and Ability Testing.

Thompson, B. (1985). Alternate methods for analyzing data from experiments. *Journal of Experimental Education, 54*, 50–55.

Thompson, B. (1986). ANOVA versus regression analysis of ATI designs: An empirical investigation. *Educational and Psychological Measurement, 46*, 917–928.

Thompson, B. (1988a). Discarding variance: A cardinal sin in research. *Measurement and Evaluation in Counseling and Development, 21*, 3–4.

Thompson, B. (1988b). Program FACSTRAP: A program that computes bootstrap estimates of factor structure. *Educational and Psychological Measurement, 48*, 681–686.

Thompson, B. (1989a). Statistical significance, result importance, and result generalizability: Three noteworthy but somewhat different issues. *Measurement and Evaluation in Counseling and Development, 22*, 2–6.

Thompson, B. (1989b). Why won't stepwise methods die? *Measurement and Evaluation in Counseling and Development, 21*(4), 146–148.

Thompson, B. (1991a). A primer on the logic and use of canonical correlation analysis. *Measurement and Evaluation in Counseling and Development, 21*, 80–95.

Thompson, B. (1991b). Review of *Data analysis for research designs*. *Educational and Psychological Measurement, 51*, 500–510.

Thompson, B. (1992a). DISCSTRA: A computer program that computes bootstrap resampling estimates of descriptive discriminant analysis function and structure coefficients and group centroids. *Educational and Psychological Measurement, 52*, 905–911.

Thompson, B. (1992b). Misuse of ANCOVA and related "statistical control" procedures. *Reading Psychology, 13*(1), iii–xviii.

Thompson, B. (1992c). Two and one-half decades of leadership in measurement and evaluation. *Journal of Counseling and Development, 70*, 434–438.

Thompson, B. (1993). The use of statistical significance tests in research: Bootstrap and other alternatives. *Journal of Experimental Education, 61*, 361–377.

Thompson, B. (1994a). Guidelines for authors. *Educational and Psychological Measurement, 54*, 837–847.

Thompson, B. (1994b). The pivotal role of replication in psychological research: Empirically evaluating the replicability of sample results. *Journal of Personality, 62,* 157–176.

Thompson, B. (1994c). Planned versus unplanned and orthogonal versus nonorthogonal contrasts: The neo-classical perspective. In B. Thompson (Ed.), *Advances in social science methodology* (Vol. 3, pp. 3–27). Greenwich, CT: JAI Press.

Thompson, B. (1995). Stepwise regression and stepwise discriminant analysis need not apply here: A guidelines editorial. *Educational and Psychological Measurement, 55,* 525–534.

Thompson, B. (1996). AERA editorial policies regarding statistical significance testing: Three suggested reforms. *Educational Researcher, 25*(2), 26–30.

Thompson, B. (1999a). If statistical significance tests are broken/misused, what practices should supplement or replace them? *Theory & Psychology, 9,* 167–183.

Thompson, B. (1999b). Journal editorial policies regarding statistical significance tests: Heat is to fire as *p* is to importance. *Educational Psychology Review, 11,* 157–169.

Thompson, B. (2000a). Canonical correlation analysis. In L. Grimm & P. Yarnold (Eds.), *Reading and understanding more multivariate statistics* (pp. 285–316). Washington, DC: American Psychological Association.

Thompson, B. (2000b). Ten commandments of structural equation modeling. In L. Grimm & P. Yarnold (Eds.), *Reading and understanding more multivariate statistics* (pp. 261–284). Washington, DC: American Psychological Association.

Thompson, B. (2001). Significance, effect sizes, stepwise methods, and other issues: Strong arguments move the field. *Journal of Experimental Education, 70,* 80–93.

Thompson, B. (2002a). "Statistical," "practical," and "clinical": How many kinds of significance do counselors need to consider? *Journal of Counseling and Development, 80,* 64–71.

Thompson, B. (2002b). What future quantitative social science research could look like: Confidence intervals for effect sizes. *Educational Researcher, 31*(3), 24–31.

Thompson, B. (Ed.). (2003). *Score reliability: Contemporary thinking on reliability issues.* Newbury Park, CA: Sage.

Thompson, B. (2004). *Exploratory and confirmatory factor analysis: Understanding concepts and applications.* Washington, DC: American Psychological Association.

Thompson, B. (in press). Research synthesis: Effect sizes. In J. Green, G. Camilli, & P. B. Elmore (Eds.), *Complementary methods for research in education.* Washington, DC: American Educational Research Association.

Thompson, B., & Borrello, G. M. (1985). The importance of structure coefficients in regression research. *Educational and Psychological Measurement, 45*, 203–209.

Thompson, B., Cook, C., & Heath, F. (2003a). Structure of perceptions of service quality in libraries: A LibQUAL+™ study. *Structural Equation Modeling, 10*, 456–464.

Thompson, B., Cook, C., & Heath, F. (2003b). Two short forms of the LibQUAL+™ survey assessing users' perceptions of library service quality. *Library Quarterly, 73*, 453–465.

Thompson, B., Diamond, K. E., McWilliam, R., Snyder, P., & Snyder, S. W. (2005). Evaluating the quality of evidence from correlational research for evidence-based practice. *Exceptional Children, 71*, 181–194.

Thompson, B., & Kieffer, K. M. (2000). Interpreting statistical significance test results: A proposed new "What if" method. *Research in the Schools, 7*(2), 3–10.

Thorndike, R. M. (1978). *Correlational procedures for research.* New York: Gardner.

Tucker, M. (1991). A conpendium of textbook views on planned versus post hoc tests. In B. Thompson (Ed.), *Advances in educational research: Substantive findings, methodological developments* (Vol. 1, pp. 107–118). Greenwich, CT: JAI Press.

Tukey, J. W. (1977). Exploratory data analysis Reading, MA: Addison-Wesley.

Tzelgov, J., & Henik, A. (1991). Suppression situations in psychological research: Definitions, implications, and applications. *Psychological Bulletin, 109*, 524–536.

Vacha-Haase, T., Henson, R. K., & Caruso, J. (2002). Reliability generalization: Moving toward improved understanding and use of score reliability. *Educational and Psychological Measurement, 62*, 562–569.

Vacha-Haase, T., Nilsson, J. E., Reetz, D. R., Lance, T. S., & Thompson, B. (2000). Reporting practices and APA editorial policies regarding statistical significance and effect size. *Theory & Psychology, 10*, 413–425.

Vacha-Haase, T., & Thompson, B. (2004). How to estimate and interpret various effect sizes. *Journal of Counseling Psychology, 51*, 473–481.

Walsh, B. D. (1996). A note on factors that attenuate the correlation coefficient and its analogs. In B. Thompson (Ed.), *Advances in social science methodology* (Vol. 4, pp. 21–32). Greenwich, CT: JAI Press.

Webb, E. J., Campbell, D. T., Schwartz, R. D., & Seechrest, L. (1966). *Unobtrusive measures: Nonreactive research in the social sciences.* Chicago: Rand McNally.

Wick, J. W., & Dirkes C. (1973). Characteristics of current doctoral dissertations in education. *Educational Researcher, 2,* 20–22.

Wilcox, R. R. (1997). *Introduction to robust estimation and hypothesis testing.* San Diego: Academic Press.

Wilcox, R. R. (1998). How many discoveries have been lost by ignoring modern statistical methods? *American Psychologist, 53,* 300–314.

Wilkinson, L., & APA Task Force on Statistical Inference. (1999). Statistical methods in psychology journals: Guidelines and explanations. *American Psychologist, 54,* 594–604.

Willson, V. L. (1980). Research techniques in *AERJ* articles: 1969 to 1978. *Educational Researcher, 9*(6), 5–10.

Witte, R. S. (1985). *Statistics* (2nd ed.). New York: Holt, Rinehart & Winston.

Wright, S. (1921). Correlation and causality. *Journal of Agricultural Research, 20,* 557–585.

Wright, S. (1934). The method of path coefficients. *Annals of Mathematical Statistics, 5,* 161–215.

Zeidner, M. (1987). Age bias in the predictive validity of scholastic aptitude tests: Some Israeli data. *Educational and Psychological Measurement, 47,* 1037–1047.

Ziliak, S. T., & McCloskey, D. N. (2004). Size matters: The standard error of regressions in the *American Economic Review. Journal of Socio-Economics, 33,* 527–546.

Zuckerman, M., Hodgins, H. S., Zuckerman, A., & Rosenthal, R. (1993). Contemporary issues in the analysis of data: A survey of 551 psychologists. *Psychological Science, 4,* 49–53.

Index

Alpha (α). *See* Statistical significance,
    p_{CRITICAL}
American Educational Research
    Association, 186
American Psychological Association (APA)
    Task Force on Statistical Inference,
    186, 201
Analysis of covariance (ANCOVA)
    difficulty in interpreting residualized
        outcome, 356
    homogeneity of regression assumption,
        355–356
    purpose of, 354
    score reliability and, 356
Analysis of variance (ANOVA)
    aptitude way, 340
    as influenced by both magnitude of mean
        differences and quality of the means,
        321–331
    balanced, defined, 311
    benefits of, 329
    complex contrasts, 327, 365
    experimentwise error in balanced designs,
        358
    factor, as synonym of way, 309
    factorial models, 343–345
    fixed effects, 346–353

frequency of use, 385–386
general superiority of the GLM
    approach, 359–392
homogeneity of variance assumption,
    319–325
hypotheses uncorrelated for balanced
    design, 335
interaction effects, 334
interaction effects, corrected means for,
    342
interaction effects, interpreting, 339–343
latent variables in the ANOVA context,
    373–375
levels, defined, 310
levels of scale required for, 303, 336
main effect, 334
mixed effects, 345–353
mutilation of interval independent
    variable, 336
nonfactorial models, 343–345
omnibus hypothesis, 309
paradox of variances measuring
    differences of means, 304, 314–315
planned contrasts. *See* General linear
    model, planned contrasts
polynomial contrasts. *See* General linear
    model, polynomial contrasts

post hoc tests, 325–329
post hoc tests, as Bonferroni-type
    corrected *t* tests, 328
post hoc tests, synonymous names for,
    326
random effects, 345–353
repeated measures ANOVA. *See* General
    linear model, repeated measures
    ANOVA
simple contrasts, 327, 365
$SOS_{BETWEEN}$, meaning of, 314
SOS_{TOTAL}, meaning of, 313
SOS_{WITHIN}, meaning of, 315–316
treatment way, 340
way, defined, 309
within-subjects ANOVA. *See* General
    linear model, repeated measures
    ANOVA
ATI design. *See* Design, ATI
Average, arithmetic. *See* Location statistics,
    mean

Beta (β) weights. *See* Regression analysis,
    standardized weights
Bivariate normality. *See* Distributions,
    bivariate normal
Bonferroni correction, 308
Bonferroni formula, 305
Box plot (box-and-whiskers plot), 92–94

Categorical scale. *See* Scale, nominal
Causality, 24, 110
Central tendency. *See* Location statistics
Centroid. *See* Location statistics, centroid
Clinical significance, 135
Cohen's *d*. *See* Effect size, Cohen's *d*
Cold fusion, 253
Collinearity, 234
Combinations, number of, 140
    pairwise, 152
Commonality analysis, 278–282
Confidence intervals (CIs)
    general computation equation, 201
    interpretation of, 203–204
    misconceptions about, 203–207
    plotting in Excel, 206

relation to standard error bars, 202
relation to statistical significance, 203,
    211
Constants
    defined in experimental design, 3
    effects on means, 50–51
    effects on *SD*, 73
    effects on shape statistics, 96
    effects of relationship statistics, 131
Continuous scale. *See* Scale, interval
Contraharmonic mean, 36
Correlation. *See* Relationship statistics
Covariance. *See* Relationship statistics,
    covariance
Criterion variable. *See* Variable, dependent
Critical ratio. *See* *t* test statistic
Crossproducts (xy_i), 118

Degrees of freedom (*df*), 158
Dependent variable. *See* Variable, dependent
Design, experimental
    ATI, 340
    double-blind, 29
    experiments defined, 24
    growth curve modeling, 26
    Solomon four group, 25
    symbols, 24
    wait-list control, 25
Deviation scores, 40–41
Discriminant analysis, predictive, 424
Discrimination, item, 127–128
Dispersion statistics
    as an outcome, 54–56
    as measures of a location statistic's
        quality, 54
    bias of, 64–66
    expectations for, 57
    mean absolute deviation (MAD), 59
    negative, 280
    question addressed by, 53
    range, 57–58
    robust, 69–70
    SOS, defined, 60
    situation specific maximum, 67–68
    standard deviation, 66–67
    sum of squares, 58–62

variance, 62–66
world of, 66
Distributions
  bivariate normal, 128–130
  Gaussian. See Distributions, normal
  leptokurtic, 82
  mesokurtic, 82
  normal, 86–91
  normal, infinitely many of, 94
  platykurtic, 82
  rectangular. See Distributions, uniform
  sampling. See Statistical significance
  score versus sampling, 135–136
  uniform, 82
Division, purpose in statistics, 42–43
Double cross-validation, 259
Dummy coding, 391–392, 394

Ecological fallacy, 199
Ecological validity, 23
Effect size
  and benchmarks for, 198
  and the unit of analysis, 199
  ANOVA, 317–319
  as being "on the average," 212–213, 380
  as measures of model fit, 215, 251, 393
  eta squared (η^2), 317
  confidence intervals for, 207–210
  context specificity of, 332
  converting score-world to area-world,
      192–193
  "corrected" or "adjusted," 195–198
  "corrected" R^2 or r^2, 249
  corrected Glass' Δ, 212
  d versus Δ, 191–192
  Cohen's d, 191
  defined, 172
  Glass' Δ, 190–191
  group overlap, 188
  interpretation of, 198–200, 251
  number-needed-to-treat, 188
  odds ratio as, 424
  omega squared (ω^2), 318
  $p_{CALCULATED}$ as unacceptable measure of,
      187–188
  probability of superiority, 188, 212–213

sampling error influences on, 193–198
small may be important, 126
standardized difference, uncorrected,
    189–192
unstandardized difference, 189
variance-accounted-for, 192–193
variance-accounted-for, negative, 198
Efficiency, 47
Einstein, relativity theory of, 219
Errors, inferential
  experimentwise, 304–309
  relationships among, 148
  testwise, 304
  Type I, 145–146
  Type I, preference for in publication,
      209–210
  Type II, 145–146
  Type IV, 341
Expected mean squares, 347
Experimental design. See Design,
      experimental

"Fan" effect, intervention, 56
F test statistic, 157–158
Fixed effects. See ANOVA, fixed effects

General linear model (GLM), 98, 359–392
  constructing planned contrasts, 368–372
  orthogonal contrasts, 363–365
  planned contrasts, 362–373
  planned contrasts, advantages of,
      367–368
  planned contrasts, synonymous names
      for, 363
  planned contrasts, using Bonferroni
      correction, 372–373
  polynomial contrasts, 375–380
  repeated measures ANOVA, 380–385
  superiority of, 386–390
  three aspects of, 360
Geometric mean, 36
Glass' Δ. See Effect size, Glass' Δ

Harmonic mean, 36
Hawthorne effect, 29
Histograms, 35–36

History, design validity threat, 27
Homogeneity of regression assumption. *See*
    Analysis of covariance, homogeneity
    of regression assumption
Homogeneity of variance assumption. *See*
    Analysis of variance, homogeneity of
    variance assumption
Homoscedasticity, 232
Hypothesis
    "accepting" the null, 148–150
    alternative, 161
    nil null, 143
    null, 143–144
    omnibus, 309
    research, 143
    testing equality of two dispersions,
        157–160
    testing equality of means of two groups,
        two-tailed, 160–163
    testing equality of means of two groups,
        one-tailed, 163–165
    testing equality of two means, unequal
        variance assumed, 165–167
    testing equality of two paired (dependent)
        means, 167–169
    testing independence of counts in a
        contingency table, 413–417
    testing whether two R^2s are equal, 271

Imputation, 50, 95, 131
Instrumentation, design validity threat, 27
Interaction effects
    ANOVA, 334
    defined, 293
    testing in regression, 293–298
International Committee of Medical Journal
    Editors, 186
Invariance coefficients, 263, 265
Ipsative measurement, 21–24
Iteration, 45, 207, 408

Jackknife. *See* Replicability analysis,
    internal, jackknife
John Henry effect, 29

Levels of scale. *See* Scale, levels of
Likert scales, 22–23

Location statistics, 33–51
    centroid, 103
    expectations, 33–34
    grand mean, 313
    graphics, 34–36
    Huber estimator, 45
    mean, 39–41
    mean, trimmed, 48–49
    mean, winsorized, 47–48
    median, 37–39
    median, as estimate of mean, 49
    mode, 36–37
    question addressed by, 33
    shape effects on, 95
Logarithms, 404–407
    common (base), 404
    linearity of, 403–407
    natural (base), 405
Loglinear analysis, 413–424
    superiority over the Pearson χ^2 test,
        417–418
Logistic regression, 394–413
    log odds, 403–407
    odds and odds ratios, 401–403
    predictive discriminant analysis (PDA) as
        alternative, 424
    result interpretation, 409–413

Main effect. *See* ANOVA, main effect
Maturation, design validity threat, 27
Maximum likelihood estimation theory,
    408
Mean. *See* Location statistics, mean
Median. *See* Location statistics, median
Mediator effects, 11, 111–112
Meta-analytic thinking, 200, 253–254
Missing data, 50. *See also* Imputation
Mixed effects. *See* ANOVA, mixed effects
Mode. *See* Location statistics, mode
Model
    "falsifiability," 289
    fit, 287–289
    specification error, 231, 247
Moderator effects, 9, 113–114
Mortality, design validity threat, 27
Multicollinearity. *See* Collinearity

Multiple regression. *See* Regression analysis
Mutilation of interval predictors, 360, 386–390

NHSST. *See* Statistical significance
Nonparametric analyses, 394
Normality. *See* Distributions, normal
Normative measurement, 20–21

Odds and odds ratios. *See* Logistic regression, odds and odds ratios
Ordinary least squares (OLS) estimation theory, 407
Outcome variable. *See* Variable, dependent
Outliers
   defined, 43–46, 194
   detection, 257–258

$p_{CALCULATED}$. *See* Statistical significance
$p_{CALCULATED}$, finding with Excel, 160
Parameter, 13
Parametric analyses, 98, 394
Parsimony, 419
Path analysis
   as partitioning correlations, 285–289
   path coefficient estimation, 284–285
Pearson contingency table χ^2 test, 413–417
   limits of, 417–418
Pearson r. *See* Relationship statistics, Pearson r
Planned contrasts. *See* General linear model, planned contrasts
Polynominal contrasts. *See* General linear model, polynomial contrasts
Population, 12
Power, statistical. *See* Statistical significance, power
Practical significance, 134, 185–213. *See also* "Effect size"
Predictor variable. *See* Variable, independent

Random effects. *See* ANOVA, random effects
Range. *See* Dispersion statistics, range
Ranked scale. *See* Scale, ordinal

Rates of learning, 25
Reactive measurement, design validity threat, 28–29
Regression analysis
   a weight, meaning of, 295
   all-possible-subsets analyses, 277
   "adjusted" or "corrected" R^2, 249
   and collinearity, 244–245
   "best case," 224–225
   Case #1, 232–234
   Case #2, 234–237
   Case #3, 237–240
   curvilinear models, 290–292
   defined, 216
   entry, hierarchical, 276
   error scores (e_i), 222
   error scores (e_i), when constants, 224
   form of the equation, 220
   formula for weights across all cases, 235
   logistic. *See* Logistic regression
   interaction effects testing, 293–298
   interpretation of, 243–244, 248–270
   purposes of, 218–219
   replicability evidence. *See* Replicability analyses
   R^2, formulas for, 230, 233
   standardized weights, 225–226, 235
   standardized weights, not being correlations, 239–240
   statistical assumptions of, 231–232
   structure coefficients, 240–244, 269–270
   suppression, 237–238
   testing larger R^2 versus smaller R^2, 271
   uncorrelated predictors, 232–234
   unstandardized weights, 221, 296
   variable types, 222
   weights, computation of, 225–227
   weights, context specificity of, 241, 247–248, 268
   weights, functions of, 222–225
   weights, "insensitivity" of, 262
   weights, standardized versus unstandardized, 267
   "worst case," 223–224
   $\hat{Y}$ scores, 222
   $\hat{Y}$ scores, mean of, 224, 245

Regression analysis *(continued)*
  $\hat{Y}$ scores, *SOS* ranges of, 224
  $\hat{Y}$ scores, when *z* scores, 246
Relationship statistics. *See also* Regression
    analysis
  and curvilinear relationships, 105–106
  and distance from centroid, 118
  and imputation, 131
  and range restriction, 114–116
  and "third variables," 110–112
  and scattergram quadrants, 117–118
  and shape, 128–130
  corrected for sampling error, 195–198
  covariance, 99–100
  direct, 103
  expected sample values for, 211–212
  multiple R^2, 230
  partial, 112
  Pearson *r*, 99–107
  Pearson *r*, as only measuring linear
      relationship, 379
  Pearson *r*, as standardized covariance, 99
  Pearson *r*, equality with covariance, 101
  Pearson *r*, features of, 101–110
  Pearson *r*, shape effects on, 119, 131
  Pearson *r*, the two questions asked by, 119
  Pearson *r*, undefined, 101
  perfect, 103
  phi (ϕ), 124–126
  point biserial (r_{pb}), 126–128
  positive. *See* Relationship statistics, direct
  Spearman's rho (ρ), 118–121
  Spearman's rho, the one question asked
      by, 130
  Spearman's rho, versus Pearson *r*, 121
Reliability, score, 61, 356
Replicability analyses
  external, 254
  internal, 254
  internal, bootstrap, 255–257
  internal, cross-validation, 258–266
  internal, jackknife, 257–258
  purpose of, 254–266
Resampling. *See* Replicability analysis,
    internal, bootstrap
Response variable. *See* Variable, dependent

Reye's syndrome, 413–423
Robustness, 47
Rounding, 41–42

Sample, 12
Sample size. *See* Statistics, precision
Sampling distributions. *See* Statistical
    significance
Sampling error variance. *See* Effect sizes,
    sampling error influences on
Scale, levels of, 13–20
  interval, 17–18
  nominal, 14–16
  ordinal, 16–17
  transforming, 19–20
Scattergram (scatterplot), 101–103
Scheffé post hoc tests, 329
Scores
  centered, 71
  centered/nonstandardized, 294
  centered/standardized, 294
  noncentered/standardized, 294
  standardized, 71
  z scores, 71
Selection, design validity threat, 26
Shape statistics
  coefficient of kurtosis, 81
  coefficient of skewness, 77
  symmetry versus skew, 76
Simpson's paradox, 9–11
Smallpox, 218
Sphericity, 383
Solomon four group. *See* Design, Solomon
    four group
$SOS_{BETWEEN}$. *See* Sum of squares, explained
SOS_{ERROR}. *See* Sum of squares,
    unexplained
SOS_{MODEL}. *See* Sum of squares, explained
$SOS_{REGRESSION}$. *See* Sum of squares,
    explained
$SOS_{RESIDUAL}$. *See* Sum of squares,
    unexplained
SOS_{WITHIN}. *See* Sum of squares,
    unexplained
Standard deviation. *See* Dispersion statistics,
    standard deviation

Standard error bars, 201
Standard error, inferential versus descriptive use of, 155
Standardized score world, 70–72
Statistic, 13
Statistical regression toward the mean, 28
Statistical significance. *See also* Errors, inferential
  and perfect effect size, 182
  and "vote counting," 190
  in regression analysis, 249
  one-tailed tests, 163–165
  $p_{CALCULATED}$, what it does *not* mean, 177–178
  $p_{CALCULATED}$, what it means, 179–181
  $p_{CRITICAL}$ or α, 137
  power against Type II error, 172–177
  process defined, 136–140
  regions of rejection, 139
  sampling distribution, 135–142
  sampling distribution, purpose of, 138
  sampling distributions, properties of, 150–154
  sampling distributions versus score distributions, 140
  standard error. *See* Statistics, standard error *(SE)* of
  two-tailed tests, 139, 161–163
Statistics
  as characterizations, 1–3
  bivariate, 31
  central tendency. *See* Location statistics
  criteria for evaluating, 46–47
  descriptive, defined, 31
  dispersion. *See* Dispersion statistics
  expectations for, 32
  inferential, defined, 134
  location. *See* Location statistics
  multivariate, 8
  precision, 169–172
  robust, 47–49
  qualified by standard errors, 201
  standard error *(SE)* of, 154–155
  test, 156–157
  test statistics, defined, 156
  test statistics, noncentral, 208

univariate, 4, 7, 31
  worlds of, 33, 62
Stem-and-leaf plots, 91–92
Stepwise analyses
  defined, 270
  sampling error in, 274
  selecting predictors that are not best, 275
  wrong degrees of freedom used in packages, 272–273
Sufficiency, 46
Sum of squares. *See also* Dispersion statistics, sum of squares
  "explained," in regression, 230
  "unexplained," in regression, 228–230
Symbols
  for designs, 24
  for parameters, 13
  for statistics, 13
  for variables 8–9

t test statistic, 155, 160
t statistics, versus F for two group means, 304
Test statistics. *See* Statistics, test
Test statistic critical ($TS_{CRITICAL}$), finding in Excel, 159
Testing, design validity threat, 27
Transistors, 219
Trend contrasts. *See* General linear model, polynomial contrasts
Tukey post hoc tests, 329

Unbiasedness, 47
Univariate statistics. *See* Statistics, univariate

Validity, design
  external, 28–29
  internal, 26–28
  threats, 26–28
  wisdom, 29–30
Variable
  defined, 3
  dependent, 5–6
  dependent, focal role of, 217–218
  incidental, 6 7

Variable *(continued)*
    independent, 5–6
    latent (or synthetic or composite), 222
    measured or observed, 222
    mediator, 11, 111–112
    moderator, 9, 113
    suppressor, 237–238
    two major classes of, 222
Variance. *See* Dispersion statistics, variance
Variance, as a covariance, 116

Variance, pooled, 161
Variance, sampling error. *See* Effect sizes,
        sampling error influences on
Venn diagrams, 300

Wald statistic. *See* *t* test statistic
"What if" analysis
    for power, 174–177
    for sample effect size expected when
        parameter effect is zero, 196, 211–212

About the Author

Bruce Thompson is Distinguished Professor of Educational Psychology and Distinguished Professor of Library Sciences, Texas A&M University, and Adjunct Professor of Family and Community Medicine, Baylor College of Medicine, Houston. He is the coeditor of the teaching, learning, and human development section of the *American Educational Research Journal* and past editor of *Educational and Psychological Measurement*, the series *Advances in Social Science Methodology*, and two other journals. He is the author or editor of 10 books, has written over 175 research articles, and has made contributions that have been influential in promoting greater emphasis on effect size reporting and interpretation, and improved understanding of score reliability.